MW01617217

HISTORY, REVOLUTION, AND ACHIEVEMENTS
OF *NOSTRA AETATE*

HISTORY, REVOLUTION, AND ACHIEVEMENTS OF *NOSTRA AETATE*

The Second Vatican Council Declaration
on the Relation of the Church
with Non-Christian Religions

Daniel Sperber

Foreword by CARDINAL KURT KOCH

Preface by Rabbi DAVID ROSEN

URIM PUBLICATIONS

KTAV PUBLISHING HOUSE
New York

History, Revolution, and Achievements of *Nostra Aetate*:
The Second Vatican Council Declaration on the Relation
of the Church with Non-Christian Religions
by Daniel Sperber
Foreword by Cardinal Kurt Koch
Preface by Rabbi David Rosen

Typeset by Ariel Walden
Printed in Israel
First Edition
ISBN 978-1-60280-518-7

Urim Publications
P.O. Box 52287,
Jerusalem 9152102 Israel
www.UrimPublications.com

KTAV Publishing House
527 Empire Blvd.
Brooklyn, NY 11225
www.ktav.com

Cover Image: *Synagoga and Ecclesia in Our Time*, original plaster, Pennsylvania Academy of the Fine Arts. The original artwork, "Synagoga and Ecclesiain In Our Time" by Joshua Koffman was commissioned by Saint Joseph's University in Philadelphia to mark the golden jubilee of the Second Vatican Council declaration, *Nostra Aetate*.

Library of Congress Cataloging-in-Publication Data

Names: Sperber, Daniel, author. | Koch, Kurt, 1950- writer of foreword. | Rosen, David, 1951- writer of preface.

Title: History, revolution, and achievements of Nostra aetate : the Declaration on the relations of the Catholic Church to non-Christian religions of the Second Vatican Council / Daniel Sperber ; foreword by Cardinal Kurt Koch ; preface by David Rosen.

Description: First edition. | Jerusalem ; New York : Urim Publications, [2023] | Summary: "A little over half a century ago, there came about a remarkable change in the Catholic Church's attitude to the Jewish people. Once an accursed nation, responsible for the death of the Redeemer, Jews became the blessed elder brother of Christianity. Nostra Aetate traces the process of this revolutionary change in detail, through its primary Catholic and Jewish sources"-- Provided by publisher.

Identifiers: LCCN 2022040108 | ISBN 9789655242966

Subjects: LCSH: Christianity and other religions. | Vatican Council (2nd : 1962-1965 : Basilica di San Pietro in Vaticano). Declaratio de ecclesiae habitudine ad religiones non-Christianas--Congresses. | Catholic Church--Relations--Judaism. | Judaism--Relations--Catholic Church.

Classification: LCC BM535 .S6845 2022 | DDC 261.2/6--dc23/eng/20221212

LC record available at https://lccn.loc.gov/2022040108

CONTENTS

Contents

6

FOREWORD

Cardinal Kurt Koch
*President to the Commission for Religious Relations
with the Jews of the Holy See*

Since the Second Vatican's Declaration "Nostra Aetate" (No. 4) in 1965 the Catholic Church has started a systematic dialogue with the Jewish people that has brought rich fruits over the last decades. It is without doubt that "Nostra Aetate" (No. 4) laid the foundation for relations between Catholics and Jews, and can therefore rightly be considered to be the "Magna Carta" of Jewish-Catholic dialogue. It was in pondering the mystery of the Church itself that the Council was drawn to exploring its relationship with the descendants of Abraham. This is a most significant affirmation. For it underlines the fact that it was due neither to a reason that is external to the life of the Church, nor to coincidental or optional motives, that Catholics were inspired to reflect on their bond with the Jewish people, but rather due to its own reflection on the mystery of the Church.

For me it is very remarkable that the orthodox Jewish Rabbi, Professor Daniel Sperber, has decided to write a book about the Catholic document of entitled "Nostra Aetate" on the background of his experiences in inter-religious dialogue. He especially highlights the philosophical conditions and presuppositions leading to the thoughts and considerations expressed in "Nostra Aetate" (No. 4). Of course, this text must be seen in connection to the relationship that the Church had with the Jewish people before the Second Vatican Council and must be put in a wider human cultural context. Perhaps we can call it a "revolution," as Rabbi Sperber has, because after "Nostra Aetate" (No. 4) there started a process that improved radically the relations between Jews and Catholics. Nowadays they see each other as friends witnessing that they are all children of the same God.

We read in the first verse of Psalm 133: "How good it is, how pleasant, where the people dwell as one!" While the original understanding of the word "people" was exclusively intended as those belonging to the people

7

of Israel, today – after Pope John Paul II called Jews the elder brothers of Christians, with Pope Francis taking over this expression – we can speak of a community of brothers and sisters among Jews and Christians. We are inseparably linked in the essential foundation of faith in the one God, and we are united by a rich common spiritual heritage and the legacy of a longstanding shared past. Christianity has its roots in Judaism; the latter constitutes the nucleus of its identity. Jesus is and remains a son of the people of Israel; he is shaped by that tradition and, for this reason, can only be truly understood in the perspective of this cultural and religious framework.

The dialogue between Catholics and Jews has created its own vision, in a spirit of fraternal and authentic friendship. It is with gratitude that I reflect that on the level of co-existence, initiatives have emerged aimed at building bridges between Jews and Christians in the spirit of "Nostra Aetate" (No. 4). Ultimately, it is a question of gaining deeper mutual understanding, always in the mutual respect of each other's religious traditions, and of nurturing the value of each other. Catholics and Jews should unceasingly aim to gain a deeper mutual familiarity. This aspect should never be neglected, particularly in the fields of education and formation.

I hope that Rabbi Daniel Sperber book reflecting on "Nostra Aetate" can contribute especially within the Jewish world to make this document, as well as the process that started after its promulgation, more widely known. "Nostra Aetate" is a success story because it really did change positively the relationship between the Jewish people and the Catholic Church.

PREFACE

Rabbi David Rosen KSG, CBE
AJC's International Director of Interreligious Relations

The 1965 document of the Second Vatican Ecumenical Council concerning the relationship of the Catholic Church to other religions, known by its opening words *Nostra Aetate*, radically transformed the approach of the Catholic Church towards Judaism and the Jewish people, as well as changing the way it viewed the other religions of the world.

There were a number of factors that led to this dramatic change, not least of all the impact of the Shoah, the Nazi Holocaust. Even though as has been well acknowledged, Nazi ideology reflected a perverted pagan world view; nevertheless the extermination of six million Jews was perpetrated overwhelmingly by baptized Christians in ostensibly Christian lands. Nazi policies could not have succeeded to the extent they did in this regard without the "teaching of contempt" towards the Jew that was part of the normative Christian teaching over the centuries.

While this background is extensively referred to in Rabbi Professor Daniel Sperber's remarkably rich work; he nevertheless places *Nostra Aetate* in a far wider human cultural context. In so doing he not only shares with us profound ideas from other world religions in all their diversity and commonality, but also provides insight into the development of human thought generally. In effect he presents *Nostra Aetate* as a reflection of human religious evolution.

The tortuous course that the statement regarding Jews and Judaism had to navigate is also referred to. In effect, it was only by broadening the scope of the statement to address other world religions, that it was possible in the end for the Church to address its relationship with Judaism and the Jewish People. As a result and perhaps somewhat paradoxically, it was in effect the latter that opened the way for Catholicism to develop a theology of religions beyond its own tradition. Accordingly while *Nostra Aetate* was indeed born out of a wider human context, the original specific motivation

9

behind it (for a radical review of its approach towards the Jews) actually served to facilitate a universal human interreligious engagement on the part of the Church.

This work also traces the transformation of specific Catholic-Jewish relationship that was greatly further enhanced during the papacy of John Paul II (as was the relationship of the Church with world religions) and flourishes today in the era of Pope Francis.

This specific transformation itself has a universal message. There was arguably no more chronic a relationship between religions with Jews portrayed as rejected and condemned on High; as odious and contemptible; even as in league with the Devil. Today this relationship is viewed so positively that the Jews are seen in the words of John Paul II, as the Church's "dearly beloved elder brother of the original Covenant never broken and never to be broken"; that the relationship of the Church with the Jewish people is "intrinsic" to the former's identity and not comparable to its relationship with any other religion. Antisemitism is identified as "a sin against God and man" and as Pope Francis has echoed his predecessors, it is "incompatible with true Christianity." If such a chronic relationship has become such a positive one, then surely there is no relationship, no matter how vitiated by destructive theology or politics, that cannot be rehabilitated and transformed positively.

Of course this does not mean that "the work is finished." Almost two millennia of negativity do not disappear in fifty years even with the best of good will. Moreover there are still places in the Catholic world where *Nostra Aetate* and the subsequent statements and teachings of the Church on this subject are not really known at all. These are not a required part of the educational syllabus for the training of priests as they should be. The ignorance is of course especially the case in parts of the Catholic world where there are no Jewish communities to speak of and thus where there is no interaction with contemporary Jewry. Much more needs to be done to ensure that this revolution in Catholic teaching concerning Jews and Judaism reaches down to the grass roots from the Olympian heights and is internalized throughout the Catholic church globally.

However for all the dangers of the age in which we live, it is one of amazingly blessed and fruitful interactions between religious communities and especially between the Catholic Church and the Jewish people that would have been unthinkable only a generation ago.

Rabbi Sperber's most stimulating work takes us into the world of ideas and their development that facilitated this transformation and enables us today to enjoy the enrichment of interreligious dialogue and in particular of the new era for Jewish-Christian relations "in our times."

INTRODUCTION

This study has an interesting history. It began as a brief lecture as part of the conference on the theme "The Church's Relations with Non-Christian Religions," which took place in the Centro Matteo Rici of the Pontifical Gregorian University Rome, convened by the Holy See's Commission for Religious Relations with the Jews, together with the Pontifical Council for Interreligious Dialogue, on October 28, 2015. I was then asked to agree to have this two page presentation published in a journal of the World Council of Churches, to which I agreed. The Pontifical Gregorian University also requested it for their publication *Pro Dialogo*, and I agreed to that too if they would accept an expanded version of the paper, since it had been far too elliptical and concentrated in its formulations. My request was viewed positively and I sent the expanded version.

Somehow or other, the study continued to grow as I realized that the subject was much broader than I had originally conceived. Additional elements suddenly became evident, the horizon broadened, and the study seemed to expand out of itself, as if it were an independent dynamic entity.

This, then, is the present product, the result of several months of intensive thinking and addictively driven research.

Here I may add that the reason I was invited to participate in the Rome conference was because for the last two decades and more I have been active in interreligious dialogue. And in one of my roles in that area, I was a representative of the Israeli Rabbinate in its "team" involved in relations with other religions, which expresses itself, inter-alia, in a Catholic-Jewish Commission, which meets to discuss theological and other issues at regular intervals. We also interacted with the Anglican Church, Moslems, Hindus and other faith groups.

It is my sincere hope that this study will make Jewish readers more aware of the remarkable changes that have taken place in the relationship between Judaism and the Catholic Church in our own generation. And perhaps not all Catholics are fully cognizant of the enormity of these changes. If the perusal of this study has such an effect upon its readers, then that be my reward.

*

Here I feel it is my duty to thank my Catholic brethren for their continuing friendship, the fellows members of the above-mentioned team; Oded Wiener – my once commanding officer during my "squarebashing" phase; organizer extra-ordinaire, Rabbi David Rosen CBE; Knight Commander of the Order of St. Gregory the Great, who leads the field in this area and offered many valuable comments; and other colleagues.

I should also like to express my thanks to Mr. Menachem Butler who made available to me a wealth of additional bibliographic material.

And, of course, this work could not have been produced without the painstaking labour of my loyal secretary, Mrs. Esther Dranger, who somehow manages to understand and put into order my messy handwritten manuscript.

My wife, Chana, who for years has been researching Christianity in the 1st century and sees many similarities to the present-day situation, has always had to bear my scholarly foibles, with their forays, into "alien" fields. Though her research takes a different tack, they too seek to achieve a deeper understanding of early Christianity, and, to find a solution to the ever-perplexing puzzle of how the spectre of Judeao-phobia – Jew-hatred – developed, and was fostered by the Church for so many generations. Perhaps she is less forgiving than I am, but in our own ways we both seek the *tikkun olam* that is mentioned in the concluding sentence of this study.

Together we strive, and hopefully complement one another with mutual love.

Daniel Sperber
2023

APOLOGIA PRO ME

Here I would like to add the following reflections.

Much has been written by prominent scholars on the remarkable nature of *Nostra Aetate*, and its subsequent extraordinary influence on Jewish-Catholic relations. Already in Oct. 2005 my good friend and colleague, Rabbi David Rosen, an expert in this field, presented an eloquent and detailed study on this subject in an essay entitled, *"Nostra Aetate,* Forty Years after Vatican II. Present and Future Perspectives (Conference of the Holy See Commission for Religious Relations with Jewry)". It contained certain reservations, but emphasized the revolutionary nature of the document. He subsequently published an important essay entitled *Fifty Years since the Second Vatican Council: Its Significance for the Christian Jewish Relations,* apud *A Jubilee for All Time: The Copernican Revolution in Jewish-Christian Relations,* ed. Gilbert S. Rosenthal, Eugene Oregon, 2014, pp. 3–13. He ends this essay (p. 13), with the optimistic statement that despite the fact that in historical terms the process has just begun, it may take generations to come to its fullest fruition:

> Nevertheless, a new era was ushered in by *Nostra Aetate*, not only overcoming the tragic past and paving the way for a rediscovery of brotherhood, but even opening up the way for us to view each other in a new way theologically, as part and parcel of the Divine blessing for humanity that we are called for ...

Similarly, Rabbi Shlomo Riskin related to this issue in his "Is Christian-Jewish Theological Dialogue Permitted? A Postscript to Rabbi Joseph B. Soloveitchik's Article 'Confrontation,'" in the section entitled "The Catholic Church Reaches out." And more recently, in 2015, Uri Bialer, Neville Lamdan and Alberto Melloni, published their papers of a symposium held in that year, entitled "Nostra Aetate: Origins, Promulgation,

Impact on Jewish Catholic Relations." Numerous others, too many to mention, wrote on the subject, some highly positive, while others had their reservations. See, for example, Yaron Hazoni (in *Torah Musings* Dec.7, 2015), "What the Vatican Didn't Say – And What it Did;" David Berger, "*Nostra Aetate* after Fifty Years: Covenant and Election of Israel," apud *A Jubilee for All Time*, p. 246.

So what have I to add to the already vast body of literature that exists on the subject? Well, the aim of this study is somewhat different, in that it attempts to trace, uncover and describe the various currents, or undercurrents, both intellectual and cultural, of the late 19th and early 20th centuries, which constituted a kind of basis for the great theological revolution that took place in the Catholic Church. So over and above the deep sense of shame and guilt that plagued the Catholic Church after the Holocaust on account of its action and/or inaction to save the Jews, additional new philosophical perspectives made possible an admissible theological change, and indeed even the radical reversal of traditional beliefs.

I am neither an expert in modern European intellectual history nor in the complexities of Catholic theology. (My own field is primarily the history of Jewish law and custom and its application in contemporary Jewish society.) Consequently, much of my study is largely derivative. So why did I take upon myself to write this study? Well, during the last decade or so, as part of my role in interreligious dialogue (with a number of different religions) I became ever more aware of the highly dramatic changes that have taken place, and indeed, continue to take place in Catholic-Jewish relations; that which Cardinal Walter Kaspar called "an astonishing transformation." (I still recall that when in the late fifties I went to school in London's Kilburn district – a predominantly rough Irish area – one of my classmates adamantly refused to believe I was a Jew, as I had no horns under my school-cap, nor cloven hoofs in my plimsoles!) And I am not a little perturbed by the fact that the vast majority of world Jewry is largely unaware of this and of its truly historic significance. Furthermore, I suspect that only a minute (perhaps elite) percentage of the vast Catholic community has any inkling of the very significant changes taking place among Jewish and Catholic thinkers. For us Jews, this is an extremely difficult process. It means casting off the burdensome shadow of some two millennia of Jewish suffering and tragedy, and banishing the spectre of Christian oppression and the Satanic image (in European Jewish eyes) of the Church.

I hope that this study will bring light and awareness to both Jew and Christian alike, so that together we can continue along that wonderfully fruitful journey initiated by *Nostra Aetate*.

CHAPTER 1

Introduction:
The Basic Premise of Western Philosophy

I<small>N THE</small> W<small>EST</small>, the concept of religious freedom is relatively new. The notion of the legitimacy of multiple truths was anathema to most forms of Western political thought, as it was in classical Greek philosophy.[1] For according to the very basic three laws of identity,[2] as first accepted by Socrates (apud Plato's dialogue *Theaetetus*, and further explicated by Aristotle in his *Metaphysics*):[3] (1) A is A, that is if something exists it has a single nature; it is what it is; (2) the law of the excluded middle – A cannot be A and not A at the same time and in the same sense; truth is not self contradictory;[4] and (3) a statement is either true or false.[5] This premise, which E.A. Burtt calls "a semi-deification of the law of contradiction"[6] in his essay "What Can Western Philosophy Learn from India?" (*Philosophy East and West*, 5/3, 1955, p. 206), also expresses itself in the Church's rejection of the doctrine of "double truth."[7] This doctrine first appears in 1277 as part of the introduction to her condemnation of heterodox ideas. In this document, Stephen Tempier, the Bishop of Paris, declares that certain masters in the Parisian Arts Faculty "hold that something is true according to philosophy but not according to the Catholic faith, as if there are two contrary truths, and as if in contradiction to the truth of Sacred Scripture there is a truth in the doctrines of the accursed pagans." The same proposition may be true and false simultaneously, true in philosophy and false in theology – such is the condemned doctrine of double truth. Unready to accept this denial of the law of contradiction, which he sees as a device to assert heresy, the bishop then lists 219 condemned errors. The masters of arts are warned not to teach them on pain of excommunication. Although the thirteenth-century Averroist Siger of Brabant, and his contemporary Boethius of Dacia are the only two masters mentioned by name in the condemnation, the list of heterodox propositions is so broad that it includes doctrines taught by Saint Thomas, (*Dictionary of the History of Ideas: Studies of Select Pivotal Ideas*, vol. 2, New York, 1973, p. 31, s.v. Double Truth).[8]

In point of fact, this is the logical-philosophical basis for the Christian concept of supersessionism, i.e. that the New Law (Christianity) supercedes and totally abrogrates the Old Law (of Judaism).[9] For these two opposing faith-systems cannot legitimately function side by side, since the one is [now] right and consequently the other is (now) wrong. It is true, as Sara Lipton writes in her *Images of Intolerance: The Representation of Jews and Judaism in the Bible, moralisée*, Berkeley, Los Angeles, London, 1999, pp. 55–57, that:

> From its very beginnings, Christianity was in a large part defined by its attitude toward Mosaic Law and the Hebrew Scriptures. Like the Jews, and in contrast to Gentile pagans, the earliest followers of Jesus and all subsequent orthodox Christians accepted the divine origins and absolute authority of the books of Moses. The historical truth of the events recorded in the Hebrew Scriptures was affirmed, and the patriarchs, judges, and prophets of the Hebrews were revered as righteous and believed to have a share in the world to come. Early Christian theologians defended the sanctity of the Hebrew Scriptures against both pagans and Manichaean and Marcionite heretics.
>
> This positive regard for the Hebrew Scriptures was balanced by a complementary aspect of Christian theology, which asserted that although given by God, the Law was no longer to be literally observed in the Christian era. Following ideas formulated in the Epistles of Paul, patristic and subsequent Christian writers held that the "Old Testament" period of a religion of works was replaced upon the incarnation of Christ by a period of righteousness through grace. According to this doctrine, the Law was given to the Chosen People to prepare them to receive the New Law of the Gospels. The ceremonies of the Mosaic law were henceforth to be interpreted spiritually: physical circumcision, for example, was replaced with "circumcision of the heart," as realized in the Church through the sacrament of baptism. [The phrase comes from the *De Alternatione Ecclessiaee et Synagogae Dialogus of* Pseudo-Augustin, PL 42, 1839.] The oxen, calves, and

goats of the Levitical sacrifices were now replaced by the Body of Christ in the form of the Eucharistic Host on the Christian altar.

This double-edged (or, in Gilbert Dahan's terminology, "bi-polar") [*Les intellectuels chrétiens et les juifs au moyen age,* Paris 1990 pp. 584–585] attitude towards the Hebrew Scriptures and Mosaic law naturally influenced, though it by no means rigidly dictated, medieval Christian approaches to Judaism and its contemporary adherents. On the one hand, the Jews' status as living testimony to the authenticity of scriptural events guaranteed them continued tolerance within Christendom. In what became the most influential formulation of Christian doctrine regarding the Jews, Augustine stated that they should be allowed to live among Christians because they preserved the original text of Holy Scripture and because their very existence served as proof and living reminder of the actuality of scriptural events. *On the other hand, the principle that Mosaic law had been abrogated by the coming of Christ led to condemnation of postbiblical Judaism,* which insisted on the ongoing validity of the letter of the law: Augustine also required that Jews be maintained in a subjugated state as testimony to the fact that they had lost spiritual legitimacy and all claim to temporal authority. [My emphasis, D.S.]

Hence, Jewish insistence on maintaining the old Law could be attributed to ignorance, insanity, or to willful malice.

Thus Stephen Langton wrote, for example:

> Unde Iudei fugient e facie Domini et Cepte plures sunt qui agunt contra conscientianm et bene sciunt Quod Dominus fuit incarnatus et passus, et tarnen Volunt sequi patres suos . . .[10]

This "abrogation" of the Old Law found visual expression as well as exegetical formulations in thirteen century sources, such as the Bible *moralisée,* as so ably demonstrated by Lipton (ibid. p. 62 et seq.). Thus, for example, folio 37c of Vienna ONO cod. 1179, has an illustration which shows Jesus destroying a pile of scrolls symbolizing the Old Law, with an accompanying illustration of Moses destroying the Tablets of the Law.

Woodcut depicting Jews being burnt. Engravings made by Wolgemut, Michael and
Wilhelm Pleydenwurf.
Printed by Anton Koberger (1443–1513). Nurnberg, 1493.

And the commentary accompanying these illustrations is:

> Moses who destroyed the tablets signifies Jesus Christ who destroyed
> the Old Law. The people who sought forgiveness, and then Moses
> retrieving some new tablets, signifies Jesus Christ who reforms the
> Holy Church, so that She might do his will (Lipton ibid. 62).

And those who tenaciously hold on to these "broken tablets" and deny the
now truly revealed truth institute a threat to the true believers, as well as
camning themselves to perdition.

And since there can be no two contradictory truths,[11] it is surely one's
moral duty to eradicate false faiths, by "redeeming" their holders from
their false understanding by persuasion or "more effective" methods. This
constituted the theological justification for forcible conversion, which
became dominantly acceptable in the mediaeval period.[12]

Indeed, we should recall that the Spanish Inquisition did not cease its persecution of heretics until 1824, and the last auto-de-fé took place in Mexico in 1850, about the time Charles Darwin set sail on the *Beagle* and Michael Faraday discovered the relationship between electricity and magnetism.

And just so that we should fully understand what that meant, I shall quote a passage from J. Swain, *The Pleasures of the Torture Chamber*, New York, 1931, citing the *Pery Anecdote*: [*Original and Select*, by Reuben and Sholto Percy, ed. Joseph Clinton Robert and Thomas Byerly, London, 1823], p. 181, and see also Sam Harris *The End of Faith: Religion, Person, and the Future of Reason*, U.K., 2005, p. 86):

> The condemned are then immediately carried to the Riberia, the place of execution, where there are as many stakes set up as there are prisoners to be burnt. The negative and relapsed being first strangled and then burnt; the professed mount their stakes by a ladder, and the Jesuits, after several repeated exhortations to be reconciled to the church, consign them to eternal destruction, and then leave them to the fiend, who they tell them stands at their elbow to carry them into torments. On this a great shout is raised, and the cry is, "Let the dogs' beards be made"; which is done by thrusting flaming bunches of furze, fastened to long poles, against their beards, till their faces are burnt black, the surrounding populace rending the air with the loudest acclamations of joy. At last fire is set to the furze at the bottom of the stake over which the victims are chained, so high that the flame seldom reaches higher than the seat they sit on, and thus they are rather roasted than burnt. Although there cannot be a more lamentable spectacle and the sufferers continually cry out as long as they are able, "Pity for the love of God!" yet it is beheld by persons of all ages and both sexes with transports of joy and satisfaction.

(See Robert Moore, *The Formation of a Persecuting Society: Authority and Deviance in Western Europe 950–1250*, Oxford, 1987.)

It even found its homiletical "source" in the New Testament parable in Luke 14: 16–24, where we are told that:

> 16. A certain man made a great supper, and bade many. 17. And sent his servant at supper time to say to them that were bidden. Come; for all things are now ready. 18. And they all with one consent began to

make excuses. . . . 21. So that servant came, and showed his lord those things. Then the master of the house being angry said to his servant, go out quickly into the streets and lanes of the city, and bring hither the poor, and the maimed, and the halt, and the blind. 22. And the servant said, Lord, it is done as thou hast commanded, and yet there is room. 23. And the Lord said unto the servant: 24. Go out into the highways and hedges, and *compel them to come in*, that my house be filled . . . [My emphasis, D.S.]

(Cf. *Theological Dictionary of the New Testament*, ed. Gerhard Kittel, vol. 1, Grand Rapids, Michigan, 1964, pp. 344–347, and vol. 7, ed. G.W. Bromiley, 1971, pp. 728–729.) Or as Macaulay put it:

I am right and you are wrong. When you are stronger, you ought to tolerate me; for it is your duty to tolerate truth. But when I am stronger, I shall persecute you, for it is my duty to persecute you. (T.B. Macaulay, *Cultural and Historical Essays*, London, 1870, p. 336.)

The degree to which this ideological position persisted may be seen, for example, in the writings of Prof. H. Van Straelen. Van Straelen, a Dutch-born priest (born 1903) who left for Japan in 1935 where he acted as a missionary for seven years, and was appointed Professor at Nanzan University in Nagoya, was also appointed by Pope Paul VI as *peritus* for the council, and was universally acclaimed as one of the leading missiologists. In November 1965 – the same year of *Nostra Aetate*, which prima facie espoused a new attitude towards non-Christian religions – he published a volume entitled *Our Attiitude Towards Other Religions* (Enderle-Herder, Tokyo). It has a preface by Cardinal Paul Marella, dated 18 Oct. 1965; in which he writes that "Certainly we, as Catholics, should not build a wall of separation between us and the devoted followers of Buddhism, Hinduism etc.; rather we should work together with them in as many ways as possible." Van Straelen also sought to deepen the nature of dialogue with non-Christian religions, and accord them respect. Nonetheless, on p. 48 he writes:

Moreover, not only are all the truths of the other religions in Christianity, but they are there balanced and corrected as they are not in the non-Christian religions. Hinduism teaches that the divine is near, that God resides within us, nay, that we are God, since we are part of the supreme, cosmic being which pervades the universe, but it denies that God is personal. Mohammedanism teaches that God is great, but forgets that He is loving. It knows that He is a king, but not that He is a father. Buddhism teaches that this earthly life is fleeting, but it forgets that God sent us to do work, and that we must do it while it is day. Confucianism teaches that we live in the midst of a great framework of sacred relationships, but it neglects the supernatural and forgets that in the midst of these we have a living help and a personal friendship with God.

One further thing is to be noted, namely, that only Christianity can conserve and perpetutate these goods. They are so intertwined with untenable and strange elements in the non-Christian religions that they will finally weaken with the systems of which they are a part. Already in nearly every land of the East, and especially in Japan, one can see the old moral and social values slipping, because the sanctions on which they rested, have dissolved and cannot be replaced. The good old values, which the non-Christian religions certainly have, it seems to me can only live in the present time within the protection and warrant of their true home in Christ.

And in a long spirited polemic discussion of K. Rahmer's *Schriften Zur Theologie*, vol. 5, which preaches a new kind of ecumenicism, Van Straelen quotes, enthusiastically, Father Danielou's essay "The Salvation of the Nations" (pp. 93–94), saying:

> Revelation must be carried to these people, so that their prayer may be a genuine prayer and so that it may be addressed to the true God.
>
> There is much that must die. The great civilizations in their positive reality – Islam, for instance, and all that is in solidarity with it; Hinduism and Buddhism, the great and diverse cultures, religions, and philosophies of the Orient remain, for all their excellencies, great obstacles between human souls and Christ. They are what the missionaries strike up against, what holds them back, what retains souls in error. We can well understand the indignation against these erroneous doctrines expressed by missionaries of former days, and the vehemence with which they spoke of them.... Beyond any doubt Islam erects a rampart against Christianity, perhaps the strongest of any – for there is

nothing rarer than the conversion of a Moslem. In the end, even Father de Foucauld failed miserably in his efforts to convert the Moslems. This defeat was more important than a victory, in that it made him understand that there was only one thing for him to do: To adore the Eucharist in the heart of the desert, to make a minute beginning and to pray in the name of the Moslems until such time as they might begin to pray themselves. All the same, the attempt to evangelize Islam appears to be a complete failure. It is like striking against a stone wall.

What is this wall? It is everything in Islam that must die, everything in Islam that is false, and everything in Islam that is (one can even go so far as to use the word) demoniacal. The great conflict between Christ and Belial that appears on every page of the Gospel goes on even today throughout the world. There is an evil power, a Satanic power, which holds souls in error and which persists." (This is true of Islamism, Hinduism and Buddhism).

We must tear souls away from Satan first of all through prayer, penance and sacrifice. That is the most crucial combat, and we can take part in it even now. As for the rest, that is Christ's concern, and He sends forth His labourers when He will. But first here is a mystical battle, a spiritual conflict, more bloody than any human battle, as Rimbaud has said somewhere. God's real combats are fought in the interior world. There, we fight furiously, trying to free ourselves from all the wretched desires within us; there, saints suffer the assault of Satan himself, of the powers of evil.

This can help us to realize the dramatic and tragic nature of the missionary problem, inasmuch as it is a struggle to tear away souls and peoples from something that is opposed to Christianity, and is to its very roots the spirit of evil.

"What obstacles do we find in India or China? We were saying that India does not believe in the reality of the visible world. For her, the only reality is the invisible world. The body is an illusion and in a certain degree evil. Therefore, the Incarnation becomes practically unthinkable. If God is conceived of as the principle opposed to matter and not, as in the authentic Christian perspective, the Creator of all things; if one starts from this dualism between spirit and matter, which is at the heart of the Hindu mentality, then the Incarnation becomes inconceivable. Then the idea of a God-made man, of a God Who

26

descends, of a God who loves what is beneath Him is practically unthinkable, because it appears to be the fall of God. . . .

In order to understand this, Hinduism would have to free itself – and this is what is so difficult – from a portion of the attitude of mind that so profoundly colours it. A crisis would be needed, for Hinduism will be converted not by winning a few individuals away from it, but by an evolution within the culture itself. Thus, men will be needed who can enter its mentality in order to transform it from within, to prove that it is unsatisfactory, that it cannot hold up, that it must be left behind, and thereby open the way to Christianity.

At bottom what keeps India away from Christ is pride. It is the refusal to recognize its insufficiency. The great idea of the Hindus is that they possess wisdom and that they alone control the wellsprings from which it flows. All else is avatar. Jesus, Mohammed, Buddha – are merely manifestations of a single message, but it is India that possesses this message in its purity and in its completeness. At bottom, Hinduism holds that there is but one wisdom and that there is no Revelation.

Hinduism must die to this pride, just as the Jews needed to die to their pride, that is, to renounce themselves. And obviously such collective renouncement is most difficult. The pride of the Brahmins astonishes those who go to India. It is what makes the Brahmins so fascinating and at the same time so reserved, so hermetically sealed within themselves. Now, only humility opens the way to Christ. In consequence, as long as this recognition of insufficiency is absent, Christ cannot enter into a soul or into a world. The day that India raises its arms to the Liberator it will be able to open itself up to Him. But until such time, its enormous riches are corrupted. India's riches are immense, but they are sealed by pride, because they do not open out upon the true Light . . . [My emphasis, D.S.]

So in spite of Van Straelen's involvement in *Nostra Aetate*, and his plea for greater understanding and respect for other religions, in *his* final analysis, those religions are wrong, false and even doomed to block the path of salvation. This has been a lengthy citation, but its import is so important in that it highlights the problems that Western theological doctrine faces.

And most recently Sam Harris, in his *The End of Faith: Religion, Terror and the Future of Reason*, U.K., 2005, has, in his passionate critique – or more correctly denunciation – of faith, i.e. all religious beliefs, argued that faith is the root-cause of terrorism, in that (p. 13):

> Our situation is this: most of the people in this world believe that the Creator of the universe has written a book. We have the misfortune of having many such books on hand, each making an exclusive claim as to its infallibility. People tend to organize themselves into factions according to which of these incompatible claims they accept – rather than on the basis of language, skin color, location of birth, or any other criterion of tribalism. Each of these texts urges its readers to adopt a variety of beliefs and practices, some of which are benign, many of which are not. All are in perverse agreement on one point of fundamental importance, however: "respect" for other faiths, or for the views of unbelievers, is not an attitude that God endorses. While all faiths have been touched, here and there, by the spirit of ecumenicalism, the central tenet of every religious tradition is that all others are mere repositories of error or, at best, dangerously incomplete. Intolerance is thus intrinsic to every creed. Once a person believes – *really* believes – that certain ideas can lead to eternal happiness, or to its antithesis, he cannot tolerate the possibility that the people he loves might be led astray by the blandishments of unbelievers. Certainty about the next life is simply incompatible with tolerance in this one.

Now, though this formulation is admittedly rather extreme, the basic logic it expresses, which he calls "reason in exile," is the same as that discussed above, namely the exclusivity of one's faith, meaning the belief in one's "truth" posits intolerance of the "faith/truth" of others.

Endnotes to Chapter 1

1. Classical Greek-originated philosophy has dominated Western thinking up to the present day. For example, E. Husserl and M. Heidegger see a need for a "complete Europeanization of the earth and mankind." (See E. Husserl, *Die Krisis der Europäischen Wissenschaften und transzendententale Phänomenologie*, ed. W. Biemel, The Hague 1954, p. 14; M. Heidegger, *Unterwegs zur Sprache*, Pfullingen 1959, p. 103). Heidegger goes so far as to say:

> The phrase "Oriental-European philosophy," which one so often hears, is in truth a tautology. Why? Because "philosophy" is in essence Greek. . . ."
> (Heidegger, *Was ist das – die Philosophie*? Pfullingen 1956, p. 13, as translated by J.L. Mehta, *India and the West*, Chicago 1985, p. 138).

See further on this theme Wilhelm Halbfass, *India and Europe: An Essay in Understanding*, New York, 1988, pp. 167–170, in his chapter "Preliminary Postscript" for a fuller understanding of this attitude of a sort of colonial dominance over non-European thought. He quotes a statement to the effect that:

> It was Hegel who contrasted the Western idea of truth as the total conceptual recovery of the world in all its variety to the Orient, and defined the Orient as a failure in the same understanding.

In that same statement we read:

> China and India are not entirely aware of what they are saying. What they need to do to have philosophies is to try to *understand* themselves and everything else.

(J.L. Mehta, *India and the West* quoting M. Merleau-Ponty, pp. 121, 185.)
Needless to say this "understanding" that they need to have is a Western philosophic one.

2. This was clearly pointed out by E.A. Burtt, in his article "What can Western Philosophy Learn from India," *Philosophy East and West* 5/3, 1955, p. 201, who writes that:

> Western Philosophy, ever since the time of Aristotle, has accepted the famous "law of thought" as practically absolute. . . . These laws have constituted

29

the basic creed of Western logical theory ever since Aristotle discussed the penalties of rejecting them in his third book on metaphysics. He speaks (p. 206) on the "semi-deification of the law of contradictions," and the need "to avoid inconsistency at all cost."

3. Cf. Harry A. Wolfson, *Studies in the History of Philosophy and Religion*, edd. I. Twersky and George H. Williams, vol. 1, Cambridge Mass. 1973, in his article "The Double Faith Theory in Saadia, Averroes, and St. Thomas" (first published in *JQR* 31, 1942, p. 213 et seq.), p. 592, where he describes Saadia Gaon's (882–942) definition of two kinds of faith, as follows:

> True faith means that a thing is known to be as it really is, the many to be many, the few to be few, the white to be white, the black to be black, the existent to be existent and the non-existent to be nonexistent. False faith means that a thing is known to be the opposite of what it really is, the many to be few, the few to be many, the white to be black, the black to be white, the existent to be nonexistent and the nonexistent to be existent. (*Emunot ve-Deot* 4).
>
> This, then, is Saadia's restatement of Aristotle's double faith theory as a purely epistemological concept.

See continuation of his analysis of the "double faith theory," according to which, for example, St. Thomas would assert that:

> Faith in its religious sense means a voluntary assent to the teachings of Scripture about which intellectually the mind may be in doubt but which are still accepted by voluntary assent: The test of such faith is the certainty which follows the assent. . . . (ibid. p. 612)

This is too broad and complex an issue to be fully discussed within this context.

Renaissance humanists were more tolerant and accommodating. Thus, for example, (Michael Eyquem de) Montaigne (1533–1592), in his famous essay "*On the Art of Conversation*" wrote:

> When I am contradicted, it arouses my attention, not my wrath. I move towards the man who contradicts me. He is instructing me. The cause of truth ought to be common to both of us.

Or as the Brazilian novelist Paulo Coelho (de Souza) (born 1947) wrote in 1997, in his *Manual de Guerreio de Luz* (*Manual of the Warrior of Light*, English version, Harper Collins 2003):

> In order to have faith in his own path, he does not need to prove that someone else's path is wrong.

4. This is called "the law of non-contradiction." See Albert North Whitehead and Bertrand Russell, *Principia Mathematica*, Cambridge 910, pp. 116–117, where it is formulated as a theorem of propositional logic. However, Ravi Zacharias, a traditional Christian evangelist, in his *A Shattered Vision: The Real Face of Atheism*, 1994, 2004, p. 176, states that most Eastern philosophers reject the law of non-contradiction. See, for example, Heinrich Dumoulin, *Zen Buddhism: A History*, vol. 1, *India and China*, Bloomington Indiana 1998, pp. 40–44, discussing, inter alia, Nagarjuna's four alternatives: affirmation, negation, double affirmation, neither affirmation nor negation. There are, however, some parallels in Eastern thinking to the law of the excluded middle (perhaps somewhat in contradiction to what we have indicated below). See, for example, F. Th. Stcherbatsky, *Buddhist Logic*, New York, 1962, vol. 2, pp. 400–443, especially pp. 416–417, bringing the translated text of the *Nyāya-bindu* by Dharmakīrti (c. 650 C.E.) with a commentary (Tīkā) by Dharmattara (847 C.E.). (See idem vol. 1, pp. 34–37 and, incidentally, see Surendranath Dasguptā.) *A History of Indian Philosophy*, vol. 1, Delhi 1975, pp. 409–410 note 1.) See also the concept of *Dialetheism*, according to which something can at the same time be both true and false (a "true contradiction"), on which see: Graham Priest, "What is so Bad about Contradictions?" *Journal of Philosophy* 95, 1998, pp. 410–426; Francesco Berto and Graham Priest., "Dialetheism" in *Stanford Encyclopedia of Philosophy*; Bruno Whilth, "Dialetheism, logical consequences and hierarchy," *Andypis* 6/4, 2004, pp. 318–326. And compare Bilal Krishna Matilal, *The Character of Logic in India*, Albany 1998, pp. 127–139, discussed in Chapter 2 on the word "*Anekantavada.*" Here I have only touched upon what is a very broad field of philosophy and logic.

It should also be noted that Aristotle, in his *De Interpretatione* stated that, "It is not impossible for contraries to hold of the same thing at the same time" (ibid. 246, 7–9, sect. 14/38).

However, we should not forget the Greek skeptics. Thus Aristocles, (cited in Eusebius 14:18, 1–5, Caizzi 53, *The Helenistic Philosophers* vol. 1, by A.A. Long & D.N. Sedley Cambridge 1987), pp. 14–15, writes:

> According to Timon, Pyrrho [of Elis] declared that things are all equally indifferent, unmeasurable and inarbitrable. For this reason neither our sensations nor our opinions tell us truths or falsehoods. Therefore for this reason we should not put our trust in them one bit, but we should be unopinionated, uncommitted, and unwavering, saying concerning each individual thing that *it is no more than it is not, or it both is and is not, or it neither is nor is not.*
> [My emphasis, D.S.]

(See editor's commentary ibid. p. 16)

5. See Hyam Maccoby, *Judaism on Trial: Jewish-Christian Disputations in the Middle Ages*, London, Washington, 1993, p. 63, who writes concerning the great 13th century Jewish authority, Nahmanides (Mosheh ben Nahman, 1194–1270), that he believed that:

> ... Human reason, limited as it was, nevertheless was a God-given gift, and partook of God's own reason. It is therefore impossible for human reason to be wrong in something which it saw clearly, such as the elementary laws of logic; and therefore, no statement could be divinely inspired if it contravened those laws. Nahmanides' love of reason is evident in everything he wrote, even in his writings on mysticism. His passionate insistence on reason in the disputation [of Barcelona, 1263) and his attack on the doctrine of Incarnation on the ground of its irrationality, are perfectly in accordance with his general outlook.

See also his note 7, on p. 217, on his "finely poised position between rationalism and antirationalism."

A kind of logical corollary of this premise is that there cannot be mutually contradictory statements in a canonic text. Thus, in Christian religious thought, St. Augustin, for example, focused his exegetical attention on devising explicit rules of interpretation, "to prove that these apparently contrary and contradictory statement [in the Bible] are neither contrary nor contradictory." (St. Augustin, letter 147, in *Augustus of Hippo: Select Writings*, transl. Marry T. Clark, New York, 1984, p. 373.) And St. Justin Martyr (died 164) remarked, "I would rather acknowledge that I do not understand what is said – than admit the existence of two contradictory passages in Scripture." (St. Justin Martyr, *Dial*, 65:2, apud Willis A. Shotwell, *The Biblical Exegesis of Justin Martyr*, London, 1965, p. 5.) And according to Origen "failure to maintain a consistent harmony of interpretation from the beginning to the end of the Bible," smacks of heresy. (Origen, Comm-in *loan* 10:4 and 10:18, apud M.F. Wiles, "Origen as Biblical Exegesis," in *Cambridge History of the Bible*, vol. 1, p. 480; and see John B. Henderson, *Scripture, Canon, and Commentary: A Comparison of Confucian and Western Exegesis*, Princeton, New Jersey, 1991, pp. 118 et seq., that this is also the case in other religious theological systems.) Thus, for instance, Moslem exegetes solved Quranic contradictions through the doctrine of abrogation, *naskh*, "according to which later pronouncements of the Prophet abrogate, i.e. declare null and void, his earlier pronouncements." (Arthur Jeffrey, *Islam*: Muhammad and His Religion, Indianapolis 1958, p. 66; and see David S. Powers, "Genre The Exegetical *nāsikh al-Qu'rān wa monsükhuhu*," apud Andrew Rippin ed., *Approaches to the History of the Interpretation of the Qur'ān*, Oxford 1988, p. 123.)

The above should be linked to the Platonic idealistic tradition, relying on Plato's theory of ideas, from which Western philosophy originated, conceiving truths as unchanging and eternal and the idea of "papal infallibility," pronounced by the

Vatican in 1869–1870, which argued that Pope Pius IX was incapable of making an error, carried this approach to the extreme. (See Patric J. Toner, "Infallibility," *The Catholic Encyclopedia 7,* New York, 1910, pp. 780–850. For a critique of this doctrine, see Shusterman, "Fallibilism and Faith," Common Knowledge 13/2–3, 2007, pp. 379–384, in which we also learn of Cardinal Joseph Ratzinger's Papal address after he became Benedictus XVI in 2005, in which he embraced notable fallibility, which is part of the process we highlight below in Chapter 10. (See also Nadav Berman Shifman's as yet unpublished article "Pragmatism and Jewish Thought: R. Berkovits's Philosophy of Halachic Fallibility," to be published in *The Journal of Jewish Thought and Philosophy*. I thank him for his prepublication copy of his article.)

Also relevant is Isadore Twersky's comment in his *Introduction to the Code of Maimonides* (*Mishneh Torah*), New Haven and London, 1980, pp. 86–87.

6. For its implications for tolerance and intolerance, see the important study of Gustav Mensching, *Tolerance and Truth in Religion,* transl. H.J. Klimkeit, Alabama 1971. The origin of German edition entitled *Toleranz und Wahrheit in der Religion,* Heidelberg, was published in 1955. The English version was augmented by the translator and the author, thus also incorporating the new understandings of *Vatican 2,* (on pp. 5–7, 53–56).

This question was very clearly and succinctly formulated in relation to Christianity by Joseph Cardinal Ratzinger (late Pope Benedict XVI) in his essay entitled "Truth-Tolerance-Freedom," Sect. 1, entitled "Faith-Truth-Tolerance," in his *Truth and Tolerance: Christian Belief and World Religions*, San Francisco, 2003, p. 210:

Are tolerance and belief in revealed truth opposites? Putting it another way: Are Christian faith and modernity compatible? If tolerance is one of the foundations of the modern age, then is not the claim to have recognized the essential truth an obsolete piece of presumption that has to be rejected if the spiral of violence that runs through the history of religions is to be broken? Today, in the encounter of Christianity with the world, this question arises ever more dramatically, and ever more widespread becomes the persuasion that renouncing the claim to truth in the Christian faith is the fundamental condition for a new universal peace, the fundamental condition for any reconciliation of Christianity with modernity.

7. The doctrine of the "double truth theory," usually associated with Latin Averroism, but actually found in the works of many thinkers who cannot be considered followers of Averroes in any definable sense, requires much more detailed and penetrating analysis. For, as Paul Oskar Kristeller writes in his *Renaissance Thought and its Sources* (New York, 1979) in "The Unity of Truth," chapter 11, p. 198:

Mediaeval thought . . . provided the Renaissance with a large arsenal of arguments, formulated in terms of many different issues, for the discussion of the relationship between faith and reason, philosophy and theology, as well as with a few general attempts to define their relationship: The harmony between faith and reason on the confirmation of faith by reason as proposed by Aquinas; the gradual withdrawal of reasons from the area of faith and the tendency to base theological doctrine on faith and authority alone . . .; and finally *the coexistence of faith and reason that grants faith a superior value* but *not the right to interfere in the domain of reason*, a position known under the crude label "double truth theory". . . .

He describes this doctrine (p. 199) "as a separation or dualism of faith and reason," and states that it "evidently considers the teachings of faith and of reason incompatible in a plain and simple sense."

He goes on to say (p. 200):

> I am inclined to admit that the dualistic theory, unsatisfactory as it may seem to us, is one of the possible attempts to deal with a genuine dilemma, and specifically with a case where there is an insoluble discrepancy between philosophy and theology, between reason and faith. I should even say that for a thinker who wanted to hold on to both reason and faith and found himself confronted with such a discrepancy, this is the most plausible manner in which he can face, if not solve, the dilemma. For somebody who is willing to do either without reason or without faith or without both, the dilemma ceases to exist, and the theory loses its purpose and meaning.

He then continues to analyze the views of such authorities as Pomponezzi, Marcilio Ficino and Pico della Mirandola, but this is already way beyond the scope of our study.

8. See continuation on pp. 31–37, (article by Martin Pine). The text of the 1277 condemnation may be found in M. Denifle and A. Chatelain, *Chartularium Universitatis Pariensis*, Paris 1889, vol. 1, pp. 543–555. See also É. Gibson, "La Doctrine de la Double Vérité," *Études de Philosophie Médiévale*, Strasbourg, 1921, pp. 51–69; T. Gregory, "Discussioni Sulla Doppia Verita," *Cultura e Scuola* 2, 1962, pp. 99–106; M. Pine, "Pietro Pomponazzi and the Problem of Double Truth," *Journal of the History of Ideas* 29, 1968, pp. 163–176, etc. See further Joshua Parens, *An Islamic Philosophy of Virtuous Religions: Introducing Alfarabi*, Albany, 2006, p. 143 note 4, who writes:

> Great scholarly controversy still abounds about the exact character of Latin Averroism. The most traditional view of thinkers such as Siger of Brabart and John of Jandun is that they believe it is possible for theology to prove truths

that contradict the truths proven in philosophy. According to this view, they seem to imply no different in rank of the respective truths.

See further Henry Charles Lea, A History of the Inquisition of the Middle Ages, vol. 3, New York, 1955, p. 557.

Beginnings of this philosophical phenomenon lie in the development of theological doubts from the 11th century onwards. This has been traced convincingly by Gavin I. Langmuir, in his important *Towards a Definition of Antisemitism*, Berkeley and Los Angeles and London, 1996, chapter 5, entitled "Doubt in Christendom," (pp. 100–133). Thus, for instance, on p. 112, he writes that:

> Ratramnus [of Crobie] was almost alone in the awareness of a conflict between what Christians were told to believe and what he could observe.

And cf. ibid. p. 89 that:

> There were doubts about either the divinity or humanity of Christ; there were denials of the efficacy of the Eucharist, prayers for the dead, and infant baptism; there were attacks on the sanctity of churches, crosses, and the clergy; and there was a countervailing insistence on the Gospels, the inspiration of the Holy Spirit, individual faith, evangelical preaching, real poverty, and chastity. A more direct attack on the dominant religiosity of the Benedictine Age would be hard to imagine, and it was met by brutal persecution from 1022 onward, primarily by lay people and lower clergy, but also by more moderate official efforts at repression. [Raoul Manselli, *Studi Sulfe eresie de secolo XII* 2nd ed., Rome 1975, pp. 19–38].

(Indeed doubt and uncertainty were in themselves close to heresy. Surely, this is the primary message of the Gospel tradition about "Doubting Thomas," or, as it was earlier called, "The incredulity of Thomas" [John 20: 24–29], and Jesus' alleged statement there [verse . . . . .], "blessed [are] they that have not seen and [yet] have believed."])

These popular religious movements were condemned by ecclesiastical authorities as heretical (ibid. p. 116). The doctrine of "double truth" sought to respond to these "doubts" offering a sort of hermeneutical casuistic solution to the contradictions between "belief" and "observation."

In the 12th century we find theological debates centering on the implicit self-contradictions in Christian faith, and the solutions offered. Thus, in *La Vie de Saint George*, apud *les Oevres de Simund de Freine*, ed. John E. Matzke, Paris, 1909 (pp. 61–117), the Roman Emperor Dorien challenged George with questions such as, "When Christ was crucified, where were the other members of the Trinity?," or "How can a God die?" and "Isn't a Virgin Birth just a contradiction in terms?" to which George replies, that the "Father and Son are as inseparable as fire and light," and the "light's birth is like sunshine passing through glass." And St. Catherine replies to her polemic denigrator, Maxence, to much the same argument that:

> You point out to us a set of contraries: if he is a man, then he isn't God. If he is God, he isn't mortal. You do not wish to concede that it could be right that Jesus could be both God and man.

(See Sarah Kay, *Courtly Contradictions: The Emergence of the Literary Object in the twelfth Century,* Stanford California, 2001, p. 126, et seq.)

Kay points out (p. 124) that the responses to the opposition admit of "two different approaches to contradictoriness, one involving the maintenance of paradox, the other its dialectical resolution." We may add, that the former is frequently found in mediaeval mystical literature, the latter among the so-called rationalists.

The theological problem can also be seen in the fact that the Biblical text was very differently interpreted by Christians and Jews. And:

Neither Jews nor Christians believed there could be valid conflicting interpretations of scripture (though there may be different layers of meaning), and both Jews and Christians believed they understood what Hebrew scripture meant, that is what God meant (ibid. p. 106).

9. See, e.g., Lactantius, *Epitome Institutionum Divinarum* (*Epitome of the Divine Institutes*), ed. transl. E. H. Blakeny, London, 1950, chapter 48, entitled, "Of the disinheriting of the Jews and the adoption of the Gentiles), pp. 96–97:

> . . . The Scriptures prove that the Jews have been disinherited, because they rejected Christ, and that we, who are of the Gentiles, have been adopted in their room. . . .

Lactantius was born c. 250 C.E. and died c. 325 C.E.

10. See Gilbert Dahan, "Exégèse et Polémique les Commentaines de la Genèse d'Etienne Langton," apud *"Les Juifs au Regard de L'histoire" Mélanges en L'honneur de Bernhard Blumenkranz,* ed. Gilbert Dahan, Paris 1984, p. 146; Lipto ibid. p. 178 note 16.

11. This is also the meaning of St. Vincent of Lérins' famous definition of (Catholic) orthodoxy, formulated against the Nestorians, as found in his *Commonitorium* 2/6 (c. 434 C.E.):

> . . . quod ubique, quod semper, quod ad omnibus creditum est.
> . . . which has been believed everywhere, always, by all.

See Reginald S. Moxon ed. *Commonitorium of Vincentius of Lerin*, Cambridge 1915, p. 10; edd. P. Schalf & H. Wace, *A Select Library of the Christian Church: Nicene and*

Post. Nicene Fathers, vol. 11, [Second Series], U.S.A., 1894, transl. C.A. Heurtley, p. 132.) The *"Commonitory"* is written under the assumed name of Peregrinus, but Gennadius of Marseilles, in his *De Scriptoribus Ecclesiastieus* (c. 495 C.E.) ascribes it to Vicentius. See Heurtley's Introduction ibid. p. 127.

12. And this paradoxically despite the words of Lactantius, (c. 250–325 C.E.), in his *Epitome of the Divine Institute*, ed. transl. E.H. Blakeney, London, 1950, chapter 54, entitled "Of religious freedom, and the cruelty of the persecutors," p. 10:

> And yet it is religion alone in which liberty has established her dwelling place. Beyond everything else religion is a matter of free choice, nor can anyone be compelled to worship what he dislikes. . . .

As late as the end of the 19th century, we hear echoes of this basic position. Thus in the encyclical of 1888 of Pope Leo XIII, entitled *Libertas Humana*, (Denziger, Schön, 3252), we read:

> Itaque ex dictus consequitur, nequaquam licere petere, defendere, largiri cogitandi, scribendi, docendi, itemque promiscuam religionum libertatem, veluti iura totidem, quae homini nature dederit. Nam si vere natura dedisset, imperium Dei detrectari ius esset, nec ulla temperari lege libertas humana posset. ("And so from what has been said it follows that *it is by no means lawful to demand, to defend and to grant indiscriminate freedom of thought, writing, teaching and likewise of belief*, as if so many rights which nature has given to Man. For if nature had truly given these, it would be right to reject God's power, and human liberty could be restrained by no law.") [My emphasis, D.S.]

See R. Panikkar, *Myth, Faith and Hermeneutics*, New York Toronto 1979, p. 459.

And this despite the statement by Theodoric the Ostrogoth (493–526) in his statement to the Jews of Genova:

> We cannot command "religion," because nobody can be forced to believe against his will. (Cassiodorus, *Variae* 2:27, apud Mommsen, *Monumenta Germaniae Historia: Auctores* Cut. XII. 62; Panikkar ibid. p. 455.)

For a further understanding of the causes and nature of the earlier mediaeval inquisitional process, see P.R.C. Brown, "St. Augustin's Attitude to Religious Coercion," *Journal of Roman Studies* 54, 1964, pp. 107–116; and see also Kenny Charles Lea, *A History of the Inquisition of the Middle Ages*, vol. 1, New York, 1955, Preface:

> The Inquisition was not an organization arbitrarily devised and imposed upon the judicial system of Christendom by the ambition or fanaticism of the Church. It was rather a natural – one may almost say an inevitable – evolution of the forces at work in the thirteenth century, and no one can rightly

appreciate the process of its development and the results of its activity without a somewhat minute consideration of the factors controlling the minds and souls of men during the ages which laid the foundation of modern civilization. To accomplish this it has been necessary to assess in review nearly all the spiritual and intellectual movements of the Middle Ages, and to glance at the condition of society in certain of its phases.

See the historical development described in detail in Chapter V. entitled "Persecution," pp. 209 et seq. Thus, for example, (pp. 209–220)

The Church had not always been an organization which considered its highest duty to be the forcible suppression of dissidence at any cost. In the simplicity of apostolic times its members were held together by the bond of love, and the spirit with which discipline was enforced is expressed in St. Paul's precept to the Galatians (VI. 1, 2) –

"Brethren, if a man be overtaken in a fault, ye which are spiritual, restore such an one in the spirit of meekness; considering thyself, lest thou also be tempted."

"Bear ye one another's burdens, and so fulfil the law of Christ."

Christ had commanded his disciples to forgive their brethren seventy times seven, and as yet his teachings had been too recent to be buried beneath a mass of observances and doctrines in which the letter which kills overpowered the spirit which saves. . . ."

Yet already was the seed scattered which was to bear so abounding a harvest of wrong and misery. St. Paul will listen to no deviation from the strictness of his teachings – "But though we, or an angel from heaven, preach any other gospel unto you than that which we have preached, let him be accursed" (Galat. I. 8); and he boasts of delivering unto Satan Hymenaeus and Alexander "that they may learn not to blaspheme" (I. Tim. 1. 20). How this spirit increased as time wore on may be seen in the apocalyptic threats with which the backsliders and heretics of the seven churches are assailed (Rev. II, III.) The process went on with accelerating rapidity. Theology could not form itself without starting a cloud of questions unsettled by the gospel: earnest disputants arose who, in the heat of controversy, magnified the points at issue till they assumed an importance rendering them the vital tests of Christianity, and men believed with the most fervid conviction that their adversaries were not Christians because they differed on some unimportant fragment of ritual or discipline, or on some infinitesimal dogma which only the mind trained in the dialectics of the schools could comprehend. . . .

The triumph of intolerance was inevitable when Christianity became the religion of the State, yet the slowness of its progress shows the difficulty of overcoming the incongruity between persecution and the gospel. Hardly had orthodoxy been defined by the Council of Nicae when Constantine brought the power of the State to bear to enforce uniformity. All heretic and schismatic priests were deprived of the privileges and immunities bestowed on the clergy and were subjected to the burdens of the State; their meeting places were confiscated for the benefit of the Church, and their assemblies, whether public or private, were prohibited . . .

Step by step the inevitable progress was made, and men easily found specious arguments to justify the indulgence of their passions. . . .

A powerful impulse to this development is to be found in the responsibility which grew upon the Church from its connection with the State. When it could influence the monarch and procure from him edicts condemning heretics to exile, deportation, to the mines, and even to death, it felt that God had put into its hands powers to be exercised and not to be neglected. . . .

It was not until 1231, in the Sicilian Constitutions, that Frederic rendered the punishment by cremation absolute. This was in force merely in his Neapolitan dominions, and the edict of Ravenna, in March, 1232, while inflicting the death penalty does not prescribe the method; but that of Cremona, in May, 1238, embodied the Sicilian law and thus rendered the fagot and stake the recognized punishment for heresy throughout the empire, as we find it subsequently embodied in both the Sachsenspiegel and the Schwabenspiegel, or municipal laws of northern and southern Germany. In Venice, after 1249, the ducal oath of office contained a pledge to burn all heretics. In 1255 Alonso the Wise of Castile decreed the stake for all Christians who apostatized to Islam or to Judaism. In France the legislation adopted by both Louis IX and Raymond of Toulouse, for carrying out the provisions of the settlement of 1229, is discreetly silent with regard to the penalty of heresy, though under it the use of the stake was universal, and it is not until Louis issued his *Établissements*, in 1270, that we find the heretic formally condemned to be burned alive, thus rendering it part of the recognized law of the land, although the terms in which Beaumanoir alludes to it show that it had long been a settled custom. . . .

The practice of burning the heretic alive was thus not the creature of positive law, but arose generally and spontaneously, and its adoption by the legislator was only the recognition of a popular custom.

The zenith of this process may be seen in the detailed description of what Lea calls "the repulsive subject of the execution itself" (pp. 551–552):

When the populace was called together to view the last agonies of the martyrs of heresy, its pious zeal was not mocked by any ill-advised devices of mercy. The culprit was not, as in the later Spanish Inquisition, strangled before the lighting of the fagots; nor had the invention of gunpowder suggested the somewhat less humane expedient of hanging a bag of that explosive around his

39

neck to shorten his torture when the flames should reach it. He was tied living to a post set high enough over a pile of combustibles to enable the faithful to watch every act of the tragedy to its awful end. Holy men accompanied him to the last, to snatch his soul if possible from Satan; and, if he were not relapsed, he could, as we have seen, save also his body at the last moment. Yet even in these final ministrations we see a fresh illustration of the curious inconsistency with which the Church imagined that it could shirk the responsibility of putting a human creature to death, for the friars who accompanied the victim were strictly warned not to exhort him to meet death promptly or to ascend firmly the ladder leading to the stake, or to submit cheerfully to the manipulations of the executioner, for if they did so they would be hastening his end and thus fall into "irregularity" – a tender scruple, it must be confessed, and one singularly out of place in those who had accomplished the judicial murder. For these occasions a holiday was usually selected, in order that the crowd might be larger and the lesson more effective; while, to prevent scandal, the sufferer was silenced, lest he might provoke the people to pity and sympathy. [Eymeric. Direct. Inquis. p. 512 – Tract. De Paup. De Lugd. (Martene Thesaur. V. 1792).]

As for minor details, we happen to have them preserved in an account by an eye-witness of the execution of John Huss at Constance, in 1415. He was made to stand upon a couple of fagots and tightly bound to a thick post with ropes, around the ankles, below the knee, above the knee, at the groin, the waist, and under the arms. A chain was also secured around the neck. Then it was observed that he faced the east, which was not fitting for a heretic, and he was shifted to the west; fagots mixed with straw were piled around him to the chin. Then the Count Palatine Louis, who superintended the execution, approached with the Marshal of Constance, and asked him for the last time to recant. On his refusal they withdrew and clapped their hands, which was the signal for the executioners to light the pile. After it had burned away there followed the revolting process requisite to utterly destroy the half-burned body – separating it in pieces, breaking up the bones and throwing the fragments and the viscera on a fresh fire of logs.

As to the later stages of the inquisition, which used much the same inquisitorial methodology, in Spain in the 15–16 centuries, see Lea's *A History of the Inquisition of Spain*, vol. III, New York, 1922, Book VIII chapter 1, entitled "Jew," pp. 231–316; idem, *The Inquisition in the Spanish Dependencies*, New York, 1922, pp. 419–427, etc.

We have treated of this subject somewhat lengthily, because of the irrationality of the Inquisition in the eyes of Jews (and, of course, heretics), and, more than that, the deep historical trauma it has left on the heavily scarred Western Jewry. This only underscored the amazing transformative changes that have taken place in recent generations. They find their singular expression in the *Declaration on Religious*

Freedom which was ratified on 19 November 1965, (and which had undergone six different schemae and at least nine public sessions) and included the solemn statement characterizing the document and giving it its historic importance, namely:

> Haec Vaticana Synodus declarat personam humanam ius habere ad libertalim religiosam.

Article 2, from which this statement comes, also declares that this right is that of freedom from coercion on the part of individuals or the state, and that no one is to be forced to act in a manner contrary to his own beliefs.

(See, in detail Pietro Paran's article entitled "Declaration of Religious Freedom," in *Commentary on the Documents of Vatican II*, ed. Herbert Vorgrimler, vol. 4, Freiburg, Montreal 1949, pp. 49–86, especially pp. 64–65.)

However, one should note that already Thomas Aquinas (1224–1274) had spoken against forcible baptism, though it might bring eternal salvation, because it could not be allowed to override natural law (or natural good). (See *Summa Theologica* 2a, 2aC, Q.10 Oct. 12, whether the children of Jews and other unbelievers ought to be baptized against their parents' Will.)

His argument was that despite the fact that a Jew is to be considered a slave of the state, he maintained that in common law the slave is protected by the moral and natural law and so is to be protected from extreme and excessive claims. (His attitudes to the Jews is set out in his short book entitled *De Regimni Judaeorum*. See also Edward Zipperstein, *Essays in Jewish Thought*, Los Angeles 1989, pp. 183–184.)

CHAPTER 2

The Eastern Philosophical Approach
to *"Coincidentia Oppositum"*

In the East, however, the notion that if I am right then you who think differently must be wrong (see above the beginning of Chapter 1) was not a basic logical axiom and there was an alternative position according to which there could be a legitimacy to the notion of multiple truths.[1] Thus, an Indian could easily state concerning the creation, that "then there was neither non-existence nor existence"[2] – a statement not rational in terms of Western logic. And, in the words of the great Japanese scholar Hajime Nakamura, in his masterly book, *The Ways of Thinking of Eastern Peoples*, Japan, 1960, p. 44:

> ... This idea of the oneness of opposite pairs held in the *Upanisads* was accepted by the Vedantins, the most influential philosophical school in India of later ages.[3]

And so, indeed, we find that this was the case in certain schools of mysticism, such as that of Meister Eckhart, including mediaeval European schools of thought, basing themselves on Heraclitus (535–475 BCE),[4] and later developed by the Neo-Platonist Nicolas of Cusa (*De Docta Ignorentia*, 1440)[5] in his principle *Coincidentia Oppositorum*.[6] Simply stated, for the most part, classical western logic did not admit to the possibility of something being both existent and non-existent,[7] or this and its opposite, just as nothing could be both black and white all over. In Hinduism[8] and the Eastern religions, however, such "opposites" were acceptable.

And so writes Heinrich von Stietencron, in his "Hindu Perspectives," apud *Christianity and the World Religions: Paths to Dialogue with Islam,*

Hinduism and Buddhism, by Josef van Ess, Heinrich von Stietecron and Heinz Bechart, ed. Hans Küng, New York, 1986, p. 146:

> A characteristic of the Great Hindu religions is that they never start out by assuming an irreconcilable opposition between two postulated truths. Any claim to an absoluteness is alien to them. They see it as narrowing the range of potential human consciousness. Wherever they find *unavoidable contradictions, they view them as lodged within the framework of complementary oppositions*, and they try to integrate them into some comprehensive connection. [My emphasis, D.S.][9]

Thus, in Hinduism we frequently find descriptions of God that are composed of opposite characteristics. See, for example, how Coomaraswamy describes God:

> God is an essence without duality (*advaita*), or as some maintain, without duality but not without relations (*visistādvaita*). He is only to be apprehended as Essence (*asti*), but this Essence subsists in a two-fold nature (*dvaitibhāva*); as being and as becoming [*tattva* and *bhava*, corresponding to the Greek *ousia* – being – and *nemesis* personification of divine wrath]. Thus, what is called the Entirety (*krtsnam, pūrnam, bhūman*) is both explicit and inexplicit (*niruktānirukata*), sonant and silent (*śabdāśabda*), characterized and uncharacterized (*saguna, nirguna*), temporal and eternal (*kālākāla*), partite and impartite (*sakalākāla*), in a likeness and not in any likeness (*mūrtāmūrta*), shewn and unshewn (*vyaktāvyakta*), mortal and immortal (*martyāmartya*), perishable and the Imperishable (*ksaraścāksarn*), and so forth. Whoever knows him in his proximate (*apara*) aspect, immanent, knows him also in his ultimate (*para*) aspect, transcendent, the Person seated in our heart, eating and drinking, is also the Person in the Sun. This sun of men, and Light of lights "whom all men see but few know with the mind," is the Universal Self (*ātman*) of all things mobile or immobile. He is both inside and outside (*bahir antaś ca bhutānām*), but uninterruptedly (*anantaram*), and therefore a total presence, undivided in divided things. He does not come from anywhere, nor does he become anyone, but only lends himself to all possible modalities of existence.[10]

In the Hindu scriptures there abound statements which are impossible in terms of western rationalism. Thus, for example, in *Chāndogya Upanisad* 3:2:2 we read of the world of Brahmā:

> It is not so there. The sun has not set; nor has he ever risen. O ye gods, by this truth, may I not fall from Brahmā.

Or in *Īśa Upanisad* 5, on the Supreme being immanent and transcendent:

> It moves and it moves not; It is far and it is near; It is within all this and it is also outside all this.[11]

And in *Katha Upanisad* 1:21:

> Sitting, he moves far; lying he goes everywhere ... – this being "The Opposite Characteristics of the Supreme"[12]

Of course, one is aware of the fact that these paradoxical statements have to be interpreted. Thus Radhakrishnan writes, "explaining" this latter statement:

> *Viruddha-dharmavan.* S. Brahman has both sides of peaceful stability and active energizing. In the former aspect He is *Brahman*; in the later *īśvara*. The latter is an active manifestation of the Absolute *Brahman*, and not the illusory one as some Advaita Vedāntins suggest.

Be that as it may, and however we seek to understand these apparently self-contradictory types of statements, so much a part of Eastern thought, they are readily accepted by the Hindu thinker, it being a part, not only of his philosophy, but also of his regular ritual "exercises." Thus, Mircea Eliade, in his *Yoga: Immortality and Freedom*, New York, 1958, writes as follows in his chapter of "Techniques for Autonomy," pp. 98–99:

> Let us note that the most important yogic and tantric experiences realize a similar paradox. In *prānāyāna*, life coexists with holding the breath (a holding that is in fact in flagrant contradiction to life); in the fundamental tantric experience (the "return of semen"), "life" coincides with "death," the "act" becomes "virtuality." [Cf. ibid. p. 170.]

It goes without saying that the paradox is implied in the very function of Indian ritual (as, of course, in every other ritual); for, by the power of ritual, some ordinary object incorporates the divinity, a "fragment" (in the case of the Vedic sacrifice, the brick of the altar) coincides with the "Whole" (the god Prajāpati), nonbeing with Being. Regarded from this point of view (that of the phenomenology of paradox), *samādhi* is seen to be situated on a line well known in the history of religions and mysticisms – that of the *coincidence of opposites*. It is true that, in this case, the coincidence is not merely symbolic, but concrete, experiential. Through *samādhi, the yogin transcends opposites* and, in a unique experience, unites emptiness and superabundance, life and death, Being and nonbeing. Nor is this all. Like all paradoxical states, *samādhi* is equivalent to a reintegration of the different modalities of the real in a single modality – the undifferentiated completeness of precreation, the primordial Unity. The yogin who attains to *asamprajñāta samādhi* also realizes a dream that has obsessed the human spirit from the beginnings of its history – to coincide with the All, to recover Unity, to re-establish the initial nonduality, to abolish time and creation (i.e., the multiplicity and heterogeneity of the cosmos); in particular, to abolish the twofold division of the real into object-subject.

It would be a gross error to regard this supreme reintegration as a mere regression to primordial nondistinction. It can never be repeated too often that Yoga, like many other mysticisms, issues on the plane of paradox and not on a commonplace and easy extinction of consciousness. . . .[13] [My emphasis, D.S.]

Indeed, Ananda Kentish Coomaraswamy, in his very intriguing essay "The Darker Side of Dawn," (Washington, April 17, 1935, *Smithsonian Miscellaneous Collections* 34/1) pp. 1–2, sees this as a characteristic of contemplative practice alike in East and West: for:

Metaphysical religion envisages a "Supreme Identity" (in the Rg Veda *tad ekam*, "That One") in which the outwardly opposing forces are one impartible principle; the lion and the lamb lying down together. The contrasted powers are separated only by the very nature of reason, which sees things apart as subject and object, affirmation and negation, act and potentiality, Heaven and Earth. Contemplative practice alike in East and West seeks to approach divinity in both aspects, avoiding a one-sided vision of the Unity; willing to know Him both as being and non-being, life and death, God and Godhead.[14]

Furthermore, Diana Eck, in her *Encountering God: A Spiritual Journal from Bozeman to Banaras*, Penguin Books, 1995, when describing how Hindu thought deals with God being One and Manyness (pp. 6–62), writes that there is an ability to symbolize consciously, taking two views at once.

> This capacity to think symbolically means that ... one does not relinquish one viewpoint for another. Plurality is not given up in favour of oneness, or oneness in favour of plurality. Both viewpoints are held – and understood to be held – simultaneously.[15]

How are we to understand this apparently self-contradictory and thus, surely, illogical way of thinking? Heinrich Zimmer, in his classic *Philosophies of India*, edited by Joseph Campbell, New York, 1951, seeks to explain this in a number of passages in his book. On pp. 312–313 he writes:

> For the ultimate and real task of philosophy, according to Indian thought, and to such classical Occidental philosophers as Plato, transcends the power and task of reason. Access to truth demands a passage beyond the compass of ordered thought. And by the same token: the teaching of transcendent truth cannot be by logic, but only by pregnant paradox and by symbol and image. Where a carefully reasoning thinker, progressing step by step, would be forced to halt (out of breath, as it were, at the confines of the stratosphere, panting for lack of oxygen, swooning with pulmonary and cardiac distress) the mind can still go on. The mind can soar and enter the supernal sphere on the wings of symbols, which represent the Truth-beyond-the-pairs-of-opposites, eluding by those wings the bird-net of the basic principle of earthbound human logic, the pedestrian principle of the incompatibility of opposites. For what "transcendent" means is the transcending (among other things) of the bounding and basic logical laws of the human mind.
>
> "Transcendent" means that a principle is in effect that comprehends the identity of apparently incompatible elements, representing a union of things which on the logical level exclude each other. Transcendent

truth comprehends an ever-recurrent "coincidence of opposites" (*coincidentia oppositorum*) and is characterized, therefore, by an everlasting dialectical process. The secret identity of incompatibles is mockingly disclosed through a constant transformation of things into their antitheses-antagonism being but the screen of a cryptic identity. Behind the screen the contending forces are in harmony, the world-dynamism quiescent, and the paradox of a union of contrary traits and forces stands realized *in toto*; for where the One and the Many are identical, eternal Being is known, which is at once the source and the force of the abundant diversity of the world's perpetual Becoming.

Though called the true and only Being (*sat*), this Transcendent is known also as non-Being (*asat*); for it is that ineffable point "wherefrom words turn back, together with the mind, not having attained" (*Taitliriya Upanisad* 2:9) – as birds flying to reach the sun are compelled to return.

And on p. 380 he writes:

.... Brāhmans brought to India ... a jubilant, monistic emphasis on the sanctity of life: a powerful and persistent assertion that the One Thing is always present as two. "I am both," asserts the Lord of Food; "I am the two: the life-force and the life-material – the two at once." The jejune disjunction of the world into matter and spirit derives from an abstraction of the intellect and should not be projected back upon reality; for it is of the nature of the mind to establish differences, to make definitions and discriminate. To declare, "There are distinctions," is only to state that there is an apprehending intellect at work. Perceived pairs-of-opposites reflect the nature not of things but of the perceiving mind. Hence thought, the intellect itself, must be transcended if true reality is to be attained. Logic is a help for preliminary clarification, but an imperfect, inadequate instrument for the final insight; its orderly notions, oppositions, and relationships must be overcome if the searching mind is to attain to any direct conception or realization of the transcendent truth. The One Thing that is the first, last, and only reality (this is the basic Brāman thesis) comprises all the pairs-of-opposites (*dvandva*) that proceed from it, whether physically, in the course of life's evolution, or conceptually, as logical distinctions occurring to the intellect coincident with thought.

And again on p. 451:

> But in the transcendent state the differentiations known to thought
> vanish, so that not even the notion of a motionless and unqualified,
> undynamic Eternal Essence can subsist. This great idea was only meant
> to inspire the beginner and guide the advanced pupil on the road to the
> true, concept-shattering experience. In itself, in the end, it proves to
> be an impediment. Where it stands, the initiate stands and is thus kept
> within the realm of contradictory pairs-of-opposites; for the notion of
> Eternity demands its opposite, that of the transient, the phenomenal,
> the illusory world. And so the initiate who has found "Eternity" still is
> entangled in the devious net of *māyā*. His remaining with such ideas
> gives proof that he has still a certain distance to go. If the one who is
> finally enlightened uses such a term, it is only by way of accommo-
> dation to the partly enlightened, more or less beclouded mind of the
> pupil who has come to him for help. The guru uses the term out of
> a mixture of indifference and sublime compassion, his own intrinsic
> and preferred attitude being silence, the silence of the Self (*maunam*,
> "silence," the quality of the *nuni*, "saint").

(See further index p. 667, s.v. "opposites, pairs of (usually dvandva.)"

Perhaps a slightly different approach is that which is found in Jaina thought.

Thus, for example, one of the most important and fundamental doctrines of Jainism, given by Mahavira (599–527 B.C.E.), is *Anekantavada*, the multiplicity of viewpoints,[16] the notion in which truth or according to modern scholarship reality, are perceived differently from diverse view-points,[17] so that no single point of view (*dristikona*) is the complete truth.[18] Hence, it encourages its adherents to consider the views and beliefs of their opposing rival parties; and warns against uncompromising doctrine as an error based on limited viewpoint.

Parenthetically, we may perhaps characterize this as a sort of "philo-sophical impressionism." Think of Claude Monet's (1840–1926) series of cathedral-façades in different shades of light-pink, blue and yellow, or perhaps more to point some 135 art works between 1899 and 1920 called Water Lilies," of his pond in Giverny.[19]

Wilhelm Halbfass, in his *India and Europe: An Essay in Understanding*, New York, 1988, p. 267, summarizes as follows:

The Philosophical consummation of the Jaina approach is reached in the perspectivistic theory of world-views (*naya*) which we find most fully developed in the works of Siddhasena Divākara and Mallavādin. Here, the enumeration of historically factual viewpoints merges with the construction of systematically possible standpoints in philosophy. Jainism is credited with a special and unique manner of coordinating, systematizing and completing the other world-views, of showing their attachment to partial truths and mere aspects, and of salvaging them from their self-imposed isolation and one-sidedness.

He further adds (ibid. p. 268) that in the view of Bhartrhani, the greatest representation of the śabdāvaita tradition (probably circa second half of the 5th century C.E.), according to his *Vākyapadīya*, as well as his commentary on Patanjali's *Mahābhāsya*:

There are various "views," or "ways of seeing," with reference to one and the same "visible" object: *ekasmin api drśye 'rthe darśanam bhidyata prthak*. The "seeing" and understanding of time varies: *bhinnaus kālasya darśanam*. We find different perspectives, different ways of seeing the same reality in many areas. There is the "perspective of unity" (*ektavadarśana*) as well as the "perspective of aggorgation" (*samsargadarśana*); in such similar compounds, *darśana* is used in a way which recalls the Jaina notion of *maya*.[20]

And is this not somewhat similar to what Karl Jaspers (1883–1969, the German-Swiss Protestant philosopher theologian and psychologist), who was very interested in Eastern thought, and in 1966 wrote a book on *Socrates, Buddha, Confucius, Jesus (The Great Philosophers*, vol. 1)? For he stated in his lecture "Philosophy and Religion" given in the University of Basel in July 1947:

Conversely: what is universally valid for all (like scientific and other logically true propositions), is for that very reason not absolute, is universally valid for all from a specific standpoint and on the basis of a definite method, hence under certain conditions and not absolutely. This kind of true proposition is cogent for all whose intelligence can grasp it. But it is relative to the standpoint and method by which it is disclosed. It is existentially indifferent, because it is finite, particular, objectively cogent, – no man can or should die for it.

In short: The absoluteness of historical truth implies the relativity of every formulation of it, and of all its historically finite manifestations. Universally valid statements can be based only upon relative standpoints and methods. Formulable faith contents must not be treated like universally true propositions; the absolute awareness of truth in faith is something fundamentally different from the comprehension of the universal validity of scientifically true propositions, which are always particular. Historical absoluteness does not carry with it the universal validity of its manifestations in word, dogman, cult, ritual, institutions. It is the confusion of the two that makes it possible to claim exclusivity for a religious truth.

Here he distinguishes between religious and historical and scientific truth. Of the latter he states:

That which is historically, existentially true is indeed absolute, but this does not mean that the expression or manifestation of it is a truth for all.

But he goes even further claiming that religious truth that claims absolute exclusivity of the apprehended truth of faith can lead to terrible consequences. Thus he writes:

We may take as an example of this Biblical religion. Christianity with its claim to absolute faith for all. Our knowledge of the extraordinary accomplishments of Christianity, of the noble figures who have lived in this faith and by this faith cannot prevent us from seeing how this fundamental perversion brought forth historical evils that wore the cloak of sacred and absolute truth.

He continues, after delineating how this claim to exclusivity led to the doctrine that "the many religions are a sum of untruths or at best partial truths," resulting in "campaigns of annihilation, crusades were unleashed," . . . so that "politics became the weapon of the churches," and the "will to power became a basic factor in this religion, which originally had nothing to do with power."

In his very forceful argumentation he declares:

I do not understand how anyone can maintain an attitude of neutrality towards the claim to exclusivity. That would be possible if intolerance could be regarded as a strange and harmless anomaly. But this is by no means the case. By its very nature it tends to assert itself through powerful institutions that keep constantly arising, and it stands forever in readiness to kindle new fire in which to burn heretics. This lies in the very claim to exclusivity in all forms of Biblical religion....

(See the continuation of this lecture for his understanding of how Christianity freed from the exlusivist claims might function).[21]

Indeed, this was well expressed by F.C. Happold (1893–1971) in his book, *Mysticism: A Study and An Anthology*, Penguin Books – two years before *Nostra Aetate* – who on p. 21 cites a poem by the Latin poet and philosopher Boethius, which translated (by Helen Waddell) begins as follows:

> This dischord in the pact of things,
> This endless war 'twixt truth and truth,
> That singly held, yet give the lie
> To him who seeks to hold them both …

He continues:

> In the world, constituted as it is, men are faced not with one single truth but with several "truths," not with one but with several pictures of reality. They are thus conscious of a "discord in the pact of things," whereby to hold to one "truth" seems to be to deny another. One part of their experience draws to one, another to another. It has been the eternal quest of mankind to find the one ultimate Truth, that final synthesis in which all partial truths are resolved. It may be that the mystic has glimpsed this synthesis.

Perhaps in a similar manner, H.G. Gadamer, writing in 1960, his *Wahrheit und Methode*, Tübingen, [English translation, *Truth and Method*, New York, 1985] states [English p. 271, German p. 288] that:

> Just as the individual is never simply an individual, because he is always involved with others, so too the closed horizon that is supposed

to enclose a culture is an abstraction. The historical movement of human life consists in the fact that it is never utterly bound to any one standpoint, and hence can never have a truly closed horizon. The horizon is, rather, something into which we move and that moves with us.

Returning, however, to Eastern thinking, Nakamura writes (ibid. pp. 163–164):

Such an attitude towards other faiths is manifest in the modern religious movements in India. A religious reformer in the nineteenth century, Rām Mohan Rai, organized a religious society called Brāhma-Samāj, and he made it a fundamental principle of the society for the followers to worship the same God irrespective of their race, class, nationality and even their religions. Rāmakrsna, who was the founder of the Ramakrishna Order declared that "all religions, pursuing different ways, will finally reach the same God," (Romain Rolland, *La vie de Ramakrishna*, p. 93). "All the religions that existed are true" (ibid. p. 186). Vivekānanda, his disciple, delivered a famous address at the International Religious Conference held in Chicago on Sept. 27, 1893, saying that: "Oh, the Sacred One, called Brahman by the Hindus, Ahura Mazdah by the Zoroastrians, Buddha by the Buddhists, Jehovah by the Hebrews and God in heaven by the Christians! May bestow inspiration upon us! Christians should neither be Buddhists nor Hindus. Buddhists and Hindus should never be Christians. Everyone, however, must grow up in accordance with their own principle, holding their individual character firmly, assimilating others' spiritual merits.... This Conference has proved that Holiness, Sereneness and Compassion should not be monopolized by any religious order. And it has also proved that there were no religions in the world which had never produced noble and spiritual personalities. I firmly believe that we will read the following passages on the flags or banners of all the religions in the future – Help each other. Don't struggle witheach other. Be reconciled with others. Don't destroy others. Keep harmony and peace. Don't compete in useless matters," (Romain Rolland, *La vie de Vivekananda*, vol. 1, pp. 47–48). "I approve of existing of religions in the past. I adore God with them" (ibid. vol. 2, p. 110)....

So the peace-loving attitude in Indian people must have come from the unique way of thinking that different philosophies and different conceptions of the world are nothing but the manifestation of the Absolute One.

It was this principle influenced Mahatama Gandhi to adopt the principles of religious tolerance, *ahimsa* non-violence and *satyagraha*, literally: insistence on truth, but which came to mean passive resistance.[22]
  And again he writes among his concluding remarks (on pp. 630–631):

> The idea of tolerance and mutual concession is based on the standpoint which admits the compatibility of manifold different philosophical views of the world.[23]
>   According to our foregoing, the Indians are prone to tolerate the co-existence of philosophical thoughts of various types from the metaphysical viewpoint; the Chinese are inclined to try to reconcile and harmonize them from a political and practical viewpoint; and the Japanese tend to emphasize the historical and physiographical features of such diverse thoughts.

And earlier on, on pp. 159–160, he had explained that:

> Generally speaking, Indian people have a tendency to recognize raison d'être in the fact that there exist many different world-views, philosophies and religions in the world. For they think that these different views which seemingly conflict with each other are based on the Absolute One. Their viewpoint is, objectively, based on the idea that all things in the universe are one, and subjectively on the reflection that all human activities originate from the metaphysical and monistic principle.[24]

And he goes on (ibid.) to compare the positions in the various Buddhisms, and in Japanese thought, highlighting the subtle differences.
  Furthermore, John J. Thatamaril, an avowed Christian-Indian-American studying Sankara, in a very revealing article entitled "Managing Multiple Religious and Scholarly Identities: An Argument for a Theological Study of Hinduism," *Journal of the American Academy of Religion*, December 2000, 68/4, pp. 791–803, quotes Mark Taylor's Critique of an implicit connection between configurations of the self and western monotheism by drawing on the notion of *imago dei*:

Throughout most of the Western tradition, being is interpreted in terms of oneness and presence. To be is to be one, and to be one is, in some sense, to be uniquely and irreducibly present. As the ultimate ground or primal source of all being, God is the transcendent One whose complete self-identity and total self-presence are realized in absolute self-consciousness. When man is represented as the image of God, the self also appears self-identical, self-present, and self-conscious. The proper theological subject is the solitary self, whose self-consciousness assumes the form of an individual "I" that defines itself in opposition to and transcendence of other isolated subjects. Such a self is primarily and essentially a unique individual. The ostensible uniqueness (*unicus*, only, sole, singular) of the autonomous subject is a function of the separation from everything else. Though divided from others, the individual (*individuus*, in, not + *dividuus*, divisible, *dividere*, to divide) itself cannot be divide.... [T]his interpretation of individuality rests on the repressive logic of identity, according to which the boundary that seems to separate discrete individuals is regarded as absolutely inviolable. (Mark C. Tayin, *Erring. A Post-Modern Theology*, Chicago, 1984, p. 130.)

Tatamaril remarks (pp. 190–797) that:

Scholarly convictions about the necessary incompatibility of religious belief and objectivity or the impossibility of multiple religious identities seem to be based on understandings of the individual of the sort that Taylor rejects. Scholarly integrity is all too often understood to require a rigorous and repressive exclusion of commitment to a particular tradition as well as separation from allegiances to multiple religious traditions.

He studied with Swami Paramārthānanda, coming to the conclusion (p. 800) that:

To account adequately for multiple identities is simply impossible so long as one holds to a unitary conception of selfhood of the sort that Taylor rejects. No person can be formed or claimed by several fundamental allegiances if he or she can have but a single centered self. Furthermore, Taylor's argument that this unitary construction of individuality is closely linked to certain varieties of western monotheism presents another powerful example of how unexamined theological conceptions constrain scholarly possibilities: assumptions about the incompatibility of being at once an outsider and insider may hinge on a limited western theological anthropology. Here again, unquestioned theological presuppositions eliminate richer views of scholarly [and I might add: theological. D.S.] integrity.

And this after raising the crucial questions as follows (pp. 799–800):

The reader may well wonder how it is possible to take seriously Advaita Vedānta's claims regarding an ultimate, nondual Self (*ātman*) while also embracing the idea of multiple religious identities. In the technical terms of Advaita two-truth theory, I understand my arguments regarding multiple religious identities to be matters of conventional truth (*vyāvahārikasatya*) and not of ultimate truth (*pāramārthikasatya*). In fact, the Advaitic understanding that the true Self is the nondual *Brahman* may in fact allow for a more flexible approach to conventional identities.

Advaitic discipline also requires students to abandon their unreflective attachment to conventional identities; such attachment will only impede progress toward liberation (*moksa*). In sum, because Advaita spiritual discipline mandates a more flexible approach to conventional identities, there is no necessary conflict between affirming the possibility of multiple scholarly and religious identities and Advaita affirmations of nonduality.

Once again, from a somewhat different point of departure, we find a philosophical approach admitting to the acceptability of "multiple religious identities," a more extreme form of pluralism, way beyond toleration.

Buddhist philosophical thinking is far too complex[25] to be described in this context, for there too we find bewildering philosophic paradoxes.[26] However, we shall confine ourselves merely to one aspect of Buddhist thought, which is extremely relevant to our discussion. It is to the notion of "limitations of experience." This is very ably elaborated upon in David J. Kalupahana's *A History of Buddhist Philosophy: Continuities and Discontinuities*, Honolulu, 1992, pp. 44–49. I shall cite sections of his highly complex exposition:

One of the important features of cognitive experience admitted by the Buddha, whether of sensory experience or of extraordinary perception, is its limitation. Neither sense experience nor extraordinary perception gives us knowledge of "everything," including the so-called obvious past and the future. The flux of experience is often confined to the immediate past and the present. Thus, in the passage describing the process of perception, when he referred to the objects of the past, present, and future, the Buddha was confining himself to concepts (*sankhā*) relating to objects, not to experience or perception (*sannā*) itself. For this reason, whenever he had to speak of experience or objects of experience, he was careful to use participles such as "has been" (*bhūta*) or "has remained" (*thita*), "made" (*kata*), "dispositionally conditioned" (*sankhata*), or "dependently arisen" (*paticcasamuppanna*)....

The avoidance of any absolutistic notions of truth does not mean the wholehearted sponsorship of skepticism, either in its absolute form, as reflected in a philosopher like Sanjaya, or in its less severe form, portrayed in the Jaina logic of syādvāda, where everything is a possibility or a "maybe." The difficulty lay in discovering a middle path between these extremes. In the first place, the Buddha had to admit that every rational human being needs to recognize certain things as true and others as false. Otherwise human life would be chaotic. Therefore, to the question of whether there is a variety of truths (regarding the same matter), the Buddha declared that "truth is one and there is no second" (*ekam hi saccam na dutiyam atthi*), [*Sutta-nipāta* 884, ed. H. Smith, London Pali Text Society, 1913]. Second, it was necessary to prevent this truth from deteriorating into an absolute truth, as reflected in the statement "This alone is true, everything else is false" (*idam eva saccam mohgam annam*). This latter statement, which the Buddha refused to recognize, has a significant bearing on his conception of truth. By rejecting it the Buddha was, in fact, renouncing several theories or conceptions of truth or reality.

The statements "This alone is true" (*idam eva saccam*) is different from the statement "this is true" (*idam saccam*). The demonstrative "this" (*idam*) emphasizes the particular or the individual, and may be taken as an instance of an empirical truth. However, the addition of the emphatic particle "alone" (*eva*) may not make it an absolute truth if the reference is to an empirical truth as substantiated by the demonstrative. Therefore, "this alone is true" can more appropriately refer

56

to an essential truth, the phrase "this alone" isolating that experience from anything else or eliminating any relationship it bears to any other thing or event. In a sense, it refers to an immediate impression, comparable to that recognized by Hume, with no fringes or relationships. Furthermore, it implies a pure perception. . . .

For the Buddha, neither perception nor conception is as pure as it was assumed to be by the pre-Buddhist Indian philosophers. His conception of truth (*sacca*) had to be presented in an altogether different manner. This seems to be why the Buddha wanted to dissolve the absolutistic true/false dichotomy and replace it with a trichotomy – the true, the confused, and the false – the first accounting for what is available in the present context, the second allowing for the possible, and the third explaining the impossible. The Buddha refers to truth as *sacca*, confusion or the confused as *musā*, and the false as *kali.*

This repudiation of the absolute true/false distinction, comparable to one unsuccessfully attempted by William James in Western philosophy, seems to leave the Buddha with a method of providing truth-value to propositions very different from the methods adopted in the essentialist or absolutistic systems.

It seems that for the Buddha, if something is empirically true, then its denial is not to be characterized as absolutely false, but as something that is simply contrary to the situation. For this contrary to appear as a contradiction, it must be pitted against either an absolute truth or a constructed universal statement that does not allow for exceptions. Thus the statements "All swans are white" and "Some swans are not white" are contradictories because the former is taken to be an absolute truth. Realizing the nature of experience as well as conception, the Buddha was not willing to grant such absolute truths. To eliminate such absolutism, he adopted two strategies. The first was to redefine the conception of "all" (*sarvam*), confining it to what has been experienced. This is clear in his discourse on "everything" or "all" (*sabbam*). The second strategy was to concretize every universal statement with the use of the demonstrative. Thus we have statements such as "All *this* is suffering" (*sabbam idam dukkham*), never "All is suffering" (*sabbam dukkham*).

In the context of such an epistemic evaluation of truth and falsity, a statement that can be counted as false is one that denies not only the empirical truth but also any possibilities.

Let us leave Kalupahana's explication at this point.

This understanding of the Buddhist position bases itself primarily on the very famous parable that Buddha tells of a king who called together all the blind men in Sāvatthī and had them assembled around an elephant. Every one of them touched one part of the elephant's body, and then were asked to describe its appearance. The king received a variety of answers. "Those among the blind men who had left the head of the elephant said 'Your Majesty, the elephant is like a cauldron.' Those who touched its ear said, 'Your Majesty, the elephant is like a shovel.' Those who felt its trunk said, 'Your Majesty, it is like the shaft of a plough.' This continued until finally, 'they attached each other with their fists, crying 'An elephant is like this, not like that'...." (*Udāna* 6.4, Oldenberg, *Reden des Buddha*, 1922, p. 134). Gustav Mensching, in his *Tolerance and Truth in Religion*, transl. M.J. Klimkeit, Alabama, 1971, explains (pp. 19–20):

> This parable has deep significance; it reveals the innermost reasons for Buddha's [tolerant] attitude. Every one of the blind man really does have contact with part of the true elephant. Transposed into religious terms, the implication is that different religions views are all based on true contact with the sacred. The concrete expressions referring to the object of contact are figurative statements, in the sense of the blind men's claim when they say the elephant is *like* this or that worldly phenomenon. The reason for the engaging in strife is the fact that every one of these blind men holds his partial insight to be universally valid. Yet in fact none of the perceptions do justice to the complete nature of the real object. This same applies to the realm of religion; no one statement can fully encompass and express the whole truth.[27]

Let it suffice here to see that in (at least some streams of) Buddhism "facts" based on sensory experience have limited truth-value, and while not every statement need be qualified by a Jain "maybe," empirical knowledge posits a "repudiation of the absolute true/false distinction," as indicated above. This, of course, opens the way to a more tolerant approach to "pluralistic truth," if one may coin such a phrase.

Here we should note that it was in the nineteenth century that Europe became acquainted with Buddhism, and from the establishment of the *Asiatic Society of Bengal in Calcutta* in 1784, by the great Sankritist Sir William Jones (1746–1794), through to the publications of the *Pali Text*

Society, founded in 1881 by T.W. Rhys Davids (1843–1922), Buddhism became a subject of intense interest among the European intellectual society of the late nineteenth and early twentieth century, giving birth to the *Theosophical Society* and other cultic groups, (discussed in part below chapter 6). This development is described in detail in John Snelling's *The Buddhist Handbook: A Complete Guide to Buddhist Schools, Teaching, Practice and History*, Rochester, Vermont, 1991, pp. 193–256, in a section entitled "Buddhism comes West."[28]

Wilhelm Halbfass, in his study *India and Europe: An Essay in Understanding*, New York, 1968, in which he explores the history of intellectual encounters between India and Europe throughout the ages, concludes (p. 440) with a discussion on the effect of globalization of Western culture; asking:

> Will the "Europeanization" of the earth be reversed? Are other cultures and traditions . . . ready to provide alternatives? In the modern plane-tary situation, Eastern and Western "cultures" . . . meet in a Westernized world, under conditions shaped by Western ways of thinking. The medium, the framework of any "dialogue" seems to be an irreducibly Western one. But is this factually inescapable "universality" the true *telos* of mankind? Could it be that the global openness of modernity is still a parochially Western-European horizon?[29]

And let us consider a basic aspect of Chinese thought, as explicated by Alan Wilson Watts (1915–1973), the popular philosophical interpreter of Eastern philosophy.

> At the very roots of Chinese thinking and feeling there lies the principle of polarity, which is not to be confused with the ideas of opposition or conflict. In the metaphors of other cultures, light is at war with darkness, life with death, good with evil, and the positive with the negative, and thus an idealism to cultivate the former and get rid of the latter flourishes throughout much of the world. To the traditional way of Chinese thinking, this is as incomprehensible as an electric current without both positive and negative poles, for polarity is the principle that + and –, north and south, are different aspects of one and the same system, and that the disappearance of either one of them would be the disappearance of the system.

To this he adds:

> People who have been brought up in the aura of Christian and Hebrew
> aspirations find this frustrating, because it seems to deny any possibil-
> ity of progress, an ideal which flows from their linear (as distinct from
> cyclic) view of time and history.

So too Li Zhilin, in his essay "On the Dual Nature of Chinese Thought and
its Modernization," apud *Culture and Modernity: East-West Perspectives*,
ed. Eliot Deutsch, Honolulu, 1991, pp. 245–247, after discussing the "Dual
Nature of Logical Thought," i.e. formal logic and dialectical logic, points
out that the "Chinese showed a constant tendency to develop dialectical
logic" (p. 245, citing Joseph Needham, *Science and Civilization in China*,
vol. 3, *Mathematics and the Sciences of the Heaven and Earth*, Boston,
1959, p. 151). He then examines the method of reasoning in traditional
Chinese thinking (pp. 246–247) thus:

> It occurs as a kind of systematic inference (that is, a system that can
> be inferred from another system), which is different from Western
> propositional inference. The Chinese inference is also full of dialectical
> concepts.
> The first concept is of dynamism. The two opposite symbols "-------"
> and "--- ---" form a dynamic system of strong and weak. Combining
> these two symbols, the *Yi Jing* (*Book of Changes*) – which signaled the
> beginning of Chinese philosophy – inferred a more complex dynamic
> system of eight trigrams and sixty-four hexagrams, with the latter
> derived from a combination of any two of the original eight trigrams.
> Thus it was said that "through the interplay of the strong and the weak,
> change and transformation become manifest."
> The second concept is of organicism. For example, *the Classic of
> Internal Medicine* says that a doctor can measure, discriminate, and
> explain the functions of a patient's internal organs simply by feeling
> the patient's pulse. Obviously it considered the "*yin-yang* and five
> elements," the five internal organs, and the patient's physiological and
> mental changes as an organic and interconnected whole.

But what is perhaps the most significant in the context of our discussion
is the third:

The third is a concept of the unity of opposites. Xun Zi pointed out that reasoning ("dialection and explanation") involved contradictions and was a process by which to comprehend "the way of movement and quiescence." And Wang Fuzhi held that reasoning was a contradictory movement between good and bad luck, joy and anger, gain and loss.

He then continues further to elucidate this third concept (ibid. pp. 249–250):

3. *The Harmony of Opposites*
This is a theoretical framework for a way of thinking about the law of development of things (*li*).

The *Yi Zhuan* (Appendixes of the Book of Changes) says: "One *yin* and one *yang* constitute what is called *Tao*," and "Through the interplay of the strong and the weak, change and transformation become manifest," assuming that though the world is full of various contradictions it has achieved a harmonious development.

Taoism advocates the idea of harmony of opposites as well. Lao Zi says: "The movement of Tao consists in reversion," holding that everything in the world is produced from opposites in contradiction – for example, *yin* (negative forces) and *yang* (positive forces – and everything moves towards its opposite: "Being and nonbeing produce each other, difficult and easy complete each other, long and short contrast each other, high and low distinguish each other, sound and voice harmonize with each other." Taoism holds that the two opposites in a contradiction are mutually conditional and interdependent. Thus it can be seen that the relationship between the two opposites in a contradiction is a sort of dynamic harmony between two things in mutual antithesis, connection, and involvement.

This kind of thinking is widely prevalent in traditional Chinese culture and provides the Chinese theory of knowledge with a multidimensional structure of antitheses: righteousness and profit, humanity and righteousness, past and present, propriety and law, Heaven and man, names and actualities, being and nonbeing, principle and desire, and so forth.

Moreover, this way of perceiving things can be popularly formulated into two propositions. One is that everything in the world can be divided into two. The other is that two can harmoniously combine into one, just as Lao Zi says: "It is on the blending of the breaths of the *yin* and the *yang* that their harmony depends." The idea of a harmony of opposites is substantially aimed at a solution to the problem of the dialectical unity of "two" with "one," and it signifies the law of the unity of opposites within things and things at their best state.

And moving to Japan, we note the expositions of Zen Buddhism by the Nobel Peace Prize winner of 1963, and great Zen philosopher Daisetz T. Suzuki (1870–1966), one of the key personalities in the spreading of Zen to the West. In one of his articles ("Knowledge and Innocence") he writes:

> Zero = infinity, and infinity = zero. The zero I speak of is not a mathematical symbol. It is the infinite – a store-house or womb (*Garbha*) of all possible good or values. The double equation is to be understood not only statistically but dynamically. It takes place between being and becoming. For they are not contradictory ideas. Emptiness is not sheer emptiness or passivity or Innocence. It is and at the same time is not. It is being, it is becoming. It is knowledge and Innocence. . . .

Clearly "It is and at the same time is not" is one of those cryptic statements so puzzling to the West, and so familiar in the East.

And perhaps we may compare the theory of language of the Japanese philosopher Shinran (1173–1262), the founder of Shin Buddhism, or, more technically Jōdo Shinshin, the "True Pure Land School," from certain aspects, to what we have found in the Jaina doctrine of *Anakantevada.* For Thomas P. Kasulis, in his study "The Origins of the Question," apud *Culture and Modernity: East-West Perspectives*, ed. Eliot Deutsch, Honolulu, 1991, pp. 218–219:

> Normally, when we think of literalist interpreters, we envision scholars who pour over the philological, historical, and contextual components of the text or, alternatively, fundamentalists who believe that the text is patently obvious and one should simply read it naively. Shinran would have good reasons for rejecting either of these models of literalism, however. The scholarly approach itself smacks of *hakarai*, the ability to figure things out by trusting one's own knowledge and technical skills. The fundamentalist approach, on the other hand, overlooks the pernicious presence of ego and its ability to delude us in our attempts to "just see what the text says."

Shinran's readings of the texts clearly fit neither model of literalism. In the opening of his *Ichinen tanen mon'i*, for example, he quotes a passage from Shan-tao, a passage that surely means by any ordinary reading of the Chinese: "May everyone always desire that *at the time of death* [the Pure Land] will appear before them" and interprets it to say instead: "Everyone should always, *up to the time of death*, desire that [the Pure Land] will appear before them."

The Key to Shinran's position is in how he understands "other-power" to inform his reading of a text. Shinran's position is that one must submit to the text, but not to its letters; one must yield to the spiritual power behind it, the power of Amida's Vow. For Shinran, the Shin Buddhist reader should approach the text without preconceptions, without special technical skills, and without the confidence that one can understand. We should see the text as something open to our entering into it.

This explains why Shinran's reading emphasizes the terms "thus" (*nyoze*), "faith" (*shin*), and "enter" (nyū) in T'an-luan's statement. In Shinran's understanding of the power of Amida's Vow, *shinjin* or faith is the dynamic through which thusness and the thus-come (*nyorai*, that is, the Buddha Amida) work naturally through the person so that the person may enter the Pure Land. By approaching the text with *shinjin*, the reader trusts not the text but the compassionate vow of Amida Buddha to help us.

How can we trust ourselves to be honest? How can we trust ourselves not to deceive ourselves? According to Shinran, we can't. Faith, which includes the denial that I can figure out things on my own, must inform the reading of the text from the start as well as follow from it. A religious reading requires of the reader that one not trust oneself: such a misplaced trust is simply own-power, *jiriki*. The only effective form of trust is the trust in Amida's Vow, and that trust is nothing other than the natural function of the Vow's power itself. From the *tariki* standpoint, I do not read the text; the text expresses itself to me and through me.

What does this mean in broader philosophical terms? Shinran's point is that there is no such thing as a religious text *per se*, but only religious *readings* of sacred texts. More precisely, if a text is read nonreligiously, it is not a religious text. If it is read religiously, it may or may not be a religious text, depending on whether it possesses the capacity to affect the reader's spiritual self-reflection. Interestingly, if the reader leaves the reading with the sense of "now I know the answer," the text read is not religious. The point of the religious text is to make us more acutely aware of our inadequacy, our failings, our limitations. Similarly, a reading that leaves the reader in utter despair also fails to qualify as religious because it has not instilled the reader with the sense of "other-power" essential to the faith necessary in spiritual development. Indeed, according to Shinran, without such faith, the text cannot be read religiously.

Does this not mean that since "the text expresses itself to me and through me," and each "me," i.e. person is different with his own individual characteristics, the text will express itself in accordance with his special self – i.e. from his own *dristikona*, in Jaina terminology?

Clearly we cannot analyze all the various themes in Japanese religious philosophy, but the above should surely suffice in highlighting some of the critical differences between Eastern and Western thinking.

As a sort of summary of what I see as a basis in Eastern thought, as opposed to Western thinking, I should like to cite the very lucid exposition of Fritjof Carpa (a theoretical physicist), in his *The Tao of Physics: An Exploration of the Parallels between Modern Physics and Eastern Mysticism,* ... ed. Boston, 2000, pp. 145–146, in chapter 11, entitled "Beyond the World of Opposites":

When the Eastern mystics tell us that they experience all things and events as manifestations of a basic oneness, this does not mean that they pronounce all things to be equal. They recognize the individuality of things, but at the same time they are aware that all differences and contrasts are relative within an all-embracing unity. Since in our normal state of consciousness, this unity of all contrasts – and especially the unity of opposites – is extremely hard to accept, it constitutes one of the most puzzling features of Eastern philosophy. It is, however, an insight which lies at the very root of the Eastern world view.

Opposites are abstract concepts belonging to the realm of thought, and as such they are relative. By the very act of focusing our attention on any one concept we create its opposite. As Lao Tzu says, "When all in the world understand beauty to be beautiful, then ugliness exists; when all understand goodness to be good, then evil exists." [Lao Tzu, *Tao Te Ching*, transl. Chu Ta-Kao, New York, 1972, chapter 1]. Mystics transcend this realm of intellectual concepts, and in transcending it become aware of the relativity and polar relationship of all opposites. They realize that good and bad, pleasure and pain, life and death, are not absolute experiences belonging to different categories, but are merely two sides of the same reality; extreme parts of a single whole. The awareness that all opposites are polar, and thus a unity, is seen as one of the highest aims of man in the spiritual traditions of the East. "Be in truth eternal, beyond earthly opposites!" is Krishna's advice in the *Bhagavad Gita*, and the same advice is given to the followers of Buddhism. Thus D. T. Suzuki writes, "The fundamental idea of Buddhism is to pass beyond the world of opposites, a world built up by intellectual distinctions and emotional defilements, and to realize the spiritual world of non-distinction, which involves achieving an absolute point of view." [D.T. Suzuki, *The Essence of Buddhism*, Kyoto, 1968, p. 18.]

The whole of Buddhist teaching – and in fact the whole of Eastern mysticism – revolves about this absolute point of view which is reached in the world of *acinty*, or "no-thought," where the unity of all opposites becomes a vivid experience. In the words of a Zen poem,

> At dusk the cock announces dawn,
> At midnight, the bright sun.
> [Quoted in A.W. Watts,
> *The Way of Zen*, New York, 1957, p. 117.]

The notion that all opposites are polar – that light and dark, winning and losing, good and evil, are merely different aspects of the same phenomenon – is one of the basic principles of the Eastern way of life. Since all opposites are interdependent, their conflict can never result in the total victory of one side, but will always be a manifestation of the interplay between the two sides. In the East, a virtuous person is therefore not one who undertakes the impossible task of striving for the good and eliminating the bad, but rather one who is able to maintain a dynamic balance between good and bad.

This notion of dynamic balance is essential to the way in which the unity of opposites is experienced in Eastern mysticism. It is never a static identity, but always a dynamic interplay between two extremes. This point has been emphasized most extensively by the Chinese sages in their symbolism of the archetypal poles *yin* and *yang*. They called the unity lying behind *yin* and *yang* the *Tao* and saw it as a process which brings about their interplay: "That which lets now the dark, now the light appear is Tao." [R. Wilhelm, *The I Ching on Book of Changes*, Princeton N.J., 1967, p. 297.]

Or in a somewhat different succinct formulation as summarized by Archie J. Bahm, in his *Comparative Philosophy: Western, Indian and Chinese Philosophies Compared.*[30] New Delhi, 1977, pp. 67–69, noting that he distinguishes between three major "schools" of thought – European, Indian and Chinese:

European thought, structured in part by Euclidean geometry and Aristotelian logic and developed through Boolean algebra and symbolic logic, has sharpened its notion of negation in terms of an ideal called "an excluded middle." Between *a* and *not-a* there is nothing, or *a* and *not-a* have nothing in common. This ideal is often formulated in terms of "exclusive disjunction:" "X is either *a* or *not-a*, but not both." The sharpness of this distinction between *a* and *not-a* has enabled thinkers to define and clarify ideas, inferences, and systems with perfect precision, and has made possible developments in science, technology, and engineering which astound all.

Indian thought, when regarding ultimate reality as without distinctions, has idealized *Nirguna Brahman* as the negation of all negation. Since any distinction kinvolves two things which are distinct from, and hence not, each other, negation is involved in every distinction. To eliminate all distinction is to eliminate all negation. Ideally, no statements can be truly made about *Nirguna Brahman*, because all statements involve distinctions. But demands by inquirers have been met with a formula which can be used for comparative purposes. Of *Nirguna Brahman* (and the same holds for anything taken as having ultimate reality) one may say: "It (X) is neither *a*, nor *not-a*, nor both *a*, and *not-a*, nor neither *a* nor *not-a*." This "principle of four-cornered negation," which one can find repeated copiously in the Pali *Pitakas*, provides a clue to something fundamental about Indian mentality.

Chinese thought, accepting both parts and wholes, and their distinctness and indistinctness, as apprehended, have come to idealize a "both-and" logic. Not only does the nature of each thing have its wholeness (*tao*) but each *tao* consists of its opposing parts *yang* and *yin* which, though distinguishable, are inseparable from it and, though distinguishable within it, are not distinct from it. Since distinguishable stages in any cycle of changes shade into each other, such that the borderline between them is not distinct, we may say that Chinese tend to idealize distinctions which are not too distinct. Neither idealizing opposites (*yang* and *yin*) as having nothing in common, since they have both *tao* in common and their partial indistinctness from each other, nor idealizing that which opposites have in common (*tao*) as itself purified from distinctions, they find themselves accepting a "both-and" logic: Not only does each thing that exists, *X*, have both *yang* and *yin* (*a* and *non-a*), which is itself both distinguishable from and yet not completely distinguishable from them, but also each opposing part (whether *yang* or *yin*) has its own opposing parts which, as diagramed by trigrams or hexigrams, form series of tiers, each of which, when added to the first, exemplifies reapplication of the "both-and" logic.

These emphases, epitomized in three formuli, have been symbolized by diagramming variations on three circles. The rationalist ideal of an excluded middle may be represented by a circle divided exactly in half, with one half pure white and the other half pure black. The Indian ideal of distinctionless *Nirguna Brahman* has been captured in the seventh of the "Ten Cow-Herding Pictures," a series of Zen paintings designed to illustrate how one needs to achieve *nirvana* before returning to practice Zen in everyday life. The Chinese ideal of *Tao* consisting of *yang* and *yin* is depicted in the well-known *Tao* symbol; when drawn correctly, the light (*yang*) and dark (*yin*) portions of the symbol are so arranged that a string placed on any diameter will include some of both, so that swinging such a string around over all diameters will never fail to include some of both. In case any doubt remains about the intent, some designers add a spot of light in the middle of the dark portion and a spot of dark in the light portion, "Both-and" prevails over the entire symbol.

In view of all of the above, I would venture to suggest that the Eastern cultural influence has had a deep penetration in certain areas of Western philosophical thought, with significant theological implications. (See below.)

Endnotes to Chapter 2

1. This may appear to be too simplistic. It is what Robert Makim, in his important book *On Religious Diversity*, Oxford 2012, calls "Exclusivism about Truth" (pp. 14 et seq.), or, as he formulates it:

> Our tradition is entirely right, but all other traditions are entirely wrong, (ETI, "E" is for exclusivism, "T" for truth, and "I" indicating his first significant proposition about truth).

However, Makim gives other alternative, postulates, such as ET4. We are generally correct, and other traditions are generally mistaken.

Or:

> ET5 Our tradition is right about all really important religious matters, and all other traditions are wrong about these matters.

Then we might be wrong, about less important matters. He continues to give other options, such as:

> ET6 The claims of our traditions are true, other traditions are correct when they accept our claims, and they are mistaken when they reject our claims.
> ET9 The claims of our traditions are true, or most of them are true; other traditions are correct when they accept our claims, and they are mistaken when they reject our claims.

On the other hand he talks of "Inclusivism about Truth" (pp. 35 et seq.) ("I"), with such statements as IT2 Others may be right about beliefs we do not hold.

He sees this position articulated in *Nostra Aetate*'s "Declaration on the Relations of the Church to Non-Christian Religions," pertaining to Hinduism, Buddhism and other non-Christian religions, which includes a passage which runs thus:

> [Then] is found among the various peoples a certain perception of that hidden power that hovers over the course of things and over the events of human history; at times some even have come to the recognition of a Supreme Being, or even of a Father. . . . The Catholic Church rejects nothing that is true and holy in these religions. She regards with sincere reverence those ways of conduct and of life, those precepts and readings which, *though differing in*

many aspects from the ones she holds and sets forth, nevertheless often inflect a ray of that truth which enlightens all men. (Makim's emphasis.)

He further quotes from J.A. DiNoia, O.P., *A Diversity of Religions: A Christian Perspective*, Washington 1992, p. 29):

> [This Declaration takes] up in turn the doctrines of the Hindu, Buddhist, Muslim, and Judaic communities at least in a general way . . . [and approves] of the truth and rightness expressed in their beliefs and precepts. . . . As it happens, the doctrines whose truth and rightness it acknowledges, turn out to be identical with Christian doctrines. [It] does not state that any strictly alien religious claims are true and right, but neither does it exclude this possibility.

Clearly we cannot give a synopsis of the argumentation of the whole book, especially the very important chapter on "Pluralism" (pp. 100 & seq.), but it is equally clear that the notion of a "Holy War" (Christian Crusade) or "Jihad" (of Islam) is based on ET1, and the moral directives for them would be greatly modified by ET9 and/ or IT2, or indeed his PT1–PT5, when "P" equals Pluralism.

This has also been clearly and succinctly explicated by E.A. Burtt, in his "What Can Western Philosophy Learn from India," *Philosophy East and West* 5/3, 1955, pp. 202–208. He also points out there that a similar conclusion was arrived at by John Wisdom, in his *Philosophy and Psychoanalysis*, Oxford 1953, pp. 87 et seq.

There she writes (pp. 202–203):

> When, for example, one examines the early Buddhist scriptures he frequently comes across stories like the following. A disciple of Buddha, Mālunkyāputta by name, suddenly finds himself dissatisfied that the Master has not taught him the right answer to certain metaphysical perplexities. He articulates his dissatisfaction thus:
>
> "These theories which The Blessed One has left unexplained, has set aside and rejected - that the world is eternal, that the world is not eternal, that the world is finite, that the world is infinite, that the soul and the body are identical, that the soul is one thing and the body another, that the saint exists after death, that the saint does not exist after death, that the saint both exists and does not exist after death, that the saint neither exists nor does not exist after death – these the Blessed One does not explain to me. And the fact that the Blessed One does not explain them to me does not please me nor suit me. . . ." (*Majjbima-nikāya, sūtra* 63, apud H.C. Warren, *Buddhism in Translation*, Cambridge Mass. 1915, pp. 117 et seq.).
>
> So, Mālunkyāputta approaches the Buddha and voices his complaint. The Master replies to him, and in the course of the ensuing dialogue all four of these possibilities in the case of each doctrine discussed are carefully and (to the Western reader) wearisomely mentioned. It is taken for granted that the

analysis would be incomplete if any one of them were omitted. And when, some centuries later, the great Buddhist dialectician Nāgārjuna sets himself to destroy the idea that *nirvāna* (man's ultimate goal as conceived by this religion) can be rationally described, he patiently analyzes each of the four alternatives: that *nirvāna* is some form of being, that it is some form of non-being, that it is both being and non-being, and that it is neither being nor non-being. These are but two illustrations out of many.

[This process of analysis and argumentation has been called by Prof. P.T. Raju the principle of "Four-Cornered Negation." See his article "The Principle of Four-Cornered Negation in India-Philosophy," *Revue of Metaphysics* 7/4, 1954, pp. 694–713.]

Burtt then continues to explain this way of thinking "that naturally puzzle[s] the Western mind," as follows:

It is vital always to remember the fact that to the Eastern thinker a proposition or statement is not an objective entity, capable of being isolated from its living context and having properties by itself, as it is to a Western logician. It is something asserted by a human being, in some situation, for some purpose; it is an epistemic act, filling its role in a sequence or pattern of acts which he is performing in relation to certain objects and events. It must be understood, therefore, in that setting. This means, among other things, that logical relationships are not examined in the purely implicative connections which they have with each other; no mathematical science of logical form as such seems to the typical Indian mind to serve any useful end. Even the most general principles of inference are considered in the context of their function in the search for knowledge or insight about man and his world.

See the continuation of his exposition.

Finally, to exemplify the epitome of the pluralistic tradition, I shall cite (his citations) on p. 101 of a statement by the 19th century Hindu thinker Rama-Krishna:

God has made different religions to suit different aspirants, times and countries. All doctrines are only so many paths . . . one can reach God if one follows any of the paths with whole-hearted devotion . . . the one Everlasting-Intelligent-Bliss is invoked by some as God, by some as Alla, by some as Jehovah, and by others as Brahman. . . . (Quoted by Rodney Stark, *One True God: Historical Consequences of Monotheism*, Princeton, NJ, 2001, p. 106.)

But, of course, this is very much in the spirit of Eastern thought (discussed above in the section on multiple truths).

2. *Nāsadasītya*, in the *Rg-Veda* 5:129.

3. See *Brahmasūtra* 4:1, 13–15. Nakamura explains that the basis of this way of thinking is the concept of the unity of all things, so that the One Absolute Being, the Brahman or the Atman is neither existent nor not existent. "This monist of the Upanisads was developed further by the Vedantin philosophers. And it forms the core of the theological system of the Hindu religious schools. Throughout the history of philosophy of this country, the monistic view has been accepted by a majority of the thinkers" (ibid. pp. 39–40).

4. See, for example, A.A. Long and D.N. Sedley, *The Hellenistic Philosophers*, vol. 1, Cambridge 1987, pp. 329–330 (a), 332, on the "Heraclitean Principles of Opposition," drawing upon Plato, *Phaedo* 60.

See also H.S. Versal, in his chapter "Three Greek Experiments in Oneness," apud One God: *Concepts of Divinity in the Ancient World*, ed. Balora Verlin Porter, 2000, pp. 97, 109:

Indeed, Versel argues (ibid. 103–104) that it is perfectly humanly normal to be able to experience as true and valid two logically contradictory predicates for qualities. He calls this the "concept of complementarity." (Cf. also ibid. pp. 101–102, and in this chapter he seeks thus to resolve the "apparent" contradictory statements of the Greek philosopher Xenophanes, VI century C.E., who, on the one hand, seems to have been a monotheist [Fragment 23], and, on the other hand, frequently speaks of "the Gods" [Fragments 1:24; 11:1; 12:1; 14:1; 15:3; 15:1; 18:1; 34:2].)

5. On this concept in the writing of Nicolas of Cusa, (in his *De visione Dei*, chapter 9), 1453, see Josef Stallmach, *Zusammenfall der Gegensätze: Die Prinzip der Dialectik bei Nicolas* Kues, Trier 1960; Kurt Flasch, *Die Metaphysik des Einen bei Nicolas von Kues; Problemgeschichlische stellung und systematische Bedeutung*, Brill 1973; and Kristeller ibid. pp. 203–204. And on Meister Eckhart, see Rudolf Otto, *Mysticism: East and West*, New York, 1936; Walter T. Stace, *The Teachings of the Mystics*, New York, 1960, pp. 139 et seq.; Frederick Charles Coplestone, *A History of Philosophy*, vol. 3/2, Garden City New York, 1963, pp. 37–54.

6. Similarly St. Bonaventure in the 13th century. See Evert H. Cousins, *Bonaventure and the Coincidentia Oppositum*, Chicago 1978, chapters 1,3,5,7. This goes back to the neo-Platonism of Plotinus (died in Italy 270 C.E.), for example, in the *Ennead* 5.2.1:

> The One is all things and no one of them; the source of all things is not all things; all things are its possession – running back, so to speak, to it – or, more correctly, not yet so, they will be.
>
> But a universe from an unbroken unity, in which there appears no diversity, not even duality?

It is precisely because there is nothing within the One that all things are from it: in order that Being may be brought about the source must be no Being but Being's generator, in what is to be thought of as the primal act of generation. Seeking nothing, possessing nothing, lacking nothing, the One is perfect, and, in our metaphor, has overflowed, and its exuberance has produced the new: this product has turned again to its begetter and been filled and has become its contemplator and so a *Nous* [Mind]. (Translation E. Bevan, *Later Greek Religion*, London & Toronto, New York, 1927, p. 193.)

For an analysis of the various semantic fields of oppositional notions, such as: contradictory, contrary, opposite, converse, reverse, negative, contrast, incompatible, and the subtle differences between them, see Shulah Abramsky, *"Nigudim Hofchiim, Nigudim Tat-Hafuchim ve-Nigudim Okvim;" Mehkarei Givah* 2012, 2013, pp. 53–74.

7. However, this is possible according to Nicolas of Cusa, *De Possest* 53:14, where *non-esse* not-being and *essendi necessitas* necessary being can both be coninciden-tal, according to his principle of *coincidentia contradictoriorum*. These concepts are not altogether identical but for our purposes they are very closely related.

8. See, e.g., Mircea Eliade, *The Quest: History and Meaning in Religion*, Chicago & London, 1969, in the section on "Polarity and Coincidentia Oppositorum," pp. 168–169:

Of course, the couple Mitra-Varuna was not the original model of all the other polarities, but only the most important expression, on the religious and myth-ological planes, of this principle in which Indian thought has recognized the fundamental structures of the cosmic totality and of human existence. Indeed, later speculation has distinguished *two* aspects of Brahman: *apara* and *para*, "inferior" and "superior," visible and invisible, manifest and nonmanifest. In other words, it is always the mystery of a polarity, all at once a bi-unity and a rhythmic alternation, that can be deciphered in the different mythological, religious, and philosophical "illustrations:" Mitra and Varuna, the visible and invisible aspects of Brahman, Brahman and *māyā*, *purusha and prakriti*, and later on Shiva and Shakti, or *Samsāra* and Nirvāna.

But some of these polarities tend to annul themselves in a *coincidentia oppositorum*, in a paradoxical unity-totality, the *Urgrund* of which I spoke of a moment ago. That it is not only a question of metaphysical speculations but also of formulas with the help of which India tried to circumscribe a peculiar mode of existence, is proved by the fact that *coincidentia oppositorum* is implied in *jivan mukta*, the "liberated in life," who continues to exist in the world even though he has attained final deliverance; or the "awakened one" for whom Nirvāna and *Samsāra* appear to be one and the same thing; or the situation of a tantric yogin able to pass from ascetism to orgy without any modification of behavior. Indian spirituality has been obsessed by the "Absolute." Now, however one may conceive the Absolute, it cannot be conceived except as beyond contraries and polarities. This is the reason why India includes the orgy among the means of attaining deliverance, while deliverance is denied to those who continue to follow the ethical rules depending on social institutions. The "Absolute," the ultimate liberation, the freedom, *moksha, mukti,* is not accessible to those who have not surpassed what the texts call the "couples of contraries," i.e., the polarities we have discussed.

Cf. idem, "La Coincidentia Oppositorum," *Eranos Jahrbuch* XXVII, 1959, pp. 202–205; and see Alon W. Wattson, *The Two Hands of God: Myths of Polarity*, New York, 1963, pass.

9. He adds that:

> In practice, this attitude has led Hindus to develop an unusual capacity for assimilating foreign influences and other religions, while maintaining their own traditions.

10. Ananda K. Coomaraswamy, *Hinduism and Buddhism*, 2nd edition, Manohar 1989, pp. 12–13.

11. For an interesting example of this "fusing" of apparent contradiction, see Ananda K. Coomaraswamy, *The GR Veda and Land-Nāma-Bok*, London, 1935, p. 24:

> Though Yama's is the dreaded path of death (*R.V.*, I, 38, 5) and Agni is the very principle of life (*āyu, ekâyu, viśvâyu,* passim), the *Rg Veda* either identifies Yama with Agni (I, 164, 46), or calls the latter Yama's darling friend (*rāmya*, X, 21, 5) or priest (*hotr*, X, 52, 3), and there is a significant aspect in which their functions coincide, viz., as "gatherer together of the kindreds" (in I, 59, I, Agni *janān . . . yayantha,* in X, 14, I. Yama is *samgamano janānm*), cf. *ekam bhū*, "to become one," i.e., "to die." *The contrasted functions are in fact united in the Golden Germ, "whose likeness is that of life, and likeness that of death" (X. 121 2), in the Year "that separates some beings and unifies others" (AA,* III, 2, 3). How these two that are the same play into each other's hands can be seen in *R.V.*, I, 163, 2–4, where the sacrificial horse (given to Death by Agni as priest and sacrificial fire of the Aśvamedha) is given by Yama in turn to Trita, that is to Agni himself *ab intra*, is yoked by Trita, ridden by Indra, and identified with Yama, Varuna (*āditya*), and Trita. All these are One for the Comprehensor, absolutely unified (*ekadh bhūlvā, B.U.,* V, 5, 12), that is, dead and buried in the Godhead. We may say then that that it is as Yama that the dying man beholds

Agni when he reaches the realm of the two kings, Yama and Varuna (X, 14, 17); and that for the Comprehensor (*vidvān*), and for any man that has done well, that one principle that some desire as life and others fear as death can be seen in either aspect as the Friend (*mitra*), the Meeting-place (*samgamana*), and Lord of the Settlers (*viśpati*); for him the paths of Agni and of Yama are one and the same *devayāna*. [My emphasis, D.S.]

12. These quotes are from S. Radhakrishnan's *The Principle Upanisads* 17th ed., New Delhi 2016, pp. 386, 571, 618. On p. 571 he remarks:

> These apparently contradictory statements are not suggestive of the mental unbalance of the writer. He is struggling to describe what he experiences through the limitations of human thought and languages. The Supreme is beyond the categories of thought. Thought is symbolic and so cannot conceive the Absolute except through negations; yet the Absolute is not a void. It is all that is in time and yet is beyond time.

And on p. 618 he comments:

> By these contradictory predicates, the impossibility of conceiving Brahman through empirical determinations is brought out. . . .

And again in the Hindu context we read in the words of the Sri Vaisnava theologian Pillai Lokācārya as he describes the grace by which the Lord enters and dwells in the image for the sake of the devotee.

> This is the greatest grace of the Lord, that being free He becomes bound, being independent He becomes dependent for all His service on his devotee. . . . In other forms the man belonged to God but behold the supreme sacrifice of Isvara, here the Almighty becomes the property of the devotee. . . . He carries Him about, fans Him, plays with Him – yea, the Infinite has become finite, that the child soul may grasp, understand and love Him. (Bharatan Kumaraffa, *The Hindu Conception of Deity as Culminating in Rāmanuja*, London, 1934, pp. 316–317; cited by Diana L. Eck, *Darśan: Seeing the Divine Image in India*, 3rd edition, New York, 1996, pp. 46, 96 note 68.)

(Is this note similar to some Christian understandings of the Christ personality?)

13. Cf. ibid. pp. 267–273, where he discusses further "the dialectic of opposites," and also pp. 205–206, and Patanjali's *vitarkabādhane pratipaksavhāvanam*, for (avoiding) "truth from doubt, establishment of the opposites," see pp. 51–52. And just to give an example of the simple acceptance of such "inconsistencies," I quote an observation by Monier Williams, in his classic *Religious Thought and Life in India*, part 1, London, 1883, p. 55, who writes of the great Śankara:

He was a Brahmacarī, or an unmarried Brāhman under a vow of perpetual celibacy; and it may be noted as one of the inconsistencies of the Hindu religion, that in no other system is the duty of marriage so strictly enjoined, and in no other system is the importance of abstaining from wedlock as a means of gaining influence for the propagation of religious opinions so frankly admitted.

14. And cf. his remarks in "On Hares and Dreams," *The Quarterly Journal of the Mythic Society* 37/1, p. 3 (referring also to Karl von Speirs, "*Die Hasenjagd,*" *Marksteine der Volkskunst* (*Jahrbuch für historische Volkskundo* 5/6, 1939, pp. 46 and 69).

R.D. Ranade, in his *Mysticism in Maharastra: Indian Mysticism*, Poona 1933, p. 410 (ao. 60), writes, citing Rāmādasā's *Darsabadkha* 7:7, 19–23, Dhulia ed. by Dev. 1905, (from the late 17th century), writes:

> Indeed it is in the nature of all mystical experience to appear contradictory. "As soon as we begin to be aware of it, we forget it. But as soon as we forget it, it comes within the ken of our consciousness . . . When we go to see God, we miss Him. But we see God without going anywhere to meet Him. This indeed is the virtue of spiritual Epochē. When we try to leave Him away, He cannot be left. We are connected with God forever, and the connection is unbreakable. God always is, and when we do not look at Him, He immediately appears before us. The means for His attainment are only the means for His disappearance, and the means for His disappearance are really the means for His attainment. Only that man can know the meaning of this, says Rāmadāsa, who has attained to spiritual experience himself."

This, then, is a general characteristic of mystical experience.

Furthermore, in Ranade's *A Constructive Survey of Upanishadic Philosophy being a systematic introduction to Indian Metaphysics*, (vol. 2, of the *Encyclopaedic History of Indian Philosophy*), Poona 1926, pp. 137–139, when discussing the size of the soul, writes:

> We have hitherto seen some of the stages in the logical, not necessarily historical, evolution of the idea of the extension of the soul. Being first regarded as merely of the size of a grain of rice or barley, it was then regarded as of the size of a thumb, and later of the size of a span, while we have also seen that the *Kaushītaki Upanishad* speaks of the soul as filling the whole extent of the body and being hidden in it as the razor is hidden in a razor-case. We now come to treat of the idea of the soul as not being restricted to any part of the body, but being verily infinite and occupying all space. The *Mundaka Upanishad* speaks of the "eternal, all-pervading, omnipresent, subtle, and imperishable Soul who is the origin of all beings, and whom the wise alone can perceive," and the

Katha Upanishad lends its support to this statement by saying that "the wise man ceases to grieve when he has known this great all-pervading Soul" (S. 17. d). The *Maitri Upkanishad*, not being able to choose between the rival theories about the size of the soul, offers an easy eclecticism by combining all of them together in a promiscuous statement. It tells us that a man "reaches the supreme state by meditating on the soul, who is smaller than an atom, or else of the size of the thumb, or of a span, or of the whole body" (S. 17. e). In this promiscuous statement it is difficult to make out which theory this *Upanishad* advocates. An alternative interpretation of the passage can also be offered, as it has been offered by Cowell and Max Müller, following the commentator Rāmatīrtha, but to say as Rāmatīrtha says that the soul is "of the size of a thumb in the span-sized heart in the body" does not lessen difficulties. That the Upanishadic philosophers felt the necessity of reconciling such contrary statements as that the soul is only of the size of a grain of rice or barley, and that it is all-pervading and omnipresent, may be seen from a passage in the *Katha Upanishad* which asks us to believe the contradiction that "the soul of the living being is subtler than the subtle, and yet greater than the great, and is placed in the cavity of the heart," a statement which, with equal seeming contradiction, is corroborated by the philosopher of the *Chāndogya Upkanishad* who says: "My soul in the heart is smaller than a gain of rice or barley, or a mustard or a canary seed; and yet my soul, which is pent up in the heart, is greater than the earth, greater than the sky, greater than the heaven, greater than all these worlds" (S. 17. f). The Nemesis of the theory which attributes a spatial extension to the soul lies just in these contradictions, and there is no way out of the difficulty except on the supposition that the soul transcends all spatial limitations.

In the above we have brought examples of different kinds of "opposites." We could bring numerous additional examples of this acceptance of such contradictory elements, but the above should suffice to make the point. Westerners may struggle to find harmonistic solutions to such "inconsistencies," but the Eastern mind can (apparently) readily accept them.

See also Champat Rai Jain, *Confluence of Opposites*, Jain Library 1922.

15. See also Wendy Doniger O'Flaherty, *Women, Androgynes, and other Mythical Beasts*, Chicago & London, 1982, p. 6, who calls this "Indian eclecticism." See further, Morres G. Carstairs, *the Twice-Born*, London, 1958, p. 91; and Romain Rolland's Foreward to Ananda K. Coomaraswamy's *The Dance of Śiva: Essays on Indian Culture*, London, 1985, p.XIII. On the difference between western and eastern thought, see, for example, Ananda K. Coomaraswamy, *Sources of Wisdom*, Sri Lanka 1981, pp. 45–46; Rudolf Otto, *Mysticism East and West: A Comparative Analysis of the Nature of Mysticism*, New York, 1926, 1932. However, see Coomaraswamy's essay, "Paths that lead to the Same Summit," in his *Bugbear of Literacy* 2nd edition 1979; Heinrich Zimmer, *Philosophies of India*, ed. Joseph Campbell, New York, 1969, p. 4.

> But the primary concern [of Indian philosophy] – in striking contrast to the interests of the modern philosophers of the West – has always been, not information, but transformation: a radical changing of man's nature and, therefore, a renovation of his understanding both of the outer world, and of his own existence, a transformation as complete as possible, such as will amount when successful to a total conversion and rebirth.

See his chapter ibid. pp. 27–34, entitled, "The Claims of Science," and also Radhakrishnan's introduction to his classic *Indian Philosophy*, vol. 1, London, 1923, and also his Preface to that volume.

See also John J. Tatanamil, "Managing Multiple Religious and Scholarly Identities: An Argument for the Theological Study of Hinduism," *Journal* of the American Academy *of Religion* 68, 2000, pp. 791–799; and Brian K. Smith, "Who can and should speak for Hinduism?" ibid. pp. 741–749.

16. For a succinct introduction to this complex concept see Padmanabh S. Jaini, *The Jaina Path of Purification*, University of California Press 1979, pp. 90–91:

> The Doctrine of Anekānta (Manifold Aspects)
>
> The Jaina term for "existent" is *sat* (literally, being). This term designates an entity comprised of three aspects: substance (*dravya*), quality (*guna*), and mode (*paryāya*). By substance the Jaina understands a support or substratum (*āśraya*) for manifold qualities (*gunas*). The qualities are free from qualities of their own (otherwise they would themselves become substances), but invariably they undergo modifications (parināma) in the form of acquiring (*utpāda*) new modes (*paryāya* or *bhāva*) and losing (*vyaya*) old modes at each moment. Thus, any existent must be seen on three levels: the modes, which last only a moment and belong to the qualities; the qualities, which undergo changes and yet in here forever in their substances; and the substance, which remains the abiding common ground of support for the qualities and their modes.
>
> A material atom (*pudgala-paramānu*) for example, is considered by the Jaina as a substance. It possesses at all times four qualities, namely, a color (*varna*), a taste (*rasa*), a smell (*gandha*), and a certain kind of palpability (*sparśa* touch). These qualities will vary from one moment to another – for example, a red color being replaced by blue, or a sweet taste by bitter – but an atom will never be found without these qualities or without some mode of each one of them. The same rule applies to an animate entity like a soul (*jīva*). A soul is designated as substance (*dravya*) in that it is the locus of innumerable

qualities such as knowledge (*jñāna*), bliss (*sukha*), energy (*vīrya*). The knowledge quality, for example, will increase and decrease, but there is never a time when the soul is without knowledge; otherwise it would become by definition a nonsoul, a material atom. The states of imperfection and perfection, expressed by such terms as *matijñāna* (mind-based knowledge) and *kevalajñāna* (omniscience), are in turn modes of this quality. The other qualities of the soul similarly undergo constant change. These changes do not take place merely on a surface level; rather, their cumulative effect so transforms the soul that we can distinguish various states – bound and free, pure and impure, and so on – and yet relate them to one and the same soul.

Because the qualities are innumerable and their modes are infinite, stretching from the beginningless past to the endless future, it is not possible for an ordinary (non-omniscient) person to perceive the existent in its entirety. At a single moment he can be aware either of the persisting unity (*ekatva*) of the substance or the transient multiplicity (*anekatva*) of its modes. This complexity of the existent – its simultaneous unity and multiplicity, eternity and transience – finds expression in the Jaina term *anekānta*, manifold aspects, which purports to fully describe the existent's nature.

And for a critical study of *anekānta-vāda*, see Satkari Mookerjee, *The Jaina Philosophy of Non-Absolutism*, Calcuta 1944. And see following note.

17. Diana L. Eck, in her book *Darśan: Seeing the Divine in India*, 3rd edition, New York, 1998, pp. 24–25, sees this as "the cultural genius [of India] for embracing diversity." She explains:

> For example, there are six philosophical traditions recognized as "orthodox." But they are not called "systems" in the sense in which we use that term. Rather, they are *darśanas*. Here the term means not the "seeing" of the deity, but the "seeing" of truth. There are many *darśanas*, many "points of view" or perspectives of the truth. And although each has its own starting point, its own theory of Causation, its own accepted enumeration of the ways by which one can arrive at valid knowledge, these "ways of seeing" share a common goal – liberation – and they share the understanding that all rivals are also "orthodox". . . . Any "point of view" implicitly assumes that another point of view is possible.

The "orthodox" traditions are called *āstika*, and the "non-orthodox" ones *nāstika*. For a further explanation of the terms *āstika* and *nāstika*, see Pandit N. Aiyaswami Sastri's sections (Part IV, sect. 22) "Sramana or Non-Brāhmanical Sects," apud *The Cultural Heritage of India*, vol. 1, Calcutta 1958, pp. 389–390:

The philosophical schools of India, speaking broadly, may be grouped as Brāhmanic and non-Brāhmanic, the former being referred to as *āstika* and the latter *nāstika*. *Āstika* denotes the systems which recognize the Vedas and their branches as supreme authority. It does not, as in the West, denote 'theism." Sāmkhya, for instance, is an atheistic philosophy, yet it is regarded as a Brāhmanic system, since it has accepted the authority of the Vedas. Buddhism and Jainism are considered to be non-Brāhmanic, because they do not recognize the authority of the Vedas. According to another interpretation, *āstika* is one who believes in the existence of the future world etc. According to this interpretation, the Buddhists and the Jains cannot be called *nāstikas*. Nāgārjuna implies it when he says, "A *nāstika* is doomed to hell," (a verse from his *Ratnāvali* cited in the *Madhyanaka-vethi* [Bib. Bud.IV], p. 135). Manu, on the other hand, defines *nāstika* as a person who challenges the authority of the Vedas (*nāstiko Vedanindakah*).

As already stated it will be a misnomer to dub the Buddhists and the Jains as *nāstikas*. It will be much more fitting and appropriate, if we call them *avaidikas* (non-Vedic sects.) Buddhist literature appears to speak of all the non-Brāhmanic systems as Śramanas in the frequent expression *"samanā vā brāhmanā vā."* Here "Brāhmana" appears to refer to orthodox schools. According to the tradition preserved in the Tamil literature, Śramana represents three sects, viz. Anuvādins (Pakudha Kaccāyana's sect)' Ājīvikas (Ājīvakas), and Jains. The Buddhists are spoken of separately as Sākyas.

Of these Śramana sects, Buddhism and Jainism occupy the foremost rank. There are materials in abundance, both literary and otherwise, to understand the real attitude taken up by them in the matter of religion and philosophy. But, side by side with Buddhism and Jainisnm, there were other sects having no independent literary documents as their scriptures. They are frequently referred to for criticism by the Buddha and Mahāvīra in their discourses. The common features of all these religious bodies were:

(1) They challenged the authority of the Vedas.

(2) They admitted into their Church all members of the community, irrespective of their social rank and religious career (*varna and āśrama*).

(3) They observed a set of ethical principles.

(4) They practiced a detached life with a view to liberating themselves from the worldly life etc.

(5) They could take to a life of renunciation (*pravrajya*) any time after passing over the minor age.

See further my forthcoming book *The Halachic Status of Hinduism*, Appendix 5.

18. See Tara Sethia, *Ahimsa, Anekānta and Jainism*, Motital Banarsidass, 2004, p. 80. Mahavira, also known as Vardhamana, was the twenty-forth *tirtharkara*, that is the omniscient teacher who preaches true *dharma*.

On the concept of *anakantavada* – non-absolutism, see, for example, the discussion of Nathmal Talia, in his Studies in *Jain Philosophy*, Jain Cultural Research Society, Banaras–5, (India), 1951, p. 22:

> Non-violent search for truth should inspire the enquiries of a thinker. He should not be prejudiced by preconceptions. It is this attitude of tolerance and justice that was responsible for the origin of the doctrine of Non-absolutism (*Anekānta*). Out of universal tolerance and peace-loving nature was born cautiousness of speech. Out of cautiousness of speech was born the habit of explaining problems with the help of *siyāvāya* (= *syādvāda*) or *vibhajavaya*, (Haribhadra, *Dharmasangraharni*, Bombay ed. 1918, gatha 921). This habit, again, developed into a non-absolutistic attitude towards reality (ibid. 915). Our thought is relative. Our expressions are relative. The whole reality in its completeness cannot be grasped by this partial thought or expression. Nor can it be comprehended by combining these thoughts or expressions. What is required is the radical change in our absolutistic attitude. The error lies with the attitude and not with the thought or expression. Attachment and repulsion are the two great enemies of philosophical thinking. A thinker should not be guided by abstractionist tendencies which are responsible for mutually contradictory systems of thought. These tendencies are born of predilections, more or less inherent. It is as much difficult to get rid of these predilections as to get rid of the other evils of life. Truth reveals itself to an impartial thinker. This origin of the doctrine of *Anekānta* can be clearly seen from a study of the solutions by Lord Mahāvīra of the problems which were left unexplained by the Buddha as stated above.

See further Talia ibid. pp. 202, 217.

To further explain this concept, which emphasizes the principle of pluralism (multiplicity of viewpoints) and the notion that truth and reality are perceived differently from diverse points of view, no single one of which is complete (*Tara Sethia* ibid. pp. 123–136, 400–407). The Jains illustrate this theory through the parable of the blind men and the elephant. Each blind man feels a different part of the elephant, its leg, trunk, ear etc. All claim to understand and explain the true appearance of the elephant, but due to their limited perspectives can only partly succeed (Sethia ibid. p. 115). See further B.K. Matilal, *The Central Philosophy of Jainism (Anekānta Vāda)*, Ahmenabad 1981, p. 18: "acceptance" and "inclusion" as characteristics of Jaina thought.

This doctrine is further extended to *Syādvāda*, (conditional assertion) etymologically constructed from the Sanskrit root *syad*, "perhaps," "maybe," or in the context of *syādvāda*, meaning "in some ways," or "from some perspective." This is an endeavour to be precise without violating *anekānta-vada* through a system known as *sapta-bhangi-naya*, the seven fold appreciations of *syāt* ("in some respect"). Directly related is the theory of partial standpoints, or viewpoints, *Nayavāda*: *Naya*, "partial viewpoint," and *vada*, "school of thought." See Vilas Aclinath Sangave, *Aspects of Jaina Religion*, 5th edition, Bharatiya Juanpith 2006, pp. 48–51; J.M. Koller, *Syādvadā as the Epistomological Key to the Jaina Middle Way Metaphysics of Anekāntavāda*, *Philosophy East and West* 50, 2000, pp. 400–407, etc.

For a very brief and comprehensive and lucid description of this concept, see *The Cultural Heritage of India*, vol. 1, Calcutta 1958, pp. 406–407, by Hiralal Jain, who writes as follows:

SYĀDVĀDA OR ANEKĀNTAVĀDA

The Jains have not been satisfied with merely emphasizing these three aspects of existence, but they have formulated on this basis a system of thought called Anekāntavāda or Syādvāda, which comes to this that we may make seven assertions, seemingly contradictory but perfectly true, about a thing: It is (*syā-dasti*); it is not (*syānnāsti*) it is and is not (*syādasti-nāsti*); it is indescribable (*syādavaktavyam*); it is and is not indescribable (*syādasti ca avaktavyam ca*); it is not and is indescribable (*syānnāsti ca avaktavyam ca*); it is, is not, and is indescribable (*syādasti nāsti ca avaktavyam ca*). A man is the father, and is not the father, and is both – are perfectly intelligible statements, if one understands the point of view from which they are made. In relation to a particular boy he is the father; in relation to another boy he is not the father; in relation to both the boys taken together he is the father and is not the father. Since both the ideas cannot be conveyed in words at the same time, he may be called indescribable; still he is the father and is indescribable; and so on. Thus, the philosophy of Anekānta is neither self-contradictory nor vague or indefinite; on the contrary, it represents a very sensible view of things in a systematized form.

There is yet another approach to the proper understanding of objects and events. When we take a coordinated view of things, we are said to be resorting to *naigama naya*. When we are inclined towards generalization, it is *sangraha naya*; and when inclined towards particularization, it is *vyavahara naya*. When a specific point or period of time is of the essence, it is *rjusutra naya*. When differentiation is made according to the usage of language and grammar, it is *śabda naya*. This is the doctrine of seven approaches (*sapta naya*) to the clarification of knowledge. The first three are grouped under *dravya naya*, and the last four under *paryāya naya*.

And for a few more detailed discussions, see Piotr Balcerowicz' opening chapter in the *Encyclopedia of Indian Philosophy*, ed. Karl H. Potter, vol. 14/2, Delhi 2012.

Francis X. Clooney, in his article Vedānta Désika's *Iśvarapariccheda* ("Definition of the Lord") and the Hindu argument about "Ultimate Reality," apud *Ultimate Realities: A Volume in the comparative religious Ideas Project*, ed. Robert Cummings Neville, New York, 2001, pp. 106–107, points out, as part of Desika's criticism of Jaina thought, that:

> According to Rangarāmānuja, who comments on the *Iśvaraparicheda*, the Jainas try to hold seven positions at once since, in their view, when an object is talked about, there are always seven ways of speaking about it: (1) It is something that exists (by nature), or (2) it is something that can be spoken about but cannot be said to exist until existence is predicated of it, or (3) it is something that is both existent and non-existent, or (4) it is something that is neither existent nor non-existent, or (5) it is something that is existent without being either existent or non-existent, or (6) it is something that is non-existent without being either existent nor nonexistent, or (7) it is something that is existent and non-existent, neither existent nor non-existent. Nothing, neither the most limited nor the ultimate reality, can be asserted unequivocally in a definitive form. It is certainly not possible to label anything "Ultimate Reality."

Here again we see the acceptance of opposites, unacceptable to Desika.

Desika [1268–1369] was an important proponent of (Viśistādvaita) Vedanta, a key theologian of the Srivaisnava community of South India.

On the distinction between, and indeed subordination of ordinary truth to "religious truth" in Advaita, non-dualist Vedanta, see Francis X. Clooney with Hugh Nicholson "From truth to Religious Truth in Hindu Philosophical Theology," apud *Religious Truth: A Volume in the comparative Religious Ideas Project*, ed. Robert Cunnings Neville, New York, 2001, p. 54 et seq.

Is the Jain doctrine, described above perhaps somewhat akin to the Buddhist Madhyamaka approach to the distinction between relative and ultimate truths? They express this aspect of correct relative truth by adding the Sanskrit word *mātra* at the end of whatever term they are using in the conventional sense. Thus, Jnānagarbha (8th century) said that a correct relative reality (or truth) is a *vastu-mātra*, "only a thing," "a mere thing" or "just a thing." (See Malcolm David Eckel, "Jānānagarbha's Commentary on the Destination between the two truths," apud *Miscellanea Buddhisa*, ed. Chr. Lidner, *Indiske Studies* 5, Copenhagen 1985, pp. 72–75. And see idem, apud Religious Truth, pp. 73, 80 note 12.)

Indeed, Nāgārjuna's most widely quoted verses about the two truths (in Kāriskās 24.8–11, 14, 18) are:

> The Buddha's teaching is based on two truths; ordinary relative truth and ultimate truth.
>
> Those who do not understand the distinction between the two truths do not understand the profound truth in the Buddha's teaching.

It is impossible to teach the ultimate without resorting to the conventional, and without understanding the ultimate, it is impossible to attain nirvana.

When emptiness is viewed incorrectly, it destroys the slow-witted, like a snake wrongly grasped or magic wrongly applied.

Everything is possible for those for whom Emptiness is possible; nothing is possible for those for whom Emptiness is not possible.

We call Dependent Origination Emptiness; it is a dependent designation, and it is the Middle Path.

There is no *dharma* that originates independently, so there is no *dharma* that is not empty.

(See M.J. Eckel, aput *Ultimate Realities*, ed. Robert Cunnings Neville, New York, 2001, pp. 140–141.)

Compare further a verse in the Sanskrit text known as *The Distinction Between the Middle and the Extreme*, (*Madhyānta-vibhanga*, trans T. Stcherbatsky, *Bibliotheca Buddhica* 30, Leningrad 1936; reprint ed. *Indian Studies Past and Present, Soviet Indology Series*, No. 5, 1971):

The Imagination of what is unreal exists, Duality does not exist in it. But emptiness does exist in it, and it exists in that [Emptiness].

Or:

The Image of what is Unreal is real. The Duality in it is not real. But the Emptiness in it is real, it is real in that [Emptiness], (*abhātaparikalpo'sti dvayam tatra na vidyata/ śūnyata vidyata tu atru tasyām api sa vidyate*).

Quoted from *Madhyānta-vibhāga-bhāsya*, ed. Mattmal Tatia and Anatalal Thakur, *Tibetan Sanskrit Works Series* 10, Patna 1967.

See Eckel, *Ultimate Realities*, pp. 132–133, 148, from which the above is cited, and see the following pages his complex explanation of this (to me, at any rate) enigmatic verse, attributed to Asanga, the commentary to Vasubandhu (ibid. note 31). See also Frederick J. Streng, *Emptiness: A Study in Religious Meaning*, Nashville, 1967, an examination of the Buddhist philosopher Nāgārjuna's expression of ultimate reality.

19. Note that one of his first paintings of his pond (1897–1899) is called "Water Lilies and the Japanese Bridge," and in a painting of 1875, we see "Madame Monet in a Japanese Kimono." See below chapter 6 on Japanese influence on European art.

20. See his notes and references ibid. p. 537 notes 20–25, especially note 20, where he refers us as follows:

On the systematic function of *naya* in Jainism, specifically in the works of Siddhasena and Mallavādin, see D. Malvania, 293–320; on *naya* in Umāsvāti: B.

Bhatt and Ch. Tripathi, "Tattvārtha Studies." ALB 38 (I1974), 71ff.; on "perspec-
tivism" as applied to Advaita Vedānta: H. Nakamura, "The Vedānta as Noticed
in Medieval Jaina Literature." *Indological Studies in Honor of W.N. Brown*. New
Haven, 1962, 186–194.

21. See his *Perennial Scope of Philosophy*, New York, 1949 pp. 81–94, et seq. Jaspers
had a Jewish wife and therefore was regarded by the Nazis as "tainted" (*jüdische
Versippung*), and having left Germany for Switzerland after the war, he wrote, in
1948, his book *The Question of German Guilt*. He was a humanist and politically
liberal, endorsing limited government, relative cultural and economic freedom, and
protection of society against unaccountable political direction, arguing that a human
polity requires a constitutional apparatus, enshrining basic rights, imposing mor-
al-legal order on the operation of the state, and restricting the prerogative powers of
the political apparatus. (See Stanford *Encyclopedia of Philosophy*, s.v. Karl Jaspers.)

22. Gandhi claimed to have been influenced in his development of the theory of
ahimsā as a political weapon, by the revered layman Raychandbhai Mehta, as
recorded in Mohandas K. Gandhi, *Collected Works of Mahatma Gandhi* (Delhi
1958–1976, vol. 32, p. 4):

> The persons have influenced me deeply (Tolestoy, Ruskin and Raychandbhai):
> Tolstoy through his books . . . and Raychandbhai through intimate contact.
> When I began to feel doubts about Hinduism as a religion, it was Raychandbhai
> who helped me restore them.

On the life and works of Raychandbhai Mehta (1868–1901), known to his devotees
as srīmad Rājacandra, see Jagdish Chandra Jain, *Life in Ancient India as Depicted in
the Jain Canons*, Bombay 1947, Introductions, pp. 1–2, (in Hindi, cited by Padnanabh
S. Jaini, *The Jaina Path of Purification*, University of California Press, 1979, pp.
314–315).

As to the acceptance of the principle of *ahimsā* by lay persons, there is a vow to
be declared, called the first *anuvrata* (minor vow pertaining only to lay people) in
ahimsā (non-harming) and *ahimsāvrata* (*vrata*, being restraint). The Jaina aspirant
gives a vow in the presence of a holy person, repeating the ancient formula as
follows:

> I will desist from the knowing or intentional destruction of all great lives [*trasa*,
> souls embodied with two or more senses]. As long as I live, I will neither kill
> nor cause others to kill. I shall strive to refrain from all such activities, whether
> of body, speech or mind.

This declaration is modeled on the words used by Mahāvīra's outstanding lay
disciple, Ananda. See Padmanabh S. Jina, ibid. pp. 172–173, 233–240.

Here we may quote what he said at the end of his great fast in Bombay, on the 15th January 1948:

> . . . Let every Hindu study the *Koran*, let Moslems ponder the meaning of the *Gita*, and the Sikhs, *Granath Sahib* . . . As we respect our own religion so must we respect other peoples'. What is just and right is just and right, whether it be inscribed in Sanskrit, Urdu, Persian or any other language. May God bestow sanity on us and the whole world. May He make us wiser and draw us closer to Him so that India and the whole world may be happy.

(See Dominique Lapierre and Larry Collins, *Freedom at Midnight*, Vicas Publishing House PVT LTD. Ed., New Delhi 1997, pp. 612–613.)

23. "The Jaina with his teaching of *anekānta* and its corollaries, *nayavāda* and *syāddvada* escapes the doctrinal necessity of having to follow a restricted path. All paths can be seen as valid in some respect . . ." (Padmanabh S. Jaina, *The Jaina Path of Purification*, University of California Press 1979, p. 97).

24. Here we should however take note of Ananda K. Coomaraswamy's comment in his *The Transformation of Nature in Art* Dover ed. New York, 1956, in the chapter entitled "The Theory of Art in Asia," p. 11:

It should be realized that from the Indian (metaphysical) and Scholastic points of view, subjective and objective are not irreconcilable categories, one of which must be regarded as real to the exclusion of the other. Reality (*satya*) subsists there where the intelligible and sensible meet in the common unity of being, and cannot be thought of as existing in itself outside and apart from, but rather *as*, knowledge or vision, that is, only in act.

25. See, for example, Th. Stcherbatsky, *Buddhist Logic* 2nd edition, New York, 1962, two volumes, and especially his discussions of "The Law of Contractions," vol. 1, pp. 400–416, vol. 2.

26. This subject is extremely complex, but, nevertheless, could be greatly augmented with citations from a variety of sources from the realm of Chinese thought. See, for example, the *Lao Tzu* (*Tao-Te Ching*), a classic of Tao philosophy probably from around the 6th century B.C.E. There we read:

> . . . The Named is the mother of all things.
> Therefore let there always be non-being so we may see their subtlety.
> And let there always be being so that we may see their outcome.
> *The two are the same*

But after they are produced, they have different names. They both may be called deep and profound.

Deeper and more profound,

The door of all subtleties. [My emphasis.]

(See *A Source Book in Chinese Philosophy*, translated and compiled by Wing-Tsit Chan, Princeton, New Jersey, 1963, p. 139, and cf. ibid. 140.)

Or again, for instance, the paradoxes of Hui Shih (280–305?) and Kung-sun Lung (born 380 B.C.E.?):

2. That which has no thickness cannot have any volume, and yet in extent it may cover a thousand *li* . . .

6. The truth has no limit and yet has a limit . . .

(Ibid. pp. 233–234, and see, translator's comment.)

And as to the *Two Levels of Truth* theory of the *Mādhyamikca* school, founded in India by Nāgārjuna (c.100–200 C.E.), introduced into China in the 4th century C.E. by Sung-chao, and systemized by Chi-tsang (549–623), there are two levels of truth: worldly truth (*lankikasatya*) or common or relative truth that things exist provisionally as depended beings or temporary names, but it is absolute truth (*paramārthasatya*) that all *dharmas* are empty. (See ibid. p. 358.)

And finally, but by no means having exhausted the sources, we call attention to the *Hua-Yah* school (Flowery Splendor) of the 5th century C.E. et seq., whose real founder was Fa-tsang (643–712), and whose origins are in India, (the *Avatamisaka sutra* in Sanskrit). In the *Hundred Gathas to the Sea of Ideas* of the *Flowery Splendour Scripture*, nos.3–5, we are confronted by a number of fascinating, but puzzling, paradoxes. Thus, we read (3):

A primary cause does not by itself cause anything to come into existence but needs subsidiary causes to do so. Subsidiary causes do not by themselves cause anything to come into existence, but need primary causes to do so. Since a thing can be said to come into existence only because it does so through causation, only when we understand that coming-into-existence has no nature [of its own] can we affirm that there is no coming-into-existence. But coming-into-existence and not-coming-into-existence fulfill and negate each other. When negated there is no coming-into-existence through causation. Because there is simultaneous fulfillment and negation, therefore at the time of coming-into-existence there is no coming-into-existence. He who understands this understands not-coming-into-existence.

(ibid. p. 416, and cf. continuation no. 5, p. 417.)

What emerges from an even more comprehensive analysis of the whole range of sources – not possible in this context – is the common use of such apparently paradoxical notions throughout both Confucianism, Taoism and Buddhism, but clearly this is beyond the scope of this study (see, e.g., index s.v. being and non-being, p. 833a).

27. See the continuation of his discussion, in which he brings additional motives for Buddha's tolerance. See also S. Radhakrishnan, *Eastern Religions and Western Thought*, 2nd edition, Oxford, London, 1940, pp. 308–309, adding that Asoka's (273–232 B.C.E.) dictum represents the Buddhist view, namely: "He who does reverence to his own sect while disparaging the sects of others wholly from attachment to his own, with intent to enhance the splendour of his own sect, in reality by such conduct inflicts the severest injury on his own sect."

28. We will just indicate some key elements in this process.

The first serious Western encounter with Madhyamaka thought appeared in Eugène Burnouf's *Introduction à l'histoire du Buddhisme indien*, published in Paris in 1844. This work appeared several decades after the earliest British translations of the Hindu scriptures, and its date serves as a reminder of how inaccessible most Indian Mahāyāna sources have been, even in the late decades of the twentieth century. Burnouf based his comments about Madhyamaka on a rare Sanskrit manuscript of Candrakīrti's commentary on Nāgārjuna's *Madhyamakakārikās* that had been discovered in Nepal by the British scholar and colonial official Brian Houghton Hodgson. Burnouf characterized what he saw in Nāgārjuna and Candrakīrti as a "scholastic nihilism." This interpretation caught Durkheim's attention in *The Elementary Forms of the Religious Life*, where he took particular note of Burnouf's claim that Buddhism "sets itself in opposition to Brahmanism as a moral system without God and an atheism without nature, [E. Durkheim, *The Elementary Forms of Religious Life*, transl. Joseph Ward, New York, 1965, p. 45]. Burnouf's nihilistic interpretation of Madhyamaka gained a certain currency in French and British scholarly circles. The most direct and uncompromising account of this interpretation was written by the great Belgian scholar Louis de La Vallée Poussin as a contribution to Hasting's *Encyclopaedia of Religion and Ethics*. The article, which was simply called "Nihilism (Buddhist)," ends with these words:

> This system may not bear criticism; but it is nevertheless an honest and able attempt to cook the last fruit of nihilism – negation of suffering and of liberation – evolved from the old nihilistic seed sown by Buddha himself, in the most orthodox juice (rasa) of the Good Law, the juice of suffering and liberation.

The La Vallée Poussin's interpretation of the Madhyamaka did not go unchallenged. In *The Conception of Buddhist Nirvana*, F. Th. Stcherbatsky interpreted Madhyamaka as a form of pan-Indian monism. He said: "In Mahāyā all parts or elements are unreal (*śūnya*), and only the whole, i.e. the Whole of the wholes (*dharmatā* = *dharma-kāval*) is real." [T. Stcherbasky, *The Conception of Buddhist Nirvana*, Leningrad 1927, p. 44].

Stcherbatsky's interpretation was taken up, polished, and defended by a series of scholars, not the least of whom was T. R. V. Murti, a śāstri and ācārya at Banaras Hindu University. Murti drew together many of the positive elements of Stcherbatsky's reading when he said: "The Mādhyamika Dialectic as negation of thought is intuition of the Absolute; as the rooting out of passions it is Freedom (Nirvāna); and it is perfection as union with the Perfect Being," [T.R.V. Murti, *The Central Philosophy of Buddhism*, 2nd ed. London, 1960, p. 143].

(See Malcolm David Eckel with John J. Tatamaril, "Cooking the Last Fruit of Nihilism: Buddhistic Approaches to Ultimate Reality," apud *Ultimate Realities: A Volume in the Comperative Religious Ideas Project*, New York, 2001, pp. 131–132, 148.)

In 1879, the journalist, Sir Edwin Arnold, published his famous epic poem, *The Light of Asia*, which was proclaimed by some to be the "best seller" of all Buddhist books in the West. A year later Madame Blavatsky (see below chapter 6) with her American colleague, Colonel Henry Steel Olcott (1831–1906), declared themselves Buddhists, and confirmed it "by taking Ponsil" – reciting the Five Precepts – at Galle in Sri Lanka (Snelling, p. 195). Later in 1924, the English Travers Christmas Humphreys (1901–1983) founded the *Buddhist Lodge*, which was an adjunct of the *Theosophical Society*, and in 1943 it became the Buddhist Society, publishing its own journal *Buddhism in England*, founded and edited by Arthur C. March, which later became *The Middle Way*, (ibid. pp. 198–199). Dr. D.T. Suzuki from Japan (1870–1966), who first visited London in 1908, at the World Congress of Faiths, is now seen as "the Man who brought Zen to the West." Zen became very fashionable in the United States, and perhaps less so in England and Europe. In 1959, following the Lhasa uprising, a great diaspora of Tibetan lamas came to the West. Among them Trungpa Rinpoché reached England in 1963. In the early sixties he gathered a considerable entourage of devoted followers, and with Akong Rinpoché established in 1967 the first Buddhist center in the West in Scotland. In 1970, after a severe crash leaving him partially paralyzed, he moved to the United States, where he founded additional centers and schools, (ibid. pp. 211–21). Snelling continues to chronicle the "penetration" of Buddhism into the West and Western thought. But the above should suffice for our purposes to show how by the early post World War II period, Buddhism, with its Eastern thinking, had become a significant force in the West.

29. Cited in Barbara Holdrege, "Hindu Jewish Encounters," *The Wiley-Blackwell Companion to Inter-Religious Dialogue*, ed. Catherine Cornille, London, 2013, pp. 413–414.)

30. This small book contains a useful listing of the various views as to the differences between Eastern and Western thought, bibliographical information on pp. 13–24.

CHAPTER 3

The Jewish Position in *Halachah, Aggadah* and *Kabbalah*

And moving to the area of Jewish thought throughout the ages, the Rabbis struggled with the concept of multiple truths. For in the area of *halachah* – Jewish law – there are almost always dissenting opinions. And can it be that in actual fact both have a measure of truth, but that for pragmatic reasons one rules according to one of those opinions – usually the majority one? Indeed, we read in the Talmud, in the Babylonian Tractate *Eruvin* 13b and *Gittin* 6b that:

> R. Abba stated in the name of Samuel: For three years there was a dispute between Beit Shamai and Beit Hillel, each claiming "the *halachah* is as we say." Then a heavenly voice declared, "These and these are the words of the living God, but the *halachah* follows the rulings of Beit Hillel."

And the Ritba – R. Yom Tov Alshvili (13–14 century) to *Eruvin,* ibid., ed. M. Goldstein Jerusalem, 1974, p. 107, writes as follows:[1]

> They asked the Rabbis of France, of blessed memory: How is it possible that both [opinions] be the words of the Living God, when the one forbids and the other permits? And they replied: When Moses went up to the heavens to receive the Torah, [the angels] showed him for every single detail 49 facets to forbid and 49 facets to permit. And he questioned the Holy One blessed be He concerning this. And He said that it would be given to the Sages of Israel in each generation [to make a determination], and the determination would be according

to their ruling. And this is correct according to the homily, but in truth there is a secret [explanation], (i.e. an esoteric one).[2]

Compare this to *Midrash Psalms* 12:7, ed. Buber, pp. 107–108, which is surely the source for this tosafistic tradition:

> Said R. Yannai: The Torah was not given "cut and dried" (*hatichin*), but for each word that God gave to Moses He gave 49 facets for [declaring] purity and 49 for impurity. Said Moses before Him, "Master of the Universe, how then will we be able to clarify the issues?" He replied to him, "We follow the majority; if the majority declare impurity, it is impure, if they declare purity, it is pure."[3]

Similarly, we read in *B. Hagigah* 3b:

> "The masters of the assemblies" (Ecclesiastes 12:11) – these are the scholars who gather together in assemblies and study Torah, some ruling pure and others ruling impure, some prohibiting and others permitting, some rejecting and others accepting. Were one to say, "How, then, can I learn Torah from now on?" The Scripture says, "They are given from one Shepherd" (Ecclesiastes ibid.). One God gave them, and One Leader stated them, in accordance with the words of the Lord of All Creation, blessed be He, as it is written "And the Lord spake all these words" (Exodus 20:1).
>
> You too, make your ear like an auricle – (i.e. hearken) and acquire an understanding heart to listen to the words of those that declare impure and to the words of those who declare pure, those who forbid and those who permit, those who reject and those who accept. . . .[4]

A somewhat similar notion is expressed, albeit in quite a different style, in *Sifrei Deuteronomy* 30b To Deuteronomy 32:2 (ed. Finkelstein-Horowitz, Berlin, 1940, p. 339):

> "My doctrine shall drop as the rain, [my speech shall distil as the dew]," (Deut. ibid.) – Just as the rain descends upon the trees and bestows upon them flavours, each one in accordance with what it is, the vine as it is, the olive as it is, the fig as it is; so too the words of the Torah are all one (i.e. are a single unified whole), and they contain

Scripture, Mishnah, Talmud, *Halachot* (legal rulings) and *Hagadot* (midrashic hermeneutis homilies).

Each of the genres listed above are very different in style, character and often lead to different explanations and conclusions, varied and even contradictory. But they all, coming from the same source, have a degree of legitimacy. They are varying flavours deriving from the same fountainhead.

R. Menahem Recanati (late 13th–early 14th century), in his commentary on the verse, "And God spoke all these words saying," (Exodus 20:1), writes as follows:

> The Rabbis said in Babylonian Talmud *Hagigah* 3b: [The words of the wise are as goads and as rails fastened] "by the masters of the assemblies ..." (Ecclesiastes ibid.) – These are the learned Sages; "assemblies," they who are studying Torah; these declare pure and these declare impure, these declare kosher and these declare not kosher, these permit and these forbid. Should a person say: How can I now know [i.e., which is correct]? This we learn, "And God spoke all these words saying" (Exodus ibid.) – they all have one Father, all were given by one Master, they were spoken by the Lord of all acts. And they said: R. Meir had one pupil who could prove the insect to be pure in 49 ways (*B. Eruvin* 13b). [And, of course, insects, vermin, are impure. D.S.] And all this is because the words spoken [by God] were [in] "a great voice which did not end" (Deuteronomy 5:19) – [a voice] which had all the facets which change and turn over from impure to pure, to forbidding and permitting, to not kosher and to kosher. Because we cannot possibly believe that that voice lacked anything. Therefore in the greatness of the voice were things that could turn in all directions. And each of the Sages received his own ["voice"], for not only the prophets received from Mount Sinai, but all Sages in every generation, each of them receives his own [message]. And this is what the verse (ibid.) tells us. "These words the Lord spoke unto *all your assemblies* [in the mount out of the midst of the fire, of the cloud, and of the thick darkness]." [My emphasis, D.S.] And in relation to this it is stated that "Both these and these are the words of the living God." For if one of them was mistaken, they would not have made this statement. And these are the 70 facets that the Torah has, which turn to all sides, for that "voice" split up into seventy branches, as we have explained in

our commentary to Psalms. Our Sages, of blessed memory taught that God gives to a great host of exponents the "word" which splits up into *seven times seven voices*, [i.e. 49 *tongues*]; [see above, *Midrash Psalms* 12:4] And R. Yehoshua ben Levi explained it, like a man who strikes the anvil and numerous sparks fly out in all directions.[5]

So too, the great host of exponents. The hammer is but one single thing, and it splits up a stone [which it smites] into many fragments. So too is "the voice" in which the Torah was given. And if you think about it, this clears up all the uncertainties.

The *Maharshal*, R. Shlomoh Luria, (1510–1573) in his (first) introduction to his *Yam shel Shelomoh* (Lublin 1630), formulates this notion as follows:

Everything that is found in the words of the Sages of the Torah, from the time of Moses up to the present day, these are the Sages concerning whom it is said, "The words of the wise are as goads" (Ecclesiastes ibid.) – they were all given by One Shepherd (*B. Hagigah* 3b). And be not surprised by the various differences of opinion, which are so very distant one from the other, if these opinions are directed to heaven ... But all are the words of the living God, as though each one of them received [his tradition] from God and from Moses, even though what came out of Moses' mouth could never be two opposite statements on one single issue. And the Kabbalists explained that all souls were present at Sinai and received [the words] through 49 channels (*tzinorot*), seven times seven purified (cf. Psalms 12:7). And these are the voices (or sounds) which they heard and saw. [Cf. Exodus 20:18, "And all the people saw the thunderings (*kolot*, voices) and the lightning."] These are the opinions that were transferred through the channels (or conduits), each one seeing through his channel in accordance with his own understanding. So each one receives in accordance with the strength of his soul ... such that one reaches one conclusion, declaring impure, and the other another one, declaring pure ..., *and all are true.* [My emphasis, D.S.] And you may understand this. And for this reason the Torah was given to the Sages of each and every generation, each according to the source of his understanding ... and in accordance with that which is shown to them from the heavens.[6]

Similarly, in our generation, R. Mosheh Feinstein, in his *Igrot Mosheh*, *Yoreh Deah* 3:92, writes:

> Our Sages describe the opposing views of halachic debates as both being "the words of the living God." This means that the Torah study of the diverse views of Sages inherently does not contain something which is not true. Thus the opposing views of Beit Shammai and Beit Hillel are both true. This rule applies also to the disputes of R. Eliezer and all the Tannaim and Amoraim. All of them were given from One Shepherd. Thus it was not untrue when the Heavenly *Bat Kol* (voice) announced that the halachah was in accord with R. Eliezer.[7] His words were inherently true – even though in this world we decide practical halachah on the basis of majority decision. And because of the inherent truth of all views of our sages, we say the blessing, "Who gave to us the Torah of truth" even if we are only learning the views that have been rejected from practical halakhah such as those of Beit Shammai or minority opinions.

And in his *Igrot Mosheh*, introduction to *Orah Hayyim*, we read:

> Both of the opposing views are the words of the "Living God" even though the actual truth as understood by Heaven is only like one of them.

This almost mystical view is echoed in a statement by the *Shlah ha-Kadosh*, R. Isaiah Horowitz (1570–1626), in his *Toledot ha-Adam: Beit Hokhmah* sect. 8:

> How do we understand the concept that all the words of our sages are the words of the Living God? We read in *B. Eruvin* 13b: For three and a half years Beit Shammai and Beit Hillel argued concerning whose views were actually *halachah*. A *Bat Kol* announced from Heaven that both views were the words of the living God, but the *halachah* was in accord with Beit Hillel. The Ritba writes in the name of the Rabbis of France that the halachah was given in 49 different ways of prohibition and 49 different ways of permission – it was left up to the Rabbis of each generation to determine what was the correct *halachah* for their generation. There is a problem with this explanation. Only when both

sides can be correct is it reasonable to say, "Both are the words of the Living God." For example, in *B. Gittin* 6b, concerning the concubine of Givah, the views are not mutually exclusive and both could be correct. However in a dispute where one side says it is prohibited and the other side says it is permitted – then surely both cannot be correct! Therefore, if we choose one side, how can we say concerning the rejected view that it is "the word of the Living God"? The rational mind is simply not satisfied with the words of the French Rabbis. In fact, the resolution of this problem is dependent – as the Ritba alluded – upon kabbalistic reasoning and secrets.... The explanation of this issue, in my humble opinion, is found in *B. Baba Metzia* 59b concerning the dispute between R. Eliezer and R. Yehoshua whether Heaven can decide the *halachah*. I already have explained that every single *mitzvah* has a source in Heaven. According to one's attachment in Heaven, that is how the *mitzvah* manifests itself in the physical world. The carrying out of the actual *mitzvah* is directly related to the nature of the attachment. However not everyone has the same level of attachment. Therefore, each rabbi will decide the *halachah* based upon his personal attachment and consequently they will not necessarily agree. The final *halachah* is decided by the majority which indicates the most representative means of attachment to Heaven.... This is so even though a particular individual might have a much higher type of attachment in Heaven. The *halachah* is determined by what is the most appropriate way that the *mitzvah* be performed physically for the majority. Thus, we can see why two mutually opposing views can both be the "words of the Living God." For example, in the dispute concerning *tefilin* between Rashi and Rabbeinu Tam, each holds that the *tefilin* (phylacteries) of the other is invalid. Would you think that one side never fulfilled the *mitzvah* of *tefilin* during his entire life?! The answer is that each side had a unique attachment to Heaven which determined their ruling about *tefilin*. However, the final *halachah* is determined by the majority.

Indeed, throughout the generations scholars struggled with the concept of multiple truths – "*eilu ve-eilu* ..." "(both these and these [are the words of the living God])"[8] seeking kabbalistic explanations, or finally admitting that such is beyond human comprehension. Thus R. Tzadok ha-Cohen of Lublin (1823–1900), in his *Dover Tzedek*, Pietrokov, 1911, p. 4, writes:

The expression *eilu ve-eilu* refers to the fact that ... all the aspects and parts are in fact a unity, and they all are the words of the Living God. However, this concept is truly beyond rational comprehension. How is it possible that complete opposites are both true? We know that it is impossible that truth is anything other than one. How can diverse and conflicting things all be a unity? ... Therefore, this concept of *eilu ve-eilu* is beyond the material intellect of man. That is also, why there is no absolutely clear *halachah* in the Oral Law that is beyond dispute – except for *halachah le-Moshe*, which is not disputed, as the Rambam states. . . .

And in yet greater detail in his *Resisei Lailah*, Bnei Brak, 1967, p. 18, (cited in Sagi, *The Open Canon*, p. 115):

Whenever the Torah is expounded, we will inevitably find on every matter views claiming one thing and its opposite (as is written, "some ruling pure and some impure" [*BT Hagigah* 3b] and "these and these are the words of the living God"), meaning that God holds all the separate forces in the world together. This explains the plural [these and these] since words of Torah are the vitality of the entire Creation ... and they split into streams, forbidding and allowing. We might think they convey the view of the sage but this is not so, because the sage too is in the hands of God, who enlightens him and tilts his heart solely according to the divine will, which is why they are called words of the living God since they are indeed words of God, may He be blessed ... as is prophecy. The only difference is that prophecy is "thus says the Lord," meaning exactly so, without bias or divergence. . . . God's speech through the prophet's mouth is truly revelation. But revelation cannot possibly be two opposites simultaneously since, as we know, human reason cannot accept this. . . . A sage, however, clings to God's wisdom ... which not only accepts that two opposites can be together simultaneously but actually compels this, because God made the whole of Creation one thing and its opposite. . . . Everything in the world is also its opposite, and we certainly find traces of this in God's wisdom, which is the source of the implementing will, except that in reality the opposites are not simultaneous – when it is day it is not night and when it is night it is not day, *but not so in the source, where all is one.*

Sagi (ibid. p. 114) explains R. Tzadok's reasoning as follows:

> The assumption of unity at the source does not imply that the divine mind is free of conflicts. Rather, the unique quality of the divine mind is manifest in its ability to bear these opposites simultaneously to become a union of opposites. Unity, then, is not synonymous with monotony and uniformity, and its expression is dialectic.
>
> Zadok argues that the divine unity of opposites transcends the normative realm and reflects the structure of reality as a whole. Reality, all of it, is made up of opposites united in the divine world, a statement he founds on ontological grounds: if the united God is the only reason for all opposites in the world then, at the divine *source*, all opposites are united.

Contrary to the divine reality, the human mind cannot bear this union of opposites and the consequence is separation and dispute – what was originally united now appears as contradictory options. Zadok argues that a perception of dispute as expressing a clash between mutually rejecting options reflects the essence and limitations of the human mind, not of actual reality.

This outlook too assumes a distinction between *Torah* and practical *Halachah*. The human endeavour of practical *Halachah* does not exhaust the *Torah* and a contradiction prevails between the *Torah*, which is a union of opposites, and *Halachah*, which is constructed through dispute. The religious task is to go beyond *Halachah* onto *Torah*, by clinging to God.

R. Tzadok is continuing in a line of thought already formulated in the writings of R. Yehudah Loew b. Betzalel, the Maharal of Prague (c.1520–1609). On the statement in *Mishnah Avot* 5:17, that "Any controversy that is for God's sake shall in the end be of lasting worth," he is puzzled by how a dispute could be "of lasting worth," and he explains:

> A dispute for God's sake prevails even when it involves opposites because He, may He be exalted and blessed, unites the two opposites. Although they are divided and opposed, from God's perspective they are nevertheless united since God, who is one, is the cause of both opposites. As the cause of both opposites, He himself is unity because otherwise He would be the cause of only one of them. As if you were to say that He is the cause of fire and were to assume, God forbid,

another cause for the opposite of fire, which is water ... Hence the controversy, which is for the sake of God: Although the dispute is between intrinsic opposites that cannot coexist, for God, who is the cause of these opposites, both are one ... because God is one and both are affected by the divine will as He wishes, may He be blessed.

(*Derech ha-Hayyim*, Jerusalem, 1971, pp. 258–9; Sagi ibid. p. 115.) Sagi explains (ibid.) that:

This unity collapses only at the level of performance, but the opposites reflect unity from the perspective of Halachah:
From the perspective of Halachah, these behaviours are mutually opposed and cannot occur simultaneously, but both actions as includes all the opposites. The study of these views, both the one that allows and the one that forbids, is the study of Torah, which is from God, (*Derech ha-Hayyim* ibid.).

And the great twentieth century rabbinic authority and thinker, R. Avraham Yitzhak ha-Cohen Cook (1865–1935), in a letter addressed to Samuel Alexandrov (*Igrot ha-Rayah*, vol. 1, Jerusalem, 1962, p. 133, (Sagi ibid. p. 119), writes as follows.

On what I wrote about the unity of opposites, Your Honour answers relying on the well-known view that two contradictory views on the same issue are impossible. As for myself, I wonder whether this is the question at all. My main contribution is the claim that, in the supernal thinking that probes the depths of all matters, reality knows no opposites. Wherever there are opposites, there is without doubt some hidden condition that, when clarified, will reveal that even when two statements appear to be contradictory, one of them will emerge as referring to one aspect of the issue and the second to another. Through the two opposites together, we see the statement from both sides and find they are definitely not contradictory. From their regard, they are not relating to the same issue since they are dealing with different aspects.

And similarly in R. Abdallah Somech's *Zivhei Tzedek*, Bagdad (1813–1829), to *Yoreh Deah* sect. 26:

Question: How could the conflicting opinions of our Sages – where one asserts that something is prohibited and another claims that it is permitted – all be given to Moshe on Mount Sinai? Answer. The answer to this question is extremely deep, and we are not able to answer it properly. Even the *Rishonim* (early mediaeval authorities) did not have a full satisfactory response to it.

He then quotes the Ritba (cited above), the Shlah, the Hida, R. Hayyim Yosef David Azulai (1724–1806), etc. finally admitting that:

Even the Ritba indicated that the genuine answer is from the mysteries of *Kabbalah*. Therefore, the bottom line is that this question is beyond our ability to understand. We see the many answers that were offered to give a little comfort – especially to the masses. Thus, they will have to suffice because the real answer is found in *Kabbalah*, which is not appropriate for either of us.

Each of these authorities seeks to explain how two contradictory views can, in a sense, both be correct. Yet they all accept the fact that opposing opinions can both be true.[9] Kanarfogel (in his above-mentioned article pp. 112–113) writes:

The Search for Truth is the study of Torah and the determination of Jewish Law, and the likely and welcome possibilities of multiple truths being discovered, are the cornerstones of all of the *Tosafot* passages and texts discussed to this point.

And having mentioned the Kabbalists we may note their use of the term *Ahdut ha-Shavah* to denote that *Ein-Sof*, the infinite God, is a "unity of opposites," one that reconciles even those aspects of the cosmos that are opposed or contradict one another.[10]

And to give one such example, I shall cite a passage from the great thirteenth century Spanish kabbalist, Joseph Gikatila's *Shaarei Orah* 41b:

When the work of the commencement was finished, [the Scripture] begins to mention YHVH Elohim with regard to the plenitude of the world. Know and believe that the secret of the [divine] Unity in its entirety is the secret of "YHVH our God, YHVH is one" (Deut. 6:4).

> It is in this way that you should know that wherever you find in the
> Torah YHVH Elohim, which is the complete Name, all things found
> in the [biblical] section where YHVH Elohim is mentioned, have been
> accomplished by all the attributes in their totality, by the attribute of
> judgment and the attribute of mercy … everything in full perfection,
> with mercy and judgment … As a function of this principle the Torah
> has said: "The Rock, perfect is its action" (Deut. 32:4), of which the
> explanation is: the Rock which decrees the verdict does not act with
> violence, does not decide the sentence with cruelty, but "perfect is its
> action," for the word "perfect" (*tamim*) is the secret of two things, it is
> as if he had said "twins" (*teumim*), but it is a polite way of saying for
> two things on high the expression *tamim* (perfect) and for two things
> below the expression *teumim* (twins) … below twins, on high perfect,
> *because below they appear as two things, a thing and its contrary*, as
> the advocate and the prosecutor, but on high everything is in a single
> direction, the advocate and the prosecutor have the same finality. [My
> emphasis, D.S.][11]

And in rabbinic literature too there are areas which seems to be outside the normal parameters of rational thought, which seem to fall into
an "Escherian" realm. Thus, for example, the Talmud in *B. Baba Batra*
98b–99a (with partial parallels in *B. Yoma 28a and B. Megillah 10b*),
basing itself on verses in 1 Kings 6: 14 et seq., describes the Holy of Holies
in Solomon's Temple as being 20 cubits in breadth with Moses' Ark of
the Law in the center being 10 cubits wide (Exodus 25:10), and being 10
cubits distance from each of the walls of the Holy of Holies – clearly
an impossible situation. And the Talmud gives a similarly impossible
description of the Cherubins in that same space. And when questioned on
this point, the response given is:

> This is in accordance with the view of R. Levi who said, and perhaps;
> it was R. Yohanan, "This is our tradition from our forefathers,[12] that
> the space of the Ark and the Cherubin is not to be accounted;" Or
> formulated differently: the material presence of the Ark and of the
> Cherubin took up no space.

Interestingly enough, the commentators do not remark on the extraordinary nature of this reply, merely giving a technical interpretation of the

Talmudic text. Perhaps they saw this as yet another example of the miraculous nature of the Ark etc., such as is found in *B. Sota* 35a, where we are told that "the Ark bore itself," i.e. it was not actually carried by its bearers, but it carried itself, bearing its own weight. It was yet another aspect of the miraculous character of the Temple to which ten (others) miracles were attributed (in *M. Avot* 5.5, and *B. Yoma* 21a). Nonetheless, returning to the *B. Baba Batra* passage (and its parallels), the situation textually described is, as was mentioned above, physically impossible. There was, however, no attempt on the part of the rabbis of ingenious harmonization, the usual exegetical methodology which to they were wont. Rather these mutually exclusive opinions are accepted, and the impossible is confirmed. Perhaps this was regarded as a sort of grey area in which the distinction between the physical and the spiritual is blurred, and in such a "twilight zone" the impossible is regnant. And additional examples of this phenomenon may be found elsewhere in the *Aggadah*.

We see, then, that in the albeit circumscribed parameters of *halachah*, *aggadah* and also the area of *kabbalah*, we find in Jewish thought an appreciation of the notion of multiple truths, and in a related, but differentiated manner, an awareness of the built-in uncertainty as to the attainment of absolute truth. (See Kanarfogel ibid. pp. 26–35, in a section entitled "Multiple Truths and Interpretations," and especially his concluding paragraphs there pp. 34–35.)

Furthermore, most recently, Efraim Hamiel, in his *"Ha-Emet ha-Kefulah: Iyyunim be-Hagut ha-Datit ha Modernit ba-Meah ha-Tesha-Ezrei u-be-Hashpaatah al ha-Hagut ha-Yehudit ba-Meah ha-Esrim.* (The Double Truth: Enquiries into Modern Religion Thinking in the Nineteenth Century and its influence on the Jewish thinking of the Twentieth Century, Jerusalem 2016, pp. 427–428, has uncovered evidence of the acceptance of such a notion, which he calls "double truth," i.e. acceptability of apparently contradictory truths, among latter-day orthodox authorities.) He gives as an example Shmuel David Luzzato (1800–1865), known by his acronym Shadal, in his comments to the Bible (to Genesis 1:1, where he writes: if one finds in [the biblical] stories matters which do not agree with scientific research, but both on this and that, one should contemplate on the innermost heart of human being ... [such that] matters speak to the heart of each individual according to what he is ... etc., and cf. Deuteronomy 1:6, etc.) as admitting the acceptance of conflicting "truths."[13] And he notes such a tendency among certain contemporary orthodox Jewish thinkers and scholars. (ibid. p. 428).

However, moving away and beyond the more proscribed areas of *halachah* and *kabbalah* and biblical exegesis, we may rightly ask ourselves whether the notions described above are applicable to the areas of religion in orthodox Jewish thought. Avi Sagi, in his important article *Ha-Dat ha-Yehudit: Sovlanut ve-Efsharut ha-Pluralism (The Jewish Religion: Tolerance and the possibility of Tolerance), Iyyun,* 1995, p. 175, categorically denies such a possibility, arguing (ibid.), "that evidence of tolerance and pluralism within the framework of the "halachic academy," which reflects theory and pragmatism, ... and a "multiplicity of views or halachic practices" only is a function within that discrete framework itself. "But all that is outside that framework is not regarded as the words of the Living God ..., but rather a deviation, to which the halachic system can not necessarily show tolerance, as even more so, a pluralistic position." Hence, for example, the *halachah* can hardly show toleration to a Jewish apostate, or sinner. However, the non-Jew, according to Jewish thinking, is not subject to Jewish law. Consequently, the Jewish relationship to other religions may reveal a degree of toleration, and certainly to the gentile. This, indeed, is the conclusion reached by A. Altman, in his *Panim shel Yahadut,* Tel-Aviv, 1983, p. 22 (cited by Sagi, ibid.). Thus, it is clearly recognized by the Church "that certain Christian beliefs are unacceptable to Judaism."[14] Or to formulate it somewhat differently: it may not be "kosher" for Jews, but it is for non-Jews, and hence is not to be regarded as polytheistic idolatry. Furthermore, Maimonides, at the end of his classically authoritative *Mishneh Torah (Hilchot Melachim* II, ad fin., (in the uncensored version of the Rome edition of 1480), regards both Christianity and Islam, with their knowledge of the *Torah* and its commandments, as paving the way to the final revelation. Additionally, core-values of other religions are recognized and respected.[15] Furthermore, the great Provençal authority, Menachem Meiri (1240–1316), defines idolatry as a religion without ethical principles and a system of law and justice, thus de-emphasizing the element of ritual practice. This was a revolutionary idea in Jewish theology, albeit a minority view, placing primary importance on *values* and life-style, rather than on *ritual* and even belief![16] The Meiri's view which actually only came to light in the mid twentieth century as was accepted (or used) by a number of latter-day authorities, such as R. Eliahu Klatzkin (19 century), R. Yehiel Weinberg, etc. Furthermore, both

Rav Kook (1865–1935) and Rav Herzog (1888–1959), who were both Chief Rabbis of Israel (1921–1935, 1936–1954), based themselves on the Meiri in the rulings granting full civil rights to Christians as well as Moslems in the Jewish State.[17]

And what is most familiar is the well-known statement that *Zachor* (commemorate) in Exodus 20:8 and *Shamor* (heed) in Deuteronomy 5:12, in the Ten Commandments, referring to the Shabbat law, were both stated [by God] "in a single utterance" (*be-dibbur ehad*), which is impossible "for the mouth to speak or the ear to hear" (*Y. Nedarim* 3:2, with parallels in *Mechilta Ba-Hodesh* 7, *Sifrei Teitzei*, 333, etc.).[18]

Returning to our main theme, we note that the *Netziv*, R. Naftali Tzvi Berliner, at the end of the 19 century, already understood that:

> In the future when the children of Esau are moved by pure spirit to recognize the people of Israel and their virtues, then we will be moved to recognize that Esau is our brother, (Commentary, *Haamek Davar*, to Genesis 33:4).

This, then, is a sort of emerging Jewish *Nostra Aetate*. And, indeed, Esau-Edom, i.e. Rome, that is to say the Catholic Church, has for her part done precisely this in *Nostra Aetate*, and subsequent declarations.

Indeed, I showed this in my introduction to Eugene Korn's (Yitzhak Dov Korn) *Ha-Natzrut be-Einei ha-Yahadut: Avar Hoveh ve-Atid*, Jerusalem, 2013. Thus, the Meiri's commentary to *Avodah Zarah* – the Tractate dealing with idolatry, was first published in 1944, *Sanhedrin* in 1930, Horayot in 1946.

Yaakov Katz "discovered" the Meiri's unique view, first discussing it in his book *Bein Yehudim le-Goyim* (*Between Jews and Gentiles*) in 1962. This publication came fortuitously shortly before the initial discussions of Vatican Two, also in 1965, which came to fruition in the formulation of *Nostra Aetate* only in 1965. However, the Meiri's view, which triggered off a very lively polemic discussion among scholars – see bibliography below – paved the way among Jewish thinkers for a new angle of thought in the relationship towards Christianity. *Nostra Aetate* was, as it were, the complementary position from the Christian viewpoint.[19]

Judaism does demonstrate partial recognition of the legitimacy of (some) other religions, and most especially with Christianity because of the "rich complementarity" (ibid.) which exists between these two religions. Thus, though trinitarianism is difficult for a Jew to understand, nevertheless leading halachic authorities throughout the ages recognized it as legitimate for Christians, though forbidden for Jews.[20]

Hence, in Judaism, freedom of religion and tolerance towards other faiths, though not necessarily being the result of the notion of multiple truths as found in halachic and kabbalistic thought, nevertheless allows a pluralistic position vis-à-vis other faiths, because of the "positive" elements incorporated in those faiths, and especially with Christianity because of this "common patrimony" of these two religions and the "fundamental kinship" between them (from the Dec. 10 declaration, sect. 24).

I believe I can do no better than add here a passage taken out of an article by Rabbi Shlomo Riskin, (published in the *Jerusalem Post*, Tuesday, March 1, 2016, p. 16).

> God does tell Abraham, "I shall make you a great nation ... and through you all the families of the earth shall be blessed" (Genesis 12:2–3), but God later defines the content of that blessing which we must share with all of humanity: "Abraham is surely to become a great and mighty nation and through him all the nations of the earth shall be blessed; for I have loved [known, chosen] him because he commands his children and his household after him that they take responsibility for the ways of the Lord, doing acts of compassionate righteousness and moral justice." (Genesis 18:18, 19).
>
> It is not only monotheism – one God – that Abraham discovered; it is specifically ethical monotheism, a God whose "ways" are compassionate righteousness and moral justice, a God of love who wants us to love every human being, a God of justice who expects every human being to be treated justly, *to be entitled to freedom of thought and conscience* as long as he/she does not violate the physical wellbeing and human integrity of the other.
>
> Our Jewish prophets, therefore, taught the world for the first time the eventual goal of peace for all humanity, painting a picture of the millennium as a time when "swords will be turned into plowshares, spears into preening hooks, nation will not lift up sword against nation, and humanity will not learn war any more" (Isaiah 2, Micah 4), a time when the inviolability of every human being created in the Divine Image will be respected by all regardless of anyone's religious ideology or ritual performance, when "all the peoples will go forth, each person

in the name of his God, but we will go forth with the Name of the Lord our God forever and ever" (Micah 4:5). Moral absolution and ritual pluralism. [My emphasis, D.S.]

I have written somewhat lengthily on the above discourse, because the issue of "freedom of religion," understood as the legitimacy of other religions, constitutes a serious challenge to Judaism as well,[21] but not, however, the *right* to the freedom to practice other religions.

Endnotes to Chapter 3

1. *Hiddushei ha-Ritba al Massechet Eruvin*, ed. M. Goldstein, Jerusalem, 1974, pp. 117–118. This is found in *Tosafot Rabbenu Peretz* to *Eruvin*, ed. S. Wilman, Bnei Brak, 1980, p. 16 (ed. Dickman, Jerusalem, 1991, p. 48). And R. Peretz b. Eliyah of Corbeil (died 1298) notes that this interpretation is found in the *Tosafot* of his teacher, R. Yehiel of Paris, who had located it in an unnamed midrash, probably *Midrash Shocher Tov* (to Psalms) cited below. See Ephraim Kanarfogel, *The Intellectual History and Rabbinic Authors of Mediaeval Ashkenaz*, Detroit, 2013, pp. 26–27. Kanarfogel dealt extensively with this theme in his very rich article "Torah Study and Truth in Mediaeval Ashkenazic Rabbinic Literature and Thought," apud *Study and Knowledge in Jewish Thought*, ed. Howard Kreisel, Beer Sheva, 2006, pp. 101–119.

2. Cf. *Tosafot Rabbenu Peretz* to *Eruvin*, ed. S. Wilman, Bnei Brak, 1980, p. 16 (ed. Dickman, Jerusalem, 1991, p. 48), where R. Peretz notes that this interpretation is to be found within the earlier *Tosafot* of his teacher, R. Yehiel of Paris, (Kanarfogel ibid. p. 102). See Moshe Halbertal's analysis *in People of the Book: Canon, Meaning, and Authority*, Cambridge, Mass. & London, 1997, pp. 63–72, on what he calls "The Constitutive View."

3. The number 49 derives from the Song of Songs 2:4, "He brought me to the banquet hall and marked me with His Love"– "and marked" – "*ve-diglo*" – has the numerical value of 49 (cf. *Y. Sanhedrin* 4:2). The number (see below) is derived from the first part of the same verse, "He brought me to the banqueting house" – literally "the house of Wine," where wine – *yayin* – has the numerical value of 70. See Kanarfogel ibid. p. 30 note 104, who refers us to R. Avigdor Katz's commentary to the Song of Songs, ed. S.A. Wertheimer, Jerusalem 1981, p. 17, interpreting this half of the verse to mean that the Almighty brought the Children of Israel to receive the Torah at Sinai, which can be interpreted in seventy facets. R. Avigdor also adds that seventy is the *gematria* (numerical value) of the word *Sod*, as in the verse in Psalms 25:14, "The secret (*Sod*) of the Lord is with them that fear Him. [And He will show them His covenant]." See further Kanarfogel's article, "Torah Study and Truth in Mediaeval Rabbinic Literature," apud *Study and Knowledge in Jewish Thought*, ed. H. Kreisel, Beer Sheva, 2006, pp. 109–113.

This text is derived from Palestinian Talmud *Sanhedrin* 4:2, 22a. Cf. *B. Eruvin*

6b. See further, R. Hayyim Vital, (1542–1620), *Shaar ha-Kavanot: Inyanei Tefilin, Derush* 6, 11a, ed. Yeshivat-ha-Mekubalim, Jerusalem n.d. but c. 2005, vol. 1, p. 199. Cf. *B. Shabbat* 88b, and *B. Sanhedrin* 34a, on Jeremiah 23:29, "It is not Thy word like fire? Saith the Lord; and like a hammer that breaketh the rock in pieces." On which *De-Bei R. Yishmael* comments: "Just as the hammer is divided into so many sparks, so each word that was entitled from the mouth of the Holy One blessed be He was divided into *seventy* tongues." (See Rashi and Tosafot ad loc.) *B. Shabbat* has "tongues" – *leshonot*, while *B. Sanhedrin* has explanations, reasons – *taamim*. *Cf. Sefer Hassidim*, ed. R. Margaliot, Jerusalem, 1957, no. 985, p. 523, "Why was the Torah formulated in brevity and without detail (*u-be-stam*)? . . . Because one verse can be explained in many ways (*yotzei le-kamah taamim*), and if it were expressed explicitly, we would not know [the] other explanations." See further *Sefer Hassidim*, ed. S. Gutman, Elad 2014, vol. 2, pp. 747–748, in his *Yalkut Peirushim*. See further *Sifrei Naso*, sect. 42, ed. H.S. Horovitz, Leipzig 1917, pp. 47–48: . . ."God hath spoken once; twice have I heard this. . . ." (Psalms 62:11), and it says, "Is not My word like as fire? Saith the Lord; and like a hammer that breaketh the rock in pieces?" I.e., one divine statement can mean more than one thing. Cf. *Mechilta Be-Shalah, Shirah* sect. 8, ed. I.A. Horowitz & I.A. Robin, 2nd edition, Jerusalem, 1960, p. 143. And see the interesting passage in *Zohar Yitro*, vol. 1, 83b, (p. 166): that when the word came forth it appeared to be one; but when it was carved into its places, that word appeared in seventy forms (*anpin*) or variations that came forth from it, and with fifty-less-one crowns on each side . . . as it is said, . . . then the verse from Jeremiah, ibid.

Hananel Mack, in his article *"Shivim Panim la-Torah," Le-Mahalacho shel Bitui*, apud M. Bar-Asher ed., *Sefer Yovel li-Chvod R. Mordechai Breuer*, Jerusalem, 1992, vol. 2, pp. 454–460, has traced the concept of the "seventy faces" as a model for multiple Torah interpretations to *Otiyyot de-R. Akiva* and the Hebrew *Book of Enoch* (3 Enoch), while most of the usage and discussion of this concept in the mediaeval period was linked to the figures and works of Spanish esotericism, including R. Azriel of Gerona and the Zohar. Kanarfogel (ibid. p. 114) adds Ibn Ezra and Nahmanides to this list (commentary to Genesis 8:4, and additional sources). Kanarfogel further notes that:

> Although *Otiyyot de-R. Aqiba* and 3 Enoch were available in medieval Ashkenaz, [see his *Peering through the Lattices*, p. 151; E. Wolfson, *Through a Speculum That Shines*, Princeton 1994, pp. 223–224] the only Ashkenazic rabbinic figures identified by Mack who cite the tradition of *shiv'im panim la-Torah* are R. Simeon b. Isaac ha-Gadol, who refers to it in one of his liturgical poems, and R. Avigdor Katz of Vienna, who mentions it in his commentary to the Song of Songs. It should be noted that both of these figures were associated with the German Pietists, R. Simeon as part of their mystical chain

of tradition from the pre-Crusade period, and R. Avigdor toward the end of their formative period. [For R. Simeon, see, e.g., *Peirushei Siddur ha-Tefillah la-Rokeah*, ed. M. Hershler, Jerusalem, 1992, pp. 228–229. For R. Avigdor, *Peering through the Lattices*, pp. 107–110, 221–227.] Moreover, R. Eleazar of Worms himself refers to this concept twice in his prayer commentary, once in his discussion of the text of the *Shema* prayer (*lefi she-tivharu ba-Torah ha-nidreshet be-shivim panim*), and once in his discussion of the *tahanun* prayer, [*Peirushei Siddur ha-Tefillah la-Rokeah*, vol. 1, p. 294, vol. 2, p. 398]. R. Eleazar's version of this prayer contained the verse (Psalms 25:14): "The secret of the Almighty is vouchsafed for those who fear Him, He will inform them of His covenant (*sod ha-Shem li-yere'av u-berito le-hodi'am*). R. Eleazar explains that the Almighty reveals His secret lore to those who fear Him by informing them of the various layers of wisdom (including the esoteric teachings) within the Torah. He concludes by noting that the *gematria* of the word *sod* equals seventy, which reflects that the Torah may be explicated according to seventy different aspects (*nidreshet be-shiv'im panim*).

4. R. Baruch ha-Levi Epstein, in his *Torah Temimah to Exodus* ibid. (p. 198 note 1), explains that this homily bases itself upon the otherwise seemingly superfluous word *Kol,* all, i.e. "And the Lord spake *all* these words" alone. He then quotes Rashi to *B. Ketubot* 57a, who explains that sometimes one reason is more relevant and on other occasions the reasoning is reversed in accordance with slight changes in the situation. He himself suggests that it is only through arguing contrary positions that the truth evolves. However, the simple explanation of the Talmudic text is that both views have a degree of truthfulness.

5. On this midrashic theme, see Hananel Mack ibid. pp.452–453; Kanarfogel ibid. p. 27. See Naftali Wieder, *The Judaea Scrolls and Karaism*, Jerusalem 2005, pp. 424–426 (first published in *JJS* 4/4, 1953, pp. 163–165):

> "Fire" as a symbolic description of the Torah [and we may add: Sparks, D.S.] is a favourite aggadic motif and occurs frequently in Talmudic-midrashic literature. Moreover, the symbolism is appropriate to the last detail: *coals*; the words of the Sages are indeed likened to "*coals* of fire," (*Avot* 2:10). "To blow fire" is thus a picturesque idiom for teaching and expounding the Torah. It should be noted that the verb *to blow* bears already in the Bible the metaphorical meaning of to *speak*, to *utter*, (cf. Prov. 6:19, 14:25).
>
> From the single elements of the metaphor let us pass to the consideration of the metaphor as a whole. Its way of depicting the scholar who teaches and expounds the Law as "blowing fire," is strikingly illuminated by a parallel in the Talmud (*B. Hulin* 137b).

The Palestinian Amora R. Yohanan bar Nappaha (d. 279) describes the halachic discussions between the Patriarch R. Judah I, the compiler of the Mishnah, and Rab, the prominent Babylonian Amora, founder of the academy in Sura, in the following manner: "*Sparks of fire* were issuing from the mouth of Rab to the mouth of the Patriarch and from the Mouth of the Patriarch to the mouth of Rab."

The same metaphorical description occurs in yet another Talmudic passage. This example shows very clearly that the metaphor was intended as a characterization of the great, outstanding scholar only. R. Zera relates how the departed R. Jose b. Hanina appeared to him in a dream and told him of the seating arrangements in the Heavenly Academy for various deceased scholars. He learned to his consternation that R. Yohanan bar Nappaha was not allocated a seat next to R. Hiyya, and asked: "Is not R. Yohanan worthy to sit next to R. Hiyya?" Whereupon R. Jose replied: "Who could allow Bar Nappaha to enter the region of *fiery sparks and flaming torches?*" (*B. Baba Metzia* 85b).

The metaphor under consideration is, however, much older than the Talmudic age. The quotation from the Talmud contains the expression "flaming torch." This graphic and most effective figure of speech goes back to Ben-Sira, where it is used to describe the superlative nature of the prophet Elijah's words. Eulogising the prophet, *Ben-Sira* says (48:1) according to the Greek version, as follows: "Until there arose a prophet like fire, whose words were like a *burning torch*."

Finally, we may draw attention to another important source which offers a striking parallel to the imagery of fire proceeding from the mouth of inspired men. We refer to the sixth vision in the *Ezra Apocalypse* (IV *Ezra*), the Vision of the Man from the sea (4 *Ezra* 12:10, ed. Charles, vol. 1 p. 617). The most interesting feature with which "the Man" (= Messiah) is invested is that *a stream of fire was coming forth from his mouth, a flaming breath from his lips and a storm of sparks from his tongue.*

In the interpretation of the Vision the fiery stream is allegorized to represent the Law "which is compared to fire."

To sum up: We have seen that the words of inspired men (the prophet, the Messiah, and outstanding teachers of the Law) are described in terms of "fire issuing from their mouths."

6. See also his responsum no. 29.

A. Grossman, *Hachmei Ashkenaz ha-Rishonim*, Jerusalem 1995, p. 85; Kanarfogel ibid. p. 27, and his "Torah Study and Truth in Mediaeval Ashkenazic Rabbinic Literature," apud *Study and Knowledge in Jewish Thought*, ed. H. Kreisal, Beer Sheva, 2006, pp. 109–113.

This seems to express the view of continued revelation, and this indeed is the view of R. Mosheh Alsheich (1507–1600) in his commentary to Proverbs 21:17. There, he has an extended discussion on what clearly for him was a very vexing provocative question, as to how two conflicting views can both be correct. His solution is also based on his Kabbalistic views. Among other things he writes (ibid. ad init.): And therefore we should not be surprised that someone with his intellect innovates in the Torah [in what is] close to prophecy.

See also Meir Raffeld, "On Some Kabbalistic Elements Underlying the Halachic Teachings of R. Shlomoh Luria," [Hebrew], *Daat* 36, pp. 21–23; Yaakov Elbaum, *Openness and Insularity* [Hebrew], Jerusalem, 1990, p. 36; Ephraim Kanarfogel, ibid. p. 26.

7. See *B. Baba Metzia* 59b, referred to below.

The text tells us that though R. Eliezer had convincing arguments, which seemed to be supported by divine miracles, his view was not accepted by the Sages, and R. Yehoshua declared: *Lo ba-Shamayim* – that the ruling is "not in heaven," meaning the final pragmatic decision is made by man and not in heaven. This passage has been the subject of numerous studies; e.g., Yohanan Silman, "The Divine Torah that is not in Heaven: A Typological Analysis," [Hebrew], in *Bar-Ilan,* 1987, Yitzhak Englard, "The 'Oven of Akhnai': Various interpretations of our Aggadah" [Hebrew], *Ha-Mishpat ha-Ivri* 1, 1974, pp. 45–56, etc.

And even though the Talmud in *B. Baba Batra* 12ab declares that prophecy (*nevuah*) ended with the destruction of the [second] Temple, there continued to be another form of revelation called *ruah ha-kodesh*, "the holy spirit," and also the *bat kol*, "the heavenly voice." See, E.E. Urbach, *Hazal:Pirkei Emunot ve-Deot*, Jerusalem, 1969, pp. 515–516, (and in his index p. 639a, s.v. *nevuah, navi, neviim*), referring us to *Tosefta Pesahim* 1:27, ed. Lieberman p. 157; B. *Eruvin* 64b; *Leviticus Rabba* 21:8, ed. Margaliot p. 485; *Y. Sheviit* 9:1, 38d, etc., (Urbach ibid. p. 516 note 10 – all *ruah ha-kodesh*). And regarding the *bat kol*, see *B. Megilah* 32a (ibid. note 12).

As to Elijah the prophet revealing things, see *B. Sanhedrin* 98a, etc.

In mediaeval times we find Rabbis giving halachic rulings through the agency of *ruah ha-kodesh*. Indeed we have a whole volume of responsa by E. Yaakov of Mervais the Tosafist, entitled *Sheelot u-Teshuvot min ha-Shamayim (Questions and Responsa from Heaven)*. See R. Reuven Margaliot's edition, Jerusalem, 1957, (and that of R. Aaron Marcus, 2nd edition, Tel Aviv 1957). In his introduction (pp. 3–24) Margaliot brings many testimonia of Rabbis ruling through dreams (e.g., R. Mosheh of Cucy, *Sefer Mitzvot Gadol* introduction, etc.) There (pp. 28–41) we also find an analysis of the differences between prophecy, *ruah ha-kodesh, bat-kol*, and *gillui Elijah*, Elijah the Prophet's revelation – i.e. Elijah's answer to a question. See also Marcus' introduction, pp. 7–18. In recent times there has been much discussion of the question whether one can make rabbinic rulings on the basis of *ruah ha-kodesh*.

See, for example, the response in my grandfather, R. David Sperber's, *Afrakasta de-Anya* 3rd edition, Brooklyn 2002, vol. 1, sect.1, pp. 37–38, vol. 2, sect. 109, pp. 267–272; R. Ovadiah Yosef, *Yabia Omer* 2nd edition, vol. 1, Jerusalem 1986, *Orah Hayyim* sect.41, pp. 142–149, (and ibid. subsection 18, p. 146, where he discusses the difference between prophecy – *nevuah* and *ruah ha-kodesh*).

This notion is central in the thought of Conservative Judaism. See Eliot Dorff, *Conservative Judaism: Our Ancestors to Our Descendants*, 1977, p. 201; idem. *The Unfolding Tradition: Jewish Law after Sinai. For the Love of God and People: A Philosophy of Jewish Law*, 2007.

Incidentally, this is also a core belief in the Bahai Faith, termed "Progressive Revelation." See Peter Smith, s.v. Progressive Revelation, apud *A Concise Encyclopedia of Bahai Faith*, Oxford, 2000, pp. 267–277.

8. On this concept see, for example, A.J. Heschel, *Torah Min ha-Shamayim be-Aspaklariah shel ha-Dorot*, vol. 3, Jerusalem, 1990, pp. 93–103; Avi Sagi, *The Open Canon: On the Meaning of Halakhic Discourse*, London, 2007; especially pp. 127 et seq.; idem, *Elu ve-Elu: Mashmaut shel ha-Siah ha-Hilchati*, Tel-Aviv, 1996; M. Rozenzweig, "*Eilu ve-Eilu Divrei Elohim Hayyim*: Halakhic Pluralism and Theories of Controversy," apud *Rabbinic Authority and Personal Autonomy*, ed. M. Sokol, Northvale, N.J., 1992, pp. 106–118. See further S. Ettinger, "*Mahlokot ve-Emet – Le Mashmaut Sheelat ha-Emet ba-Halachah*," *Shenaton ha-Mishpat ha-Ivri* 21, 1998–2000, pp. 37–57, with some slightly different explications of some of these texts.

There is some discussion among early and late authorities relating to the statement of Rav in *B. Makkot* 11a that Rav Hiyya wore *tefillin* that were sewn with flaxen thread, whereas the *halachah* is that they must be sewn with Kosher animal sinews (*B. Shabbat* 28b, *Shulhan Aruch, Orah Hayyim* 32:49). Surely we do not assume that Rav Hiyya never carried out the *mitzvah* of *tefillin*, because he wore defective ones!? See *Ben Ish Hai*, that is R. Yosef Hayyim of Bagdhad, *Rav Poalim*, vol. 4, Jerusalem, 1964, *Orah Hayyim* 2, who discusses the problem of one who unwittingly wore halachic defective *tefillin* all his life. Do we assume that he never really carried out the *mitzvah*? He refers us to the *Hida* (R. Hayyim Yosef David Azulai), *Devash le-Fi* 4.4 [where I did not find what he refers to], who cites an ancient source quoted by *Shibolei ha-Leket* in MS, that if the intention is positive, the *mitzvah* has been fulfilled. R. Tzvi Pesach Frank, *Har Tzvi* vol. 1, Jerusalem, 1987, sect. 35, pp. 32–33, suggests that Rav Hiyya's ruling, though not accepted by subsequent generations, that is to say by the majority of (later) Rabbis, was valid for his time, thus rendering his *tefillin* as ritually fit. Surely, once again we find evidence that the majority decision determined subsequent practice, but not necessarily the absolute truth of the requirement, and that Rav Hiyya's view also was "correct."

9. See on this subject in my article in *Conversations* 23, 2015, pp. 1–28, entitled "How to Lean Towards Leniency: Halachic Methodology for the *Posek.*"

10. See, Gershon Scholem, *Kabbalah*, Jerusalem, 1974, p. 88; idem, *Origins of Kabbalah*, Princeton, 1987, pp. 312–313, 423, 441–442, from Azriel of Gerona. This concept is found frequently in Kabbalistic writings, probably beginning with *sefer Pliyah* (=*ha-Karah*), *Netiv* 2, and *Netiv* 5, discussed in the Raavad's introduction to *Sefer Yetzirah*, and in *Raza de-Yetzirah* 23, where the differences between these two texts are explained.

Kanarfogel summarizes his analysis of the Tosafistic sources on this theme as follows (p. 116):

> What emerges from our discussion is that the notion of *shiv'm panim la-Torah* reflects principally the sublime completeness of the Torah and the fact that every part of the Torah can be broken down into numerous different and distinct aspects, including the various levels of esoteric interpretation. The notion of "forty nine faces of the Torah" (*mem tet panim la-Torah*), however, refers invariably to the way the Jewish people received and experienced the truth of the Torah at Sinai (through forty nine different channels) and concomitantly, to the varied and pluralistic ways by which they would be able to interpret the halakhic possibilities and truths of the Torah. The Tosafists and other Ashkenazic halakhists, whether or not they were personally inclined toward mystical studies and conceptions, tended to favor this latter model. Those who were more inclined toward (kabbalistic) theosophy in particular (including the Spanish Kabbalists and the German Pietists) typically embraced the model and phrase of *shiv'im panim la-Torah*. [See W. Kolbremmer, "Hermeneutics and Dispute in the Rabbinic Tradition," *AJS Review* 28, 1994, pp. 283–285.]

He further notes (p. 117) that:

> . . . In the medieval Jewish mindset in general, and especially within medieval Ashkenaz, *peshat, derash, remez* (and perhaps even *sod*) were equally valid ways of ascertaining and presenting the truths of the Torah, given the possibility of multiple interpretations inherent within the Torah itself, on matters of Jewish law and beyond. As opposed to the rules of modern interpretation, Ashkenazic rabbinic scholars believed that truth could be revealed quite effectively by non-*peshat* approaches as well.
>
> Ta-Shma, *Ha-Sifrut ha-Parshanit la-Talmud*, v. 1, Jerusalem 1999, pp. 16–21. Thus, Rashbam and other Ashkenazic figures could engage in "enlightened" *peshat* and additional forms of critical biblical interpretation while maintaining their roles as leading Talmudists. Cf. H. H. Ben-Sasson's review of Urbach's *Ba'alei ha-Tosafot* ("*Hanhagatah shel Torah*") in *Behinot be-Biqqoret*

ha-Sifrut 9, 1956, pp. 39–53; Isadore Twersky, "Religion and Law," apud S.D. Goitein ed. *Religion in a Religious Age*, Cambridge, MA, 1973, pp. 69–82; I. Ta-Shma, *Knesset Mehkarim* Jerusalem, 2004, vol. 1, pp. 273–301; and Rashi's introduction to his commentary on Song of Songs.)

It is interesting to note that this concept of PARDES (i.e. *Peshat Remez Derash Sod*), so ever-present in Jewish biblical commentary, both mystical and rational, finds a kind of parallel in Christian thought. For Origen (3rd century) in his *Homilies on Leviticus*, transl. ed. G.W. Barkley, Washington D.C., 1990, p. 29 speaks of the Word of God being covered with a veil of flesh so that the letter is seen as flesh, but the spiritual sense hiding within it is perceived as divinity. Thus, God's word comes to us disguised, wrapped up in a physical layer that has to be stripped away in order to reveal the true spiritual message. (See Marc Hirshman, "Learning as Speech: Tosefta Pesahim the Light of Plotinus and Origen," apud *Study and Knowledge in Jewish Thought*, ed. Howard Kreisel, Beer Sheva, 2006, p. 27.)

A similar notion is to be found in the later Hasidic literature. Thus in Habad teaching we often find the cliché "two opposites in one subject" – *shnei hafachim be-nosei ehad*. This notion has been discussed in Eliot R. Wolfson's recent *A Dream Interpreted Within a Dream: Oneiropoiesis and the Prism of Imagination*, New York, 2011, pp. 207–208, (422–423 note 140 for references), this, in the chapter entitled "*Coincidentia Oppositorum* and the Mythologic of the Dream" (pp. 179–217).

Here we may also call attention to the source he brings on pp. 154–155, from *Midrash ha-Gaddol to Genesis*, ed. M. Margaliot, vol. 1, Jerusalem, 1975, Introduction p. 39:

> There are the rules by which the aggadah is interpreted, and the multifaceted explanations of Scripture emerge from them. And thus it says "Behold, my word is like fire – declares the Lord – and like a hammer that shatters rock!" (Jeremiah 23:29). The house of R. Ishmael taught: just as this hammer divides into several sparks, so one verse can yield several explanations, but one explanation is not derived from two verses. Hence it says "Just as a dream comes with much brooding" (Ecclesiastes 5:2), and the matter [can be explained by the method of] *a minori ad maius*: If with respect to the words of dreams that have no effect, one dream can yield several explanations, how much more so with respect to the words of Torah, which are more significant, that one verse will yield several explanations. And thus it says "For this is not a trifling thing for you" (Deuteronomy 32:47). There is no letter in the Torah, and all the more so no word, and all the more so no verse, and all the more so no chapter that does not yield several meanings and that is interpreted in several ways.

And in relation to this comparison between interpreting dreams and the interpretation of Torah, see the passage in *B. Berachot* 55b (Wolfson, p. 152) where it is related that R. Berechiah records that:

> There were twenty-four interpreters of dreams [*potrei halomot*] in Jerusalem. One time I dreamt a dream and I went to all of them, and what one interpreted for me was not what the other interpreted – yet all of them were fulfilled in me, to substantiate what is said, "all dreams follow the mouth." Is the statement that "all dreams follow the mouth" scriptural? Yes, as stated by R. Eleazar, for R. Eleazar said: Whence do we know that all dreams follow the mouth? As it says, "as he [Joseph] interpreted to us, so it was" (Genesis 41:13). Rava said: This is only if he interpreted it in accord with one's dream, as it says, "according to each man's dream did he interpret" (ibid. 12).

See on this passage Hayyim Weiss, "'Twenty-Four Dream Interpreters Were in Jerusalem . . .' On Dream-Interpreters and the Approaches to Dream-Interpretation in the "Tratise on Dreams in the Babylonian Talmud," *Madda'ei ha-Yahadut* 44, 2007, pp. 39–40, 44–46.

11. Cited also in Charles Mopsik's article, "Union and Unity in Kabbalah," apud *Between Jerusalem and Banares: Comparative Studies in Judaism, and Hinduism,* ed. Hananya Goodman, Albany, 1994, p. 231. Perhaps there is a partial parallelism to this in the Hindu notion of the union of Śiva and sacti; (Tantric "Divine bi-unity"); see K. Sivaraman, *Saivism in Philosophical Perspective: A Study of the Formative Couples of Saivan Siddhanta,* Delhi, 1977, pp. 177, 199; Coomaraswamy, "Vedic Monotheism," *Journal of Indian History* 15, 1936, pp. 84–92.

12. On *aggadot* received by tradition, see Z.H. Chajes, *The Student's Guide through the Talmud,* transl. and annotated by J.J. Shachter, London, 1952, pp. 148–153. And cf. ibid. p. 142, 246–247.

13. See further what he wrote in his *"Ha-Derech ha-Memutzaat" ke-Reishit Tzemichat ha Datit ha-Modernit: Teguvot la-Modernah shel Maharatz Chayes, R.S. Hirsch, ve-Shadal,* ("The Middle Way" as the beginning of the "Growth of Modern Orthodoxy." Reactions to the Modernity of Maharatz Chajes, RSh"R Hirsch and Shadal), Jerusalem, 2011, pp. 330–339.

14. A statement of Pope Francis, incorporated into the most recent Conciliar declaration, "The Gifts and the Calling of God are Irrevocable (Rom. 11:29); A Reflection on Theological Questions Pertaining to Catholic-Jewish Relations on the Occasion of the 50th Anniversary of *Nostra Aetate*" (No. 4), from Dec.10, 2015, sect.13.

15. This is expressed in R. Mosheh Rivkis' (*Beer ha-Golah*) gloss to *Shulhan Aruch, Hoshen Mishpat* 425:5, who writes, "The people among whom we are scattered believe in all these essentials of religion," namely One Creator of Heaven and Earth, Jewish Sacred Scripture, values of life, family, compassionate righteousness, justice etc.

One should also take account of the fact that Judaism never saw revelation as being exclusively for Jews alone. Note, for example, the biblical story of Balaam in Numbers 22–24. For, according to the Rabbis he was no less a prophet than Moses himself. (See Louis Ginzberg, *The Legends of the Jews*, vol. 3, Philadelphia, 1954, p. 356, and ibid. vol. 6, Philadelphia, 1946, p. 125 note 727, and cf. vol. 3, p. 380, and vol. 6, p. 133–134, notes 782–784. Indeed, his ass had a revelation, see Numbers 22:28–30, Ginzberg vol. 3, pp. 363, 366. For other non-Jewish prophets see *B. Avodah Zarah* 3a, (and for their names Ginzberg, vol. 2, p. 240, vol. 3, pp. 205, 354, 355–356, 371; vol. 4, 411, vol. 5, 381, vol. 6, 124, 125.). Indeed, according to the Rabbis, God offered the Torah to all the Gentiles of the World, who refused it; see Ginzberg, vol. 3, pp. 80–82, vol. 6, pp. 30–31 note 181.

This again is too broad a topic to be treated here, but let these references suffice.

16. See M. Halbertal and Avishai Margalit, *Idolatry*, pp. 212–213; M. Halbertal, "Ones Possessed of Religion: Religious Tolerance in the Teaching of the Meiri," *Edah Journal* 1/1, 2000, pp. 1–24. Y. Katz, *Zion* 1953, pp. 15–30 etc. Further, on the Meiri's attitude toward Christianity, and a discussion on how far it was revolutionary, and the extent of its practical halachic implications, see Y. Ta-Shma, *Tarbiz* 47, 1978, pp. 197–210, ibid. 49, 1980, pp. 218–219; E. Urbach, *Sefer ha Yovel le-Katz*, Jerusalem, 1980, pp. 34–44; Y. Blidstein, *Zion* 51, 1984, pp. 153–166; D.Z. Hilman, *Tzefunot* 1/1, 1989 pp. 65–72; S.Z. Havlin's edition of the Meiri's *Sefer ha-Kabbalah*, Jerusalem, 1995, pp. 21–22 note 70; idem ed. *Bet ha-Behirah Avot*, Jerusalem, 1995, p. 129 note 127; M. Halbertal, *Bein Torah le-Hokhmah: R. Menachem ha-Meiri ve-Baalei Halachah ha-Maimoniim be-Provence,* Jerusalem, 2000, pp. 80–108; Aviezer Ravitzky, "Tolerance in the Jewish Tradition," *Hazon Nahum*, ed. Y. Elman and J.G. Gurock, New York, 1997, pp. 388–389; and more recently Gregg Stern, *Philosophy and Rabbinic Culture: Jewish Interpretation and Controversy in Mediaeval Languedoc*, Abington Oxon, 2009, pp. 93–94, and Katrin Kogman-Appel, *Kabbalah* ibid. pp. 102–105. See further J.D. Bleich, "Entering a Non-Jewish House of Worship," *Tradition* 44/2, 2011, pp. 77–83, for an extensive, very reserved, summary of the different views on the subject.

It should further be noted that R. Yehiel of Paris (died 1286), in his debate with Nicolas Donin from the mid 13th century, makes much the same argument, and there he states, albeit in a polemic debate which necessitated apologetic arguments, that all "goyim" – gentiles – in the Talmud refer to the seven biblical nations who were driven out of Canaan by the Israelites. But the term does not refer to contemporary

Christians, who protect the Jewish community from all harm. (See J.D. Eisenstein, *Otzar ha-Vikuchimn*, 2nd edition, Jerusalem, 1969, p. 85 col. b.)

We should also call attention to the responsum of R. Hayyim Geliffah (15th century), published by R. Hayyim Rapoport in *Or Yisrael* 14/4 (56), 2009, in which he states explicitly concerning Christians that they are not idolaters, and believe in a single God, and that the belief in the trinity is not idolatry, but that they do not fully understand the nature of God. Likewise, the Rashba (R. Shlomoh ben Aderet) in his famous responsum, published in the *Or ha-Mizrah* ed. Jerusalem, 2005, (from manuscripts) no. 368 p. 266, brings a parable of a king who appointed officers over different parts of his kingdom, commanding the citizens to abide by the orders of their officers, but knowing that the authority ultimately comes from the king. So too, those who worship the stars who rule over a certain area are not idolaters, for they know that that star has no power of its own, but its rule derives from the Almighty who placed it in authority over that region.

17. On Rav Kook see *Igrot ha-Reiyah* vol. 1, Jerusalem, 1981, p. 99, in his letter to his disciple, Dr. Zeidel. See further Hagi ben Artzi, *He-Hadash Yitkadash, Ha-Rav Kook ke-Posek Mehadash*, Tel-Aviv, 2010, pp. 99. As to Rav Herzog, see *Ha-Hukah le-Yisrael al-Pi ha-Torah*, vol. 1, ed. Itamar Warhaftig, (*Sidrei Shilton u-Mishpat ba-Medinah ha-Yehudit*), pp. 12–17. See also *Shu"t: Teshuvot Mevuarot mi-Gedolei ha-Poskim Benei Zemaneinu. Ha-Rav Yitzhak Isaak ha-Levi Herzog: Nochrim be-Medinah Yehudit*, edd. Itamar Warhaftig and Ariel Pikar, Jerusalem, 2008.

The Meiri's view was accepted or used by a number of notable latter-day authorities, such as R. Eliyahu Klatzkin (Lublin 19th century) *Shut Imrei Shefer*, Warsaw, 1895, sect. 92; also R. Yehiel Weinberg, in his article published in *Li-Frakim*, second series 2003, pp. 275–298; R. Yosef Eliyahu Henkin, *Kovetz ha-Pardes* 31/1, p. 43, reprinted in his *Lev Ibra*, New York, 1957, p. 116; R. Yoel Ashkenazi *Shut Mahari Ashkenazi*, Muncacz, 1893, *Yoreh Deah* sect. 39, 40 ad fin.; and so too his disciple R. Shalom Mordechai ha-Cohen from Brezan (called *Maharsham*), *Shut Maharsham* vol. 5, Jerusalem, 1973, sect. 41; R. Avraham Eliyahu Kaplan, *Divrei Talmud*, Jerusalem, 1958, responsum 13/4, etc, (who refers to the Meiri as a minority view, *daat yahid*); R. Ovadia Yosef, *Yabia Omer* vol. 10, Jerusalem, 2004, *Yoreh Deah* 51/5, p. 276.

And though some scholars have questioned the authenticity of the Meiri's position, David Tzvi Hilman, in his article in *Tzfunot* 1/1, 1989, pp. 65–72 demonstrated quite conclusively its authenticity. (The Meiri's view is also cited in R. Betzalel Ashkenazi's *Shitah Mekubetzet* to *Baba Kama* 38b and 113a.)

18. That text brings a number of additional examples of such conflicting rulings, which were given *be-dibbur ehad*, such as the case of *Shatnez*, sacrifices on Shabbat etc. However, not all the examples are of the same nature, and the text requires careful analysis. See the discussion in Y. Tamar, *Alei Tamar* to *Nashim*, Givataim, 1981, p. 298.

Interestingly enough, this provocatively tantalizing statement was the subject of a variety of different kinds of interpretation, quasi-rational, mystical etc. See, for example, R. Abraham Isaak ha-Cohen Kook, (1865–1935), in his commentary to the prayer-book, *Olat Reiyah*, Jerusalem, 1989, vol. 2, p. 49, for his highly complex hermeneutic exposition of this text:

> **And on the Sabbath day, two lambs, a year old, "tamim" (perfect, unblemished).**
>
> Doubled is the matter of the *kedushah* (holiness) of Shabbat. Positive *kedushah* and negative *kedushah* is formed within it. The negative *kedusha* is the one that negates the influence of the secular (weekday) and its darkness from having reign over the world, in life and in people; internally and externally. And the positive *kedushah* is that which causes to flow the holy light; the delicate spirit of the living God, and the shining countenance of God's honor, with the essence of the pleasant joyousness of God's *kedushah* upon all existence.
>
> The secret of "*Zachor* and *Shamor*" in one articulation were said together with, "And on the Sabbath day, two, one year old lambs," corresponding to the two *Kedushot*, come the two *Mussaf* (extra) offerings, two lambs, portraying renewal of *kedushah* that penetrates [down] into the roots of the animal life force and elevates its growth of *kedushah* from the beginnings of its growth and suckling, of one year.
>
> And the "temimus" (perfection, unblemished) which goes with every sacrifice, combines here (with the other characteristics), to acknowledge that even though in this world it is not possible for the supernal notion of "a day of all Shabbat" to be displayed in its completeness, nonetheless, what light that derives from the *kedushah* of Shabbat in the "*mikdash*" is pure *kedushah* (*kedushah temimah*).

Of course this is far from being the plain meaning (*pshat*) of the statement, but it does indicate the struggle to understand it. (My thanks to Mr. Josef Septimus of New York who brought this text to my attention.)

19. The above-mentioned study of Eugene Korn discusses this issue in detail, giving a very full list of rabbinic authorities who agree that Christianity is not *polytheistic* idolatry. Korn's study first appeared in English in *Jewish Theology and World Religions*, ed. Alon Goshen-Gottstein and Eugene Korn, Oxford and Portland Oregon, 2012.

To underscore the revolutionary change in attitude of Jews towards Christianity, we may call attention to some of the mediaeval rabbinic formulations on the Church. For Christianity was routinely referred to as "idolatry," and the Church of the Holy

Sepulcher as "the house of idolatry" (*beit ha-tarfut*), (based on Genesis 31:19; see A.M. Haberman, *Sefer Gezerot Ashkenaz ve-Tzorfat*, Jerusalem, 1945, pp. 24, 26, 38, 44, 77, etc.). Baptismal waters were the "waters of stench" (*mei tzahanah*), (Haberman ibid. pp. 38, 46) . . . Christians are "uncircumcised and impure" (*areilim u-temeim*), (Haberman ibid. pp. 35, 45, 55, 103). . . . "Over all this hovered the awareness that Christianity was based upon the adoration of a dead man, whose body imported the most severe form of *tumah* (impurity), that of a corpse (*tumat meit*)," (Haberman ibid. p. 16 line 17). See on this (in Jeffry R. Woolf, *The Fabric of Religious Life in Mediaeval Ashkenaz* (1000–1300), Leiden, Boston 2015, p. 193). And such statements could be vastly multiplied, but these should suffice to clarify our point.

Additional sources reflecting somewhat crude language relating to Christianity may be found in David Berger's edition of *Nizzahon Vetus* (*The Jewish Christian Debate in the Middle Ages*, Philadelphia, 1979); and in Daniel J. Lasker and Sarah Stroumsa, *The Polemic of Nestor the Priest*, vol. 1, Jerusalem, 1996. See also Lasker's article "Mediaeval Critiques of Christianity," *Journal of Jewish Thought and Philosophy* 8/2 1999, pp. 249, 252, and the whole article (pp. 243–259) on the question of when Jewish polemicists used vulgar attacks and philosophical argumentations.

20. I have discussed this issue in considerable detail in my forthcoming book *On the Halachic Status of Hinduism*. Here I shall give a brief survey and select bibliographic information.

See the discussion of Rabbi J.D. Bleich, in his recent book The Philosophic Question of Philosophy, Ethics, Law and Halakhah, Jerusalem, 1913. In his chapter 3, "Divine Unity in Maimonides, the Tosafists, and the Meiri," he writes as follows on pp. 36–37: (The discussion relates, of course, to Christianity, but is relevant for our purpose in defining attitude to gentile religious and determining whether they be idolatrous or not.)

> A nuanced view of Christianity is ascribed to the Tosafists (12th–13th centuries) in their comments on *Sanhedrin* 63b and *Bekhorot* 25, (with parallel statements in *Rosh Sanhedrin* 7:3; Rabbenu Yerucham, *Sefer Adam Ve-Havah* 17:5). A literal reading indicates that they hold that acceptance of a doctrine of *shittuf* (association) is permitted to non-Jews. The doctrine involves a belief in the "Creator of the heavens," but links a belief in the Creator with a belief in some other being or entity. The term *shituf* is not uncommon in medieval philosophical literature and connotes plurality in the Godhead, (see David Kaufmann, *Geschichte der Attributen lehre*, Gotha, 1877, p. 460 note 148). *Tosafot* refer explicitly to the gentiles of their day, and the most obvious example of *shittuf*, clearly the doctrine which *Tosafot* seek to legitimize for non-Jews, is Trinitarianism.

He continues to say that "this interpretation of the *Tosafot* is by no means universally accepted," citing the *Noda-bi-Yehudah* (*Tinyana, Yoreh Deah* no.148), concluding that,

> It is probably correct to say that the majority of latter-day authorities interpret *Tosafot* more broadly as declaring that *shittuf* does not constitute idolatry for Noahides. (*Sha'ar Efraim*, no. 24; *Me'il Tzedakah*, no. 22; *Teshuvot ve-Shev ha-Kohen*, no. 38; *Teshuvot Hadashot le-Rabbeinu Akiva Eger* (Jerusalem, 5738), pp. 164–66; *Pri Megadim, Yoreh De'ah, Siftei Da'at* 65:11; idem, *Orah Hayyim, Eshel Avraham* 156:2; and *Mahatzit ha-Shekel, Orah Hayyim* 156:2.)

We may add the following references: M.M. Kasher, *Torah Shelemah, Yitro*, vol. 16, New York, 1955, pp. 230–233; David Tzvi Mecklenburg, *Ha-Ktav ve-ha-Kabbalah*, New York, 1946 (ed. Princ. Leipzig 1839), Deut. pp. 7–8.

21. See Avi Sagi's searching analysis, in his article cited above pp. 175–192. See further his article in *Dinei Yisrael* 15, 1999–2000, *Baayat ha-Hachraah ha-Hilchatit ve-ha-Emet ha-Hilchatit*.

For a further clarification of this important point I would quote what Eugene Korn wrote in his essay "Rethinking Christianity: Rabbinic Positions and Possibilities," apud *Jewish Theology and World Religions*, ed. A. Goshen-Gottstein and Eugene Korn, Oxford, Portland, Oregon, 2012, p. 212:

> It must be emphasized that although both Heschel [cf. below chapter 14] and Greenberg [Irving Greenberg, *For the Sake of Heaven and Earth*, Philadelphia, 2009]
> accept theological pluralism, each insists that Judaism is true absolutely for Jews and that it is contrary to God's will for Jews to cross the line to Christianity. Conflating their theological pluralism with any philosophical relativism that mocks religious truth or permanent difference is a logical confusion that both distorts and demeans their thought. Heschel even travelled to the Vatican in September 1965 when Church officials were drafting the initial versions of *Nostra Aetate* to insist that there be no hint of Jewish conversion in the document. He emotionally professed to Vatican authorities: "If faced with the choice of baptism or the crematoria of Auschwitz, I would choose Auschwitz."

See Judith Hershcopf, *American Jewish Year Book* (New York, 1965) 128; Reuven Kimelman, 'Rabbis Joseph B. Soloveitchik and Abraham Joshua Heschel on Jewish-Christian Relations, *Modern Judaism*, 24 (2004), 255. Greenberg also rejected relativism and sharply distinguished between them logically (*For the Sake of Heaven and Earth*, 196, 201–3, cited by Jospe in Chapter 3, above, pp. 99–100.)

CHAPTER 4

Back to Western Rationalism

However, in the traditional rationalist West for the most part, if I had the truth, and you thought otherwise, you were wrong, and had to be corrected, either through persuasion or through force. Indeed, this "persuasion" was your moral responsibility. That is what the Inquisition preached and practiced, with forcible conversion being the more common mode.[1] For how could one tolerate heresy,[2] sacrilege "Host desecration,"[3] and apostasy! That had to be either corrected or punished, biblically-expunging the evil from one's midst. Indeed, the notion of tolerance is actually paradoxical.[4]

Of course, in Polytheism, where gods usually had regional control, religious pluralism was acceptable. But Monotheism introduces difficulties into the notion of theological pluralism.[5]

Endnotes to Chapter 4

1. Archbishop Patrick O'Boyle of Washington, in the "debate" on the preliminary drafts of *Nostra Aetate*, in 1964, stated that:

> The word "conversion" awakens in the hearts of Jews memories of perse-cutions, sufferings, and forced denials of all the truths that a Jew loves with sincerity and good faith.

See John H. Oesterreicher, *The New Encounter: Between Christians and Jews*, New York, 1986, pp. 199–201. It is interesting to note that Msgr. John H. Oesterreicher, was born of Jewish parents in Moravia; his parents perished in a concentration camp, while he (born in 1904) fled Europe in 1940, and converted to Catholicism at the age of twenty and was subsequently ordained. After the war he was regarded as one of the Church's experts on the mission to the Jews, was convinced that Jewish conversion was necessary for the fulfillment of salvation history, but suggested that mention of the conversion of the Jews in an early draft of *Nostra Aetate* be removed. He apparently was involved in the formulation of the final draft. (See *Commonweal*, "The Study Behind 'Nostra Aetate'," by Paul Banmann, March 30, 3015, based on a lecture by University of California, Berkeley Professor, John Connelly, at the annual Catholic-Jewish Engagement lecture at Fairfield University, March 2015.) It appears that the Jewish Jules Isaac (1877–1963) also was involved in the formulation of that document. See John W. O'Malley, *What Happened in Vatican* II? Harvard University Press, 2008. (See below chapter 13.)

The very significant part played by Oesterreicher (1914–1991) in effecting the sort of theological change that enabled the formulation of *Nostra Aetate*, together with that of Karl Thieme (1902–2002), has been demonstrated by John Connelly in his important book, *From Enemy to Brother*, Cambridge Mass. 2012. (And on Thieme, see Ellias H. Fullenbach, *Das Katholisch-judische Verhältnis in 20 Jahrhundert* . . ., Paderborn 2010. See also what Fullenbach wrote on Oesterreicher in his article "Shoah, Reward, Crisis: Catholic Reflections on the Shoah," apud *Antisemitism, Christian Ambivalence and the Holocaust*, ed. Kevin P. Spicer, Bloomington Indiana 2007, pp. 201–234.

Returning to the issue of religious and forcible coercion (see above, near note 5), in point of fact, they make little or no theological sense. For can one coerce a person to believe that in which he does not believe, and that which is in clear opposition to his personal belief system?! One can perhaps coerce a person to declaim certain formulae, but those declamations would be lies in his heart. One can force a person to carry out certain actual acts, but they would be acts of deceit, or even meaningless gestures. And proof positive of this is the phenomenon of the Conversos, those Jews who were forcibly converted to Christianity, and preserved the Jewish identity in secret for hundreds of years, even to the present day. See, for example, the magnificent study of David M. Gittlitz, *Secrecy and Deceit: The Religion of the Crypto-Jews*, Philadelphia and Jerusalem, 1996.

And when one read poems of seventeenth century Marrano Poets, one feels the sense of guilt together with the hope of personal redemption as well as the ultimate punishment of their cruel oppressors. See, for example, the autobiographical poem of João Pinto Delgado (c. 1580–1653, from Lisbon to Amsterdam, where in 1636–1637, he became one of the seven parnasim (governors) of the Talmud Torah Seminary in Amsterdam, entitled "A la Salide de Lisboa" (On leaving Lisbon). On lines 25–350 he writes:

> If our sins do oblige us
> To undergo such cruelty,
> Remember that the Lord, though he
> Cloaks his intent, will punish you.
> If it seems that he forgets
> To castigate his enemy,
> It is only that his punishment is to be greater than in life.

See Marrano Poets of the Seventh Century: An Anthology of the Poetry of João Pinto Delgado, Antonio Enriques Gomez, and Miguel de Barrios, edited and translated by Timothy Delman, Rutherford, Madison, Teaneck, 1982. Such feelings are reflected throughout their poetry, (e.g., pp. 193, 261 etc.). But here too we have strayed afar from our main theme.

Returning to the issue of forcible coercion and its inherent irrationality, this was, indeed, known to the Church, and already explicitly stated by Tertullian (c.165–240) in his *Ad Scapulam* 2:

> It is one of the rights of man and privileges of nature that everyone should worship according to his own convictions. One man's religion neither harms nor helps another's. It is no part of religion to compel religion, which should rest upon free choice and not upon force – since even sacrificial victims are required to be of a willing mind.

(This passage must, however, be seen in its context. For the letter was written to Scapula, c. 212 C.E., Proconsul of Africa, who had begun to persecute Christians. Tertullian reminds him of the fate of other persecuters, and this particular context, speaks of those willing to die for their beliefs. But, of course, the same argument should apply to all religions.)

Many a pope, from Gregory I (the Great, 590–604, in a letter to its painarch of Constantinople that found its way into Gratian's *Decretum*) forbade forced baptism. However, Innocent II in 1201, recognized such conversions, while Innocent IV in 1216, forbade it. There is a considerable literature on the subject. See, for example: B. Blumenkranz, *Juifs et Chrétiens dans le Monde Occidental*, 1960, index, s.v. baptems; S. Grazel, *The Church and the Jews in the XIII century* (1961, second ed.) s.v. Baptism, Involuntary and Conversion of Jews; *Forced Baptisms*, Marina Caffiero, (English transl. Lydia Conchrane, University of California, 2012 (on 16th–19th century); Eugene J. Fisher, "Historical Developments of the Theology of Christian Mission," apud *Christian Mission – Jewish Mission*, edd. Martin A. Cohen and Helga Croner, New York, 1982, pp. 25–26. And for a list forced conversions, see James Parkes, *The Conflict of the Church and the Synagogue: A Study in the Origins of Antisemitism*, New York, 1969, p. 421 index s.v. "Baptism, forced," and, of course, Henry Charles Lea's three volumes "*A History of the Inquisition in the Middle Ages*," New York, 1953.

Indeed the papal bull of *Sicut Judaeis*, setting the official position of the papacy regarding the treatment of Jews, first issued by Callixtus II around 1120, forbade forcible conversion. It was reaffirmed many times by subsequent Popes, and, for example in the bull of Pope Alexander III: (1159–1181) we read:

> For We make the law that no Christian compel them, unwilling or refusing, by violence to come to baptism. . . . Indeed, he is not to be considered to possess the true faith of Christianity who is not recognized to have come to Christian baptism, not spontaneously, but unwillingly.

See Edward Synan, *The Popes and the Jews in the Middle Ages*, 2008, pp. 231–232. See further, Herbert Thurston, "History of Toleration," *The Catholic Encyclopedia*, vol. 14; Shlomo Simonsohn, *The Apostolic See and the Jews: Documents 192, 1404*, Pontifical Institute of Mediaeval Studies, 1988, pass. "Sicut Judaeis" was discussed in detail by Solomon Grayzel, in *Studies and Essays in Honour of Abraham Neuman*, edd. M. Ben-Horin, B.D. Weinrib, and Solomon Zeitlin, 1962, pp. 243–80, and reprinted in *Essential Papers on Judaism and Christianity in Conflict, from Antiquity to the Reformation*, ed. Jeremy Cohen, New York and London, 1991, pp. 231–259, under the title "The Papal Bull *Sicut Judaeis.*"

He further examined this subject in his "Popes, Jews, and the Inquisition from 'Sicut' to Turbalo," apud *Essays on the Occasion of the Seventieth Anniversary of Dropsie University*, edd. I Katsch and Leon Nemoy, Philadelphia, 1979, pp. 151–188, reprinted in vol. 2 of his *The Church and the Jews in the XIII Century*, ed. Kenneth Stow, New York, 1989, pp. 3–45. Grayzel (in his *Church and the Jews*) worked a mild revolution. For while he spoke forthrightly, as on one occasion when he declared that certain papal attitudes moved "in the direction of eliminating the Jew from society," he was equally prepared, unlike his predecessors to point to consistent efforts made by the popes on behalf of the Jews . . ." (from Stow's "In Memoriam," vol. 2, pp. X–XI.) On papal protection of Jews, see, for example, John XXII's letter of July 9, 1320, ibid. p. 314, and similarly from May 9, 1326, ibid. p. 331, etc. However, these are by no means representations of his policy. See ibid. pp. 301–340. We should further note that the revised edition of *The Church and the Jews* vol. 1, came out in 1966 (Herman Press, New York), just one year after *Nostra Aetate*, and in his "Preface to the Second Edition" Grayzel wrote, "Recent events have changed this [i.e. the traditional] view radically . . ."

This was again stressed in Article 2 of the Constitution "*De Ecclesia.*" See Pietro Pavan, "Declaration on Religious Freedom," apud *Commentary on the Documents of Vatican II*, ed. Herbert Vorgrimler, vol. 4, Freiburg Montreal 1969, pp. 64–65: the Declaration runs as follows:

> 1. Every man has a right to religious freedom because he is a person.
> 2. The object or content of this right is freedom from coercion on the part of individuals or of social groups or any human power.
> 3. This freedom from coercion has a double meaning: "in matters religious no one is to be forced to act in a manner contrary to his own beliefs;" within due limits no one is "to be restrained from acting in accordance with his own beliefs, whether privately or publicly, whether alone or in association with others."
> 4. This right has its foundation in the dignity of the human person, such as it is known in the light of revelation and by reason.
> 5. It is a right of the person which is to be recognized as a civil right in the constitutional law of the political society.
>
> "Haec Vaticana Synodus declarat personam humanam ius habere ad libertatem religiosam" is a solemn statement which characterizes the document and gives it its historical importance.

And we should hearken to the words of the Greek philosopher Themistius (317–387?), who in his consular oration to the Emperor Jovian (364), writes:

> Be certain, O Emperor, that the author and ruler of the universe is pleased with such variety: he loves to have the Syrians use certain rites and the Egyptians others. And the Syrians themselves are not bound by the same laws, and the form of their institutions is divided into two types. And since no one feels in his heart precisely what his neighbor feels, and this one approves one thing, and that one another, why do we wish to attempt with violence that which can in no way be achieved?

(See Luigi Luzzatti, *God in Freedom* (transl. Alfonso Arbit-Costa, New York, 1930,

p. 28; apud Joseph L. Baron, *Stars and Sand: Jewish Notes by Non-Jewish Notables*, Philadelphia, 1948, pp. 337–338.)

It should, however, be noted that already Pope Gregory (590–604) used the words *Sicut Judaeis* ("and thus to the Jews") in a letter addressed to the Bishop of Naples, emphasizing that "Jews were entitled to the lawful liberty," (Herbert Thurston, "History of Toleration," *The Catholic Encyclopedia*, vol. 14, New York, 1913; William Nicholls, *Christian Antisemitism: A History of Hate*, Northvale, New Jersey and London, 1963, pp. 221–224; Synan ibid. p. 46). This became the title of a sacred bull, first issued in 1120 by Pope Callixtus II (1065–1124), and was intended to protect the Jews. It was prompted by the First Crusade, in which over 5,000 Jews were slaughtered in Europe. It was subsequently reconfirmed continually by many Popes, and forbade Christians, on the pain of excommunication, from forcing Jews to convert, etc. (See Shlomo Simonsohn, *The Apostolic See and the Jews: History*, Toronto, Ontario, 1991, pp. 42–45, 52–58, 64–70; idem, *Documents 492–1404*, Pontifical Institute of Mediaeval Studies 1998, Documents 44,46,49,63,64; Edward Synan, *The Popes and the Jews in the Middle Ages*, 2008; James Parkes, *The Jew in the Medieval Community: A Study of His Political and Economic Situation*, 2nd edition, New York, 1976, pp. 136–149; S.W. Baron, *A Social and Religious History of the Jew*, 2nd edition, vol. 4, New York, 1957, pp. 7–11, 235–236 note 3, 240 note 15; Solomon Grayzel, *The Church and The Jews in the XIIIth Century*, New York, 1966, pp. 92 et seq., and pp. 76 et seq.) *The Constitutio pro Judaeis (=Sicut Judaeis)* was renewed probably around 1179, by Alexander III in connection with the Third Lutheran Council of that year, and was then regularly renewed by Clement III (1189–1191), Celestine III (1191–1198) and Innocent III in 1199. (Baron ibid. p. 8). On *Sicut Judaeis* Simonsohn writes (*History* p. 44):

> The initial versions of the Bull made the following points: Christians must not employ force to bring Jews to the baptismal font. Christians shall not wound or kill Jews, or rob them of their money, or change the good customs which they have enjoyed in the past, unless given permission to do so by the authorities. Jews must not be disturbed in the celebration of their festivals, nor should they be expected to render services which they have not rendered in the past. Christians must not desecrate Jewish cemeteries, nor exhume bodies of Jews to extort money. Offenders were threatened with loss of honour and office or excommunication. As we have seen, Innocent III added an introduction to his *Constitutio pro Judeis*. Although this introduction was dropped in succeeding editions of the Bull, the addition at the end, making the Bull's validity contingent on the Jews refraining from plotting against Christianity, was retained. The publication of the Bull in 1199 by Innocent III apparently did not suffice; the Pope felt called upon to publish another protective Bull

ordering the prelates of France to prohibit all Christians, especially crusaders, from harming Jews or their families.

He also notes that (ibid. note 10):

> It has been hinted that the close ties which Alexander II and Calixtus II had with the convert family of Roman bankers, the Pierleoni (Anacletus II was an offspring of that family) may be linked to their protection of the Jews. It has also been suggested that the first two or so editions of the Bull were granted Roman Jewry, and that only later was the Bull's application extended to the rest of European Jewry. While Roman Jewry were very likely instrumental in obtaining the Bull, the later editions contain nothing to show an extension. By the same token, nothing is known to have taken place in Rome itself at the beginning of the twelfth century to explain why the local Jewish community suddenly needed comprehensive protection. Recipients of the Bull outside Italy are first mentioned in relation to the edition of Alexander III. Since the texts of the Bulls of Calixtus II and Eugenius III have not survived, there is no conclusive proof either way. . . .

The freedom of each person to his own belief was again stated by Pope Pius XI, in his *Mit Brenneder Sorge* (*With Deep Anxiety*) 31, in March 14, 1937. He said:

> The believer has an absolute right to profess his own faith according to its own dictates. Laws which impede this profession and practice of faith are against natural law.

And although he was probably primarily concerned with oppression of Christians, the principle surely applies to all people of diverse faiths. Cf. further below note 64.

2. See Joshua Trachtenberg, *The Devil and the Jews: The Mediaeval Conception of the Jew and its Relation to Modern Antisemitism*, New York, 1943, pp. 171–187.

3. See M. Rubin, *Gentile tales: The Narrative Assault in the Medieval Jew*, New Haven 1999.

4. See D.D. Raphael, "The Intolerable," apud S. Mendus ed., *Justifying Tolerance: Conceptual and Historical Perspectives*, New York, 1988; Sagi, (referred to below) p. 176.

5. Here I should like to call attention to the description of the notion "toleration," found in James Hastings, *Encyclopaedia of Religion and Ethics*, vol XII, New York, 1928, p. 360b (entry by W.F. Ademey), and some of its limitations:

The word "toleration" in its legal, ecclesiastical, and doctrinal application has a peculiarly limited signification. It connotes a refraining from prohibition and persecution. Nevertheless it suggests a latent disapproval, and it usually refers to a condition in which the freedom which it permits is both limited and conditional. Toleration is not equivalent to religious liberty, and it falls far short of religious equality. It assumes the existence of an authority which might have been coercive, but which for reasons of its own is not pushed to extremes. It implies a voluntary inaction, a politic leniency. The motives that induce a policy of toleration are various, such as mere weakness and inability to enforce prohibitory measures, lazy indifference, the desire to secure conciliation by concessions, the wisdom to perceive that "force is no remedy," the intellectual breadth and humility that shrink from a claim to infallibility, the charity that endures the objectionable, respect for the right of private judgment.

However lamentable the fact may be, it should not surprise us that greater intolerance has been found in Christian nations than among any other peoples. Polytheism allows of an indefinitely enlarging pantheon. Its theology admits the existence of separate national gods among the various nations. But monotheism not only denies the existence of any such divinities; it regards the homage offered to them as a derogation from the worship due to the true God. Christianity, therefore, as well as the Judaism on which it is based, is necessarily intellectually intolerant. The same idea applies to Muhammadanism, which is always an intolerant religion as regards doctrine, even when it is not actively persecuting alien faiths. Then both Christianity and Muhammandanism claim to be universal religions; they are essentially aggressive; and the positive missionary work which this fact implies easily passes over into overt acts for the repression of idolatry and polytheism contrary as they are to the genuine Christian temper. And to this the fact that moral earnestness, at its best mounting to enthusiasm, in extreme cases degenerating into fanaticism, urges the devotees of a missionary religion towards a militancy which the hereditary adherents of non-aggressive religions have less inducements to adopt. When paganism is not tolerant, this is generally due to resentment against those who have attacked it, unless political motives are the real grounds of action. The persecution of Elijah and the adherents of Jahweh by Jezebel was occasioned by the prophet's vehement opposition to the introduction of the rites of the Phoenician Baal into Israel. The persecution of the Jews by Antiochus Epiphanes was due to their refusal to admit Hellenizing practices into their national life.

And cf. the following note.

CHAPTER 5

The Birth of Liberalism and the Notion of "Toleration"

However, with the birth of liberalism in the modern period, toleration was seen as a compromise position, not necessarily ideal, but at least humane.[1]

For, as Owen Chadwick wrote in his *The Secularization of the European Mind in the Nineteenth Century* (The Gifford Lecture in the University of Edinburgh from 1973–1974, Cambridge, 1975), p. 21:

> From the moment that European opinion decided for toleration, it decided for the eventual free market in opinion. Once concede equality to a distinctive group, you could not confine it to that group.... A free market in some opinions became a free market in all opinions.

Chadwick continues (pp. 23–24):

> Christian conscience was the force which began to make Europe secular; that is, to allow many religions or no religion in a state, and repudiate any kind of pressure upon the man who rejected the accepted and inherited axioms of society. My conscience is my own. It is private. Though it is formed and guided by inherited wisdom and by public attitudes and even by circumstances which surround me, no man may intrude upon it. It is the most important part of a man, that which forms the roots of his character and personality. How I may be true to it, whether I may be true to it, whether allegiance to it is compatible with comfort or with happiness, these decisions are for me and no one else. It shows me that I cannot trample upon other people's consciences, provided they are true to them, provided they do not seek to trample upon mine, and provided they will work with me to ensure that our

differing consciences do not undermine by their differences the social order and at last the stat. This last proviso reaches far. But it reaches not so far as the earlier doctrine that all men must conform in faith to that which society approves.

And he continues (p. 25):

> The ultimate freedom was liberty to worship God as the conscience called. Modern ideas of freedom, as they stemmed from John Locke in the later seventeenth century, were founded in religious toleration.[2]
>
> Locke's intention, after the age of intolerance and party conflict which he experienced as a young man, was to justify religious toleration. He based his argument, not upon policy – such as, we cannot hold England together as a state unless we allow Protestant dissenters to worship God as they please – but upon the principle of a natural right. Man has a natural right to freedom of conscience, and no government has a right to tamper. But this right carries other rights, freedom of opinion, freedom to meet, freedom to express. Of course Locke depended on a long tradition of political thought in Europe. But his statement of it founded liberal convictions in the form in which they conquered the Europe of the nineteenth century. The expression of them was widened, adjusted, expanded to new circumstances. But this way of thinking about freedom and the power of government ran henceforth in a continuous tradition.

And on p. 29 he writes:

> The idea of liberty had moved. Only a generation earlier it was seen as an instrument to justice; or to good government; or to the enterprise and prosperity of society; or to satisfaction of the consciences of dissenters. Now it was a quality of life; not an instrument, but a good in itself, a quality of man and of society which enabled moral personality, moral development, self-realization. A mature man is a free man. He has the right to be persuaded and convinced. Society is under obligation to listen to his opinion if he wishes to express it. Society is not just to tolerate individuality, to allow it because it can do no other. It should foster it. Our fellow-men press upon us and push us to dress in line. To the contrary, they should encourage our differences, not for the sake

of difference but so that any man may be himself, sentient, thinking, choosing, responsible. So is man a civilized being, society a civilized society. We are not to let custom, or consensus, pick our way of life for us. Morally it is better for each of us to employ all his faculties to discern the right way for himself as an individual. [John Stuart]. Mill rose up to his lovely and lyrical hymn of praise for the individual human being, so man's copy; cultivating his faculties of sensibility and discrimination; seeking truth; contemptuous of convention; diversifying human life; becoming at last a noble object of contemplation, risen above the mediocrity which surrounds him.

A distinction emerged between the person and his belief. The belief may be unacceptable, but the person still had the right to be wrong.[3] And in more religious terms, he might be misguided, but he was still God's creature, created in His Image. This, of course, was a form of condescension towards his false beliefs, which nonetheless gave him the freedom to retain his misguided faith.

Endnotes to Chapter 5

1. On "toleration" and its limitations, see the important collection of essays edited by Cary J. Nederman, John Christian Laursen, Lonham, Boulder, New York and London, 1996, entitled *Difference and Dissent: Theories of Toleration in Mediaeval and Early Modern Europe*.

2. In his *Letter Concerning Toleration* of 1689 he stated that:

> The toleration of those who differ from other in matters of religion is so agreeable to the Gospel of Jesus Christ, and to the genuine reason of mankind, that it seems monstrous for men to be so blind as not to perceive the necessity and advantage of it in so clear a light.

He even cited the Jews as an example of a religious minority that ought to be tolerated by the State, and this became a touchstone in the discussion of Enlightenment philosophers on tolerance. See Shmuel Ettinger, "The Beginnings of the Change in the Attitude of European Society to Jews," apud S. Ettinger, *Antisemitism in the Modern Era*, Tel Aviv, 1978, pp. 57–88; David Sorkin, "Jews, Enlightenment, and Religious Toleration: Some Reflections," *Year Book of the Leo Baeck Institute 37*, 1992, pp. 3–16; Shmuel Feiner, *The Jewish Enlightenment,* transl. Chaya Naor, Philadelphia, 2002, pp. 112–114, 392. Cf. Jefferson's ruling on religious tolerance in 1785; S. Jacoby, *Freethinkers, A History of American Secularism*, New York, 2004, pp. 24–25.

3. This indeed was explicitly stated in Pope Paul VI's *Dignitatis Humanae*, promulgated on December 7, 1965. There in the second paragraph we read that:

> . . . the human person has a right to religious freedom. This freedom means that all men are to be immune from coercion on the part of individuals or of social groups and of any human power, in such wise that . . . is to be forced to act in a manner contrary to his own beliefs, whether privately or publically, whether alone or in association with others, *within due limits.*

As Rev Dr. Christian M. Rutishauser expressed so clearly in his presentation in Rome, Oct. 27, 2015, in an anniversary conference on *Nostra Aetate* regarding Catholicism:

> Since Vatican II, the Catholic Church became a prominent promoter of human rights in diverse social, cultural, and political contexts all over the world. Religious freedom is just one of the different rights following out of the concept of the dignity of the human person.

Note that Protestanism also "recognizes the right and duty of every citizen to worship God, or refrain from such worship, as his conscience dictates," (Henry P. Van Dusen, apud Leo Rosten, *A Guide to the Religions of America*, New York, 1955, p. 115).

This, of course, is part of the heritage of the later renaissance age of enlightenment such as the writings of John Locke (1632–1704), who in his "*Letter Concerning Toleration*" (1689), (second ed. London, 1690, pp. 20 ff), wrote:

> If a Jew does not believe the New Testament to be the Word of God, he does not thereby alter anything in men's civil rights. If a heathen doubt of both testaments, he is not therefore to be punished as a pernicious citizen.
>
> The power of the magistrate, and the estate of the people may be equally secure, whether any man believe these things or no. I readily grant that these opinions are false and absurd, but the business of Laws is not to provide for the truth of opinions, but for the safety and security of the commonwealth, and of every particular man's goods and person. And so it ought to be. . . .

But then Rutishauser raises the very significant question, moving from *ad extra* to *ad intra*, "in what sense and in what scale are the different human rights applied within the faith community itself? And in the more specific sense: what does religious freedom mean for the individual facing the Church's authority? Does it make sense to speak of religious freedom on this level?" Judaism faces the same questions. Does the individual have the right to dissent from rabbinic rulings? And, for example, what right does a Jew have, in orthodox thinking, to convert to another religion? We leave these as open questions of a different nature, albeit partially related to our main theme.

CHAPTER 6

The Influence of Eastern Thought and Culture[1]

A more positive approach was emerging in the later 19th and early 20th century under the influence of Eastern thinking,[2] such as the religious philosophy of the Catholic Raimondo Panikkar (1918–2010). He developed his famous parable of two people looking at the same view through different windows. Each sees something different, because of the angles of the view, the different light, even different eyesight, etc.[3] Each describes what he sees absolutely truthfully, but different descriptions emerge, both of which are accurate – although subjective.[4] This parable echoes the notion of *Anekantavada* and certain aspects of Buddhist thought mentioned above (chapter 2). And, we may add, that even a single person sees things alter their shape and colour as he draws nearer or further from them[5] or as the light changes, so that the dialogue may even be, as it were, internal. Inter-religious dialogue, according to Pannikar consists of the one viewer's trying to understand, believe and accept his fellow-viewer's description though it differs from his own. Such an approach, of course, distinguishes between subjective and objective truth. But humanity can, perhaps, at least in the case of religion, never liberate itself from the subjective element. This realization leads naturally to a liberal attitude, and it was just this attitude that was accepted by Buddha (as we saw above in chapter 2).

Radhakrishnan, *Eastern Religions and Western Thought*, 2nd edition, Oxford London, 1940, explains that, "the light of absolute truth is said to be refracted as it passes through the distorting medium of human nature" (ibid. p. 308). He continues (ibid. p. 311) that, "the most we can hope for is a relative truth, a provisional hypothesis, [but] we cannot claim finality or absoluteness for any view. [Hence,] faith for the Hindu does not mean dogmatism ... [and even] while full of unquestioning belief, the Hidden is at the same time devoid of harsh judgement." Similarly Sri Ramakrishna stated: yata mata, tata patha, meaning: there are as many ways as there are points of view.

Even "prophets," who may be the sources of sacred texts, are conduits whose messages, willy-nilly, are fashioned by their personality – i.e. the "shape" of the conduit.

This is surely indicated in a very beautifully suggestive passage in *Mishnat R. Eliezer*, ed. H.G. Enelow, New York, 1933, p. 266. This (anonymous) passage states that in four different aspects the second tables of the Law were superior to the first ones. The third aspect listed is that:

> The first tables [of the Law] did not have the image of Moses glittering through them, whereas in the last (i.e. second) ones the image of Moses glittered in them.

The Midrash wishes to indicate that somehow or other the human element – image of Moses – was incorporated into the divinely inscribed ten commandments, making them more suitable, more humane, for humanity.[6]

And the language in which they express themselves creates its own limitations which again give a certain form to the statements. Furthermore, the sacred texts of the various religions are in different languages, and not necessarily translatable to the fullest sense, so that translation is, in effect, interpretation, and is often very misleading to one who has no real access to the original text.[7]

And to all of the above we should perhaps add yet another important component. The nineteenth century, as is well known, saw a newly emerging interest in the East, in Eastern culture, Eastern philosophy[8] and Eastern art.[9]

A variety of different elements somehow combined to create this new "fascination for the Orient."

To show the degree to which "Eastern wisdom" had penetrated into Western culture, we should perhaps start with (F.W.J.) Schelling (1775–1854) and (A.) Schopenhauer (1788–1860), both of whom were younger contemporaries of (G.W.F.) Hegel (1770–1831)[10] who himself was influenced by (F.) Schlegel (1772–1829) both of whose interest in India was that of the Romantics. Hegel had in his early years written and lectured on India and China, making full use of the then available translations, such as those of (H.Th.) Colebrooke (1765–1837), whose *On the Philosophy of Hinduism* appeared in 1828–1830 (in *Transactions of the Asiatic London*

Society vol. 1), and cf. his *Miscellaneous Essays* vol. 1, London, 1837, and studies such as those of W. von Humboldt on the *Bhagavad Gītā*. Hegel (1770–1831)[11] and Schelling (1775–1854) were fellow students, and Schelling too was influenced by Schlegel. Schelling saw in the *Vedānta,* "nothing but the most exalted idealism and spirituality" (*Sämmtliche Werke* 11/2, Stuttgart and Augsburg 1857, p. 482).[12] He discussed critically the *Upanisads* in more than a hundred pages of his *Philosophy of Mythology*, Berlin 1845–1846, several of which were translated for him by Max Müller, the great Indologist. Schopenhauer's (1788–1860) interest in India[13] was awakened by the Orientalist F. Majer, himself influenced by Herder. He too depended for his writings on translations, such as those of Colebrooke and others, especially those of Rommohan Roy (mentioned below). He repeatedly referred to the Buddhist concept of *nirvana*,[14] which agreed with his own goal of liberation from the blind force of will. His basic proposition was that, "in general, the sages of all times have always said the same," and that, "Buddha, Eckhardt and I all teach essentially the same." I shall not continue to enlarge upon this theme which has been most meticulously documented and analyzed by Wilhelm Halbfass, in his *India and Europe: An Essay* in *Understanding*, New York, 1968, chapters 5–8, pp. 69–144, 475–499. There he unfolds before us a highly detailed description of the developmental influence of Indian and Eastern thought as European philosophy from Hegel till Max Weber (1864–1920).

To the above we should add the perhaps more narrowly directed studies contained in a volume by Dale Riepe, *The Philosophy of India and its Impact on American Thought*, Springfield, Illinois, 1970, especially chapters 10–11 (pp. 221–279) entitled, "Developments in the Diffusion of Indian Thought since the Korean War," i.e. in the 1950s.[15] It should, however, be stressed that several of the personalities he mentions had an influence far beyond America. This was certainly the case with Aldous Huxley – see, for example, B.L. Chukov, *Aldous Huxley and Eastern Wisdom*, New Jersey, 1981 – and Christopher Isherwood, etc. To their very full expositions, which, however, are primarily directed towards philosophy and philosophers, we shall give a somewhat random list of personalities of this period with perhaps a broader perspective to those who demonstrate this influence. Laurence Binyon [1869–1943] studied Chinese and Japanese painting.[16]

Chinese Art comes to the West.

And already in 1844 Eugène Burnouf (born 1801) had published his mammoth *L'Introduction à L'histoire du Hindduisme Indian*, which offered Europe the first detailed scientific survey of Indian Buddhist history, relying entirely on unknown Sanskrit and Tibetan texts.[17] And in 1833, at the conclusion of his inaugural lecture at the Collège du France, he declared:

> We should not close our eyes to the most brilliant light that may ever have come from the Orient, and we shall attempt to comprehend the grand spectacle offered to our gaze.... It is more than India, gentlemen, it is a page from the origins of the world, of the primitive history of the human spirit, that we shall try to decipher together.[18]

The impact of his work was both throughout European and American society, influencing so diverse an audience as the historian Michelet, the composer Wagner, the American transcendentalist Thoreau,[19] etc.[20]

And in 1871 John Freeman Clarke, published his *Ten Great Religions*, with part 2 in 1883, a book that achieved immediate acclaim, the chapters on Eastern religions being a revelation. The major novelty in his work was its sympathetic attitude towards Oriental religions, which other authors had always characterized as "heathen." He seemed especially appreciative of Buddhism.[21]

In the twentieth century Anagarika Dharmapalo came to London and opened a branch of the Moha-Bodhi Society, a meeting place for lay Buddhists, in 1933 the first European Buddhist Congress was convened in Berlin, held at the Maha-Bodhi Society from September 22–23, followed by the famous World Congress of Faiths, chaired by its founder, Sir Francis Younghusband.

In May 1925, Alexandre David-Neal came to France, being the first Western woman to have reached Lhasa, and was invited to lecture throughout Europe, publishing in rapid succession a series of volumes giving a detailed sympathetic account of culture and religions of Tibetan Buddhism.

The "spirit of the East" was pervading throughout Europe, and even filtered through to Italy. Thus, the outstanding orientalist Gueseppe Tucci, who had lived in India from 1925–1930, when he taught at Tagore's university in ShantiniKetan, and conducted his first expedition to Tibet, became Professor of Indian and Far Eastern Studies in *Rome* (in 1932), and in the following year founded his own Institute of Far Eastern Studies (ISMEO), which collapsed when the war broke out in 1939. He himself had a shrine in his house, and regarded himself as a practicing Buddhist of the Kagya school. (See for much of the above the very rich material to be found in Stephan Batchelor, *The Awakening of the West: The Encounter of Buddhism and Western Culture*, Berkeley California, 1994.)[22]

Continuing this (perhaps somewhat haphazard) mosaic of prominent personalities (which could be greatly expanded), are Florence Farr (1860–1917), who became principle of the Ramanathan Girls College in Ceylon, after being deeply involved in the Theosophical Society in London, and Sturge Moore (1870–1944) who studied Buddhism; Ezra Pound (1885–1972) and Arthur Wayley (1889–1966, incidentally born as Arthur David Schloss, an Ashkenazi Jew, who E.C. Brooks characterized as "the ambassador from East to West for the first half of the twentieth century"), translated Chinese and Japanese; and in America, T.S. Eliot

(1888–1965) applied himself to Sanskrit, (while at Harvard [1911–1914]). Mainly through Pound's translations of the *Noh* plays of Japan,[23] William Butler Yeats (1865–1939) discovered in 1914 the dramatic form in which he was to couch almost all his remaining plays ... (Richard Ellman, *The Identity of Yeats*, New York, 1964, pp. 182–183). In fact Ellman has shown the degree to which that great Irish poet Yeats was so deeply affected by Eastern culture. For so he writes on pp. 182–185:

> His study of the connections and disconnections of the two cultures began in boyhood. First he became convinced from Indian literature, and from the living proof of Mohini Chatterjee, that a man could live by doctrines wholly unacceptable to most Westerners. Then, under the influence of the Theosophical Society, which had headquarters at Adyar but most of its membership in Europe and America, and of Madame Blavatsky herself, Yeats dreamed of sowing the West with Eastern thought. ...
>
> From about 1912 through 1915, Yeats felt his blood stirred, as he said, by Rabindranath Tagore. Two qualities in Tagore's work appealed to him: his poems were "the work of a supreme culture," yet seemed "as much the growth of the common soil as the grass and the rushes;" and he brought together purity and passion in a way which seemed to Yeats un-European. The *Gitanjali* or "song offerings" for which Yeats wrote an introduction in 1915 were love poems but love poems of a special sort addressed to God. In them he discovered what European saints, with the exception of St. Francis, lacked, and what Blake so definitely possessed in far greater measure, a union of "the cry of the flesh and the cry of the soul." In Tagore, "This is no longer the sanctity of the cell and of the scourge, but a lifting up, as it were, into a greater intensity of the mood of the painter, painting the dust and the sunlight." Tagore's attitude was summed up in the statement, "And because I love this file, I know I shall love death as well." Eventually Tagore proved a disappointment to his admirers in England as he grew prolix and revealed a want of English style, but Yeats pondered the lessons of his work and kept an eye cocked for other Eastern sages.
>
> In 1931 he first met Shri Purohit, a swami who was visiting England. At the time Purohit was working with Sturge Moore on some translations, but after a quarrel Yeats took Moore's place, and spent much time in the swami's company. Purohit was a strange mixture of sensuality

138

and asceticism in his personal life, and philosophically seemed to occupy, like Tagore, some intermediate place between a bias towards the soul and a bias towards the body. He and Yeats went to Majorca for five months in 1935 and translated the ten principal *Upanishads*, Yeats contributing the nuances of English prose to balance the swami's knowledge of Sanskrit. The poet also wrote an introduction to an autobiography written by Purohit's teacher, Bhagwan Shri Hamsa, and another to Purohit's translation of *Patanjali's Aphorisms of Yoga*. His poetry began to show signs of their association. . . .

In his introduction to the *Upanishads* he remarked that we have to discover in the East:

"Something ancestral in ourselves, something we must bring into the light before we can appease a religious instinct that for the first time in our civilization demands the satisfaction of the whole man." It was as if Asia was part of the human soul and could therefore not be neglected. The conviction that the most ancient wisdom is probably the truest, which leads Eliot to quote the *Vedas* in *The Waste Land*, makes Yeats return again and again to Asia in his last years.

See further R.C. Shah, Yeats and Eliot: *Perspectives on India* (1983), chapter 2, entitled "Yeats' Encounter with a Wisdom of Contraries," where we read that a Western authority on Indian eschatology stated that:

The orderly Western mind is perturbed and confused by too many equally valid possibilities side by side. The Indian mind, on the other hand, rejoiced in dynamic changes and divergent possibilities as a congenial expression of divine productivity ... [The Indian thinks that] nothing perfects itself without turning into its opposite, and as such starts a new way of development – endless and forever insatiable. . . . (A statement of Betty Heimann.)

(See also B. Wilson, "'From Mirror after Mirror': Yeats and Eastern Thought," *Comparative Literature* 34/1, 1982; H.E. McCarthy, "T.S. Eliot and Buddhism," *Philosophy East and West*, 2/1, 1952.)

So the West thinks linearly and the East cyclically. Summarizing, and relating this to Yeat's thinking, Shah writes:

> The West begins with units and unities; India begins by acknowledging the diversity and assigning *equal value to every item* in that diversity. [My emphasis, D.S.]

Or as was formulated by Margaret Chaterjee, in her essay, "Religious Pluralism in the Indian Context," apud *Culture and Modernity: East-West Philosophic Perspectives*, ed. Eliot Deutsch, Honolulu, 1991, p. 390:

> Differences are not correlated with "rival truths claims" and are even regarded as "not mattering," that is, the differences do not surface in a sense that "I am right and you are wrong."

And J.L. Mehta wrote of the Indian cultural tradition (in *The Worlds Religious Traditions*, Edinburgh, 1984) that:

> It has at no time *defined itself* in relation to the other, nor acknowledged the other in its unassimilable otherness, nor in consequence occupied itself with the problem of relationship as it arises in any concrete encounter with the other.

Chatterjee adds (ibid. p. 389):

> Religious plurality, on such a view, does not present itself as a problem to the Hindu, but something which in India has always been primarily a *fact*, a matter which poses adjustment at the behavioral level rather than provokes intellectual challenge of ideas in the realm of theorizing.

So in the early 20th century the "East" was vanquishing the westernmost country of Europe, as well as elements in America.

Similarly, Mary Baker Eddy (1821–1910), the expounder of "Christian Science," in her various writings admitted to the harmony between Vedantin philosophy and Christian Science. She even quoted certain passages from the English edition of the *Bhagavad-Gita*, which for some reason were omitted in the 34th edition of the book *Science and Health with Key to Scripture* (first published 1910).[24]

And in 1939, the great Indian philosopher Radhakrishnan wrote, underscoring the penetration of Eastern thought into the West (and, in his opinion, vice-versa with regard to science), as follows:

For the first time in the history of mankind, the consciousness of the unity of the world has dawned on us. *Whether we like it or not, East and West have come together and can no more part. The spatial nearness is preparing the way for a spiritual approximation and interchange of treasures of mind and imagination.* If we are nurtured exclusively on the past of Europe or of Asia we cannot consider ourselves to be cultivated. The thought and experience of one-half of humanity cannot be neglected without peril. If we are to correct the narrowness resulting from a one-sided and exclusive preoccupation with either Eastern or Western thought, if we are to fortify our inner life with the dignity of a more perfect and universal experience, and understanding of each other's cultures is essential. It is a foolish pride that impels some of us to combat all external influences. Every spiritual or scientific advance which any branch of the human family achieves is achieved not for itself alone, but for all mankind. Besides, there is no power possessed by any race of men that is not possessed in some measure by all. The difference is one of degree. The mysticism of ancient India or the rationalism of modern Europe is only a fuller development of something which belongs to man as man. To the observer of the essential drifts of the dawning world, it is clear that we are in an age when cultures are in fusion. [My emphasis, D.S.] (*Eastern Religion and Western Thought*, Oxford London, 1939, pp. 115–116.)[25]

The reasons for the emergence of Orientalism[26] were numerous and complex. The "Eastern Question"[27] – Europe's role in the East – became increasingly significant in European foreign policy causing stormy debates. Bonapart's expedition to Egypt, the control of the route to the Indies, all contributed to the gradual weakening of the once mighty Ottoman Empire. Opportunities for travel improved along with trade; sea-transport became cheap and reliable. Published tourist guides soon multiplied[28] and a new "grand tour of the entire eastern seaboard of the Mediterranean" became popular, [see *The Orient in Western Art*, by Gérald-George Lemaire, with a preface by Geneviève Lacambre, Paris, 2000],[29] and the horizon was pushed further into the Far East. Japan was opened up to the West in 1853, following the American fleet's Matthew Perry's "black ships" sailing in Tokyo Bay.[30] Hokusei (died 1849), the great Japanese print maker, became known to the West, and influenced Monet and Degas' painting prints.[31] The East India Company thrived till it was dissolved in 1874, having controlled large sections of India, China and other "colonial" settlements in the East. Edward Lane's (1801–1876) translation of the *Arabian Nights* first published between 1838–1840,[32] was even reflected, albeit very partially, in the Great Exhibition of 1851 in London's Crystal Palace.[33]

Of course Richard Burton's translation of 1885 superseded Lane's and was hugely popular, running into numerous editions.

But perhaps more significant for our purpose is the new interest in Eastern literary texts,[34] primarily Indian (Sanskrit)[35] and Buddhist texts (in Pali). Thus, in 1870 there began in France the publication of the *Bibliothèque Orientale*, and four years later the great orientalist scholar Friedreich Max- Müller (1823–1900) began editing the magnificent fifty-volume series entitled *Sacred Books of the East* (1879–1910), comprising the basic texts of Hinduism, Buddhism, Taoism, Confusionism, Zoroastrianism, Jainism and Islam.[36] (Note that just six years earlier was established the international Congress of Orientalists which met annually from 1873 onwards.) These "ancient sources" had a profound influence on a number of prominent thinkers, and served as the basis of the newly developing trends of "Universalism," transcedentalism, "Natural Religion," resulting, inter alia, in the establishment of the *Theosophical Society*, founded in 1875, by Madame Helen Blavatsky (1831–1891), and others, followed by Annie Bezant (1847–1933), – note, for example, her *Yoga: The Hatha Yoga and the Raja Yoga of India*, Madras, 1954–, and perhaps culminating in the encapsulated formulation of Aldous Huxley's (1894–1963) *The Perrenial Philosophy*,[37] published in 1945, and which was enormously popular at that time.[38] Huxley's writings, especially his *Ends and Means* of 1937, also affected the influential Catholic trappist monk, prolific writer, poet and mystic Thomas Merton (1915–1968), who began a dialogue with P.T. Suzuki in 1959, dialogued later with the Dalai Lama and the Buddhist monk Buddhadasa, and throughout his very productive life became increasingly involved in non-Western traditions, as is evident in his poetry and writings. See, e.g., his *Mystics and Zen Masters*, 1961, The *Way of Chuang-Tsu*, 1965, *Zen and the Book of Paradise*, 1965 etc. (See Bonnei B. Thurston, *Thomas Merton and Eastern Religions*.)

Theosophy, with its roots also in Schopenhauer's notion of "natural religion," which also captivated Müller's interest, viewed each of the world's religious traditions as sharing a single universal truth on which foundation all religious knowledge and doctrine has grown.

And to the above we should also add the fascinating phenomenon of the Jesuit paleontologist-geologist-philosopher-theologian, Teilhard de Chardin (1881–1955), admittedly a marginalized outcast from the Catholic Church during his own lifetime, but reinstated posthumously by Pope Benedict XVI, and cited by Pope Francis in his 2015 encyclical *Landato si* ("*Our Care for our Common Home*".) Having spent much of his life in the East (1905–1908, Egypt, 1923; 1926–1935, intermittently in China, 1935, India, etc.), he was deeply influenced by Eastern thought, as is evident in his posthumously published books *Le Phénomène Humain*, 1955 (written in 1938–1940), and his *Le Milieu Divine* 1957 (written in 1926–1927), *L'Energie Humaine*, 1962 (written in 1931–1935), etc.[39]

And earlier in 1893 in Chicago, as part of World Columbia Exposition, there opened the Parliament of the World's Religions (from September 11–27),[40] recognized as the occasion of the birth of formal interreligious dialogue world-wide. Representing Hinduism was Vivekananda, 1867–1902, who established hundreds of branches of the Vedanta Society in England and the United States. He, following in the steps of his master Ramakrishna,[41] who religious devotion included Jesus and Mohammat, as the incarnation of the comprehensive openness and tolerating Hinduism, proclaimed the non-dualistic spirituality of Vedāntā as the metaphysical root of universal tolerance and brotherhood. He declared:

> Ours is the universal religion. It is inclusive enough, it is broad enough to include all ideals. All the ideals of religion that already exist in the word can be immediately included, and we patiently wait for all the ideals that come in the future to be taken in the same fashion, embraced in the infinite arms of the religion of the Vedānta. (*Vivekananda, Complete Works*, vol. 3, p. 251; cf. ibid. 1, p. 119; cited by Wilhelm Halbfass, *India and Europe: An Essay in Understanding*, New York, 1988, pp. 408–409.)

This, indeed, encapsulates the notion of the *Perrenial Philosophy* mentioned above.[42]

Putting together all the different strands which are intertwined in myriad different ways[43] – e.g., Burton and Müller's connections with the East India Company, Müller's agreement with Schopenhauer's understanding of Kant's *Critique of Pure Reason*, Annie Bezant in India, etc., we see that the ground had been prepared for a more pluralistic view – some might say more anthropological - view of religion, encouraging a greater respect for the faith of the "other." (And see below section 8, entitled "Disparate Elements forming theological basis of *Nostra Aetate*," on the influence of Eastern thought in the area of New Physics.)

Endnotes to Chapter 6

1. On various aspects of the influence of Eastern philosophy and culture on the West, see Alexander Macfee, *Eastern Influence on Western Philosophy, A Reader*, Edinburgh, 2003.

In the introduction (pp. 1–2) we read of two major schools of thought; the one which takes it for granted that in the modern period Oriental Ideas have had a significant affect upon European (Western) thought, and the other which doubts this influence, or sees it as minor. One of the leading protagonists of the former school is Raymond Schwab, in his *La Renaissance Orientale*, 1950, and J.J. Clarke, *Oriental Enlightenment: The Encounter Between Asian and Western Thought*, 1997. Among the latter we find Raghavan Iyer ed. *The Glass Curtain Between Asia and Europa*, 1965, and, of course, Edward Said, *Orientalism: Western Conceptions of the Orient*, 1978. The whole introduction (pp. 1–28) is most enlightening, and rich in bibliographic information. The reader will see that I tend towards the former school of thought.

2. On various aspects of the influence of Eastern philosophy and culture on the West, see Alexander Lyon Macfie, *Eastern Influence on Western philosophy*, Edinburgh, 2003.

And for a very personal expression of the apparent negative aspects of Eastern culture on the West, see the letter of Mr. Gordon Graig, from 1915, cited in the Introduction to *The Mirror of Gesture: Being the Abhinaya Darpana of Nondikesvova*, transl. Ananda Coomaraswamy and Gopalo Kristnayya Duggirala, Cambridge, Mass., 1917, p. 1:

> If there are books of technical instruction, tell them to me I pray you. The day may come when I could afford to have one or two translated for my own private study and assistance. I dread (seeing what it has already done in other arts here) the influence of the finished article of the East; But I crave the instruction of the instructors of the East. The disastrous effect the Chinese porcelain and the Japanese print has had on us in painting we must try to avoid in this theatre art. . . .
>
> You know how I reverence and love with all my best the miracles of your land, but I dread for *my* men lest they go blind suddenly attempting to see God's face. You know well what I mean, I think. So I want to cautiously open this

precious and dangerous (only to us queer folk) book of technical instruction before the men go crazy over the lovely dancers of the King of Cambodia, before the "quaintness" tickles them, before they see a short cut to a sensation. If only you knew how unwilling these men of the theatre (most of all those dissatisfied with the old sloppy order) were to face the odds, and how they long to escape obligations (your phrase in Sati') you would almost make a yearly tour of England crying, "Shun the East and the mysteries of the East."

3. It is perhaps suitable to quote two short passages from Panikkar's essay "What Is Comparative Philosophy Comparing?" apud *Interpreting Across Boundaries: New Essays in Comparative Philosophy*, edd. G.J. Larson and E. Deutsch, Princeton 1988, p. 130, and p. 134:

> Pluralism is not concerned with multiplicity or diversity as such, but with the incommensurability of human constructs on homologous issues. The problem of pluralism touches the limits of the intelligible (not just for us but in itself. . . . It touches the shores of the ineffable and thus of silence. . . .
>
> Comparative philosophy, qua philosophy, makes us aware of our own myth by introducing us to the myth of others and by this fact changes our own horizon . . . It saves us from falling into the fallacy of believing that all others live in myths except us.

See Frederick J. Streng's comments on this in his essay "The Transcendental in a Comparative Context," apud *Culture and Modernity: East-West Philosophic Perspectives*, ed. Eliot Deutsch, Honolulu, 1991, p. 370.

Perhaps we can compare this with the Buddhist law of Otherness (*vioudha-dharma-samsarga*), according to which every variation of place, time and quality makes the object "another" object. This law reduces everything to point-instances and cancels individual identity altogether. See Th. Stcherbatsky, *Buddhist Logic*, vol. 2, Leningrad, 1930, p. 8 note 2, 197 note 2.

We may perhaps compare this with Arthur S. Eddington's description of the external world, as "a synthesis of appearances from all possible points of view." See his essay entitled, "The Domain of Physical Science," apud *Science Religion and Reality*, ed. Joseph Needham, New York, 1955, (first published Cambridge, 1925), p. 197. He goes on to explain this concept, which is scientific extension of Pannikar's theological position:

> In the main, modern science accepts this principle and arrives at its adopted conception of our environment by following it. The man and the microbe afford only one example of the possible variety of points of view. Recently physicists have been much occupied in comparing the points of view of observers travelling with different motions, *e.g.*, attached to different stars. The result has been

entirely to revolutionise the conception of space and time in the external world. The detailed frame of space and time in which we are accustomed to locate the events happening around us belongs not to the external world but to a particular presentation of it – namely, to those observers who are travelling with the same velocity as the earth. A being on a star with different velocity would, if he followed our methods and assumptions, obtain a different reckoning of space and time, and his location of external events would be a distorted version of our own. *In the external world, which is a synthesis of all points of view, we cannot give preference to one version rather than the other*; space and time, in the form in which we commonly represent them, cannot belong to the external world. The work of Einstein and Minkowski has shown how the synthesis is to be made; it leads to the conception of a four-dimensional space-time (*i.e.*, a fourfold order of events) in which there is no straight-cut separation into space and time, although there is a definite structural arrangement on a rather simple plan which is the genesis of the separation by the various possible observers. [My emphasis, D.S.]

4. This is also the case in optical illusions, especially the category of cognitive illusions /ambiguous illusions. A most famous example is M.C. Escher's "Ascending and Descending." (1960) See, the analysis of E.H. Gombridge, *Art and Illusion: A Study in the psychology of pictorial representation*, London, 1960, pp. 198–235.

See further on Escher's impossible worlds by Bruno Ernst, *The Magic Mirror of M.C. Escher*, London, 1994, p. 92 et seq., under the headings, "Explanations into Perspective" (pp. 42–55), "Creating Impossible Worlds" (pp. 63–67), "Simultaneous Worlds" (pp. 73–80), and "Worlds that Cannot Exist" (pp. 80–92). In a sense, many of his illustrations are a kind of visualization of *concidentum oppositorum*.

See further Henry Unger, "Presentation and Representation in Escher's Lithographs: The Logic and Aesthetics of Pictorial Nonsense," *Assaf: Studies in Art History*, 4, 1999, pp. 171–190. On the possibility of "contradictory worlds" see G. Priest, Logic of Paradox, *Journal of Philosophic Logic* 8, 1979, pp. 219–241; idem, *Paraconsistent Logic: Essays on the Inconsistent*, Philosophia Verlag, 1989. On "possible-worlds semantics" and the validation of counterfactual cognitions, see J. Hintikka, "Exploring Possible Worlds," apud S. Allen, ed., *Possible Worlds in Humanities, Arts and Sciences, Proceedings of Nobel Symposium* 65, Berlin and New York, 1989, pp. 52–81.

For further examples of images of ambiguous illusion, see *www.just-riddles.net/ ambiguous-illusions*. We cannot elaborate on this subject within the framework of this study.

5. See, for instance, the findings of Aude Oliva from MIT. On illusions and the interpretation of images from the point of view of the neuroscience of perception, see Richard Gregory, *The Intelligent Eye*, 1970.

6. Louis Jacobs, in his *Principles of Jewish Faith: An Analytical Study*, London, 1964, (in chapter 7, "The Sixth Principle: *Prophecy*"), p. 191, cites the Spanish philosopher Yosef Albo (c.1380–1444), who writes in his *Sefer ha-Ikkarim* 3:9, which deals with the question of how God reveals himself to different prophets in different ways, that just as a man's form is seen differently in mirrors of different shapes and sizes, so does God appear to the prophets under many forms according to the brightness and purity of the media, though God himself does not multiply or change. Here the Rabbis say: Many prophets have one idea, though no two prophets use the same expression (*B. Sanhedrin* 89a). Compare with Pannikar's parable in chapter 6. And cf. *Leviticus Rabba* 1:14 that Moses saw his prophecy through polished glass (vision – *aspaklaria metzuhtzehet*) while other prophets did so through dim glass (*aspaklaria meluchlechet*). And cf. *B. Yevamot* 49b, and Reuven Margaliot, *Shaarei Zohar*, Jerusalem, 1956, pp. 132–133, on the notion of *aspaklaria meira*, the "*illuminating lense,*" that was Moses' prophecy as opposed to that of the other prophets. The nature of prophecy in Jewish thought is too vast a theme to be discussed here. See, however, Jacobs ibid. pp. 184–215, with his rich bibliographies on pp. 196–198, 203–205, and 213–215.

Cf. Zohar 1:170b, *Tikkunei ha-Zohar*, *Tikkun* 40, 80a; Zohar 2:42b; when the being (i.e. God) descends upon humans and spreads out upon them, it will appear to each of them in accordance with their own appearance and similarity; and that is the meaning of "[I have spoken by the prophets], and I have multiplies visions, and used similitudes by the ministry of the prophets" (Hosea 12:11). (Cf. R. Reuven Margaliot's note 2, ibid. p. 84). Zohar 1:149a, "Each prophet saw his prophecy according to his [spiritual] level, (*madreigah*)"; cf. ibid. 3:110a; 2:130b, etc.

See also Abraham J. Heschel, *The Prophets*, New York and Evanston, 1962, pp. 25–26:

> The Prophet is not a mouthpiece, but a person; not an instrument, but a partner, an associate of God. Prophetic sympathy is a response to transcendental sensibility.

This again is too broad a subject to be dealt with here.

7. The great Indian philosopher, Radhakrishnan, in his Preface to his classic *Indian Philosophy*, New York, 1923, writes (col.1, p. 8):

The special nomenclature of Indian philosophy which cannot easily be rendered into English accounts for the apparent strangeness of the intellectual landscape.

See also Ilkka Niniluato, apud *Culture and Modernity: East-West Philosophic Perspectives*, ed. Eliot Deutsch, Honolulu, 1991, p. 608, who writes that "the vocabularies of Western and Eastern languages are radically different and, hence, non-translatable from one to the other." And though this may be somewhat exaggerated, there certainly is some truth in this statement.

A fine example of this may be found in a fascinating book published in Delhi in 1991, where the *Various Interpretations of the Rbhu-hymns in the Rgveda* – the title of the book – were given in fourteen different translations/interpretations by Miss Ct. V. Davane. The translations range from the fourteenth century (from Sāyana's Sanskrit Commentary), to Louis Renou's from 1965 (published in *Études Vediques et Paniniennes* 15). And just to make the point abundantly clear, I shall cite some random translations of the first verse.

Félix Nève (p. 19)
> Addressed to a divine generation this hymn, dispenser of richest treasures, has come out of the mouth of the Signers.

R.T.H. Griffith (p. 152):
> For the Celestial Race this song of praise which gives wealth lavishly, was made by singers with their lips.

Karl Friedrichgelder (p. 184):
> This song of praise that brings much reward has been prepared for the divine race by those skilled in speech, with their lips.

Louis Renou (p. 260):
> Here is a collection of praise addressed to the divine race, (which) has just been prepared by inspired orators, with (their) mouth, (praise) which confers treasures (better than anything else).

S.A. Langlois (p. 77)
> In honour of a divine race, the mouth of the priests sing this hymn, which should bring generous recognition (of these gods) . . . etc.

And this is only the very simple first line of the hymn!

8. See, e.g., Stephen Batchelor, *The Awakening of the West: The Ecounter of Buddhism and Western Culture*, London, 1994; see also Raymond Schwab, The *Oriental Renaissance: Europe: Discovery of India and the East 1680–1880*, English transl. New York, 1984, (first published 1950). The influence of the "East" was central in the development of a number of late 19th and 20th century esoteric movements, some emerging out of the new acquaintance with Buddhism; (see above Chapter

2). Thus Madame (Helena P.) Blavatsky, who had visited Turkey, Greece, Egypt and France, before arriving in London in 1851, and was one of the founders of the *Theosophical Society*, described her teachers as Indian gurus, namely Mahatma Morya – known as "Master M" – from Punjab, and Mahatma Koot Hoomi ("Master KH") from Kashmir. (See K. Paul Johnson, *The Masters Revealed: Madame Blavatsky and the Myth of the Great Whits Lodge*, Albany, 1994.)

The aims of the Theosophical Society were defined as follows:

1) To form the nucleus of a universal brotherhood of humanity, without distinction of race, creed, sex, caste or colour.
2) The study of ancient and modern religions, philosophies and sciences.
3) The investigations of the unexplained laws of nature and physical powers latent in man.

Thus the *Theosophical Society* sought to bridge esotericism, comparative study of philology and religion and the heritage of the Enlightenment.

In 1878 she travelled to India, settled in Bombay, and in 1882, the headquarters of the society were moved to Adyar, near Madras. The influence of the theosophists in India and Ceylon had such strong political implications, that Radhkrihanan (1888–1975), the philosopher and President of India (1962–1967), stated that:

> . . . the theosophical movement rendered great service by vindicating those values and ideas [of the values and vitality of Indian culture]. The influence of the theosophical movement on general Indian society is incalculable.

(See Sylvia Cranston, H.P.B. *The Extraordinary Life and Influence of Helena Blavatsky, Founder of the Modern Theosophical Movement*, New York, 1995, p. 192). Mahatma Gandhi was also influenced by the movement, with which he became acquainted during his Law Studies in London in 1889.

After Blavatsky's death on 8 May 1891, Annie Besant (1847–1933), who first met Blavatsky in 1890, came to the fore, becoming president of the *Theosophical Society* in 1907. She established the Central Hindu College at Banaras in 1898, the Hydrabad (Sind) National Collegiate Board in Mumbai in 1902, and was very active politically in India's striving for freedom. But very significantly, after a chance encounter by her associate Charles Webster Leadbeater, at Adyar with a young Indian boy called Jiddu Krishnamurti (1895–1986), Bezant adopted him, and he became a world-famous guru, until he died in Ojai California.

And we should not forget Rudolf Steiner (1861–1925), who in 1902 became the first General Secretary of the *Theosophical Society* in Germany, and in 1913 founded his own *Anthroposophical Society*. He moved away from the "Oriental wisdom-teachings" of theosophy, and his book *Die Philosophie der Freiheit* (The Philosophy of Freedom) 1894, demonstrates the influences of Max Stirner and Friedrich Nietzsche.

Similarly, Mary Baker Eddy (1821–1910), the expounder of "Christian Science," in her various writings admitted to the harmony between Vedantin philosophy and Christian Science. She even quoted certain passages from the English edition of the *Bhagavad-Gita*, which for some reason were omitted in the 34th edition of the book *Science and Health with Key to Scripture* (first published 1910).

And see Radhakrishnan's statement, cited below near note 51.

These are but some of the indications of the influence of Eastern thought on the West during the later 19th and early 20th century. This again, is a very broad subject, which I have merely touched upon. See, for example, the fine study of Kocku von Stuckrad, *Western Esoterism: A Brief History of Secret Knowledge*, London, 2005, pp. 113–132. And, of course, we should be fully aware of the influence of some of these esoteric movements on Nazism. See, e.g., Nicholas Nicholas Goodrick-Clark, *The Occult Roots of Nazim: Secret Aryan Cults and Their Influence on Nazi Ideology*, London, New York, 2004; idem, *Black Sun: Aryan Cults, Esoteric Nazism and the Policies of Identity*, New York, London, 2002.

9. See E. Gombrich, *Art and Illusion*, Princeton, New Jersey, 1960, p. 150, who writes:

> The language of which we [in the West] discuss pictures differs so radically from the Far East that all attempts to translate from one into the other are frustrated.

Interest in the East did not begin in the 19th century. It only intensified then. Already in the 17th century we find such interest. See, for example, B. Sprague Adam, *Tides in English Taste* (1619–1800), New York, 1969, vol. 1, pp. 180–223, interest in China (porcelain, lacquer, wall paper, etc.) and vol. 2, pp. 3–42, (India and China). See also Michell Edwardes, East West Passage: The Travel of Ideas, Arts and Inventions between Asia and the Western World, New York, 1971.

10. The Eastern influences on Schelling, Schopenhauer and Hegel (see M. Hulin, *Hegel et l'Orient*, Paris, 1979) have been analyzed in detail by Wilhelm Halbfass, in his essays on these personalities in *Eastern Influences on Western Philosophy: A Reader*, ed. A.L. Macfie, Edinburgh, 2003, pp. 141–219. See also Moira Nicholls, "Influences of Eastern Thought on Schopenhauer," apud The *Cambridge Companion to Schopenhauer*, ed. Christopher Janaway, Cambridge, 1999, pp. 171–212, reprinted in *Eastern Influences etc.*, pp. 187–219, where pp. 208–213, in an Appendix, there is listed Schopenhauer's Oriental sources.

11. See Ignatius Viyagappa, G.W.F. Hegel's *Concept of Indian Philosophy*, Rome 1980; W. Halbfass, *India and Europe: An Essay in Understanding*, Akary, 1988, chapter 6, pp. 84–99.

12. William Halbfass, in his *India and Europe: An Essay in Understanding*, Albany, 1988, p. 95, writes:

> Hegel's interest in India is inseparable from his anti-Romantic attitude and his criticism of the Romantic glorification of India. . . . Furthermore, Schlegel's criticism of Hegel sometimes reminds us of, and even seems to echo, Hegel's own polemics against Schlegel. While Hegel finds "infinite absolute negativity" in Schlegel's thought, Schlegel in turn finds "the evil spirit of negation and contradiction" in Hegel; both accuse each other of abstractness. . . . Schelling's philosophy, too, is included in Hegel's criticism of India. . . . [K]ey terms of Hegel's interpretation of India, such as "substantiality," the abstract "One," the empty absolute, were first developed or employed in Hegel's critique of Schelling.

See also Dorothy H. Figueira, *The Exotic: A Decadent Quest,* Albany, 1994, pp. 72–73; Richard King, *Orientalism and Religion: Postcolonial theory, India and the "Mystic East,"* London and New York, 1999, pp. 124–125.

13. He read the *Upanisads* from Anquetil du Perron's transl. from the Persian translation. He regarded it as "the greatest gift of our century," and in his classic *Die Welt als Wille Vorstellung* (The World as Will and Representation), vol. 1, 1818–1819, vol. 2, 1844, he mentions *tat tvam asī* many times. He also saw the Buddhist Four Truths as similar to his doctrine of will.

For a detailed discussion of this subject, see Bhikkhu Nānajivako, *Schopenhauer and Buddhism*, Kandy Ceylon, 1970, with a rich selection of quotations from Schopenhauer's writings relating to Buddhism.

As an example of Schopenhauer's later involvement with Buddhism, we may quote a passage from his *The World as Will and Representation* vol. 2, 1859, chapter 17, p. 169, (the English translation by E.F.J. Payne, New York, 1966):

> It almost seems that, as the oldest languages are the most perfect, so too are the oldest religions. If I wished to take the results of my philosophy as the standard of truth, I should have to concede to Buddhism pre-eminence over the others. In any case, it must be a pleasure to me to see my doctrine in such close argument with a religion that the majority of men on earth hold as their own, for this numbers far more followers than others.

Nanajivako (ibid. pp. 13 et seq.) points out that both Schopenhauer and his older contemporaries, Goethe and Schelling, attended the lectures of Prof. Friedrich Maier, one of the best known German orientalists; and in 1813, while submitting his doctoral thesis at the University of Jana, he obtained from Maier his copy of OUPNEK'HAT, a Latin translation of the *Upanisads* by Anquetil - Duperron, based on the excellently edited Persian version. See further Raymond Schwab, *La Renaissance Orientale*, Paris, 1950, for the history of European Indology.

14. In Buddhism, *nirvana* is the ultimate goal of spiritual practice. It requires the overcoming of three unwholesome roots – desire, hatred and delusion (*akushala*) and the coming to rest of active volition (samskāra). In Mahāyā Buddhism it is conceived as oneness with the absolute, bliss in cognizing one's identity with the absolute, and as freedom from attachment to illusions, affects and desires. In the various other Buddhist sects it has slightly different connotations. See *The Encyclopedia of Eastern Philosophy and Religion: Buddhism, Taoism, Zen, Hinduism*, Boston, 1994, pp. 248–250.

It is to be understood within the context of the Doctrine of two-fold Truth, as Patricia Walsh-Franks formulates it in Asian Philosophy, March 1996, 6/1, p. 9:

> This doctrine provides a way of explaining the relationship between *samsara* and *nirvana*, but it should not be taken simply as a literary device. *Samsara* is the material world of the everyday, it is the world into which we are born and then leave in death, [Phru Khantipalo *Tolerance*, 1965, p. 163 note 22]. *Samsara* is filled with ignorance and suffering because our ego-centric view prevails in it. Its falsity is even expressed in words which, by their nature, set limits to our experience. Words describe our erroneous beliefs and, thus, perpetuate our ignorance of the true nature of Being. *Nirvana*, on the other hand, is the ideal world of enlightenment. It is free of ignorance and suffering. Yet, it is not a material world as *samsara* is. Rather, it is "the ultimate goal of Buddhist striving, a suprapersonal and non-dual experience of voidness which is the end of all *duhkha* and the highest happiness" [ibid. p. 102]. If *samsara* is ruled by ignorance, *nirvana* is the home of perfect wisdom. Nagao explains the equation between wisdom and *nirvana*; through wisdom *nirvana* is met, [Gadjim M. Nagao, *Madhyamika* and *Yogacara*, transl. Lelslie S. Kawamura, Albany, 1991, p. 32 note 23]. The limits of language make it difficult to explain *nirvana* because it is unexplainable. To reduce *nirvana* to linguistic formulations objectifies it yet, it is not an object but an extraordinary experience. Language places limits, yet, *nirvana* is unlimitable. Thus, in a sense, language puts an end to *nirvana*'s existence. In silence alone *nirvana* is.

15. See also his article "Emerson and Indian Philosophy," *Journal of the History of Ideas* 28:1, 1967, pp. 115–122; F.I. Carpenter, *Emerson and Asia*, Cambridge Mass.,

1930; Russells Goodman, "East-West Philosophy in Nineteenth Century America: Emerson and Hinduism," *Journal of the History of Ideas* 51/4, 1990, pp. 625–645.

16. Here I would like to quote what the great orientalist Laurence Binyon wrote in his classic *The Spirit of Man in Asian Art* (being the Charles Eliot Norton Lectures delivered in Harvard University, 1933–1934), Harvard, 1935, pp. 188–190:

> About 1860 some stray Japanese colourprints found their way to Europe. (Specimens came to Holland in the late eighteenth and early nineteenth centuries, but they seem mostly to have disappeared; at any rate, they caused no excitement.) The first prints which arrived in Paris are said to have been used as wrappings for articles of commerce; for these prints were cheap things in Japan, not highly prized at all. Some artists seized on them with cries of joy. More prints were sent for; collectors contended for them. We all know how much they meant to the art of Degas and of Whistler. They also transformed the whole art of the poster. They showed how telling economy of line and colour could be. It was the Japanese prints which first made people in the West surmise that Asian art might be something more than exquisite handicraft and the adornment of things of use. It was supposed at first that the prints represented the culmination of the pictorial art of Japan; and Japanese art was assumed to be the one Oriental art capable of comparison with the art of the West. Edmond de Goncourt pronounced that Hokusai and Utamaro were the greatest of Japanese masters.
>
> America was more fortunate. A few men of enlightenment, especially Fenollosa, seized the truth that the really great art of Japan was the art of far earlier periods, and that the still greater art of China lay behind that. Nor must we forget in England William Anderson, whose collection of Japanese and Chinese paintings was bought by the British Museum in 1880, and who certainly discerned things in their true perspective.
>
> In fifty years how much has been discovered! Japanese publications with their marvelous reproductions opened up to us all the classics of Japanese painting and sculpture, and the splendid examples of Chinese art preserved in Japan. Collectors began to turn to China. Chinese paintings began to be imported into Europe and America. Archaeologists of many countries were sent to China and Chinese Turkestan; and all the wealth of Chinese Buddhist sculpture, still surviving in spite of the vast amount of destruction that has been wrought, was revealed.
>
> The Buddhist art of China inevitably led to the Buddhist art of India, and so to Indian art in general. For though Indian sculpture and architecture had been known to Europeans for some centuries, Indian art had been regarded merely as "heathen idols," the hideous study of the ethnologist. It is only in

this century, too, and in quite recent years, that Persian art has begun, or rather is beginning, to receive anything like its due, Persian painting in particular. Thus it was the art of the Farthest East that first opened the eyes of the West, and the art of the Nearer East that is the last to be appreciated.

What had happened to change the Western attitude? It was not only the discoveries themselves, it was something that had overtaken Western art.

We may further explain the historical development of this trend. In 1853 Japanese ports were reopened to trade with the West. On 1 April 1867 there was the *Exposition Universelle* on the Champ de Mar in Paris, which had a Japanese pavilion, with, inter alia, a showcase of *ukiyo-e* prints. Claude Monet attended this exposition, and subsequently amassed a collection of some 250 prints, 23 by Kokusai Katsushiko (1760–1849), which greatly influenced his subsequent paintings. His garden at Giverny was modeled directly after a Japanese print, right down to the arching bridge and bamboo. Degas and Mary Cassatt quote from Hokusai's *manga* which they saw at the Louvre. So too Toulouse-Louhee's posters were influenced by Japanese art.

The first champion of "Japonisme," as it came to be called, was Felix Braquemond (1833–1914), who in 1856 found Hokusai's *manga* sketches in Paris, and extolled them before his impressionist colleagues, Monnet, Bernard, Degas etc. (The *manga* is a woodblock print.)

In 1987 Van Gogh produced a copy of Hiroshige's in his "Le Cortisane." Hokusai's "Great Wave" made such an impression in the West, that it appeared on the cover of Debussy's score of "La Mer," and even Tintin's cry "Mon vieux Milon, nous sommes perdues," in "The Tiger of the Pharaoh."

In the 20th century, Frank Lloyd Wright (1867–1959) was a Japanophile and had a major collection of Japanese prints.

Arthur C. Danto wrote in his article "The shape of Artistic Pasts, East and West," apud *Culture and Modernity: East-West Perspectives*, ed. Eliot Deutsch, Honolulu 1991, p. 339:

> For me, the deep change, and indeed the beginning of modernism, begins in the West when Japanese prints became objects not of curiosity but of influence. Monet collected Japanese prints, as Matisse and Derain collected African masks and figures. But Van Gogh and Gauguin decided to constitute the masters of the Ukiyoe print as their predecessors, as Picasso determined a tradition in the Ethnographic Museum of the Palais de Trocadero to be the relevant past for the Demoiselles d'Avignon. It was, in the case of Japanese art, not simply that these stopped being objects of charm and curiosity and exoticism, connoting, as in Odette's overheated interior, pleasures forbidden by the moral world embodied in the bourgeois décor she was anxious, as a high-class courtesan, to put at a distance; it was that these prints showed the right way to represent in art, and if these were right, an entire artistic tradition was wrong and an entire

progress was beside the point. Part of this had to do with the treatment of space, part with the ideal of an illusion that three-dimensional space, whose conquest was the glory of Western art, made possible. Gauguin drew everything toward the surface, rejected chiaroscuro, flattened his forms by bounding them with heavy lines – though like Odette, who took it for granted that she should use gas to illuminate her lantern. Gauguin benefited from the easy availability of manufactured pigments to get colors in a relatively pure state, defined as "coming from the tube." (It was by and large chemical pigments that finished off the Japanese print.) In desituating his own art from his own tradition, accepting as influences the Japanese masters, Gaugin simultaneously was engaged in a piece of cultural criticism; he explicitly said, when he considered relocating to Tonkin, that "The West is rotten."

And this as opposed to an earlier period, when (ibid. p. 338):

. . . works of art were imported into the West from the first establishment of mercantile routes; Chinese porcelains appear in the Dutch still lifes of the seventeenth century, but merely as objects to hold fruit, though of course there was a demand for pottery in the Chinese style, as we know from the fact that it was broadly imitated around 1700 by the potters of Delft. There can be a great deal of such importation and imitation without the premises on which cultural complacency rests being greatly shaken. Who can forget the atmosphere of exotisme/erotisme of Odette's drawing room, with its Japanese lanterns and Chinese pots, its screens and fans and cushions of Japanese silks, the innumerable lamps made of porcelain vases (and some Turkish beads), though the marvelous lantern, suspended by a silken cord, was lit from inside by a gas jet "so that her visitors should not have to complain of the want of any of the latest comforts of Western Civilization," as Proust writes archly, (Moriel Proust, *Swann's Way*, transl. CK. Scott-Moncrieff, apud *Rememberance of Things Past*, New York, 1934, p. 168). The superiority of Western Civilization was never doubted, and one of the premises of Victorian anthropology was in effect that there is a moral direction in history as there is in evolution, that societies and species evolve toward optimality, and that Western Europe was history's masterpiece just as *Homo sapiens* was Nature's. The relationship to the outside would be fundamentally one of curiosity. The outside was the object of curiosity in the double sense of embodying strangeness, as in "curio," and as something to understand as an object of scientific curiosity.

We may add that:

At its peak [the Dutch East India Company had] 40,000 Dutch, other Europeans and Asian employees, a fleet of more than one hundred ships, and over six

156

hundred stations, in its charter area, spanning from the Cape of Good Hope to Japan.

(Martine Gosselink, *The Dutch East India Company in the East*, pp. 21–30, especially p. 21; apud *Asia in Amsterdam: The Culture of Luxury in the Golden Age*, edd. K. H. Corrigan, Jan van Campen, Femke Diercks, Janet C. Blyberg, Yale University Press, 2016.)

See further Gerald Reitlinger, *The Economics of Taste: The Rise and Fall of Picture Prices* 1760–1960, vol. 2, New York, 1963, (reprint New York, 1982), pp. 189–224, in Chapter 7, entitled "The Orient Rediscovered, 1815–1915," and also Rana Kabbani, *Europe's Myths of the Orient,* Bloomington Indiana 1986, pass; V.V. Barthold, *La Découverte de l'Asia: Histoire de l'Orientalisme en Europe et en Russie*, Paris, 1947.

We may point to yet another interesting point. Classical logic (cf. chapter 1) with its simplicity and a kind of logical symmetry was in a way paralleled by classical art and architecture, with its simplicity and symmetry. Sir Christopher Wren, the great English architect defined beauty, inter alia as,

> Natural is from Geometry, consisting of Uniformity [that is Equality] . . . Always the true test is natural or geometrical Beauty Geometrical Figures are naturally more beautiful than any other irregular; in this all consent, as to a Law of Nature.

(*Parentalia*, cited in L. Weaver, *Sir Christipher Wren*, 1923, p. 150.)

Similarly John Dennis wrote of poetry in 1704:

> The works of men must needs be more perfect, the more they resemble his Maker's. Now the works of God, though infinitely various, are extremely regular. The Universe is regular in all its parts, and it is to that regularity that it owes its admirable beauty. ("The Grounds of Criticism in Poetry," in *Durham, Critical Essays*, 1700–1725.)

However, Arthur O. Lovejoy, in his *Essays in the History of Ideas*, Baltimore and London, 1948, in chapter VII, entitled "The Chinese Origin of a Romanticism," pp. 99–135, demonstrates how in the course of the 18th century a dramatic change in aesthetic standards took place,

> When regularity, uniformity, clearly recognizable balance and parallelism come to be regarded as capital defects in a work of art, and irregularity, asymmetry, variety, surprise, an avoidance of that simplicity and unity which render a whole design comprehensible at a glance, took rank as aesthetic virtues of a high order (p. 100).

And he shows that one of the causes for this change was "the admiration for the

Chinese garden, and in a less degree, for the architecture and other artistic achievements of the Chinese" (p. 101). He traces in detail the influence of China through the reports of voyagers and missionaries, even, regarding Chinese are preeminent in science, art, politics and morality (pp. 104–105). During the 18th century the design of the English garden (see pp. 122 et seq.) was deeply influenced by Chinese gardens with their irregularity, termed *sharawadgi*. And this is also a component in the development of the "First Gothic revival" (see ibid. pp. 136–165). So China had some influence already in the early 18th century.

This European admiration for Chinese culture goes back to as early as the later sixteenth century as indeed Lovejoy points out. He gives the following bibliographic references (p. 101 note 4):

> On this see Reichwein, *China und Europa,* 1923 (Engl. Tr., 1925); G. Atkinson, *Les relations de voyages du 17 siècle* (n.s.), chap. V; and the following, which have appeared since this essay was written: V. Pinot, *La Chine et la formation de l'esprit philosophique en France, 1640–1740* (1931); A. H. Rowbotham, *Missionary and Mandarin* (1942), chaps. XVI–XVII; Lewis S. Maverick, *China a model for Europe* (1946). Pinot's and Maverick's volumes contain extensive bibliographies.

See also Daniel J. Cook and Henry Rosemant Jr., "The Pre-Established Harmony Between Leibnitz [1646–1716] and Chinese Thought," *Journal of the History of Ideas* 42/2, 1981, pp. 253–267; Donald F. Lach, "The Sinophilism of Christian Wolff (1679–1754)," *Journal of the History of Ideas* 14/4, 1953, pp. 561–574; Basil Guy, *The French Image of China Before and After Voltaire*, Geneva, 1963, especially pp. 214–218, 243–276; Nolan Pliny Jacobson, "The Possibility of Oriental Influence on Hume's Philosophy" *Philosophy East and West* 19/1, 1969, pp. 17–37, etc. And of the above show earlier influences of Oriental culture on Western thought. But its impact was far more felt, I believe, in the following centuries.

17. And even earlier, the English soldier-scholar Edward Moor (1771–1848) had published his *The Hindu Pantheon*, London, 1810, which influenced, among others, Percy Bysshe Shelley (1792–1822), who showed considerable interest in India and Hinduism. (See Insan-ur-Rahim, Malik, "The Image of India in Shelley," *The Criterion* 51/4, 1990, pp. 625–645; Jalal Uddin Khan, "Shelley's Orientalia: Indian Elements in his Poetry," *Atlantis* 30/1, 2008, pp. 35–51.) And although he himself could not read *"the sacred books of the Brahmas,"* he freely availed himself "of the labours . . . of the learned gentlemen . . . Mr. Wilkins, Mr. Colebrooke, Mr. Wilford and others . . . [and] Sir William Jones (alas!)" (Preface p.x). It was reprinted in 1861, and in 1864 (in Madras) with additional notes by the Rev W.O. Simsan, referring to new scholarship and emphasis the Christian viewpoint. It is of further interest to note that on p. 1 he writes:

Strictly speaking *the religion of the Hindus is monotheism*. They worship God in unity, and express their conception of the Divine Being and his attributes in the most awful and sublime terms. God, thus adored, is called Brahm: the One Eternal Mind: the self-existing, in comprehensible Spirit.

18. Stephen Batchelor, *The Awakening of the West: The Encounter of Buddhism and Western Culture*, London, 1994, pp. 239–240.

19. Henry David Thoreau (1817–1862), the transcendentalist writer was deeply influenced by Indian literature and philosophy. During his two years at Walden Pond, which he sees as his sacred Ganga (Ganges) he tried to live as a Yogi. He wrote:

> In the morning I bathe my intellect in the stupendous and cosmogonal philosophy of the Bhagavat Gita, since whose composition years of the gods have elapsed, and in comparison with which our modern world and its literature seem puny and trivial; and I doubt if that philosophy is not to be referred to a previous state of existence, so remote in its sublimity from our conceptions. I lay down the book and go to my well of water, and lo! There I meet the servant of the Brahmin, priest of Brahma and Vishnu and Indra, who sits in his temple on the River Ganga reading the Vedas, or swells at the root of a tree with his crust and avater jug. I meet his servant come to draw water for his master, and our buckets as it were grate together in the same well. The pure Walden water is mingled with the sacred water of the Ganga (Ganges), (*The Writings of Henry D. Walden*, Princeton 1989, p. 298).

He expressed his disenchantment with Hebraism and his love of Hinduism in a number of passages (e.g., ibid. p. 57; Umesh Patri, *Hindu Scriptures and American Transcendentalism*, South Asia Books, 1987, pp. 98–240; Swami Abhadanada, *India and Her People*, 1906, pp. 235–266; B.G. Gokhale, *India in the American Mind*, 1989, pp. 22–27, 235–236, J.J. Clarke, *Oriental Enlightenment: The Encounter Between Asia and Western Thought,* 1997, pp. 86–87; David H. Albert, "Thoreau's India: The Import of Reading in a Crisis," *Proceedings of the American Philosophical Society* 125/2, 1981, pp. 104–109, etc.)

He in turn had been influenced by Ralph Waldo Emerson (1803–1882), who had written of Vedic thought that:

> It is sublime as night and a breathless ocean. It contains every religious sentiment, all the grand ethics which visit in turn each noble poetic mind . . ., (Nani R. Palkhivala, *India's Priceless Heritage,* 1980, pp. 9–24).

Emerson's profound harmony with the Indian scriptures is best illustrated in his poem "Brahma," derived from Kalidasa, composed in 1956. And in his *Essays*, vol. 5, pp. 258–259) he wrote:

By the law of contraries, I look for the inimitable taste for Orientalism in Britain.

And a little poem entitled Maya begins:

Illusion works inpenetrable
Wearing webs innumerable.

Maya, is, of course, the Hindu Goddess who keeps mankind under the spell of illusion. (See also Leyla Goren, *Elements of Brahmism in the Transcedentalism of Emerson*, pp. 42–45; Fredrik Ives Carpenter, *Emerson and Asia*, Haskell House Publ. 1930, etc.) See Dale Riepe, "Emerson and Indian Philosophy," *Journal of the History of ideas* 28/1, 1967, pp. 115–122.

And the list continues, but is far beyond the scope of this study.

20. As indicated at the end of the preceding note, there were many more notable personalities who were deeply influenced by Hinduism. For example, Sir William Jones (1746–1794), (see *Objects of Enquiry: The Life, Contribution and Influence of Sir William Jones* edd. Garland Cannon and Kevin R. Brine, New York and London, 1995, pp. 141–160); Wilhelm Humboldt (1767–1835) started studying Sanskrit in 1821, and was enthralled by Schlegel's edition of the *Bhagavad Gita*, on which he wrote an extensive study (in *Proceedings of the Academy of Berlin* 1825–1826). Of course, Arthur Schopenhauer (1788–1860) did much to bring the knowledge of Hindu thought to Europe. (See Wilhelm Halbfass, *India and Europe: A Essay in Understanding*, New York, 1988, p. 436.) Arnold Joseph Toynbee (1889–1975) predicted that at the close of this century, the world will be dominated by the West, but in the 21st century "India will conquer her conqueror" (Swami Prabhavananda, *Spiritual Heritage of India*, Vedanta Press, 1997). He is said to have stated that:

"There may or may not be only one single truth and only one single Ultimate way of salvation. We do not know. But we do know that there are more approaches to truth than one, and more means of salvation than one."

This is a hard say for adherents of the Judaic family (Judaism, Christianity, and Islam), but it is a truism for Hindus. (*Britannia Perspectives*, quoted by T.V.R. Shenoy, in Secularism *is not for Hindus alone*).

We may further add Richard Wagner's (1812–1883) use of the *Ramayana* by the Hindu poet Valmiki (c. 400 B.C.E.) as an episode in his Parsifal (1882), and his attraction to Buddhist ideas, which he acquired from Burnouf. See M. Edwardes, *East-West Passage: The Travel of Ideas, Arts and Inventions Between Asia and the Western World*, New York, 1971, pp. 165–166. And there (p. 167) he also notes Tolstoy's (1828–1910) interest in Eastern religions, especially Buddhism from where he took the concept of non-violence, which he adapted to the needs of modern political man, and it was through his influence on Mahatama Gandhi, that this concept of *ahimsa* became so central in Gandhi's policy.

To the above we could add William James, Herman Melville and Walt Whitman, William Blake all of whom, with many others, were influenced by the *Vedas*, the *Upanishads*, and the *Bhagavad Gita*. (See e.g., David Weir, *Brahma in the West: William Blake and the Oriental Renaissance,* Albany, 2003; Naresh Guha, *W.B. Yeats: An Indian Approach*, Calcutta, 1968, etc.)

We should further note that a "major example of Indian influence on European architecture in the nineteenth century is the Brighton Pavilion [1815–23], which is extraordinary for England – or anywhere else for that matter," which had "a Chinese interior within a fabulous Indian Shell" [Ralph Dulton, *The English Interior, 1500–1900*, B.T. Batsford, Ltd., New York, 1948]. Yet "another rich example of this pseudo-Indian architecture is Sir Charles Cockerell; Sezincote House in Gloucestershire, which was built to satisfy his desire for something in the Indian style" (c. 1805). See *Selected Lectures of Rudolf Wittkower: The Impact of Non-European Civilizations on the Art of the West*, compiled and edited by Donald Martin Reynolds, Cambridge University Press, 1989, pp. 194–199, with additional examples of the "Indian influence."

21. See *Dictionary of the History of Ideas: Studies of Select Pivotal Ideas*, New York, 1973, vol. 3, pp. 432–433, entry by Carl J. Jackson.

22. See also Richard King, *Orientalism and Religion: Postcolonial Theory*, India and "The Mystic East," London and New York, 1999, chapter 7, pp. 143–160, entitled "Orientalism and the discovery of 'Buddhism.'"

This is the period of the great discoverers of the East, such as Sven Hedin, whose *Southern Tibet: Discoveries in Former Times Compared with my Own Researches in 1906–1908*, in thirteen magnificent volumes, nine text, two map folios, and one of panoramics folio. Straakholm, 1910–1922, covers Traushimalaya, Karakorunand Chong – Tong. Chinese knowledge of Central Asia and journeys to the Eastern Pamir. Similarly Marc Aurel Stein, *On Ancient Central-Asian Tracks: Brief Summary of Three Expeditions in Innermost Asia* and *North-Western China*, London, 1933; *On Alexander's Track to the Indus Personal Narrative of Explorations on the North-West Frontier of India carried out under the Orders of H.M. Indian Government*, London, 1929; Ruins of Desert Cathay: *Personal Narrative of Explorations in Central Asia and Innermost China*, London, 1912; *Old Routes of Western Iran: Narrative of an Archeological Journey Carried Out and Recorded by . . . with the Assistance of Fred H. Andrews . . .* , London, 1940; *Archeological Reconnaissances in North-Western India and South-Eastern Iran . . .* , London, 1937, etc., and many others. The list is too lengthy to even contemplate recording here, but the above should give an inkling as to the atmosphere of the time.

23. And if we mentioned the Japanese *Noh* plays, we also note that Berthold Brecht, known for his famous teachings of "alienation," which sought to break up the inertion of empathy, published in 1960, "Kurze Beschreibung einer neuer Technik der Schauspielkunst, die einen Verfremdungseffekt heovorbrigt," (*Versuche*, 1960, pp. 89–105). See also *Schriften Zum Theater: über eine nicht-aristotelische Dramatik*, 1960, particularly pp. 74–89: "Verfremdungselfekt in der Chinesischen Schauspielkunst," explaining that the Chinese actor makes familiar ehavior look unfamiliar. He later qualified the doctrine, originally conceived as the opposite of empathy, in *Gespräch über die nötingung zur Einfühlung*, 1953 (reprinted in *Schriften zum Theater*, pp. 210 et seq.) See on this in Edgar Wind, *Art and Anarchy* 3rd edition, North Western University Press, 1985, pp. 8, 98 note 14.

Let us also note that between the years 1957 and 1960 there appeared the tetralogy of Lawrence Durell, *The Alexandria Quartet*. And in an interview he gave in 1959, he described the ideas behind the *Quartet* in terms of *a convergence of Eastern and Western metaphysics*, based on Einstein's overturning of the old view of the material universe, and Freud's doing the same for the concept of stable personalities, yielding a new concept of reality. (See *The Paris Review*, 23 April 1959, in an interview with Gene Andrewsky and Julian Mitchell, entitled "Lawrence Durell: The Art of Fiction, no. 23 [interview]." Durrell explained in the preface to the second volume of the *Quartet* that the four novels are an explanation of relativity and the notions of continuance and subject-object relation.

A similar theme is to be found in Kurosawa's Japanese film *Rashomon*, which appeared at the Venice Film Festival in 1951, and won both the Italian Critics Award and the Golden Lion Award, and in the United States it was released at the end of 1951, and received an Academy Honorary Award in 1952, for being "the most outstanding foreign language film released in the U.S.A. during 1951."

24. See, e.g., *Swami Prajanananda*, Calcutta, 1971, p. 164; Damodar Singhal, *Modern Indian Society and Culture*, Meenakshi Prakashan, 1981, p. 136; Wendell Thomas, *Hinduism Invades America*, The Beacon Press Inc., 1930, pp. 228–234; Stephen Gottschalk, (1941–2005, a lifelong Christian Scientist), The *Emergence of Christian Science in American Religious Life*, University of California Press, 1973, pp. 152–153, etc.

25. Here I should like to quote a statement from R.J. Zwi Werblowsky's *Beyond Tradition and Modernity: Changing Religions in a Changing World*, London, 1976, p. 84.

> I shall have to say something later about the view, advocated more especially by some modernist Hindu thinkers, that all religions are essentially one and only outwardly appear to be different. Whatever the merits or demerits of this

philosophical and theological doctrine – for it is that, and certainly not a generalization derived from an empirical study of the historical religions – students
of religion tend to be far more impressed by the truth of an opposite observation, to the effect that religions, however different they may be in their origins,
fundamental insights and doctrinal structures do, in fact, tend to become
similar. This phenomenon was forcefully pointed out not by a professional
historian of religion but by a British psychologist, Robert Thouless (Robert
H. Thouless, *Conventionalization and Assimilation in Religious Movements as
Problems in Social Psychology*, 1940, p. 1). Nobody would dream of denying
the differences between Christianity and Buddhism, but they are not terribly
relevant when comparing the ehavior of a pious Catholic passing by a roadside
cross or shrine, and that of a pious Buddhist passing by a temple or stupa.
The sangha is certainly something very different from Christian clergy; yet
occasionally their functions and roles are disconcertingly similar.

26. See A.L. Macfie, *Orientalism: A Reader*, Edinburg, 2000. See further Urs App,
The Birth of Orientalism, Philadelphia, Oxford, 2010; G. Prakash, "Orientalism
Now," *History and Theory* 34/3, 1995.

27. See A.b. Macfie, *The Eastern Question: 1774–1928*, London and New York,
1966.
We shall point to some key events in the opening of the East to the West in the
late 18th and early 19th century.
On July 25, 1792, the first British embassy reached the month of the Pei-ho in
China, under the ambassadorship of Viscount George Macartney, together with some
ninety-four additional people. It took some time for the entourage to reach Peking
when the embassy was established. This is one of the key events in the relations
between Britain and China. As for Annan (now Vietnam), in 1862 the Emperor signed
a treaty with the French recognizing their territorial rights over the three lower
provinces of Cochin China, where France already possessed the city of Saigon. In
1865 the French decided to launch a decisive expedition of reconnaissance into the
interior of Indo-China to expand their control in this region. And, of course, there is
the history of Britain in India. . . . To the above we may further add the remarkable
discoveries that opened up Central Asia, Mongolia and Tibet etc. by the great
explorer Marc Aurel Stein (1862–1943), with his five great trecks between the years
1900 and 1920, Sven Hedin (1865–1952), with his three dangerous journeys between
1894 and 1908, and Sir Francis Edward Younghusband (1863–1942). Their writings
and their tales enhanced the allure of the Oriental Adventure. (See the delightfully
readable and illustrated book by Timothy Severin, entitled *The Oriental Adventure:
Explorers of the East*, U.K. 1976.)

28. As a random example we may call attention to William Frederick Meyer and N[icholas] [elfiald] Dennys' *The treaty ports of China and Japan: A complete guide to the open parts of those countries, together with Pekin, Yedo, Hongkong and Macao. Forming a guide book and vade mecum for travelers, merchants, and residents in General,* London. It was published both in Hong Kong and London, and its editor, Dennys (1820–1899) claimed that it was the first such comprehensive handbook printed for public distribution. It was originally typeset in China, allowing place names and other words to be pointed in Chinese characters. The specially commissioned maps were also engraved in China. The book includes physical descriptions and brief histories of over twenty cities, details of schools, population statistics and much practical information. (See Shapiro: Rare Books, catalogue *Fire and Ice* no. 77.)

29. This work deals mainly with Middle-Eastern Art. We shall not enter into the acrid polemic discussion over Edward Said's famous 1973 book, *Orientalism*, and the critiques of his thesis by Bernard Lewis and others. See also William V. Spanos, *The Legacy of Edward Said*, Urbana & Chicago, 2009. Of tangential interest is the book by Barbara Hodgson, *Dreaming of East: Western Women and the Exotic Allure of the East,* Berkeley, 2005.

But briefly let us say that Said's *Orientalism* was the source of considerable discussion among the scholarly world. His thesis that Western Scholarship had presented Oriental culture in a patronizing, colonial fashion, and that this scholarship was inextricably tied to imperialist societies who portrayed it, was severely criticized by many prominent scholars, such as the internationally known British orientalist Bernard Lewis (see e.g., Lewis' *Islam and the West*, London, 1993, pp. 99–118, "The Question of Orientalism"; likewise, *The Muslim Discovery of Europe*, New York, 1982. See also Martin Kiamor's review-article of Robert Irwin's *Dangerous Knowledge,* 2007, entitled "Enough Said," *Commentary,* March 2007; Oleg Grabar, "Edward Said, Bernard Lewis, "Orientalist: An Exchange," New York Review of Books, 29/12, August 1982.) Said responded to Lewis' criticisms in an "Afterword" in his 1995 edition of Orientalism, pp. 329–352, and again in a "Preface" to the 2003 ed., pp.XI–XXIII. See also Jacob Barnai, *Sabbateanism*: *Social Perspectives*, Jerusalem, 2000, pp. 31–32 (Hebrew).

Of additional interest is Rana Kabbani's *Europe's Myths of Orient*, London, 1986, dealing with several aspects of East-West interplay and "Orientalism" in general. Of additional interest is the London Tate exhibition catalogue of 2008, entitled "The Lure of the East: British Orientalist Painting."

30. Japanese culture was then revealed to the West at the Paris Exposition of 1867. In 1856 Townsend Harris went to Japan as the first American consul and in 1863 the first Japanese embassy was established in Europe. In 1868 began the remarkable period of Westernization in Japan known as the Meiji, named after the Emperor who was in that year restored as the actual as well as the nominal ruler of the country.

By 1860, Sardou, a king among constructors of the well-made play, had already introduced fan, parasol, and double suicide into a play, and in1861 Baudelaire was receiving prints from Japan. [After the Exposition of 1867, there began a movement of Japanophilia.] Verlaine reported that he had woodcuts . . . The Goncourt brothers wrote studies on Hokusai and Utamaru. . . . Saint-Saëns and Lecocq composed "Japanese" operettas, Heredia wrote the sonnet "Samurai," and Loti evoked a false, but picturesque, Japan . . . in *Madame Chrysanthème*. Judith Gautier wrote dramas with names such as *Yellow Princess, The Cherry Trees of the Suma, The Vendor of Smiles*, and *Princess of Love*.

See Leonard Cabell Pronko, *Theater East & West: Perspectives Toward a Total Theater*, Berkeley and Los Angeles, 1967, pp. 113 et seq., in a chapter entitled "Kabuki: Inroads in the West."

31. The Hokusei Ukiyo-e style also influenced Mary Cassat, 1844–1926, and Henri de Toulous-Lautre, 1864–1901. It is said that he was first discovered by Félix Bracquemond, (1833–1914), around the year 1856 in Paris. (In 1862 Japanese ambassadors were received by the European Napoleon III, but the colour-print, Japan's most significant envoy, had already arrived in France in the form of wrappings round vases and fans.) What specifically influenced Degas and others were his *Mange drawings*. He himself was a collector of Japanese prints. See S. Wichmann, *Japonisme: The Japanese influence on Western Art since 1858*; New York, 1999; Lionel Lanbourne, *Japonisme: Cultural Crossings Between Japan and the West*; Colta Feller Ives, *The Influence of Japanese Woodcuts on French Prints*, New York, 1974; Gregory Irvine, *Japonism and the Rise of the Modern Art Movement: The Art of the Meiji*; Gabriel P. Weisberg, *Japonism: Japanese Influence on French Art 1854–1910*; Jill deVonyar, *Degas and the Art of Japan, 2007*, etc. Hokusei is mentioned several times by Van Gogh in his letters to his son Theo, in the years 1888–1889. See *The Complete Letters of Van Gogh*, London, 1950, vol. 2, p. 674, vol. 3, pp. 29, 52. Gauguin too was influenced by both Hokusei and Hiroshige; See *Gauguin*, by George Boudaille, London, 1984 (transl. by Alisa Jaffa, first French ed. Paris, 1963), pp. 83–85. There Boudaille writes, "The whole groups of Pont-Aven looked upon the Japanese print as an example and an authority." See further John Rewald, *Post Impressionism from Van Gogh to Gauguin*, New York, 1962, index p. 613b, s.v. Japan. There are also numerous articles on this subject, too many to record here.

And while on the subject of "Japanisme" we may note that Emile Zola (1840–1902) was an enthusiastic collector of Japanese prints. His staircase was decorated with Japanese prints whose erotic subject-matter he described as "furious fornications."

Manet's famous portrait of him from 1868 has a Japanese Screen in the background, as well as a Japanese *ukiy-e* woodblock print by Utagawa Kuniaki II (c. 1840) of a wrestler. Similarly Van Gogh's portrait of Pere Tanguy (1887) also has a background of Japanese prints.

Odilon Redon (1840–1916), born Bertrand Jean Redon, had an interest in Hindu and Buddhist religion and culture, and the Buddha-image figures prominently in his art, e.g., *Death of Buddha* 1899, *The Buddha* 1906, etc. In 1899 Baron Robert de Domecy (1867–1946) commissioned seventeen decorative panels for the din-ing-room of Chateau de Domecy sur-le-Vault in Burgundy, and they are influenced, both in format and colour, by Japanese painting-style in folding screens, *byābu.* (They are now in the Musée d'Orsay.)

Michael Edwardes, in his *East West Passage*, New York, 1971, p. 123 remarks that:

> Many Symbolist poets adopted impressionist techniques, calling their poems "impressions" and frequently using Japanese allusions. There was also a real attempt actually to *imitate* Japanese poetic style. This development was significant, because it began to move literary *japonisme* out of the exotic towards a genuine appreciation of Japanese forms. The publication in 1910 of an important anthology of Japanese literature, in translation, inspired French poets like Paul Fort and Oaul Eluard to imitate even the syllabic arrangements of the Japanese nature lyrics known as *haiku.* One authority has suggested that the discovery of *haiku* by French poets was as important to them as was the discovery of the sonnet to the poets of Renaissance England.
>
> From even this brief survey it can be seen how *japonisme* entered the veins of French art. The excitement Japan caused in Paris, the capital of the world of art, soon spread out to other parts of Europe and to America.

He then goes on to discuss the influence of Japanese prints on Whistler.

We should also note that Gilbert (1836–1911) and Sullivan (1842–1900) produced in 1885 the Opera *Mikado*, shown at the Savoy Theater, which was their most suc-cessful one, with 672 performances, in London alone, and this reflects the popular enthusiasm for "*japonaiserie.*"

And as an amusing aside, this time in reference to China, Sax Rohmer, (Arthur Henry Sarsfield Ward, 1883–1959) produced a whole series of highly successful nov-els (1912/13–1917, 1931–1959) on the character of the Chinese villain Dr. Fu Manchu.

We could continue this list, but the above selection should suffice to make its point.

And from Japan (and China) to India we may here add that this is the period when major museums are beginning seriously to collect Indian art. Thus in 1883 the Bibliothèque Nationale, Paris, bought a volume of Indian miniatures sold by Prisse d'Avenres. In the nineteenth century the Rijksmuseum and Tropenmuseum of Amsterdam and the Volkskunde Museum of Leiden and the Haarlem Kolonial

Institute were acquiring Indian pieces and collections of Indian industrial arts. Likewise major British museums. (See Partha Mitter, *Much Maligned Monsters: A History of European Reactions to Indian Art*, Oxford, 2013, pp. 266, 300–303.) In 1879 William Morris gave a lecture in Birmingham entitled, "The Art of the People," in which we get a glimpse of his admiration for the industrial arts of India, disagreeing in this with Ruskin (ibid. pp. 260–262). The discoveries in the West of great archeological sites, such as Sanchi, Amaravati, and Ajanta were of great interest. A detailed description of Elephanta was published in 1843, in Don Jaão de Castro's *Primiero Roteiro de Costa da India desde Goa ate Dio*, pp. 65–81, (ibid. pp. 304–308). Gustav Morcau used a proliferation of Indian temples as a backdrop to his symbolic painting, *Triomphe d'Alexandre* (ibid. 264; cf. P. Jullian, *Dreamers of Decadence*, London, 1871, pp. 131 et seq.) and "the veritable *apotheosis* of Elephanta" came in 1875, when a grand banquet was held in the main cave in honour of the Prince of Wales who was visiting India, "the brightest jewel in the Imperial crown." It was entirely opposite that *L'Exposition Universella* of 1900 which announced the ground opening of our century, displayed in its architectural *Ponorama-du Tout du Monde* a composite Indian building derived from different periods (ibid. pp. 264–266). Rodin was a great admirer of Indian art, and his paeon on Śiva Natarāja may be found in *Sculptures Civaites*, by A.K. Coomaraswamy, E.B. Havell and A. Rodin, Brussels and Paris 1921, p. 9 et seq (ibid. pp. 264, 359 note 7).

32. Rana Kabbani, in her *Europe's Myths of Orient*, London, 1986, demonstrates that a radical change towards the Orient takes place in Europe in the mid 19th century. Formerly, from the late 18th century until the mid-19th century the attitude to the orient had been a romantic one, expressing erotic longings which provided a respite from Victorian sexual repressiveness, and the "East" served as a metaphor for sensuality (as in Coleridge's poetry etc. pp. 35–36), while a change took place in the mid-19th century when the vogue for romance was on the wane since it was "at variance with the spirit of the age." For so wrote Lane in an article published in the *Athenaeum*, 25 September 1841:

> The nineteenth century is distinguished by a craving for the positive and the real – it is essentially an age of analysis and criticism.

Indeed Lane's version of the *Arabian Nights*, as opposed to earlier versions, catered to such a craving for the real.

> He had made a self-conscious efforts to place the stories in an historical and sociological framework by appending extensive notes to them. He considered the stories' value to lie in the "fullness and fidelity with which they describe the character manners and customs of the Arabs," (Edward W. Lane, *The Thousand and One Nights*, London, 1839–1841, 3 vols., vol. 3, p. 685).

(See Kabbani ibid. p. 37 et seq.)

And in his Introduction to his *Manners and Customs of the Modern Egyptians*, London, 1836, p. iii), he wrote:

What I have principally aimed at, in this work, is correctness; And I do not scruple to assert that I am not conscious of having endeavoured to render interesting any manner that I have related by the slightest sacrifice of truth (Kabbani ibid. p. 38.).

33. On the Great Exhibition of 1851 see the Commemorative *Album* of that event, issued by the Victor and Albert Museum in London, 1950, compiled by Mr. C.H. Gibbs-Smith, Keeper of the Department of Museum Extension Services, with the assistance of members of the department. It contains a detailed description of the construction of the building Crystal Palace, arrangement of the exhibits, contemporary comments etc., and a hundred or so (catalogue) pages of illustrations. I quote two passages of somewhat random interests.

> p. 27: (Paxton's comment):
> No means were so beneficial to the human race as those which brought men in contact with each other, thus rubbing off the rust of prejudice and ill-will, and cementing them together by feelings of amity and mutual consideration for each other's prosperity and happiness. If that was good as between man and man, how infinitely greater the benefit as between nation and nation. Fancy a Brotherhood of Nations!

And the somewhat amusing incident recorded on p. 70:

> 'Whilst the Hallelujah Chorus was being performed [at the Opening Ceremony], a Chinese, touched apparently by the solemnity of the scene, came forward and made a profound obeisance to the Queen. "This live importation from the Celestial Empire," the reporter of the *Examiner* records, "managed to render himself extremely conspicuous, and one could not help admiring his perfect composure and nonchalance of manner." (He came in a blue satin robe and was met by Capt. Owen, R.E., who with presence of mind recollecting there was no representative of China, admitted him, and he occupies a front place among the foreigners in Selous's picture). He talked with nobody, yet he seemed perfectly at home, and on the most friendly terms with all. A most amusing advantage was taken of his appearance, for, when the procession was formed, the diplomatic body had no Chinese representative, and our stray celestial friend was quietly impounded, and made to march in the rear of the ambassadors. He submitted to this arrangement with the same calm indifference which marked the whole course of his proceedings, and bore himself with a steadiness and gravity that fully justified the course which had been adopted. His ehavior throughout was that of "a citizen of the world" as perfect as Goldsmith's

philosopher himself. This famous Chinaman, whose name was Hee Sing (and who is seen in the illustration on page 57), was later discovered to have hoaxed everyone. "He was a sea captain," wrote Cole tartly, "who brought his junk into the Thames for exhibition, and got a good deal of money."

See on p. 116, fig. 157, an illustration of Indian ceramic objects, with the following description:

> Group of Indian objects, principally enameled. "In the Indian collection we find no struggle after an effect, every ornament arises quietly and naturally from the object decorated, inspired by some true feeling or embellishing some real want. The same guiding principle, the same evidence of thought and feeling in the artist, is everywhere present; . . . With them the construction is decorated; decoration is never, as with us purposely constructed."

However, these items were, apparently, not yet exhibited in the 1851 exhibition, neither was "the irony throne and foot-stool presented to Queen Victoria by the Rajah of Travancore" (India), ibid. p. 120 fig. 169, neither of which appears in the "*Crystal Palace Exhibition Illustrated Catalogue*," London, 1851 ("An Unabridged Replication of the Art-Journal special issue"), if indeed this catalogue included all the objects. One may further note that in the Catalogue's essay, "The Exhibitions as a lesson in Taste," by Ralph Nicholson Wornum, pp. 1 xxx – 11 xxx, there is no mention of Far-Eastern art, only of Saracenic, or "Jewish and other Asian ornament like the Egyptian" (ibid. p. 11 xxx), but, strangely enough, Indian China and Japan do not yet appear, though objects from their countries were already readily available. This must surely be indicative of how "elitist" British art connoisseurship evaluated these forms of art.

However, in the International Exhibition of 1862, in London, which went on for some six months (from 1 May till 1 November), which event some 6.1 million people attended, the Japanese Court aroused very considerable attention, and very soon, rooms full of Japanese objects were to be found in almost every middle-class house.

It is worth noting that there was an efflorescence of research and notable publications on Eastern art in the post-World War II years. And to give an impression of what was going on in Europe and the U.S.A., we give just a random sampling of such of the important publications (and exhibitions) that preceded *Nostra Aetate*. This list is by no means comprehensive and can be greatly expanded:

> *Catalogue of the Exhibition at the Royal Academy of Arts*, London, 1947–1948,
> Sir Leigh Ashton, ed., *The Arts of India and Pakistan*, London, 1950,
> René Grousset, *Le Chine et son Art,* Paris c. 1951.
> Sir Henry Garner, *Oriented Blue and White*, London, 1954,
> John A. Pope, *Chinese Porcelains from Ardabill Shrine*, Washington D.C., 1956,

Dietrich Sekal, *Emakimmo: The Art of Japanese Pointed Hand Scrolls*, New York, 1959,

Arts Council of Great Britain, *The Arts of the Ming Dynasty.* . . . Nov.–Dec. 1957, London, 1958,

William Willetts, *Chinese Art*, 2 vol., London, 1958,

James Cahill, *Chinese Painting*, New York, 1960,

Laurence Binyon and J.J. O'Brien Sexton, *Japanese Colour Prints*, ed. B. Gray, second ed. London, 1960,

Michael Sullivan, *The Birth of Landscape Painting in China*, London, 1962.

34. See, for example, C. Bouquet, *The Christian Faith and Non-Christian Religions*, Digwell Place, Welwyn Herts, 1958, pp. 356 et seq., especially pp. 373 et seq.; Nicol Macnicol, *Indian Theism from Vedic to the Muhammadan Period*, Dentworth Press, 1915, pp. 373 et seq.

35. See Rosane Rocker, Alexander Hamilton (1762–1824): A Chapter in the Early History of Sanskrit Philology, (American Oriental Series 51), New Haven 1969. Thus, for instance, Henry D. Thoreau (1817–1862) in his famous *Walden* (first published in 1854) has references to the *Bhagavat gītā*, and he translated passages from the *Laws of Manu* (See Joseph J. Moldenhauer, Edwin Masev, Alexander Korn, *The Writings of Henry D. Thoreau: Essays and Miscellaneous*, Princeton, 1975, pp. 129–139; cf. ibid. pp. 140–142, Sayings of Confusion.) And in his *A Week on the Concord and Merrimac Rivers* (1849) he ruminates on the *Gita*, thus:

> In the morning I bathe my intellect in the stupendous and cosmogonal philosophy of the Bhagvat-Geeta, since whose composition years of the gods have elapsed, and in comparison with which our modern world and its literature seem puny and trivial . . . I lay down my book and go to my well for water, and lo! There I meet the servant of the Brahmin . . . come to draw water for his master, and our buckets as it were grate together in the same well. The pure Walden water is mingled with the sacred water of the Ganges.

After the Wilkins translation, used by Emerson and Thoreau, many others were made.

See John Algeo, "The Bhagavad Gita in East and West," *The Quest,* 1989, p. 98, The whole article (pp. 74–80) is highly instructive, and as he remarks on p. 79:

> The interaction of Eastern and Western thought about and from the *Gita* is one of the curiosities of literary and social relations.

For a description of how the Sanskrit language and texts became even more available and influential in the West from about 1780, when the Brahmins of Bengal were given orders to translate into English (through the intermediary of Persian language) the ancient law and sacred writings of India, through William Jonas' realization of Sanskrit's affinities with Greek and Latin – he was appointed a Justice of the High Court of Bengal – and the publication of his findings in 1788 (in *Essai sur les Moeurs et l'Esprit des Nations; Traité de Metaphysique*, etc.), see Leon Poliakov, *The Aryan Myth: A History of Racist and Nationalist Ideas in Europe*, transl. Edward Howard, Sussex University Press, Edinburgh, 1971, chapter 9 (pp. 182–214, especially pp. 189–190 et seq.). Paradoxically, this development, while on the one hand being an important component in the movement towards the notion of the "Perrenial Philosophy," an extreme form of theological-philosophical pluralism, also led to emergence of the Aryan Myth, through Schelling, Schlagel and others, which constituted the basis of the Nazi radical anti-Semitic racist philosophy, which is the main thesis of Poliakov's brilliant book.

36. Swami Vivekananda made an extraordinary tribute to Müller and his love of India, quoted in Nirad Chaudhuri, *Scholar Extraordinary: The Life of Professor the Rt. Hon. Friedrich Max Müller, P.C.* Delhi, Oxford University Press, 1974, p. 204:

> Although a world-moving scholar and philosopher, his learning and philosophy have only led him higher and higher to the realization of the spirit; his lower knowledge has, indeed, helped him to reach the higher. This is real learning. Knowledge gives rise to humility. Of what use is knowledge if it does not show us the way to the highest?
>
> And what love he bears towards India! I wish I had a hundredth part of that love for my own motherland. An extraordinary and at the same time intensely active mind has lived and moved in the world of Indian thought for fifty years or more and watched the sharp interchange of light and shade in the interminable forest of Sanskrit literature with keen interest and heart-felt love, till they have all sunk into his whole soul and coloured his whole being.
>
> Max Müller is Vedantist of Vedantists. He has indeed caught the real soul of the melody of the Vedanta in the midst of all its settings of harmonies or discords – the one light that lightens up the sects and creeds of the world, the Vedanta, the one principle of which all religions are only applications.
>
> His life has been a blessing to the world; may it be many, many years more, before he changes the present plane of his existence.

Cited in Ibn Warraq's book is a very rich repository of information on Indian Orientalists (pp. 167–7–214), on Orientalism in painting, culture, music and literature (part 3 of the book, pp. 297–7–406), besides being a trenchant criticism of Edward Said's *Orientalism*. His information and bibliographic dates only serves to holster my thesis on the influence of the East on Western thought, adding numerous additional examples. Here we may add that in 1875 James Fergusson published his

History of Indian and Eastern Architecture, the first important work on the subject, which is still of value today.

37. This whole movement has most recently been described in rich detail in chapter 5 of Michael J. Altman's *Heathen, Hindoo, Hindu: American Representations of India*, 1721–1893, Oxford, 2017, pp. 98–119, and see the following chapter on the "World's Parliament," on pp. 120–136, (all with copious bibliography). As an interesting comparative comment, I would refer to Jonathan Garb, in his essay *"Modern Kabbalah As an Autonomous Domain of Research,"* Los Angeles, 2016, [Hebrew], English introduction p. XII, who writes of R. Abraham Isaac ha-Cohen Kook (1865–1935), the first Chief Rabbi of Israel, and one of the major Jewish thinkers of the early 20th century:

> In a striking text on modern "new forms of awareness," R. Kook describes globalization as rendering the mystical insight of world-wide interconnections as a manifestation of the unity of the human spirit, apprehensible to the masses.

And cf. ibid. p. 82 note 13.

38. See P.J. Saher, *Eastern Wisdom and Western Thought*, New York, 1970, part 2, for a reevaluation of Aldoux Huxley's depths of thought. The most preeminent exponents of "Perennialism" were René Guénon (1886–1951), Ananda Coomaraswamy (1877–1947), and Frithjof Schuon (1907–1998). This school should be distinguished from the so-called perennialism found in theosophy and some forms of neo-Hinduism. See, e.g., Harry Oldmeadow, "The Comparative Study of Eastern and Western Metaphysics: A Perennialist Perspective," *Sophia* 46, 2007, p. 54. It may also be noted that there were much earlier antecedents to this notion of a Perrenial philosophy. For already between the years 1642 and 1645 Herbert of Cherbury wrote his *De religione gertilium* (On the religion of the Heathens), published in 1663, as a supplement to his earlier *De Veritate* ("On Truth"), 1624, in which he set forth the idea of "a religion of pure reason and Suprahistorical Catholicity" He used the expression *notitia communis* and *consensus gentium* to characterize what he regarded as basic religious truths. The five constituent articles of faith are: The belief in one God; the duty to honour Him; His moral worship in the form of pius attitudes and virtuous conduct (*virtus cum pietate coniunctā*); the pain of sin; and the belief in an afterlife in which good and evil are rewarded. Christianity, according to him, was only one of a number of religions which had been nurtured on the fountainhead of the universal, pan-human revelation of reason. He offered a framework in which the reports about the religion and philosophy of Indra found their place. (See William Halbfass, *India and Europe: An Essay in Understanding*, New York, 1981, pp. 55; H. Scholz, *Die Religionsphilosophy des Herbert von Cherbury*, Giessen, 1914, p. 20ff.)

Halbfass, continues (ibid.) to document other earlier examples of this phenomenon, such as a "natural philosophy" of Raymond of Sabunde, Thomas More's concept of "rational religion" (*Utopia*, 1516). [Is it by chance that Lucas Cranach the Elder's *The Golden Age* was painted c. 1330 (Munich, Alte Pinakothe), and earlier Hieronymus Bosch's *Earthly Paradise*, the left panel of his Garden of *Earthly Delights*, (Madrid, Prado), was produced c 1495–1505?] Auqustinces Steuchus on *philosophia perennis* (*De perenni philosophia*, 1540, ed. B. Schmitt, New York, London, 1972); J. Böhm, *Mores, Leger, et Ritus Omnium gentium*, Lyon, 1520; Sebastian Franck, *Cosmographia, Weltbuch*, (Tübingen, 1534), etc. The whole of Halbfass' chapter, entitled "*Deis, Enlightement, and Early History*" (ibid. pp. 54–68) is a fascinating and rich description of this development, with, of course, a stress on the India element. It is doubtful if Huxley knew anything of all this.

39. See Ursula King, *Teilhard de Chardin and Eastern Religions*, Paulist Press, 1977.

40. J.H. Barrows, ed., *The World's Parliament of Religions*, 2 volumes, Chicago 1893. See also C. Lancaster, *The Incredible World's Parliament of Religions*, 1987. We should add to what we have written above (and below) the observations of Wilhelm Halbfass, in his *India and Europe: An Essay in Understanding*, New York, 1988, pp. 162–163:

> Since the end of the nineteenth century, Harvard University has developed a certain tradition of including India in the teaching of philosophy. W. James (1842–1910) often referred to Indian thought in his lectures and publications, although his attitude was not particularly sympathetic (D. Riepe, *The Philosophy of India and its Impact on American Thought*, Springfield 1970, pp. 77 et seq.), J. Royce (1855–1916), G. Santayana (1863–1952); and W.E. Hocking (1873–1966), who were also associated with Harvard, showed a remarkable interest in and appreciation of the Indian tradition, (ibid. pp. 82 et seq. Hocking attended the World Parliament of Religions in Chicago, and Leored Vivekananda). J.H. Woods (1864–1935), who taught in the Department of Philosophy at Harvard and served as its chairman, devoted his scholarly energies primarily to Indian thought. His most significant contribution was published in 1914 under the title *The Yoga System of Patanjali*; it is a translation of the *Yogasūtras* together with the commentaries of Vyāsa and Vācaspatimiśra. In his own way, Woods tried to continue the work of P. Deussen, who was one of his teachers (ibid. p. 91 et seq.).
>
> Numerous other representatives of academic philosophy in America have dealt with Indian ideas more or less explicitly, for instance W.B. Savery, E.A. Burtt, F.S.C. Northrop, Ch. Hartshorne, A. Danto, and – again at Harvard – R. Nozick (R. Nozick, *Philosophical Explanations*, Cambridge, Mass., 1981), *The*

Encyclopedia of Indian Philosophies, edited by K.H. Potter (vol. 2, Princeton, 1977), is primarily meant for Western philosophers taking an interest in Indian thought ("It is to be stressed that the work is addressed to philosophers primarily, and indologists secondarily," ibid. p. XII). Moreover, American universities, unlike European universities, employ a considerable number of Indian and other Asian scholars teaching Indian, Western and "comparative" philosophy, (such as J.N. Mohanty, D. Sinha, and K.N. Upadhyaya).

An increasing number of Western scholars try to do justice to Indian philosophy by treating it simply "as philosophy," regardless of its cultural and historical origin and context, and dealing with it in terms of truth and validity. In most cases, this amounts to an application of methods and criteria of modern logic and epistemology or, more specifically, of current Anglo-Saxon analytic philosophy. This perspective focuses on the technical, systematic achievements of Indian philosophy, and it tries to measure and clarify them by using the "most advanced" standards of modern Western thought. Almost inevitably, Indian thought appears as a more or less successful approximation to these standards.

Others expect from India alternatives to the Western attitudes and preoccupations. They hope to find human possibilities and dimensions of meaning which are less developed or even absent in the West. They look for synthesis, dialogue, mutual supplementation, even therapy. In this sense, F.S.C. Northrop invokes "the meeting of East and West," (Cf. P.S.C. Northrop, *The Meeting of East and West*, New York, 1946), W.E. Hocking says that "we need not only two but many eyes," and he refers to a hierarchy of three historic attitudes towards foreign cultures, specifically the East: 1. "This is strange and alien – avoid it." 2. "This is strange and alien – investigate it." 3. "This appears strange and alien – but it is human; it is therefore kindred to me and potentially my own – learn from it" (W.E. Hocking, "The Value of Comparative Study of Philosophy," apud *Philosophy – East and West*, ed. Ch. A. Moore, Princeton, 1944, pp. 1–11, especially p. 11). [This journal was established in 1951 by Charles A. Moore, as an outgrowth of the work of the East-West Philosopher's Conferences established in 1947, by the University of Hawaii's Dep. Of Philosophy. The conferences and the journal are active to the present day. D.S.]

Hocking's statements appeared in a volume edited by Ch. A. Moore (1901–1967), who was one of the most dedicated advocates of a "meeting" of Asia, specifically India, and the West. Since 1939, he organized "East West Philosophers' Conferences" at the University of Hawaii. He also founded the journal *Philosophy East* and *West* and edited *A Source Book in Indian Philosophy* (with S. Radhakrishnan; first published in 1957). Throughout his career, he tried to further the cause of "synthesis" and "comparison" and to naturalize Indian thought in American academic and scholarly life, (Riepe ibid. pp. 210 et seq.). Moore's unbroken optimism, his faith in the philosophical and "synthetic" potential of organized meetings, his unquestioning reliance on "personal representatives" of Eastern religious and philosophical traditions, his immunity from hermeneutical scruples – this in itself is a remarkable and symptomatic phenomenon. In a sense, Moore's efforts continued the tradition of the first "World Parliament of Religions" which was held in Chicago in 1893. (See Moore, *The Indian Mind*, Honolulu, 1967, p. VIII. Note also J. Needleman, The New Religions, Garden City, 1970; idem, *A Sense of Cosmos: The Encounter of Modern Science with Ancient Truth*, Garden City, 1975.)

41. On Ramakrishna and his influence, see what Swami Nirvedananda wrote in a chapter entitled "Sri Ramakrishna and Spiritual Renaissance," apud *The Cultural Heritage of India*, vol. 4, ed. Haridas Bhattaharyya, Calcutta 1956, pp. 653–728.

42. One of the leaders in this area was Frithjof Schuon (1907–1998); see, e.g., Harry Oldmeadow, *Frithof Schuon and the Perenial Philosophy*, 2010. Of interest is Huston Smith article "Is there a perennial philosophy?" in *Journal of American Academy of Religion* 55/3, 1987, pp. 553–566.

43. We might call attention to the rambling comments of Paul Bruton (1898–1981), the British theosophist and spiritualist (whose real name was Raphael Hurst), in vol. 10, of his *Notebooks*, entitled *The Orient: Its legacy to the West,* New York, 1987, pp. 4–6:

> 7
>
> Dr. Neumann's *Reden des Gotamos*, a translation into German of many of the Buddha's sayings, lay in manuscript for more than thirty years because it could not find a publisher. Then, in 1919, this lengthy volume was published in Berlin and immediately became a bestseller among the middle classes. Buddhism, with its highly ascetic outlook, its over-emphasis on suffering, its denial of earthly hope, could offer this ruined people only an inward peace at most. Yet the intellectual elements among them clutched at it in their despair. There was at the same time a wave of interest in Eastern wisdom and Oriental thought among the intelligentsia. But, when economic conditions improved in a few years, most of the interest fell away. Again when Rabindranath Tagore visited Europe in 1921, bringing, as he himself said, the spiritual message of the East to the West; it was in postwar Germany that he achieved a sensational success; it was in postwar Germany that his lectures and writing gained an appreciation tremendously greater than they gained anywhere else. During that year nearly a million copies of his translated books were sold, and there were always many more applicants than seats at his lectures.

8

The likelihood of increased interest in Indian yoga makes it more important than in prewar days to understand its real character and present condition.

9

These oriental teachings have filtered down from the first scholarly translations to the latest vulgarized easy-reading surface-views journalistically conveyed to mass readers in the West. It is only since the last war that this has gone on so quickly.

13

Yoga is on the way in the West to becoming respectable. What began with human curiosity is moving toward human acclamation.

17

It is interesting to note that, in the last periods of their lifetimes, poets like W.B. Yeats and James Stephans and psychoanalysts like Carl G. Jung and Karen Horney took to the serious study of Indian or Japanese-Indian philosophy.

18

We witness today much more interest in these subjects of mysticism, meditation, and Oriental religion not only among the general public, but also among college students and even among scientists who wish to investigate.

19

Appreciation of the teachings of Hinduism and its highest expression, the Advaita, is increasing in the West. And, thanks to T.M.P. Mahadevan, His Holiness' faithful, competent, and brilliant disciple, it is being expounded through books and articles with great accuracy and authoritativeness. Mahadevan enjoys the grace of His Holiness. [Shankaracharya of Kamakoti]

20

The continued effect of this infiltration of Eastern ideas on Western minds is now becoming visible, but we have not come farther than a fraction of the distance it will yet go.

And see, indeed, the whole first section on "Meetings of the East and West," pp. 3–60, for additional insights, such as (p. 26 no. 143):

We cannot shake our Greek heritage out of us, nor should we want to. The wisdom of the East must intertwine with the wisdom of the West.

CHAPTER 7

The Emergence of the Philosophy of Individual Rights

It has been said that the most controversial document of the whole Council was the *"Declaration of Religious Freedom: On the Right of the Person and of Communities to Social and Civil Freedom in Matters Religious."* And the source of the controversy was "because it raised with sharp emphasis the issue that lay continually below the surface of all conciliar debates – the issue of *development of doctrine*" [my emphasis, D.S.], (John Courtney Murray S.J., apud *The Documents of Vatican II*, edd. W.M. Abbot and J. Gallagher, American Press, 1966, p. 673). And it was for precisely this reason that Pope John Paul VI called this Declaration, "one of the major texts of the Council" (ibid. p. 674). Murray writes (ibid. p. 673):

> The notion of development, not the notion of religious freedom, was the real sticking-point for many of those who opposed the Declaration even to the end. The course of the development between the *Syllabus of Errors* (1864) and *Dignitatis Humanae Personae* (1965) still remains to be explained by theologians. But the Council formally sanctioned the validity of the development itself; and this was a doctrinal event of high importance for theological thought in many other areas.

He continues (ibid.):

> Moreover, taken in conjunction with the Pastoral Constitution on the Church in the Modern World, the Declaration opens a new era in the relations between the People of God and the People Temporal. A long-standing ambiguity has finally been cleared up. The Church does not deal with the secular order in terms of a double standard – freedom

for the Church when Catholics are a majority. The Declaration has opened the way toward new confidence in ecumenical relationships, and a new straightforwardness in relationships between the Church and the world.

And as he rightly points out (ibid.):

It can hardly be maintained that the Declaration is a mile-stone in human history – moral, political, or intellectual. The principle of religious freedom has long been recognized in constitutional law, to the point where even Marxist-Leninist political ideology is obliged to pay lip-service to it. In all honesty it must be admitted that the Church is late in acknowledging the validity of the principle.

Indeed this *Declaration* affirms a principle of wider import, namely that the dignity of man – the Jewish notion of *Kevod ha-Briyot* – consists in his responsible use of freedom. This is explicitly stated at the beginning of the *Declaration*:

1. A sense of the dignity of the human person has been impressing itself more and more deeply on the consciousness of contemporary man. [Cf. John XXIII, encyclical "Pacem in Terris," Apr.11, 1963: AAS 55 (1963), p. 279; ibid. p. 265; Pius XII, radio message, Dec. 24, 1944: AAS 37 (1945) p. 14, Pius XI, encyclical "*Mit Brennender Sorge,*" March 14, 1937; *AAS* 29 (1937), p. 160; Leo XIII, encyclical "Libertas Praestantissimum," June 20, 1888; *Acts of Leo XIII* (1888), pp. 237–238.] And the demand is increasingly made that men should act on their own judgment, enjoying and making use of a responsible freedom, not driven by coercion but motivated by a sense of duty. The demand is also made that constitutional limits should be set to the powers of government, in order that there may be no encroachment on the rightful freedom of the person and of associations.
    This demand for freedom in human society chiefly regards the quest for the values proper to the human spirit. It regards, in the first place, the free exercise of religion in society.

The editor (ibid. pp. 675–676 note 2) remarks, most significantly, to my mind, that:

Vatican II has been characterized by a sense of history, an awareness of the concrete world of fact, and a disposition to see in historical facts certain "signs of the times." Hence the Declaration begins by noting two facts. The first is the recent rise of man's personal consciousness, his sense of selfhood. This increasing awareness of the dignity of the human person marks a progress of civilization. It is the good which has come out of the great evil of totalitarianism, which brutally refuses to acknowledge the reality of man's selfhood. The second fact is the related rise of man's political consciousness, his aspiration to live as a free man under a limited government which puts no obstacles to his pursuit of truth and virtue, and, in particular, leaves him unhindered in the free exercise of religion in society. (Happily, the Declaration adopts the classical phrase which the Founding Fathers likewise adopted when framing the First Amendment in 1791.)

In thus acknowledging certain realities of contemporary life, the Declaration also establishes direct continuity with two basic doctrinal themes of John XXIII in the encyclical "Pacem in Terris:" the dignity of the human person and the consequent necessity of constitutional limits to the powers of government. The language of these opening sentences is, in fact, taken from this great encyclical.

It is this "sense of history and the legitimization of doctrinal development"[1] that lies at the core of *Nostra Aetate*'s "Copernican revolution," as it has been called.

And this acceptance of the paramount value of individual right, religious and civil, goes back to later nineteenth century philosophical thinking, namely the very considerable influence of the writing of John Stuart Mill (1806–1873), considered by many to have been "the most influential English-speaking philosopher of the nineteenth century," (according to the *Stanford Encyclopedia of Philosophy*). (Incidentally, he was god-father to Bertand Russel.) His essay "On Liberty," published in 1859, no doubt partially under the influence of John Locke's (1632–1704) three "Letters Concerning *Toleration* (1689–1692),"[2] had an enormous influence on subsequent political and religious thought. (He himself was an avowed atheist.)[3]

One may perhaps add the influence of the great English philosopher David Hume (1711–1776) and his views on religious toleration.[4] He too may have been influenced by Oriental philosophy.[5]

And just to give a taste of his thinking, we may consider the following brief quotation from "On Liberty:"

> First: the opinion which it is attempted to suppress by authority may possibly be true. Those who desire to suppress it, of course deny its truth; but they are not infallible. They have no authority to decide the question for all mankind, and exclude every other person from the means of judging. To refuse a hearing to an opinion, because they are sure that it is false, is to assume that *their* certainty is the same thing as *absolute* certainty. All silencing of discussion is an assumption of infallibility. Its condemnation may be allowed to rest on this common argument, not the worse for being common.
> (W.W. Norton's critical edition, ed. David Spitz, New York, 1975, p. 18.)

And, of course, earlier on, Thomas Paine wrote in his famous and influential pamphlet *Common Sense* (1776), in his "Continental Charter" that:

> ... the purpose of government is securing freedom and property to all men and above all the free *exercise of religion*, according to the dictates of conscience....[6] [My emphasis, D.S. Thomas Paine, *Common Sense*, ed. Isaac Kramnick, London, 1976, p. 97.][7]

There is over here the element of skepticism as to ultimate values, but not necessarily its "enthronement," (see Richard Walheim, "Without Doubt or Dogma, The Logic of Liberalism," The *Nation* 183, July 28, 1956, pp. 74–76).

On November 4, 1950, the European Convention on Human Rights which was signed at Rome, and came into force on September 3, 1953, stated (in act. 9. [1]) that:

> Everyone has the right to freedom of thought, conscience and religion; this right includes freedom to change his religion or belief, and freedom, either alone or in community with others and in public of private, to manifest his religion or belief, in worship, teaching, practice and observance.

(However, there are some jurisprudential differences made within these rights, between the so-called *forum internum*, or private sphere, and the *forum extertium*, the public sphere; (see Carolyn Evans, *Freedom of Religion under the European Convention on Human Rights*, Oxford, 2001, pp. 72 et seq.).

And here it should be noted that in 1951, Jacques Maritain, the most distinguished Catholic philosopher of his time, published his classic *Man and the State* (Charles R. Walgreen Foundation Lectures, Chicago, 1951), in which Chapter 10 (pp. 76–107), entitled "The Rights of Man," seeks to tackle the problems of radically different ideological positions reaching a practical agreement on this basic notion. Let us consider at least some of his discussions on the complexities of this issue. And though these are long passages they are of cardinal importance, most especially since they come from a Catholic thinker (pp. 76–79).

MEN MUTUALLY OPPOSED IN THEIR THEORETICAL CONCEPTIONS CAN COME TO A MERELY PRACTICAL AGREEMENT REGARDING A LIST OF HUMAN RIGHTS

Owing to the historical development of mankind, to ever widening crises in the modern world, and to the advance, however precarious, of moral conscience and reflection, men have today become aware, more fully than before, though still imperfectly, of a number of practical truths regarding their life in common upon which they can agree, but which are derived in the thought of each of them – depending upon their ideological allegiances, their philosophical and religious traditions, their cultural backgrounds and their historical experiences – from extremely different, or even basically opposed, theoretical conceptions. As the International Declaration of Rights published by the United Nations in 1948 showed very clearly, it is doubtless not easy but it is possible to establish a common formulation of such *practical conclusions*, or in other words, of the various rights possessed by man in his personal and social existence. Yet it would be quite futile to look for a common *rational justification* of these practical conclusions and these rights. If we did so, we would run the risk of imposing arbitrary dogmatism or of being stopped short by irreconcilable differences. The question raised at this point is that of the practical agreement among men who are theoretically opposed to one another.

Here we are confronted by the paradox that rational justifications are *indispensable* and at the same time *powerless* to create agreement among men. They are indispensable, because each of us believes instinctively in truth and only wishes to give his consent to what he has recognized as true and rationally valid. Yet rational justifications are powerless to create agreement among men, because they are basically different, even opposed to each other; and is this surprising? The problems raised by rational justifications are difficult, and the philosophical traditions in which those justifications originate have been in opposition for a long time.

He continues to analyze the complex paradox he is dealing with as follows:

During one of the meetings of the French National Commission of UNESCO at which the Rights of Man were being discussed, someone was astonished that certain proponents of violently opposed ideologies had agreed on the draft of a list of rights. Yes, they replied, we agree on these rights, *providing we are not asked why*. With the "why," the dispute begins.

The subject of the Rights of Man provides us with an eminent example of the situation that I tried to describe in an address to the second International Conference of UNESCO, from which I take the liberty of quoting a few passages. "How," I asked, "is an agreement conceivable among men assembled for the purpose of jointly accomplishing a task dealing with the future of the mind, who come from the four corners of the earth and who belong not only to different cultures and civilizations, but to different spiritual families and antagonistic schools of thought? Since the aim of UNESCO is a practical aim, agreement among its members can be spontaneously achieved, not on common speculative notions, but on common practical notions, not on the affirmation of the same conception of the world, man, and knowledge, but on the affirmation of the same set of convictions concerning action. This is doubtless very little, it is the last refuge of intellectual agreement among men. It is, however, enough to undertake a great work; and it would mean a great deal to become aware of this body of common practical convictions."

"I should like to note here that the word *ideology* and the word *principle* can be understood in two very different ways. I have just said that the present state of intellectual division among men does not permit agreement on a common *speculative* ideology, nor on common *explanatory* principles. However, when it concerns, on the contrary, the basic *practical* ideology and the basic principles of *action* implicitly recognized today, in a vital if not a formulated manner, by the consciousness of free peoples, this happens to constitute *grosso modo* a sort of common residue, a sort of unwritten common law, at the point of practical convergence of extremely different theoretical ideologies and spiritual traditions. To understand that, it is sufficient to distinguish properly between the rational justifications, inseparable from the spiritual dynamism of a philosophical doctrine or religious faith, and the practical conclusions which, separately justified for each, are, for all, analogically common principles of action. *I am fully convinced that my way of justifying the belief in the rights of man and the ideal of freedom, equality, and fraternity is the only one which is solidly based on truth. That does not prevent me from agreeing on these practical tenets with those who are convinced that their way of justifying them, entirely different from mine or even opposed to mine in its theoretical dynamism, is likewise the only one that is based on truth.* Assuming they both believe in the democratic charter, a Christian and a rationalist will, nevertheless, give justifications that are incompatible with each other, to which their souls, their minds, and their blood are committed, and about these justifications they will fight. And God keep me from saying that it is not important to know which of the two is right! That is essentially important. They remain, however, in agreement on the practical affirmation of that charter, and they can formulate together common principles of action." (Mexico City, November 1947.) [My emphasis, D.S.]

(The rest of the chapter is well worth studying, but is beyond the framework of this study.)

And these expressions of the philosophy of individual rights led to what took place on November 20, 1963, only two years before the publication of *Nostra Aetate*, when the General Assembly of the United Nations adopted and proclaimed unanimously[8] a *Declaration on the Elimination of All Forms of Racial Discrimination*. The Declaration was first drafted by the Sub-Commission on the Prevention of Discrimination and Protection of Minorities and the text which it prepared, and was later amended by the Commission on Human Rights and the Third Committee. A final amendment was introduced in the Assembly itself. One of the Articles to which considerable time and discussion were devoted was the controversial Article 9 of the Declaration, which states:

> 1. All propaganda and organizations based on ideas or theories of the superiority of one race or group of persons of one color or ethnic origin with a view to justifying or promoting racial discrimination in any form shall be severely condemned.
> 2. All incitement to or acts of violence, whether by individuals or organizations, against any race or group of persons of another color or ethnic origin shall be considered an offense against society and punishable under law.
> 3. In order to put into effect the purposes and principles of the present Declaration, all States shall take immediate and positive measures, including legislative and other measures, to prosecute and/or outlaw organizations which promote or incite to racial discrimination or incite to or use violence for the purposes of discrimination based on race, color or ethnic origin.[9]

And let us not forget the heroic efforts in far-off America of Martin Luther King Jr. (1920–1968) and his colleagues, who fought during the years so valiantly to combat racial inequality. Perhaps the pinnacle of his career was his world-famous oration at the March on Washington on August 28, 1963, known widely as "I have a dream." He ended his heart-stirring peroration with the words:

> ... Let freedom ring from every hill and Molehill of Mississippi. From every mountainside, let transforming.
>
> And when this happens, when we allow freedom to ring from every village and every hamlet, from every state and every city, we will be able to speed up the day when all of God's children, black men and white men, Jews and Gentiles, Protestants and Catholics, will be able to join hands and sing in the words of the old Negro spiritual "Free at last! Free at last! Thank God the Almighty, we are free at last."

The speech had a tremendous public impact, so much so that *Time Magazine* named him as "Man of the Year" for 1963.

And on October 14, 1964, he received the Nobel Prize for his efforts in combating racial inequality, being the youngest person ever awarded this prize.

He, of course, was concerned primarily with the rights of the American Negro. But, in effect, his words resonated to encompass all forms of racial discrimination.

Actually, already as far back as 1948, The World Jewish Congress as a whole had taken a stand on the matter of anti-racialism and freedom of human rights, obviously will an emphasis on combating anti-Semitism. Its second Plenary Assembly, meeting in Montreux, Switzerland, had adopted a resolution in which, inter alia, the Congress:

> Reminds all governments and peoples of the world of the recognized and established facts:
>
> That racialism and anti-Semitism are everywhere the forerunners of Fascism;
>
> That the preaching of these doctrines is being used by the foes of democracy as one of the main instruments to destroy democracy;
>
> That racial and anti-Semitic propaganda inevitably undermines respect of human rights and fundamental freedoms by fostering the spirit of intolerance and hatred which must endanger the security of all minority groups and friendship between nations; ...
>
> That the efficacy of a legislative program for combating such subversive movements has been amply proven.
>
> The Congress, therefore, appeals to all governments and nations of the world to outlaw racialism and anti-Semitism, especially by:
>
> Making incitement to hatred against racial and religious groups a punishable offense under domestic law;
>
> Prohibiting the misuse of freedom of speech, press or assembly for the spreading of racialism and anti-Semitism by banning the teaching of racialism and anti-Semitism and by examining the text-books of all educational institutions with this purpose in view. ...

This stand of the World Jewish Congress was ratified by the Special European Conference on Anti-Semitism and the Nazi-Fascist Revival, convened in London by the European Executive of the World Jewish Congress, in December, 1962.[10]

The conference gave its fullest support to the World Jewish Congress

> In its policy and action to secure the adoption, by the United Nations, of international Covenants obliging Member States to make legally effective the human rights and fundamental freedoms laid down in the governing principles of the UN Charter and set out in the Universal Declaration of Human Rights and to render illegal and punishable all acts and activities designed to incite racial hatred, violence, discrimination and prejudice.

In point of fact, the World Jewish Congress was instrumental in the adoption of a U.N. resolution condemning anti-Semitism a few years ago, at the time of the world-wide outbreak of swastika smearings and other racist manifestations.

And we should also take account of the fact that already in 1940 H.G. Wells had written a highly influential tract on the Rights of Man, which set the groundwork for the 1948 Universal Declaration of Human Rights, though it was only adopted by the United Nations' General Assembly on December 16, 1966. And this was before the 1954 international Covenant on Civil and Political Rights (ICCPR). It formed a part of *The International Bill of Human Rights* along with *The International Covenant on Economic and Social Rights* (*ICESCR*) and *The Universal Declaration of Human Rights* (*UDHR*), which later had been adopted on December 10, 1948. Part 3 article 18 of the *ICCPR* included freedom of "thought, conscience and religion."[11]

Indeed, David Berger already pointed this out a decade and a half ago (in his article "From Crusades to Blood Libels to Expulsions: Some New Approaches to Medieval Antisemitism," *The Second Victor J. Selmanowitz Memorial Lecture*, Touro College Graduate School of Jewish Studies, New York, 1997, 5–6, reprinted in David Berger, *Persecution, Polemic, and Dialogue: Essays in Jewish-Christian Relations* (Boston: University Studies Press, 2010), 15–39, at 19–20, where he wrote:

> Vatican II was convened in a post-colonial age marked by a new regard for self-determination and a new respect for cultural diversity – as well as minority rights. Exclusivist claims did not sit well in this environment, and harsh punishment, even divine punishment, for religious dissent surely did not. A telling expression of the inner struggle triggered by the clash of this liberal, humanistic sensibility with a narrower, more forbidding tradition was formulated by a playwright hostile to

Catholicism whose bitter work, *Sister Mary Ignatius Explains It All To You*, nonetheless has its very funny moments. Sister Mary, an old-fashioned nun teaching in the aftermath of Vatican II, defines "limbo" for her classroom/audience. If I remember correctly, she displays a picture of a baby trapped behind the bars of a crib and declares, "Limbo is where unbaptized children went before the Ecumenical Council."

The historical and theological precision of this statement may leave something to be desired, but it brilliantly captures a central feature of the ideological atmosphere of the Council, which had nothing to do with Jews and next to nothing to do with the Holocaust. It was this spirit that animated the adoption of a more positive attitude toward Islam and the religions of the East, the assertion that salvation is possible outside the Church – and *Nostra Aetate, No. 4*. One who locates the fundamental impetus of the historic declaration of the Jews in the specifics of the Jewish-Catholic relationship loses sight of the larger process and misses the key point.

Later he somewhat modified this statement by saying that:

On reflection, the assertion that this larger reassessment had "next to nothing to do with the Holocaust" was too strong, perhaps much too strong, since even the broader transformation in the Church and beyond may well have been influenced by the Holocaust, but the basic point, I think, remains valid. We are dealing with a watershed in the history of the Church that far transcends the Jewish question, and the reassessment of that question is a part of that larger phenomenon rather than an essentially independent development.[12]

Endnotes to Chapter 7

1. In note 4, on pp. 677–678 he further emphasizes this point:

> In no other conciliar document is it so explicitly stated that the intention of
> the council is to "develop" Catholic doctrine. This is significant, since it is
> an avowal that the tradition of the Church is a tradition of progress in under-
> standing the truth. The basic truth here is the concept of the "citizen" as stated
> by Pius XII – the man who "feels within himself a consciousness of his own
> personality, of his duties, and of his rights, joined with a respect for the freedom
> of others" (Christmas Discourse, 1945). This conception, as the Declaration
> will say, is deeply rooted both in the Christian tradition and in the tradition
> of reason. In recent times, it was Leo XIII (in "Rerum Novarum") who first
> began to move it, as it were, to the forefront of Catholic social teaching. Pius
> XII continued this development, drawing out the implications of the dignity of
> man in terms of his duties and rights. He also brought forward the correlative
> truth that the primary function of government is to acknowledge, protect,
> vindicate, and facilitate the exercise of the rights of man. Both of these truths
> were taken up by John XXIII, chiefly in "Pacem in Terris," in which they are
> given an almost systematic form of statement.
>
> However, in regard to the right of man to religious freedom, even "Pacem in
> Terris," is unclear and even ambiguous. What precisely does religious freedom
> mean? Does it find place among the inalienable rights of man? These are the
> questions to which, for the first time, the Church gives an unmistakably clear
> and entirely unambiguous answer. The council brings forth out of the treasury
> of truth a doctrine that is at once new and also in harmony with traditional
> teaching.

This issue of "history" or "event" versus "spirit," and what has been termed
"Doctrinal Discontinuity" has recently been discussed in depth by Gavin D'Costa,
in his *Vatican II: Catholic Doctrines on Jews and Muslims*, Oxford 2014 pp. 19 et seq.

2. Locke's principle source in the area of Church and Slate is the Anglican . . . of
the previous century, Richard Hooker (1554–1600). Against the Puritan desire for
a single-faith society ruled by the righteous, Hooker argued for a spirit of charity
and reciprocity between people of different religious persuasions and against any

attempt to establish the Kingdom of God on earth in a righteous parliament run by Puritans. He wrote:

> My desire therefore to be loved by my equals in nature, as much as possible may be, *imposeth upon me a natural duty of bearing to . . . fully like affections*, from which relations of equality between ourselves and them, that are as ourselves, what several rules and canons, natural reason hath drawn for direction of life, no man is ignorant. (*Of the Laws of Ecclasiastical Polity*, Book 1, chapter 8, cited by Locke, *Second Treatise of Government* 2:5).

See Roger Ruston, "Religious truths and Human Coexistence," apud "*Does God Believe in Human Rights? Essays on Religion and Human Rights*," edd. N. Ghanea, A Stephans, R. Walden, Leiden Boston, 2007, p. 38.

3. See Linda G. Raeder, "*Spirit of the Age," John Stuart Mill and the Religion of Humanity*, University of Missouri Press, 2002. See also Isaiah Berlin's essay, "John Stuart Mill and the End of Life," being the forth lecture of his "Five Lectures on Liberty," apud *Liberty: Isaiah Berlin*, ed. Henry Hardy, Oxford 1969, pp. 218–259. We may further note that Locke's philosophy gained little notice until the end of the eighteenth and the beginning of the nineteenth centuries. See Alister McGrath, *History and Theology: The Making of Modern Identity*, Oxford 1998, pp. 214–215. As an incidental point of interest, Mill's father James, wrote a highly successful three volume *History of British India* 1818, and eventually directed India House. He was never actually in India, and was a severe critic of Indian culture.

These philosophical positions go back to the renaissance, as indicated above, and to the influence of the writings of Thomas Hobbes (1588–1679), Voltaire (1694–1778) and Jean Jacque Rousseau (1712–1774). See W.H. Contes, H.V. White and J.S. Schapiro, *The Emergence of Liberal Humanism: An Intellectual History of Western Europe*, vol. 1, New York, 1966, Chapter 3, entitled "The New Religious Outlook: Toleration and Intellectual Freedom," pp. 67–90; and chapter 9, entitled "Intellectual and Religious Freedom," pp. 246–274, for a fine analysis of the early contributory factors. We should also be cognizant of the enormous adulation for Thomas Jefferson in the early post World War II era, an adulation cultivated by Franklin D. Roosevelt. Roosevelt on July 4, 1936, the 160th anniversary of *The Declaration of Independence*, had already cited the famous Jefferson quote, the one most prominently engraved on the Jefferson Memorial:

> I have sworn on the altar of God eternal hostility against any force of tyranny over the mind of man.

And though in the context of Roosevelt's speech this was intended to address the dangers of dictatorial governments etc., it still resonated of intellectual freedom. And yet another of Jefferson's famous proverbs was:

All men are created equal, regardless of race creed, or colour, and whether a man be Jew or Gentile, he may think what he deems fit.

(Mika Edelstein, Representative of Manhattan's Lower East Side, quoted this statement in the House of Representatives on June 6, 1941, responding to Representative John E. Rankin, the stern isolationist. Shortly after leaving the hall of the house, he slumped dead of a heart attack, *Time Magazine* June 16, 1941, p. 16.)

4. See Richard H. Dees, "'The Paradoxical Principle and Cartulary Practice:' Hume on Toleration," *Hume Studies* 31/1, 2005, pp. 145–164. This phrase comes from *Hume's History of England* 1786, vol. 4, p. 168. See also Henry A.F. Kamen, *The Rise of Toleration*, New York, 1967, p. 217.

5. See Alison Gopnik, "Could Hume Have Known Buddhism? Charles François Dolu, the Royal College of La Flèch, and the Global Jesuit Network," *Hume Studies* 35/1–2, 2009, pp. 5–28.

6. However, it has been pointed out (*The Documents of Vatican II*, edd. W.M. Abbot and J. Gallagher, American Press 1966, p. 679 note 5) that:

It is to be noted that the word "conscience," found in the Latin text, is used in its generic sense, sanctioned by usage, of "beliefs," "convictions," "persuasions." Hence the unbeliever or atheist makes with equal right this claim to immunity from coercion in religious matters. It is further to be noted that, in assigning a negative content to the right to religious freedom (that is, in making it formally a "freedom from" and not a "freedom for"), the Declaration is in harmony with the sense of the First Amendment to the American Constitution. In guaranteeing the free exercise of religion, the First Amendment guarantees to the American citizen immunity from all coercion in matters religious. Neither the Declaration nor the American Constitution affirms that a man has a right to believe what is false or to do what is wrong. This would be moral nonsense. Neither error nor evil can be the object of a right, only what is true and good. It is, however, true and good that a man should enjoy freedom from coercion in matters religious.

This brings up the second question, concerning the foundation of the right. The reason why every man may claim immunity from coercion in matters religious is precisely his inalienable dignity as a human person. Surely, in matters religious, if anywhere, the free human person is required and entitled to act on his own judgment and to assume personal responsibility for his action or omission. A man's religious decisions, or his decision against religion, are inescapably his own. No one else can make them for him or compel him to make this decision or that, or restrain him from putting his decisions into practice, privately or publicly, alone or in company with others. In all these cases, the dignity of man would be diminished because of the denial to him of that inalienable responsibility for his own decisions and actions which is the essential counterpart of his freedom.

It is worth noting that the Declaration does not base the right to the free exercise of religion on "freedom of conscience." Nowhere does this phrase occur. And the declaration nowhere lends its authority to the theory for which the phrase frequently stands, namely, that I have the right to do what my conscience tells me to do, implies because my conscience tells me to do it. This is a perilous theory. Its particular peril is subjectivism-the notion that, in the end, it is my conscience, and not the objective truth, which determines what is right or wrong, true or false.

7. Compare Moses Mendelsohn's 1783 demand for the right to be different, in his *Jerusalem* (cited from Moses Mendelsohn *Jerusalem, or, on Religious Power and Judaism*, transl. Alan Arkush, with introduction and commentary by Alexander Altman, Hanover, 1983, pp. 138–139, and cf. *The Jew in the Modern World: A Documentary History*, 3rd edition, edd. Paul Mendes-Flohr Jehuda Reinharz, New York, Oxford, 2011, p. 73):

> Brothers, if you care for true piety, let us not feign agreement where diversity is evidently the plan and purpose of Providence. None of us thinks and feels exactly like his fellow man; why then do we wish to deceive each other with delusive words? We already do this, unfortunately, in our daily intercourse, in our conversations, which are of no particular importance, why then also in matters that have to do with our temporal and eternal welfare, our whole destiny? Why should we make ourselves unrecognizable to each other in the most important concerns of our life by masquerading, since God has stamped everyone, not without reason, with his own facial features? Does this not amount to doing our very best to resist Providence, to frustrate, if it be possible, the purpose of creation? Is this not deliberately to contravene our calling, our destiny in this life and the next – Rulers of the earth! If it be permitted to an insignificant fellow inhabitant thereof to lift up his voice to you: do not trust the counselors who wish to mislead you by smooth words to so harmful an undertaking. They are either blind themselves, and do not see the enemy of mankind lurking in the ambush, or they seek to blind you. Our noblest treasure, the liberty to think, will be forfeited if you listen to them. For the sake of your felicity and ours *a union of faiths is not tolerance*; it is diametrically *opposed to true tolerance*! For the sake of your felicity and ours, do not use your powerful authority to transform some *eternal truth*, without which *civil society can exist, into a law, some religious opinion*, which is a matter of indifference to the state, *into an ordinance of the land*! Pay heed to the right conduct of men; upon this

bring to bear the tribunal of wise laws, *and leave us thought and speech which the Father of us all assigned to us as an inalienable heritage and granted to us as an immutable right* . . . At least pave the way for a happy posterity toward that height of culture toward that *universal tolerance of man* for which reason still sighs in vain! Reward and punish no doctrine, tempt and bribe no one to adopt any religious opinion! Let everyone be permitted to speak as he thinks, to invoke God after his own manner or that of his fathers, and to seek eternal salvation where he thinks he may find it, as long as he does not disturb public felicity and acts honestly toward the civil laws toward you and his citizens. Let no one in your states be a searcher of hearts and a judge of thoughts, let no one assume a right that the Omniscient has reserved to himself alone! If we render unto *Caesar* what is *Caesar's*, then do you yourselves render unto *God what is God's! Love truth! Love peace!*

And just a short while before that Mendelssohn's friend, Gotthold Ephraim Lessing (1729–1781), published his *Nathan the Wise* in 1779 (transl. Williams Jacks, Glasgow 1894), in which he gives his beautiful "Parable of Toleration" (act 3 scene 7), which I cannot refrain from quoting in full. (The play is based on the parable of the three rings in Giovanni Boccaccio's *Decamaron* (composed between 1348–1353). The play presents Judaism, Christianity and Islam as three sons of a benevolent father who gave each an identical ring, and although each claims that his alone is authentic, Nathan the Jew is made spokesman for the ideals of the Enlightenment: tolerance, brotherhood and love of Humanity. It is thought that Lessing modeled Nathan after his good friend Mendelsohnn:

> NATHAN: In days of yore a man lived in the East, who owned a ring of marvelous worth, given to him by a hand beloved. The stone was opal, and shed a hundred lovely rays. But mostly it possessed the secret power to make the owner loved of God and man, if he but wore it in this faith and confidence. What wonder then that this man in the East ne'er from his finger took the ring. *And so arranged it should forever with his house remain.* Namely, thus: He bequeathed it to the most beloved of his sons, firmly prescribing that he in turn should leave it to the dearest of his sons; And always thus the dearest, without respect to birth, became the head and chieftain of the house by virtue of the ring alone. You understand me, Sultan?
>
> SALADIN: I understand, proceed.
>
> NATHAN: The ring, descending from son to son, came to the father of three sons at last. All three of whom obeyed him equally, and all of whom he therefore loved alike. From time to time indeed, now one seemed worthiest of the ring and now another, now the third. Just as it happened one or other with him were alone, and his o'erflowing heart was not divided with the other two, and so to each one of the three he gave the promise – in pious

192

weakness alone – he should possess this wondrous ring. This then went on as long as it could, but then at last it came to dying, which brings the father into sore perplexity. It pains him much to practice such deceit upon two sons who rested so upon his word. What can be done? In secret he seeks out a skillful artist, and from him orders two other rings, just to the pattern of his own, and urges him to spare neither pains nor gold, to make a perfect match. The artist so succeeded in his task, that, when he brought the jewels home, the father even failed to tell which was the pattern ring. Now, glad and joyous, he calls his sons – but separately of course – gives each a special blessing with his ring, and died. You hear me, Sultan?

SALADIN ; (*Somewhat moved, turns from him*)

I hear, I hear. But pray get ended with your tale. You soon will be?

NATHAN: I'm at the end, for what follows is self-understood. Scarce was the father dead, when each one with his ring appears, claiming each the leadership of the house. Inspections, quarrelling and complaints ensue, but all in vain, the veritable ring was not distinguishable. –

(After a pause, during which he expects the Sultan's answer) Almost as indistinguishable as to us, is now – the true religion.

SALADIN: What? Is that meant as answer to my question?

NATHAN: This meant but to excuse myself, because I lack the boldness to discriminate between the rings, which the father by express intent had made so that they might not be distinguished.

SALADIN: The rings! Don't play with me. I thought the faiths which I have named were easily distinguishable, even to their raiment, even to meat and drink.

NATHAN: But not yet as regards their proofs, for do not all rest upon history, written or traditional? And history can also be accepted only on faith and trust. Is it not so? Now, whose faith and confidence do we least misdoubt? That of our relatives? Of those whose flesh and blood we ate, of those who from our childhood have lavished on us proofs of love, who ne'er deceived us, unless 'twere wholesome for us so? How can I place less faith in my forefathers than in yours? Or the reverse? Can I desire of you to load your ancestors with lies, so that you contradict not mine? Or the reverse? And to the Christian the same applies.

SALADIN: By the living God, the man is right, I must be dumb.

NATHAN: Let us return unto our rings. As said, the sons accused each other, and each one swore before the judge he had received his ring directly from his father's hand – which was quite true – and that, indeed, after having long his promise held to enjoy eventually the ring's prerogative, which was no less the truth. Each one insisted that it was impossible his father could play false with him, and ere he could suspect so dear and true a father, he

193

was compelled, howe'er inclined to think the best of them, to accuse his brothers of this treacherous act, to unmask the traitors, and avenge himself.

SALADIN: Well, and the judge? I'm curious to hear what you will give the judge to say. Go on.

NATHAN: The judge said this; produce your father here at once, or I'll dismiss you from this court. Think you I'm here but to solve riddles? Or would you wait till the true ring itself will speak? But stop, I've just been told that the right ring contains the wondrous gift to make its wearer beloved, agreeable alike to God and man. That must decide, for the false rings will not have the power. Now which one do the other two love most? Come, speak out; you're silent? Do the rings work only backwards and not outwardly? Does each one love himself the best? Then you're all three deceived deceivers; none of your rings are genuine. The genuine ring is no doubt lost. To hide the loss and to supply its place the father ordered the other three.

SALADIN: Splendid, splendid!

NATHAN: The judge went further on to say: If you will have my judgment, not my advice, then go. But my advice is this: You take the matter as it stands. If each one had his ring straight from his father, so let each believe his ring the true one. T'is possible your father would no longer tolerate the tyranny of this one ring in his family, and surely loved you *all – and all* alike. And that he would not two oppress by favouring the third. Now then, let each one emulate in affection untouched by prejudice. Let each one strive to gain the prize of proving by results the virtue of his ring, and aid its powers with gentleness and heartiest friendliness, with benevolence and true devotedness to God; and if the virtue of the ring will then have proved itself among your children's children, I summon them to appear again before this judgment seat, after a thousand thousand years. Here then will sit a judge more wise than I, who will pronounce, Go you. So said the modest judge.

SALADIN: God, oh God!

NATHAN: Saladin, if no you feel yourself to be that promised sage –

SALADIN: (*Rushes to him and seizes his hand, which to the end he does not let go*) I, dust? I, nothing? Oh God!

NATHAN: What ails thee, Sultan?

SALADIN: Nathan, dear Nathan, your Jude's thousand thousand years have not yet fled, his judgment seat's not become mine. Go, Go, but be my friend.

8. South Africa did not participate in the voting of the draft resolution, because of the fact that South African policy is specifically singled out in the document for condemnation. (Statement of the South African representative to the U.N. November 10, 1963.)

Here we should also note the contribution of René Cassin to the subject of human rights. Already on the 4th December 1948 he presented to the plenary session of the General Assembly of the United Nations the *Universal Declaration of Human Rights*. See Jay Winter and Antoine Prost, *René Cassin and Human Rights: From the Great War to the Universal Declaration*, Cambridge 2013, (original French edition appeared in 2011).

9. This article was the subject of considerable controversy in that it would appear to curtail certain human rights, and that "the mere expression of views and opinions is not punishable, however much we may dislike or condemn them." (Mr. Ralph Enckell, representative of Finland, on behalf of Scandinavian delegation.) See on all of the above, Natan Lerner, *The Crime of Incitement to Group Hatred.* World Jewish Congress, New York, published in March 1965, just seven months before *Nostra Aetate* was issued on 28 October 1965. For a further discussion of the UN *Declaration* and its precursors, see Lerner pass.

10. For a full report on the proceedings of the Conference, see *World Jewry*, London, January–February, 1963. We should also take account of Gerhart M. Riegner's contribution in the area of universal individual rights and civil liberties. See his *Ne Jamais Désespérer*, Paris, 1998, pp. 243–249.

11. Article 18 reads as follows:
1. Everyone shall have the right to freedom of thought, conscience and religion. This right shall include freedom to have or to adopt a religion or belief of his choice, and freedom, either individually or in community with others and in public or private, to manifest his religion or belief in worship, observance, practice and teaching.
2. No one shall be subject to coercion which would impair his freedom to have or adopt a religion or belief of his choice.
3. Freedom to manifest one's religion or beliefs may be subject only to such limitations as prescribed by law and are necessary to protect public safety, order, health, or morals as fundamental rights and freedoms of others.

There is a very considerable literature on human rights, and on the specific declarations. Javaid Rehmon, in his article "Conflicting Values or Misplaced Interpretations?" apud *"Does God Believe in Human Rights?"* edd. N. Ghanea, A. Stephans and R. Walden, Leiden Boston, 2007, p. 71, writes:

> If the jurisprudential debate is bewildering and complex, an agreement on the substance of human rights has proved impossible. Diversity, dissensions from religious and cultural relativism continually rupture the finely crafted fabric of international human rights law. . . .

We are there referred (note 15) to the following studies on the subject:

See E. Brems, *Human Rights: Universality and Diversity* (The Hague: Kluwer Law International, 2001); A.D. Renteln, *International Human Rights: Universalism versus Relativism* (Newbury Park: Sage Publications, 1990); A.D. Renteln, "The Unanswered Challenge of Relativism and Consequences of Human Rights," *Human Rights Quarterly*, 7 (1985), 514; H. Gros-Espiell, "The Evolving Concept of Human Rights: Western, Socialist and Third World Approaches" in B.G. Ramcharan (ed.), *Human Rights: Thirty Years after the Universal Declaration: Commemorative Volume on the Occasion of the Thirtieth Anniversary of the Universal Declaration of Human Rights* (The Hague: Martinus Nijhoff Publishers, 1979), 41–65; D. Donoho, "Relativism Versus Universalism in Human Rights: The Search for Meaningful Standards," *Stanford Law Journal*, 27 (1991) 345; A. Eide, "Making Human Rights Universal: Unfinished Business," *Nordic Journal of Human Rights*, 6 (1988), 51; J. Donnelly, "Cultural Relativism and Universal Human Rights," *Human Rights Quarterly*, 5 (1984), 40b M.D. Evans, "Human Rights and the Universality Debate," in R. O'Dair and A. Lewis (eds), above n. 2, 205–26.

Here again, this is too vast and specialized a subject to be treated here. But the aforementioned book deals with several significant aspects of the human rights issue, and is a fine starting point.

See also the useful pamphlet by Avishalom Westreich, entitled *Human Rights, Jewish Law, and Humankind*, Israel Democracy Institute, 2012, in Hebrew.

And as to specifically Jewish civil rights, see Raphael Mahler, *Jewish Emancipation: A Selection of Documents*, New York, 1941, pass. See, for example, p. 51 no. 35 a document from June 19, 1848, granting complete religious-equality in Sardinia:

> We, by virtue of the authority delegated in us, have ordered and hereby order as follows:
> Differences of religion constitute no exception for the enjoyment of civil and political rights and to admissibility to civil and military ports.

And earlier in no. 84, from March 29 of that same year:

> The Israelites of the Kingdom [of Sardinia] shall enjoy from the date of these presents all civil rights and the capacity to obtain academic degrees, without any innovations with regard to the exercise of their cult and the school directed by them.

These rulings derive from the famous *French Declaration of the Rights of Man and of the Citizen* from 26 August 1789, which included the sentence:

> No person shall be molested for his opinions, even such as are religious, provided that the manifestations of these opinions does not disturb the public order by the law (ibid. p. 25).

And, most ironically (?), on December 27, 1848, the law concerning the fundamental rights of the German people was passed in the *Reich* (*!*), which included (Art. 5 sect.14):

> Every German has full freedom of faith and conscience. Nobody shall be forced to disclose his religious creed (ibid. pp. 48–49).

See further *Religious Diversity and Human Rights*, edd. Irene Bloom, J. Paul Martin, and Wayne L. Proudfoot, New York, 1996; Paul M. Taylor, *Freedom of Religion: UN and European Human Rights Law and Practice*, Cambridge, 2006. And see the very interesting study of Robert Erlewine, *Monotheism and Tolerance: Recovering a Religion of Reason*, Bloomington and Indianapolis, 2010, where he analyzes the views of Mendelssohn, Kant and Hermann Cohen, finding in them a way to universal tolerance. (But his analysis of Cohen has been seen to be somewhat flawed.)

12. See his article in *A Jubilee for All Time: The Copernican Revolution in Jewish-Christian Relations*, ed. Gilbert S. Rosenthal, Eugene, Oregon 2015, pp. 233–234, article entitled "*Nostra Aetate* after Fifty Years: Covenant and Election Of Israel." The whole article (pp. 233–247) merits careful study. Berger again visited this issue in his article in *Tablet*, Dec.15, 2015, entitled "Vatican II at 50: Assessing the impact of 'Nostra Aetate' on Jewish-Christian Relations."

CHAPTER 8

Disparate Elements Forming the Theological Basis for *Nostra Aetate*

So there appears to have been a confluence of a variety of disparate elements that come together to cultivate a basis for the theological foundation of *Nostra Aetate*: The penetration of Eastern thought and culture into the West, emergence of the primary rights of the individual and the attendant justification of the morality of tolerance, and international legislation on the issue of racial discrimination, anti-Semitism and its horrific expression in the holocaust, the subsequent feelings of guilt among many Christians, and also the establishment of the State of Israel in 1948 – all the above and no doubt many others,[1] formed the backdrop against which the drama of *Nostra Aetate* was configured and scripted.

I am not suggesting that all these elements were consciously in the minds of those who crafted this revolutionary document, but only that they contributed to a general atmosphere, sometimes called "the spirit of the age"[2] that was conductive to such "new thinking."[3]

However, it should be noted that this document did also relate directly to Hinduism and Buddhism, evidence of the drafters' clear awareness of these developments.[4]

In much the same way as Thomas Paine wrote:

> Our style and manner of thinking have undergone a revolution. We see with our eyes; we hear with our ears; and we think with our thoughts, [other] than we formally used. [Tom Paine, "Letters to Abbé Raynal on the Affairs of North America," in *Writings of Thomas Paine*, ed. M.D. Conway and C. Putman, New York, 1906, vol. 2, p. 105.]

Or what Owen Chadwick, in his *The Secularization of the European Mind in the Nineteenth Century*, Cambridge, 1975, p. 192, called "the historical consciousness," which was "a new kind of consciousness ... distinguishable from [consciously] amassing new information – rather as 'scientific method' or 'scientific consciousness' might be alleged to have become a habit of mind in persons who knew no science."

Indeed, this was differently expressed by Pietro Pavan, in his essay on the *Declaration on Religious Freedom*.[5] There, in his *Commentary to Article 1*, he writes on the first part that it:

> Emphasizes a characteristic phenomenon of modern times. Men are becoming increasingly conscious of their own personal dignity, which shows itself as a claim to greater freedom, regarded as an exercise of responsibility. Such a claim is particularly evident in the sphere of intellectual and spiritual values, especially also in the religious sphere. This is, moreover, also a claim concerning the function and organization of public authorities, which may legitimately be exercised only within legally defined limits. Hence these must be laid down as clearly as possible in order to guarantee the necessary space for the freedom of the citizens.
>
> In such a historical situation there will be a new conception of religious freedom: in social relations it appears as a mutual right. It must, therefore, be understood as an expression of personal dignity and as an exercise of responsibility. Hence freedom is both duty and love, especially as regards spiritual values and above all with regard to God. This is why the Council has dealt with religious freedom and has issued a Declaration on it.

And in his introduction (p. 53) he writes in much the same vein concerning the third schema (i.e. draft – there were six).

> It begins with the statement that modern men are becoming ever more conscious of their own personal dignity. In the new schema this dignity is the basic motif, but it is understood above all as responsibility of action.
>
> The increased consciousness of their own dignity led men to want greater freedom in all spheres, especially in religious matters, and hence to demand that this freedom should be guaranteed by setting

well-defined limits to the authority of the state. Thus the constitutional state came into being.

Consequently religious freedom, too, was seen in a new context. This is why the Council considered it right to think about it and produce a Declaration on the subject. Religious freedom is proclaimed to be a right of the person; it consists in freedom from coercion, whether on the part of individuals or of public authority. This freedom is twofold: in matters of religion no one may be compelled to act against his conscience, and no one may be prevented from acting according to his conscience.

He ends his *Commentary* on the following note (p. 86):

The later paragraphs of the final article deal with other aspects of the present historical situation. There is a constant progress towards the unity of the human race which is due to the factors of our modern civilization, especially to the enormous technological advances and their effects in the economic, social, political, cultural, moral and religious spheres.

This progress towards unity results in the fact that "men of different cultures and religions are being brought together in closer relationships" (Article 15, para. 3). Hence religious pluralism is on the increase within the existing political communities and even more in the developing ones. In such a situation the document declares, "in order that relationships of peace and harmony may be established and maintained within the whole of mankind, it is necessary that religious freedom be everywhere provided with an effective constitutional guarantee, and that respect be shown for the high duty and right of man freely to lead his religious life in society" (Article 15, para.4).

However, he adds, as a caveat, for theological reasons no doubt:

These historical facts have certainly contributed to the decision of the Council fathers to proclaim religious freedom as a right of the person *today*; but this right is based, as has been said before, not on historical facts but on the claim due to the dignity of the human person.

So "the spirit of the age," or "aspects of the present historical situation," were certainly elements in the impetus towards "new thinking," or as Thomas Carlyle had observed that new historical events do not spring from one single cause but from a whole web of causation, from "all other events, prior or contemporaneous," ("Thomas Carlyle 'On History,'" in *Critical and Miscellaneous Essays collected and Republished*, London, 1872, vol. 2, p. 257).

Indeed, the Church was keenly aware of changes that were taking place both in social, economic and scientific fields, as is very evident in Pope John XXII's 1961 encyclical, entitled *Mater et Magistre* (which in turn was a further development on the thema promulgated in earlier encyclicals, such as *Rerum Novarum* of Pope Leo XII from 1891 and *Quadragesimo Anno* of Pope Pius XI, from 1931).[6]

This was also hinted at by Msgr. Jorge Mejia (Executive Secretary to the Vatican Commission for Religious Relations with the Jews), in his essay in "More Stepping Stones to Jewish-Christians Relations," ed. Helga Croner, New York, 1985, p. 8, when he wrote that:

Again, this is not to deny that "external" factors may have had an influence in determining the fact and orientation of this examination [i.e. leading to *Nostra Aetate*].

Furthermore on pp. 6–7 he writes (rather surprisingly):

Yes, the Catastrophe was behind us. But I confess that I knew next to nothing about it when I left Argentina for Rome in November 1946, and it was only very gradually that I became conscious of the magnitude of the tragedy. Others perhaps knew better, at least from a certain point in time on. But my argument is that this knowledge, upsetting and terribly poignant as it certainly was, would not have had the transforming effect it has had, were it not because of the soil already tilled (at least to a certain extent) that it found.

(However, he points to different kinds of background which "tilled the soil.")

Of course, pluralism and tolerance are by no means identical, and there is a considerable distance between tolerance and pluralism. Tolerance is willing to suffer the dissenting view, without giving it legitimacy, while pluralism gives legitimacy, or at least partial legitimacy, to the view of the others, sometimes through the feeling of ultimate inactivity.

Thus, beyond "condescension" there also emerges a degree of uncertainty – skepticism – as to how to understand and relate to "the other's" religious faith, a sort of theological form of Heisenberg's "Uncertainty Theorum."

And the great twentieth century physicist, Neils Bohr, who was the pathfinder in the wave-particle theory of light, stated that superficial truths are those whose opposites are false, but that "deep truths" are such that their opposites or apparent contradictions are true as well. And it should be noted that the Church too was aware of those important changes in scientific thinking, as is clear from the aforementioned 1961 encyclical of Pope John XXIII, *Mate et Magistra*, nos. 47 and 196–197.

Perhaps we can compare this with Arthur Eddington's remarks (1892–1944) in his *The Nature of a Physical World*, London, 1928, as brought by Arthur O. Lovejoy, in his *The Revolt Against Dualism: An Inquiry Concerning the Existence of ideas*, La Salle Illinois, 1955, p. 180:

> Eddington, when finding that it is not altogether easy to give a plain answer to the question whether it is "really true that a moving rod becomes shorter in the direction of its motion," nevertheless gives an answer. The proposition is *"true* but it is not *really true."* And this somewhat oddly phrased distinction signifies that the proposition "is not a statement about reality (the absolute), but is a true statement about appearance in the frame of reference."

I believe this last comment requires some further elaboration. For Werner Heisenberg[7] (1912–1976) in his Principle of Indeterminacy (better known as Heisenberg's Uncertainty theorem) had reached the outer limits of scientific possibilities by doing away with determinism and simultaneously the position and velocity of a partical, for the greater the precision of the one the greater the imprecision of the other. The deeper one penetrates into the microcosmic world, the more difficult or even impossible, is direct observation. For the observation itself *interferes* with the behaviour of the phenomenon. Or in his own words, ". . . we cannot make observations without disturbing the phenomena – the quantum effects we introduce with our observation introduce a degree of uncertainty into the phenomena to be observed" (Heisenberg, *Physics and Beyond*, London, 1971, p. 104).

And when the margin of uncertainty is calculated, it turns out that it is always a function of that greatest of all mysteries; Max Planck's constant quantum. This is a sort of *Anekantaveda* of physics.[8] Or as J. Bronowsky wrote in his classic *The Ascent of Man*, London, 1973, p. 367:

> The Principle of Uncertainty or, in my phrase, the Principle of Tolerance fixed for all the realization that all knowledge is limited.

Niels Bohr's coat-of-arms. Note the use of the Chinese "Yang-Yin" symbol in the center of the coat-of-arms.

Furthermore Heisenberg pointed out that, "It may well be that a description of the living organism that could be called complete from the standpoint of the physicist cannot be given, since it would require experiments that interfere with the biological functions," (Heisenberg, *Physics and Philosophy*, London, 1959, p. 135). And Erwin Schrödinger (1887–1961), who has had lifelong interest in *Vedant* philosophy, which deeply influenced his speculations (as expressed in his *"What is Life,"* McMillan, 1944, and *"What is Life: Mind and Matter,"* Cambridge, 1974), clinched the issue by reminding us that:

> ... incredibly small groups of atoms, much too small to display exact statistical laws, do play a dominating role in the very orderly and lawful events within a living organism. They have control of the observable large-scale features which the organism acquires in the course of its development. (Schrödinger, *What is Life*, p. 17).[9]

Hence, the gap between organic and inorganic matter cannot be spanned.[10] Amaury de Riencourt writes in his chapter "Orientalisation" that:

> It is highly symbolic that such an eminent physicist as Erwin Schrödinger should lend his powerful voice to a persuasive defense of Eastern monism as against Western monotheism, in the light of the fundamental Oneness displayed at the microcosmic level of physics where all phenomena are interrelated and cannot be viewed as autonomous and isolated events or processes. He points out that the plurality perceived by us is an illusion, quoting Vedantic philosophy and its famous analogy of the universe assimilated to a many-faceted crystal which shows multitudes of pictures of what is a single reality, without multiplying it. [Schrödinger, *My View of the World*, Cambridge, 1964, p. 18]. We have just seen that some schools of Mahāyāna Buddhism have used the same simile. He adds, in true Eastern fashion, that this has to be "... experienced, not simply given a notional acknowledgement" [ibid. pp. 19–21]. While he refuses to accept Spinoza's pantheism, he claims that all conscious beings are "all in all" and that each one of our lives is not just a fragment of existence but, in a way, the *whole* of it – a whole constituted in such a way, however, that it cannot be seen at one glance [ibid. pp. 21–22].
>
> His basic theme is that consciousness is One and cannot be found in the plural, which plurality is an illusion. This illusion, in turn, triggered in Western philosophic thought a conflict between an inevitable idealism denying the existence of matter à la Berkeley and its complete uselessness in dealing with the objective physical world. He dismisses the conflict by referring specifically to one of the cardinal tenets of the *Upanisads* according to which the external world and consciousness

are one and the same, being constituted of the same basic elements – which leads him to say that the fact that there is only One external world amounts to stating that there is only *one* consciousness [ibid. pp. 31, 37].

This ancient wisdom is not limited to the *Upanisads* and *Vedānta*. The Chinese Taoists long ago expressed the same monistic viewpoint; the *Tao Te Ching* states that "Therefore the sage embraces the Oneness (of the universe), making it his testing-instrument for everything under Heaven." Or we read in the *Kuan Tzu* book: "Only the *chün-tzu* (gentleman) holding to the idea of the One can bring about changes in things and affairs." [See J. Needham, *Science and Civilization in China*, vol. 2, Cambridge, 1956, p. 46.]

This leads Schrödinger to abandon the dualism of thought and existence, or mind and matter. This has been unsuccessfully attempted before in the West, although, as he remarks, "... it is odd that it has usually been done on a materialistic basis.... But this is no good. If we decide to have only one sphere, it has got to be the psychic one, since that exists anyway [ibid. pp. 61–63]."

Another cardinal element is now introduced in this orientalization of the world-view of physics: the virtual disappearance of a sharp separation between object and subject, observer and thing observed, since the observer, like the mystic, is an active "participant" in the experiment and forms one whole with whatever is being observed. Schrödinger, in sum, states that the reduction of the whole of reality to mental experience is itself an *idea*, a mental construction; he emphasizes, however, that he objects to the "... assertion that there must be also, externally to it or alongside it ... an object of which it is the idea and by which it is caused [ibid. p. 64]."[11]

A further aspect in what Rienholt calls "the Orientalization of physics" (ibid. pp. 161–162) is:

The impact of the increasing contribution of Eastern scientists from India, China and Japan, among others. An early indication of this trend was the collaboration of Indian physicist S.N. Bose with Einstein on a concept which became known as the "Bose-Einstein Statistics." After the two World Wars, Heisenberg noted that the great scientific contribution to theoretical physics that had come from Japan may well have been due to an affinity between the traditional philosophies of the Orient and the implications of the Quantum Theory – probably due to the fact that it must have been easier for Easterners to adapt to the quantum-theoretical idea of reality because they had not "... gone through the naïve materialistic way of thinking that still prevailed in Europe in the first decades of this century" [Heisenberg, *Physics and Philosophy*, p. 173].

Many Easterners agree, and some find an Eastern flavour in the vision of the new physics. For instance, Nobel prize-winning Japanese physicist Hideki Yukawa, referring to Relativity, asserts that, "Here, time resolves itself into the fourth dimension, on a par with space, where harmony prevails in an eternal state of rest ... and one may sense something close to the Oriental outlook." [See H. Yukawa, *Creativity and Intuition*, Tokyo, 1973, p. 60.] Another striking example of the outright impact of the Eastern cultural influence is the discovery of the non-conservation of parity in the case of weak interactions by two Chinese physicists, Tsung Dao Lee and Chen Ning Yang, who received the Nobel Prize in 1957. Western physicists were prompt to wonder whether the cultural heritage of the Orient had made it easier for them to doubt the symmetry of natural law. [See M. Gardner, *The Ambidextrous Universe*, New York, 1964, p. 249.] It is a fact that the prime *yin-yang* symbol of China is asymmetrical (it is not superposable on its mirror-image, whereas the Christian Cross, for instance, is indeed left-right symmetrical). This "familiar asymmetry of the oriental symbol, so much part of Chinese culture, may have played a subtle, unconscious role in making it a bit easier for Lee and Yang to go against the grain of scientific orthodoxy, to propose a test which their more symmetric-minded Western colleague had thought scarcely worth the effort" [Gardner ibid. p. 252].

We have elaborated somewhat lengthily on this issue, not only to underscore the influence of the East on Western thinking,[12] even in the field of physics, but also once again to call attention to the newly emerging notions – in science – of intrinsic uncertainty, so much so that Carl Friedrichson von Weizacker (1922–2007) talks of a scale or hierarchy of degrees of reality, which he terms "degrees of truth" [Heisenberg, *Physics and Philosophy*, pp. 157–158). Thus, whereas in classical physics a thing either is or is not, following Aristotelian logic (*tertiam non datur*), in which there is no room for a third possibility, at the subatomic level this is no longer the case, as was pointed out by Robert Oppenheimer, in the following given situation:

> If we ask, for instance, whether the position of the electron remain the same, we must say "no;" if we ask whether the electron's position change with time, we must say "no;" if we ask whether the electron is at rest we must say "no;" if we ask whether it is in motion, we must say "no" (Robert Oppenheimer, *Science and Common Understanding*, Oxford, 1954, pp. 42–43; Reincourt, p. 164).

Oppenheimer himself concluded that, "The Buddha has given such answers when interrogated as to the conditions of man's Self after his death, but they are not familiar answers for the tradition of seventeenth and eighteenth century science."

Indeed, he had learned Sanskrit in Berkeley with the hindologist Arthur W. Ryder in 1933, and read in the original language the *Bhagavad Gita*. Indeed, when in June 16, 1945, the first artificial nuclear explosion was carried at "Trinity" (new Alanogordol), as he witnessed the explosion, he claims that he thought of the verse in the *Bhagavad Gita* (XI:12), "if the radiance of a thousand suns were to burst into the sky, that would be like the splendour of the mighty one. . . ." Later he also said that another verse from the *Gita* entered his head at that moment, namely: "I am become Death, the destroyer of worlds" (XI:32).[13]

His close confidant and colleague Isidor Rabi said of him:

> Oppenheimer was overeducated in those fields, which lie outside the scientific traditions.

Such was his interest in religion, in the Hindu religion in particular, which resulted in a feeling of the mystery of the universe that surrounded him like a fog. He saw physics clearly, looking toward what he had already done, but at the border he tended to feel there was much more of the mysterious and the novel than there actually was. . . . [He turned away from the hard crude methods of theoretical physics into a mysterious realm of broad intuition (I. Rabi, *Oppenheimer*, 1969, p. 7; cited in Hijiya, 2000, p. 166)].

So his turning to Hinduism and Buddhism to seek answers to "the mysterious realm of broad intuition" which may transcend opposites, should not surprise us.

Indeed, consider a statement of Buddha, which transcends the strictly logical pairs of opposites, but is a series of negative paradoxes. Thus,

> There is no Self outside of its parts.
> There is a path to walk on, there is walking being done, but there is no traveler. There are deeds being done, but there is no doer.
> As there is no Self, there is no transmigration of Self; but there are deeds and the continued effect of deeds.
> There is no entity that migrates, no Self is transferred from one place to another; but there is a voice uttered here and the echo of it comes back.
>
> (P. Carm, The Gospel of Buddha, London, 1915, p. XL.)

One could greatly multiply such examples, such as the case of Fritjof Capra, who wrote in 1975, *The Tao of Physics: An Explanation of Parallels between Modern Physics and Eastern Mysticism*, a book that ran into 43 editions in 23 languages. What we have tried to show is that great European scientists during the first half of the twentieth century were developing a new kind of physics, which was in many ways close in its "non-rational rationale," if I may suggest such a classification to Eastern "logic." A new kind of thinking was emerging in the West (under the influence of the East) in which both uncertainty of the absolute truth, the varying degrees of truth, or the multiplicity of truths was becoming recognized as acceptable notions.[14] All this, then, should be added to what we noted above in section 6, entitled, "The Influence of Eastern Thought on Culture." And it should be noted that almost all our quotations come from books that were published before 1965. And this mode of thinking influenced theologians as well, with what we have earlier called "a sort of theological form of Heisenberg 'Uncertainty Theorum.'"

And just to give a somewhat random selection of Buddhist "paradoxical" examples, I will quote sections from Mahāyāna Sutra texts (apud *Buddhist Texts through the Ages*, edd. B. Conze, J.B. Horner, D. Snellgrove, A. Waley, Hooper ed. New York and Evanston, 1964).

> ... The lack of a basis of apprehension in all Dharmas, that is called "perfect wisdom." When there is no perception, appellation, conception or conventional expression, there one speaks of "perfect wisdom."

(*Ashtasāhastrikā prajnāpāramita* VII.177; *Buddhist texts* no.143, p. 150.)

Or:

> Manjustri: What are the qualities and what the advantages of a per-fection of wisdom which is without qualities? How can one speak of the qualities or advantages of a perfect wisdom which is incapable of doing anything, neither raises up nor destroys anything, neither accepts nor rejects any dharma, is powerless to act and not at all busy, if its own-being cannot be cognized, if its own-being cannot be seen, if it does not bestow any dharma, and does not obstruct any dharma, if it brings about the non-separateness of all dharmas, does not exalt the single oneness of all dharmas, does not affect the separateness of all dharmas, if it is not made, not something to be done, not passed, if it does not destroy anything, if it is not a donor of the dharmas of the common people, of the dharmas of the Arhats, of the dharmas of the Pratyekabuddhas, of the dharmas of the Bodhisattvas, and not even of the dharmas of a Buddha, and does not take them away, if it does not toil in birth-and-death, nor cease toiling in Nirvana, neither bestows nor destroys the dharmas of a Buddha, if it is unthinkable and inconceivable, not something to be done, not something to be undone, if it neither produces nor stops any dharmas, neither annihilates them nor makes them eternal, if it neither causes to come nor to go, brings about neither detachment nor non-detachment, neither duality nor non-duality, and if, finally, it is non-existent?
>
> The Lord: Well have you, Manjusri, described the qualities of per-fect wisdom.... (*Saptaśatikā* 32b–34a, ibid. pp. 150–151, no.145.)

Or again:

> Sariputra: That thought which is non-thought, is that something which is?
>
> Subhuti: Can one find, or apprehend, in this state of absence of thought, either a "there is" or a "there is not."
>
> (*Satasāhasrikā prajñāramita* III, 495–502, ibid. p. 176, no.163.)

Or yet again:

> Sariputra: For what reason should a Bodhisattva be known as not lacking in perfect wisdom:

Subhuti: Form is lacking in the own being of form. And so for all things.

Sariputra: What then is the own being of form, etc.?

Subhuti: Non-positivity is the own being of form, etc. It is in this sense that form is lacking in the own-being of form. And so with the other skandhas. Moreover, form is lacking in the mark which is characteristic of form. The mark, again, is lacking in the own being of a mark. The own being, again, is lacking in the mark of (being) own being.

Sariputra: A Bodhisattva who trains himself in this method, will he go forth to the knowledge of all modes:

Subhuti: He will. Because all dharmas are unborn and do not go forth.

Sariputra: For what reason are all dharmas unborn, and do not go forth?

Subhuti: Form is empty of the own being of form. And so are all other dharmas. With regard to them no birth or going forth can be apprehended. It is thus that a Bodhisattva who practises perfect wisdom comes near to the knowledge of all modes.

(*Pancavimśatisāhasrikā prajnapāramita* 136–38, ibid. p. 175, no.162.)

Or again, as in a Yogācāra statement:

This is why it is said that everything is non-empty and everything is not non-empty, because [the imagination] exists, [Duality] does not exist, and [emptiness] exists. This is the Middle Path.

(Cited in Malcolm David Eckel's essay, entitled "Buddhist Approaches to Ultimate Reality," apud *Ultimate Relations*, ed. Robert Cummings Neville, Albany, 2001, p. 135, quoted from T. Stcherbatsky, *Bibliotheca Buddhica* 30, Leningrad, 1936; see Eckel, ibid. p. 148 note 29, and see Eckel's interpretation of this cryptic statement.)

And finally, for this highly incomplete selection: cf. p. 278: "All words are true," said Manjusri. "Are lies then also true?" asked Brahma. "They are," said Manjusri. "And why? Good sir, all words are empty, vain and belong to no point in space. To be empty and vain and to belong to no point in space is the characteristic of Absolute truth. So in that sense all words are true ..." (*Viśesha – cinta Brahma-paripsecehā-Takakusa*, xv, 50 and 82, ibid. p. 278, no. 200).[15]

And this "Easternizing" process, took place not merely in the areas of science and the arts, but also in the development of new theological thinking. Thus, for instance, the great and enormously influential Lutheran theologian, Rudolph Otto (1869–1937), was deeply interested in Eastern thought. He wrote a number of books on this subject, such as: *Christianity and the Indian Religion of Grace*, Madras, 1928; *India's Religion of Grace and Christianity Compared and Contrasted* (transl. F.H. Foster), New York, 1930; *Mysticism East and West: A Comparative Analysis of the Nature of Mysticism* (transl. B.L. Bracy and P.C. Payn), New York, 1926. And he, in turn influenced several major theological thinkers, such as Martin Heidegger (1899–1937), who was in contact with several leading Japanese intellectuals, such as Hajime Tanake and Kuki Shūzo, and wrote a study entitled, "A Dialogue on Language between a Japanese and an Inquirer" (apud *On the Way to Language*, New York, 1971). Reinhard May's *Heidegger's Hidden Sources: East Asian Influences on his Work*, London, 1996, traces the Taoist and Zen elements in his thinking. (See also G. Parkes ed., *Heidegger and Asian Thoughts,* Honolulu, 1987.) Likewise, the Trappist mystic monk Thomas Merton (1915–1968) was deeply influenced by Eastern religions, especially Daoism, and published many books on the subject, somehow combining his own Catholism with Eastern esoteric thinking. Vatican II took into account these very different forms of religious thinking, expressing itself in the section on Non-Christians (Sect 1) thus:

> The Church therefore has this exhortation for persons: Prudently and lovingly, through dialogue and collaboration with the followers of other religions, and in the witness of Christians' faith and life, acknowledge, preserve, and promote the spiritual and moral goods found among these men, as well as the values in their society and culture.

And yet another major Lutheran thinker influenced by Otto was Paul Tillich (1886–1965), in whose writings we can also discern the elements of Eastern thought affecting his theological analysis. Thus, for example, he writes in his classic *Systematic Theology*, vol. 2, Chicago, 1957, p. 12:

... In such a state, the God of both religious and theological language disappears. But something remains, namely the seriousness
of that doubt in which meaning within meaninglessness is affirmed.
The source of this affirmation of meaning within meaninglessness, of
certitude within doubt is not the God of traditional theism, but the "God
above God," the power of being, which works through those who have
no name for it, not even the name God.

And of course we can hardly overlook the work of Carl Jung (1875–1961),
who actually visited India in 1937 (where he became seriously sick), and
was deeply involved in Hindu and Buddhist thought from his own particular and unique perspective, and in 1978 published his Psychology and
the East. (See, e.g., J. Wouter Hanagraaff, *New Age Religion and Western
Culture: Esoterism in the Mirror of Secular Thought*, Leiden New York,
1996.) He was deeply influenced by the psychologist-sinologist Richard
Wilhelm (1873–1930), whose translation of *I Ching*, which took him
ten years, appeared in 1923, and who promulgated a "shared philosophy
for human kind," a sort of philosophical "fusion," which peaked in the
celebration of a sacrificial ceremony to Beethoven according to the rites
of Zhou, in 1927. (See M. Stein, "Some Reflections on the influence
of Chinese thought on Jung and his psychological theory," *Journal of
Analytical Psychology*, 51 (2), 2005, pp. 209–222.)[16]

And let us not forget Joseph Campell (1904–1987), who had met with
Jiddu Krishnamurti, in 1924, and who during the years 1955–1956 lived in
both South India and Japan. He was influenced by Jung, but also by the
Tibetan Book of the Dead (*Bordo Thodol*). He edited the works of the great
Indologist Heinrich Zimmer, and his *The Hero with a Thousand Faces* first
appeared in 1949, and was followed by The *Masks of God* in four volumes
through 1959 to 1968. His works were, and still are, enormously popular
and greatly influential.

Similarly Mircea Eliade (1907–1986), who lived in India between 1928–
1932, and studied under the Indian philosopher Suhendranath Dasgupta,
was influenced by Otto, and was deeply involved in Vedanta thought,
writing copiously on comparisons between Eastern and Western thought,
as was also Renée Guénon, of Catholic background (1886–1951), who in
1921 wrote his *Introduction to the Study of Hindu Doctrine*, and in his
many writings emphasized the great divide between Eastern and Western
thought, which he attempted to bridge.

So many things were happening during this fascinating period. Karl Barth, one of the foremost Protestant theologians of the twentieth century issued the Darmstadt Statement in 1947, which was basically a Christian apologia for the holocaust, and went beyond the earlier Stuttgart Declaration of 1945.

Albert Schweitzer, who was also influenced by Indian thought, and even wrote a book entitled *Indian Thought and its Development*, Boston, 1935, and in his lifetime activities lived the Jain principle of *ahimsa* – non-violence, received in 1952 the Nobel Prize for his "Reverence for Life." Teilhard de Chardin (1881–1955) the Jesuit priest, who was at this time criticized by the Catholic Church, was developing a new theology of Christianity taking into account contemporary scientific developments. (See, e.g., *R.C. Zaener, Matter and Spirit: Their Convergance in Eastern Religions, Marx, and Teilhard de Chardin, New York, 1963.*) Jacques Maritain (1882–1973), the Catholic philosopher, who served as French Ambassador to the Vatican during the years 1945–1948, and who is known for his doctrine of "Integral Humanism," (book published in 1936), played a key role in developing *The Universal Declaration of Human Rights*, passed by the General Assembly of the United Nations. He struggled with what we might call the holocaust guilt syndrome.[17]

And the list continues …

But returning to our main theme – the penetration of Eastern thought into Western thinking, be it scientific, philosophic or theological – introduced, as we have sought to show above, elements of uncertainty as to the nature of absolute truth, and indeed if there actually is such a thing. The further corollary of this new mode of thinking in the field of ethics was "moral uncertitude," now often termed "moral relativism."[18] Maritain attempted to counter this perplexing moral dilemma, by positing his view of "Integral Humanism." He saw ethical norms as rooted in human nature, and "natural law" known through "connaturality," meaning knowledge acquired by acquaintance. Natural rights are rooted in natural law, and moral philosophy must be seen in the context of theology.[19] And it was in this context that he was involved in the drafting of the *Universal Declaration of Human Rights*, as mentioned above. But an element of philosophical skepticism pervades much of the thinking of this period, and with it also pangs of guilt.

Let me further stress that this uncertainly, this skepticism, is not an uncertainty in the legitimacy of one's own faith, but in its *exclusivity*.

This "uncertainty" further encourages liberalism, but, as stated above, a liberalism that can be "beyond condescension;" and beyond condescension bringing one to what may even be a realization that the other may *also* be true. For indeed, to think that one is the exclusive monopoly stakeholder in the absolute truth surely is *hubris*,[20] though, of course, there is a difference between rational thinking (called "philosophy") and faith (called "revelation").

However, here we must add an important caveat. There are some objective facts, be they historical or material, which may perhaps be subject to various interpretations. But they have a core truth, which if denied or strayed away from, lead to falsity. Moses, irrespective of whether actually he existed or not, was according to the "correct" tradition a man and not a woman. Thus, for example, the statement/tradition in Alexander Polyhestor (1st century B.C.E.) that "a Hebrew woman [named] Moso ... composed the laws of the Hebrews" is plainly false.[21] Similarly, I am certain that Isaac, and not Ishmael was the son who was almost sacrificed by Abraham, so that those Islamic commentators who interpret a Quranic passage as suggesting that it was Ishmael are mistaken.

> (As a matter of fact, there are among Muslim sources two views as to which son Abraham was commanded to sacrifice. See *'Arā'is Al-Majālis fi-Qisas al-Anbiyā: or Lives of the Prophets*, as recounted by Abū Ishāq ibn Muhammad ibn Ibrāhīm al-Tha'labi, [died 1036], transl. and annotated by William M. Brinner, Leiden, Boston, Köln, 2002, pp. 154–158. Cf. Reuven Firestone, "Exegesis on Abraham's Sacrifice in the Light of Jewish, Christian, and Sunni Muslim Tradition," *Journal of the Academy of Religion* 66, 1998, pp. 193–116.)

In other words, even if we accept the notion of multiple truths, nonetheless not *every* belief is true, and there are false interpretations, which cannot be accepted by the critical believer. Or as Christian M. Rutishauer stated in the aforementioned source:

> The so-called world religions seem to be all at the same level of truth. But the view of the sciences of religion which approach the different religions in a neutral, distant and objective way cannot be adopted [in his case, D.S.] by the Christian faith uncritically.

214

However, having said all that, and not denying the importance of an ev-er-critical eye, there is, nonetheless, a sense in which there may be validity to different belief systems.[22]

Endnotes to Chapter 8

1. See, for example, Ulrich L. Lehner, *On the Way to Vatican II: Catholic Enlightenment and the Reform of the Church*, Minnesota, 2016, for philosophical antecedents.

2. Here we may note that Joseph Cardinal Ratzinger, later Pope Benedict XVI, was influenced by Indian philosophy. This is an article first published in 1964 (!) in a Festschrift in honour of Karl Rahmer's sixtieth birthday, and reprinted in his volume *Truth and Tolerance: Christian Belief and World Religions*, San Francisco, 2003, p. 24, in which he wrote:

> No one, to date, has been able to offer our generation a more impressive, warmer, or more persuasive picture of a religion of the future, which in its turn would be able to bring about a "future for religion," than the President of India, Radhakrishnan, whose written works ever and again lead up to a vista of the coming religion of the spirit, which will be able to unite fundamental unity with the most varied differentiation. Over against such prophetic utterances, with their unmistakable weight of human and religious authority, the Christian theologian looks like a dogmatic stick-in-the-mud, who cannot get away from his know-it-all attitude, whether he expresses it in the swaggering manner of apologists in past times or whether in the friendly manner of contemporary theologians, who acknowledge to the other person to what extent he is already a Christian without being aware of it.

In note 11 ibid. he refers us to the following bibliographic information:

> See especially his books *The Hindu View of Life* (1926); *Eastern Religions and Western Thought* (1939); *Religion and Society* (1974); *Recovery of Faith* (1956). For a critical examination of Radhakrishnan, especially P. Hacker, "Ein Prasthnatraya-Kommentar des Neuhinduismus: Bemerkungen zum Werk Radhakrishnans" [A neo-Hindu Prasth-Natrays commentary: Observations on the work of Radakrishnan], *Orientalische Literatur-Zeitung* 56 (1961): 565–76; for a popular view: J. Neuner, "Gespräch mit Radhakrishnan" [Conversation with Radhakrishnan], *Stimme der Zeit* 87 (1962): 241–54. See also Kraemer, *Religions and Christian Faith* (in German trans., *Religion und christlicher Glaube* [Göttingen, 1959], pp. 95–134).

And on p. 47, he brings a long passage from H. Bürckle, *Mensch auf der Suche nach Gott* (pp. 130 et seq.) on modern Hinduism's idea of man. And cf. further ibid. pp. 33–35, 83, 122–125, 144, 162 (the elephant parable), 197. Throughout we see his knowledge, acquaintance and debt to Radhakrisnan and Hinduism in general.

Likewise he is interested in Buddhism, and refers to it several times in the book, always positively. See, e.g., pp. 49, 68,162,175–176,194, 217, 226–227. And cf. ibid. pp. 121–122.

3. And as a single, but very pertinent example of this "new thinking" – a different attitude to the notion of religion and its "individual exclusivity" – i.e. that the one excludes the other, which permeated the Western world. We may point to the very influential writings of Wilfred Cantwell Smith (1916–200), who had lived in India in 1940–1947 and published his first book, *Modern Islam in India: A Social Analysis*, London, 1943, *whose The Meaning and End of Religion*, London, 1962, made an enormous impact on comparative religious thinking. Likewise in 1963, his *The Faiths of Other Men*, (the first part of which consists of seven radio talks given early in 1962 over the national network of the Canadian Broadcasting Corporation, in its series "The . . . of the Air," and the second part of which was a lecture delivered in Montreal in 1961) and which appeared in June 1965 (in New York and London), he wrote (pp. 82–83):

> Perhaps it will be interesting to add, too, that it was from my study of Hindus, and of the Taoists of China, that I have learned most clearly the limitations and dangers of mysticism. Or to take another example from the other side of the arena, my Calvinist background has certainly helped me to understand and appreciate the more rigid Islamic theologians; but in turn, my study of these has illuminated for me, and helped me greatly to understand, the conservative Christian thinker Karl Barth, the power of whose position I have only lately come to appreciate.
>
> It may be objected that other Christians have understood and appreciated Barth without having been led to it by orientalist routes. Of course this is true, and proves the very point that I am trying to make; namely, that one may arrive at an understanding of truth by various paths. This includes Christian truths. The influence on contemporary Christian theology of the modern Jewish thinker Martin Buber is also relevant here.

(And see his very insightful discussion in the chapters on "Hindus," "Buddhists" and "The Chinese" ibid.).

And a later work, *Questions of Religious Truth*, which appeared in London in 1967, was based on the Taylor Lecture delivered at Yale Divinity School in 1963, in which was included a very important chapter "Can Religion be True or False?" (pp. 65–95), he concluded that chapter as follows (pp. 94–95):

Another way of phrasing this same point is perhaps simpler, though its implications reach just as far, in all directions. Might we say that the statement "the
Qur'an is the word of God," rather than being in itself true or false, at a generic
or abstract level, impersonally, can become true – in the life of a particular
person; and further, that it has become true in the lives of many persons; and
further, that it has become more true in the lives of certain persons, at certain
times, than others. It becomes true through faith. (It can also become false.)

I leave with you the question as to whether this applies to all religious
statements, including our Christian ones: that they have become true for some
men, and that they may become true for me, that they may become more true
for me than they yet have.

If this were so, another question would perhaps follow; namely, can some
religious statements become more true than others? To discuss this collabora-
tively would open up the possibility of a new era, perhaps, in inter-community
discourse and inter-community understanding. I would still insist that we relate
it to the lives and the faith of persons.

We may answer our last chapter's question, then, by saying that the Qur'an
has become the word of God to some men, not to others – and of the former,
those to whom it has become so, it has become so more truly to some than
to others.

Now the interesting things about this type of answer are two. The first is
that this way of looking at the matter appears, to me at least, as observer and
theorist, to be nearer the truth; and my argument has endeavored to make this
persuasive. True statements, in the religious realm, are significant and are
worth striving after – even if they are not as important as, or anyway are not
a substitute for, true lives.

The second point is that this type of statement would seem potentially
capable of being accepted eventually by both Muslims and Christians.

The two points are, of course, related. So long as we disagree, one at least
of us is wrong; or, both are inadequate. And there is perhaps some reason to
imagine that the latter is the case. Contrariwise, if anyone can really arrive at
a statement that approximates the truth, should be able and happy to adopt it.

Probably I have failed. Yet, even if, in the process, I have illustrated what
is required, that in itself may be an advance.

And this very thoughtful, but highly complex statement, by the Director of Harvard
University's Center for the Study of World Religions (1964–1973), rated by the
Howard Gazette as "one of the field's most influential figures of the past century,"
and a prominent member of albeit. . . . United Church of Canada, indicates the
(perhaps indirect) influence of Eastern thought on Western Christian thinking.

Undoubtedly, there were other contributory factors too, economic, political, religious and ideological. See, for example, Salvatore Abbruzzose's Chapter (10) entitled "Religion and Post War Generation in Italy," apud *The Post-War Generation and Establishment Religion*, edd. Wade Clark Roof, Jackson W. Carroll, David A. Roozen, Boulder, San Francisco, Oxford, 1995, pp. 207–223, and most especially p. 213:

> . . . The transition from collateralism to Vatican II and thus to the religious choice of the Azione Catholica at the end of the 1950s caused a big change in the Catholic movement. . . .

4. See the section entitled "Declaration on the Relationship of the Church to Non-Christian Religions:"

> 2. From ancient times down to the present, there has existed among diverse peoples a certain perception of that hidden power which hovers over the course of things and over the events of human life; at times, indeed, recognition can be found of a Supreme Divinity and of a Supreme Father too. Such a perception and such a recognition instill the lives of these peoples with a profound religious sense. Religions bound up with cultural advancement have struggled to reply to these same questions with more refined concepts and in more highly developed language.
>
> Thus in Hinduism men contemplate the divine mystery and express it through an unspent fruitfulness of myths and through searching philosophical inquiry. They seek release from the anguish of our condition through ascetical practices or deep meditation or a loving, trusting flight toward God.
>
> Here, the Declaration selects certain key elements of Hinduism without attempting the impossible task of describing in a short space the complex nature of Hinduism, the distinctions between Vedanta (scriptures) and Puranas (lesser sacred books), the six philosophical systems, the innumerable sects, etc. Mention might have been made of the similarities between Hindu and Christian beliefs – e.g., the concept of God's appearance on earth; the concept of grace; sacraments; and similarities between the Christian Trinity and the Hindu ultimate reality – but all this, it was legitimately felt, could be left to the work of dialogue that is endorsed and commended at the end of the Article.

(See *The Documents of Vatican II*, ed. Walter M. Abbott, S.J., New York, 1966, pp. 661–662 note 7.)

And as to Buddhism, we read ibid:

> Buddhism in its multiple forms acknowledges the radical insufficiency of this shifting world. It teaches a path by which men, in a devout and confident spirit, can either reach a state of absolute freedom or attain supreme enlightenment by their own efforts or by higher assistance.

Here again, as with Hinduism, so with Buddhism – a whole library of knowledge opens up at the mention of the word. Instead of attempting to give detailed summaries of the common areas of interest, the Declaration touches on general themes and leaves the rest to development in competent dialogue. (*The Documents of Vatican II*, p. 662 note 8.)

There is a clear, though understated admission of the awareness of the "signs of the times" in the statement *La Scale Evangeliche*, of January 1981. It begins:

The "signs of the times" offer an incentive for the renewal of the evangelical option of the religious life.

And section 14 states that:

The cultural, social and political changes which have affected, at times adversely, peoples and continents spur the Church to an evangelical response to the wide range of the aspirations and hopes of humanity.

This intense pastoral concern was reinforced by the discussions and objectives of the Second Vatican Council and has reemerged in the Synods of Bishops and in papal exhortations.

(See *Vatican Collection* vol. 2: *Vatican Council II: More Post Conciliar Documents*, ed. Austin Flannery, O.P., New York, 1982, no. 94, pp. 260, 271.)

5. *Commentary on the Documents of Vatican II*, ed. Herbert Vorglinler, vol. 4, Freiburg, Montreal 1969, p. 63.

Let us note that while I do not know how consciously aware of these various elements the authors of *Nostra Aetate* were in the sixties, they certainly were in the year 2000, when in August 6 of that year the Vatican authorities published a declaration entitled "*Dominus Iesus: On the Unicity and Salvic Universality of Jesus Christ and the Church.*" This declaration was signed by Joseph Cardinal Ratzingers Prefect, and Tarcisio Bertone S.D.B., Archbishop Emeritus of Vercelli, Secretary. In the introduction, paragraph 4, the declaration states that:

The roots of these problems – i.e. the relativistic theory which seek to justify religious pluralism, thus endangering the Church's constant missionary proclamation – are to be found in certain presuppositions of both a philosophical and theological nature, which hinder the understanding and acceptance of the revealed truth, even by Christian revelation; relativistic attitudes towards truth itself, according to which what is true for some would not be true for others; the radical opposition posited between the logical mentality of the West and symbolic mentality of the East; the subjectivism which by regarding reason as the only source of knowledge, becomes incapable of raising its "gaze to the heights, not daring to rise to the truth of being," [John Paul II, Encyclical letter *Fides et ratio*, 5, *AAS* 91, 1999, pp. 5–88], the difficulty in understanding and accepting the presence of definitive and eschatological events in history; the metaphysical emptying of the historical incarnation of the Eternal Logos, reduced to a mere appearing of God in history; the eclecticism of those who in theological research, uncritically absorb ideas from a variety of philosophical and theological contexts without regard to consistency, suplematic connection, on compatibility with Christian truth; finally the tendency to read and introspect Sacred Scripture outside the tradition and Magisterium of the Church.

The whole Declaration, which would seem to refute and reject all of which I have suggested in this study, appears to be something of a retraction, through reinterpretation, of the spirit of *Nostra Aetate*, perhaps in the wake of subsequent criticism. Furthermore, since its main theme is the "unicity" of the church, meaning that Catholicism is the only true Christianity, and it only tangentially relates to other religions, which, in any case, were never accepted as real truths by Catholicism, (see section VI, paragraphs 20–22), it appears to be mainly directed to other Christian denominations, and was, therefore, understandably forcefully rejected by a significant group of Protestant pastors, in their "Analysis of Dominus Iesus" (http//www.cwrc-rz. org/analysisofdi.html).

This document does indeed require careful and critical analysis in its relation to *Nostra Aetate*.

6. See further the Catachism of the Catholic Church no.159:

Faith and science: "Thought faith is above reason, there can never be a real discrepancy between faith and reason. Since the same God who reveals mysteries and infuses faith was bestowed the light of reason on the human mind, God cannot deny himself, nor can truth ever contradict truth. Consequently, methodical. . . . All branches of knowledge, provided it is carried out in a truly scientific manner and does not override moral laws, can never conflict with faiths, because the things of the world and the things of faith derive from the same God. The humble and persevering investigator of the secrets of nature is being led, as it were, by the hand of God in spite of himself, for it is God, the conserver of all things who made them what they are."

And already in 1893 Pope Leo XIII wrote in an encyclical:

. . . No real disagreement can exist between the theologian and the scientist provided each keeps within his limits . . . (Leo XIII, *Providentissimas* Deus 18).

And the Jesuit Teilhard de Chardin (1881–1955), wrote in his influential 1959 book, *The Phenomenon of Man* that science and religion were two vital sides of a same phenomenon: a quest for perfect knowledge. (The book was finished in 1930, but published posthumously in 1955. Initially the Catholic Church prohibited its publication on the grounds it contradicted orthodoxy. It deals, inter-alia with evolution. However, later his views were regarded by the Church as acceptable, (e.g., Pope Benedict XV in his reflections on the *Episte to the Romans* in July 2009; see John L. Allen, Jr., 28 July 2009, *National Catholic Reporter*).

Many changes have taken place in the Church's attitude to science. The Galileo affair is well known. And in 1939 Pope Pius XII, in his speech to the Pontifical Academy of Sienna, spoke of Galileo as among "the most audacious heroes of research . . .," while Cardinal Ratzinger, on 15 February 1990, said in a speech delivered in the Sapienza University at Rome that some current views of the Galileo affair form "a symptomatic case that permits us to see how deep self-doubt of the modern age, of science and technology go today." By 1992 Pope John Paul II expressed regret for how the Galileo affair was handled, and Galileo himself underwent complete rehabilitation even to the extent that a statue of him was erected within the Vatican walls. (See Richard Owen and Sarah Delaney, "Vatican recants with statue of Galileo," *London Times Online News*, 2008.)

(On the "Galileo affair," see Pietro Redondi, *Galileo: Heretic*, transl. Raymond Rosenthal, Princeton, N.J., 1987; and Jerome J. Langford, Galileo, *Science and the Church*, 3rd ed., Ann Arbor, 2001.)

This again is a vastly complex subject (for Jewish theology too) that cannot be dealt with here. But see, for example:

> David C. Lindberg and Ronald L. *Numbers, When Science and Christianity Meet*, Chicago, 2003; Phillip M. Thompson, *Between Science and Religion: The Engagement of Catholic Intellectuals with Science and Technology in the Twentieth Century*, Lanham Md., 2009; Benjamin Wicker, *The Catholic Church and Science: Answering the Questions, Exposing the Myths*, Tan Books, 2001; Peter M.J. Hess and Paul L. Allen, *Catholicism and Science*, Greenword, 2008;Dan O'Leary, *Roman Catholicism and Modern Science: A History*, Blumbury Academic, 2006, etc.

Furthermore, in paragraph 62 of *Vatican* II, in the section on "Harmony between culture and Christian Formulation," it is explicitly stated that the faithful should:

> . . . blend modern science and its theories and the understanding of the most recent discoveries with Christian morality and doctrine. Thus their religious practice and morality can keep pace with their scientific knowledge and with an ever-advancing technology.

The editor in *The Documents of Vatican II*, Walter M. Abbott, S.J., America Press 1966, pp. 269–270 note 203, remarks as follows:

Here, as elsewhere, it is easy to recognize the compatibility of insights developed by thinkers such as Teilhard de Chardin in his "Divine Milieu" (Harper, 1960) with the fundamental outlook of the Council. In a sense, this statement of the Constitution ratifies the basic inspiration of the "nouvelle théologie" of the 1940s. For those familiar with some of the controversy over the "nouvelle théologie" at that time it may be of interest to note that several of its leading promoters, including Fathers Henri de Lubac, Jean Daniélou, and Yves Congar, served as expert consultants to the commission responsible for drafting this Constitution.

7. When mentioning Heisenberg, I cannot but call attention to the very ambivalent relationship he had with the Nazi regime. This has been examined in detail, with somewhat ambiguous conclusions by John Cornwall, in his *Hitler's Scientists: Science, War and the Devils' Pact*, London, 2003, see index s.v. Heisenberg, Werner, p. 521a. But what is clear is that he declined invitations to become an émigré at the beginning of the war (p. 230), he was active in Germany atom bomb project (ibid. pp. 199 et seq.), he supported Hitler's war aims (ibid. p. 407), and never openly expressed regret for having worked for him and contributing to the morale of Nazism (ibid.). Cornwall summarizes his uncertain "verdict" (ibid. p. 406).

So what are we to make, finally, of Werner Heizenberg? Was he the brilliant hero who would have deprived Hitler of the atom bomb had he known how? [Cf. ibid. pp. 310–319, 397.] In Michael Frayn's play Copenhagen there is an attempt to draw a parallel between Heisenberg's uncertainty principle in quantum physics and the uncertainties of history and biography. The play is a fictional account of an actual event in which Heisenberg and Nils Bohr met in Copenhagen in 1941. It was first performed in London in 1988, with great success, and subsequently in New York, etc. And, incidentally, see Joseph Cardinal Ratzinger (afterwards Pope Benedict XVI)'s remarks on Heisenberg's attitude to religion in his *Truth and Tolerance: Christian Belief and World Religion*, San Francisco, 2004, pp. 139–141, referring to Heisenberg's *Der Teil und der Ganze: Gesprach in Umkreis der Atom-physik*, Munich, 1969 [*Physics and Beyond: Encounters and Conversations*, transl. Arthur J. Pomerans, New York, 1971]. The conversation with Max Planck (ibid. p. 117), was in 1927, and compare his post-Nazi conversation in 1952 (ibid. p. 288 et seq.).

8. See on this Amaury de Reincourt, *The Eye of Shiva, Eastern Mysticism and Science*, New York, 1981, pp. 24–26.

See J. Bronowsky, *The Ascent of Man*, London, 1973, p. 358 for a fine popular explanation of Heisenberg's theorem and its antecedents in the findings of Karl Friedrich Gauss (late 18th century). He writes:

> When an observer looks at a star, he knows that there is a multitude of causes for error. So he takes several readings, and he hopes, naturally, that the best estimate of the star's position is the average – the centre of the scatter. So far, so obvious. But Gauss pushed on to ask what the *scatter* of the errors tells

us. He devised the Gaussian curve in which the scatter is summarized by the deviation, or spread, of the curve. And from this came a far-reaching idea: the scatter marks an area of uncertainty. We are not sure that the true position is the centre. All we can say is that it lies *in the area of uncertainty*, and the area is calculable from the observed scatter of the individual observations.

And on p. 356 he writes:

. . . We have one step more left to take, to the electron microscope, where the rays are so concentrated that we no longer know whether to call them waves or particles. Electrons are fired at an object, and they trace its outline like a knife-thrower at a fair. The smallest object that has ever been seen is a single atom of thorium. It is spectacular. And yet the soft image confirms that, like the knives that graze the girl at the fair, even the hardest electrons do not give a hard outline. The perfect image is still as remote as the distant stars.

We are here face to face with the crucial paradox of knowledge. Year by year we devise more precise instruments with which to observe nature with more fineness. And when we look at the observations, we are discomfited to see that they are still fuzzy, and we feel that they are as uncertain as ever. We seem to be running after a foal which lurches away from us to infinity every time we come within sight of it.

He continues to describe the evolution of the idea of uncertainty with the early twentieth century Max Born etc. in an almost lyrical style, as follows:

Max Born meant that the new ideas in physics amount to a different view of reality. The world is not a fixed, solid array of objects, out there, for it cannot be fully separated from our perception of it. It shifts under our gaze, it interacts with us, and the knowledge that it yields has to be interpreted by us. There is no way of exchanging information that does not demand an act of judgment. Is the electron a particle? It behaves like one in the Bohr atom. But de Broglie in 1924 made a beautiful wave model, in which the orbits are the places where an exact, whole number of waves closes round the nucleus. Max Born thought of a train of electrons as if each were riding on a crankshaft, so that collectively they constitute a series of Gaussian curves, a wave of probability. A new conception was being made . . . that whatever fundamental units the world is put together from, they are more delicate, more fugitive, more startling than we catch in the butterfly net of our senses.

And he ends with Heisenberg and the statement stated in the text below. (See further J.Z. Yourg, *Doubt and Certainty in Science*, London, 1953.)

A further observation of great interest that Bronovsky makes in connection with the development of physics in the late 19th and 20th century is its influence on art. Thus he writes on pp. 350–351:

> And that is why the turning-point comes in 1897, when J.J. Thomson in Cambridge discovers the electron. Yes, the atom has constituent parts; it is not indivisible, as its Greek name had implied. The electron is a tiny part of its mass or weight, but a real part, and it carries a single electric charge. Each element is characterized by the number of electrons in its atoms. And their number is exactly equal to the number of the place in Mendeleev's table that that element occupies when hydrogen and helium are included in first and second place. That is, lithium has three electrons, beryllium has four electrons, boron has five, and so on steadily all through the table. The place in the table that an element occupies is called its atomic number, and now that turned out to stand for a physical reality within its atom – the number of electrons there. The picture has shifted from atomic weight to atomic number, and that means, essentially, to atomic structure.
>
> That is the intellectual breakthrough with which modern physics begins. Here the great age opens. Physics becomes in those years the greatest collective work of science – no, more than that, the great collective work of art of the twentieth century.
>
> I say "work of art," because the notion that there is an underlying structure, a world within the world of the atom, captured the imagination of artists at once. Art from the year 1900 on is different from the art before it, as can be seen in any original painter of the time: Umberto Boccioni, for instance, in *The Forces of a Street*, or his *Dynamism of a Cyclist*. Modern art begins at the same time as modern physics because it begins in the same ideas.
>
> Since the time of Newton's *Opticks*, painters had been entranced by the coloured surface of things. The twentieth century changed that. Like the X-ray pictures of Röntgen, it looked for the bone beneath the skin, and for the deeper, solid structure that builds up from the inside the total form of an object or a body. A painter like Juan Gris is engaged in the analysis of structure, whether he is looking at natural forms in *Still Life* or at the human form in *Pierrot*.
>
> The Cubist painters, for example, are obviously inspired by the families of crystals. They see in them the shape of a village on a hillside, as Georges Braque did in his *Houses at L'Estaque*, or a group of women as Picasso painted them in *Les Demoiselles d'Avignon*. In Pablo Picasso's famous beginning to Cubist painting – a single face, *the Portrait of Daniel-Henry Kahnweiler* – the interest has shifted from the skin and the features to the underlying geometry. The head has been taken apart into mathematical shapes and then put together as a reconstruction, a re-creation, from the inside out.

This new search for the hidden structure is striking in the painters of Northern Europe: Franz Marc, for example, looking at the natural landscape in *Deer in a Forest*; and (a favourite with scientists) the Cubist Jean Metzinger, whose *Woman on a Horse* was owned by Niels Bohr, who collected pictures in his house in Copenhagen.

He ends this section somewhat whimsically, thus:

> There are two clear differences between a work of art and a scientific paper. One is that in the work of art the painter is visibly taking the world to pieces and putting it together of the same canvas. And the other is that you can watch him thinking while he is doing it. (For example, Georges Seurat putting one coloured dot beside another of a different colour to get the total effect in *Young Woman with a Powder Puff* and *Le Bec*.) In both those respects the scientific paper is often deficient. It often is only analytic; and it almost always hides the process of thought in its impersonal language.

9. See also his *My View of the World*, Oxford, 1983, chapter 4, in which he indicates that individual consciousness is only a manifestation of the unitary consciousness pervading the world. Indeed, his essay "The Spirit of Science," apud *Spirit and Nature, Eranos Yearbook*, New York, 1954, (first written in 1946, pp. 322–341) begins with a quote from Sankara's commentary to *Vedanta-Sutras*, and then goes on to refer to Buddhist thought.

10. See de Riencourt ibid. p. 178. And see further Frederick Sontag, *Uncertain Truth*, Lanham, 1995, who states that a situation of cultural and intellectual uncertainty characterizes the 20th century context of the search for truth, attributing this to developments in quantum and theoretical physics, as well as philosophy and linguistics.

See, for example, the view of C.S. Peirce, who formulated the notion of "fallibilism" in the context of his unique occupation with the philosophy of science. (See his "Some Consequences of Four Incapacities," *Collected Papers of Charles Sanders Peirce*, edd. C. Hartshorne and P. Weiss, vol. 5, Cambridge, Mass., 1958, pp. 264–265.), according to which there are three things human beings cannot achieve: "Absolute certainty, absolute exactitude, absolute universality" (CP 1 1931, p. 141, see his "Fallibilities, Continuity, and Evolution" ibid.). Indeed, any knowledge we have is by definition fallible and partial, even without taking the dynamics of itself into account:

> For fallibilism is the doctrine that our knowledge is never absolute but always swims, as it were, in a continuum of uncertainty and indeterminacy. Now the doctrine of continuity is that all things so swim in continua. (CP 1: p.171)

(See Nadav Berman Shifman, "Pragmatism and Jewish Thought: R. Eliezer Berkovits's Philosophy of Halakhic Fallibility," in the section of the "Introduction: Jewish Thought and American Pragmatism," in which he discusses Peirce's fallibilism, with a full bibliography. His article will shortly appear in *The Journal of Jewish Thought and Philosophy*, and I thank him for sending me a prepublication copy.)

11. Riencourt ibid. pp. 167–169.

12. Such Eastern views clearly were known to the leaders of the Catholic Church. *Nostra Aetate* related explicitly to Eastern religions. Already in 1960 Engaku Taisio and the Fudenji of Taiten Guariscki, disciple of Taisen Deshimoru founded the Italian Buddhist Association (*Associazione Buddhista Italiana*). (See W.L. King, *Buddhism and Christianity: Some Bridges of Understanding*, Philadelphia 1963.) And, admittedly later, Pope John Paul II (1920–2005), in his *Crossing the Threshold of Hope*, published in New York in 1994, writes concerning Buddhism, quoting the Second Vatican Council, which mentioned "a common soteriological root present in all religions," but that "the Buddhist tradition and methods deriving from it have an almost exclusively element of soteriology" (ibid. p. 85). This greatly angered Buddhist leaders, so that Thinley Nosbu Rinpoche (of Tibetan Buddhism) responded with an essay entitled *Welcoming Flowers from across the Cleansed Threshold of Hope: An Answer to the Pope's Criticism of Buddhism* (Jewel Pub. House, 1997).

Similarly Ven Bhikru Bodhi, of the Theravade Buddhists published an essay (in 2010) entitled *Towards a Threshold of Understanding*, intended as a corrective to the Pope's demeaning characterization of Buddhism." Further on the influence of Buddhism on the West, see Richard King, *Orientalism and Religion: Postcolonial Theory, India and the "Mystic East,"* London and New York, 1944, pp. 143–160, chapter entitled "Orientalism and the Discovery of 'Buddhism.'"

Here again, there is much more to be said on this subject, but let this suffice.

13. See James A. Hajiya, *"The Gita of Robert Oppenheimer,"* Proceedings of the American Philosophical Society 244(2), 2000, pp. 133–166; Richard Rhodes, "I Am Become Death" . . . The Agony of J. Robert Oppenheiumer," *American Heritage*, Oct. 1977, see also idem, *The Making of the Atomic Bomb*, New York, 1986.

14. See Riencourt ibid. pp. 156–197.

15. We can gain some kind of understanding of these strange (to us) enigmatic paradoxical statements, by reading Edward Conze, *Buddhism*, Oxford, 1953, pass.; *The Living Thoughts of Gotama the Buddha*, presented by Ananda K. Coomaraswamy and I.B. Hotner, London, Toronto, Melbourne and Sidney 1948, pp. 1–43, etc.

16. See further Howard Coward, *Jung and Eastern Thought*, Albany, 1985; idem, "Taoism and Jung: Synchronicity and the Self," *Philosophy East and West* 46/4, 1996, pp. 477–495, where he demonstrates that, "Jung's central and often misunderstood concepts – "synchronicity" and "the self" – were strongly influenced in their initial formulation by his reading of Taoist thought."

See also J.J. Clark, *Jung and Eastern Thought: A Dialogue with the Orient*, 1994. So too R. Moacanin, *Jung's Psychology and Tibetan Buddhism: Western and Eastern Paths to the Heart*, Wislow, 1986.

17. Maritain's theological attitude towards the Jews changed in the post-holocaust period. Thomas A. Idinopulos, in his aricle "How the Shoah Affects Christian Belief," apud *Contemporary Christian Religious Responses to the Shoah, Studies in the Shoah* vol. 6, ed. Steven L. Jacobs, Lanham, New York, London, 1993, pp. 115–116, highlights this change:

> In an essay of 1937, "The Mystery of Israel," [reprinted in *The Social and Political Philosophy of Jacques Maritain*, edd. Joseph Evans and Leo Ward, N.Y., 1956, pp. 194–212] Maritain refers to "the basic weakness of the mystical communion of Israel," which is "its failure to understand the cross, its refusal of the cross." He also speaks of the passion or historical suffering of the Jewish people:
>
> It is the passion of a scapegoat, enmeshed in the earthly destiny of the world and in ways of the world mixed with sin, a scapegoat against which the impure sufferings of the world strike back, when the world seeks vengeance for the misfortunes of its history upon what activates that history. Israel thus suffers the repercussion of the activation it produces, or which the world feels it is destined to produce. . . .
>
> When one looks beneath the involution of the writing, one recognizes that the author repeats the argument of the ancient church fathers: The Jewish people, in rejecting Christ, antagonizes the Christian world, thereby bringing down on itself calamity and woe. The clear implication is that if the Jewish people accepts the message of the victorious cross, if Israel ceases to be *Israel*, anti-Semitism will stop, Jewish suffering will cease.
>
> It is impossible to know if the events of the Second World War and the *Shoah* made Maritain seem somehow more realistic in his attitude toward suffering, particularly Jewish suffering. There is the first hint that some suffering is unexplainable, useless, serving no higher, no greater purpose. In an essay of 1946 ["Blessed are the Persecuted," reprinted in *The Range of Reasons*, New York, 1952, pp. 219–226], which takes its title from Jesus' eighth beatitude, "Blessed are they that suffer persecution for justice's sake: for theirs is the kingdom of heaven," Maritain speaks of the classical Christian equation

between suffering and salvation. Those who choose to suffer in imitation of Christ's cross, share his victory, inheriting the kingdom of heaven. But what of those who do not so choose: indeed, what of those who were never permitted a choice? After reciting instances of Nazi atrocities, including references to the destruction of the Jews, Maritain asks:

Where lay the consolation of these persecuted innocents? And how many others died completely forsaken? They did not give their lives; their lives were taken from them, and under the shadow of horror. They suffered without having wanted to suffer. They did not know why they died. Those who know why they die are greatly privileged.

What is significant about this statement is its spirit: it represents that rare instance in which a Christian thinker felt compelled to search within his own theological system for a specific answer to the specific question raised by the knowledge of manifestly useless suffering. What is remarkable is not the answer given, but the honest facing of the question.

Reflecting on the meaningless suffering of innocent people, Maritain speaks differently of the relationship between Jews and Christians. Now they constitute a kind of fellowship of suffering. "Like strange companions," he writes, they "have together journeyed along the road to Calvary." He continues, "The great mysterious fact is that the sufferings of Israel have more and more distinctly taken the shape of the cross." Here the point is no longer Jewish suffering caused by the rejection of Christ; there is a new emphasis on the Jew's sharing of Christ's cross as the result of this innocent, unjustified suffering. Perhaps it is only that – a change of emphasis, not an essentially altering of the mind. One cannot be sure.

See also Richard Francis Crane, "Heart-Rending Ambivalence: Jacques Maritain and the Complexity of the Post-War Catholic Philosemitism," *Studies in Christian-Jewish Relations 6,* 2011; *Jacques Maritain and the Jews,* ed. Robert Royal, Notre Dame, Indiana, 1994, pass.

Here we should like to quote a very significant statement of Maritain, found in his *On the Church of Christ*, transl. Joseph W. Evans, Notra Dame, Indiana, 1973, p. 174:

It seems to me very significant that those two events of such great bearings – on the Jewish side the return of a portion of the people to the Promised Land, on the Christian Side the Second Council of the Vatican – took place at the same time, the first in 1948, the second in 1962–1965. They mark, each in its own way, a reorientation of history.

(Cited in Michael Novak's important essay, "Maritain and the Jews," in *Jacques Maritain and the Jews,* p. 123. The whole essay is on pp. 123–137.) Maritain's juxtaposition of these "reorientalizing" events suggests that the establishment of the State of Israel was also a significant component in the development resulting in the formulation of *Nostra Aetate*.

18. See, for example, James Q. Wilson, *The Moral Sense*, New York, 1993, p. 8, and Roy F. Baumeister's somewhat problematic study, *Evil: Inside Human Cruelty and Violence*, New York, 1997.

19. See J. Maritain, *An Essay on Christian philosophy*, New York, 1955, pp. 38 et seq.

20. Joshua Parens, in his book *An Islamic Philosophy of Virtuous Religions: Introducing Alferabi*, New York, 2006, in a chapter [six] entitled, "The Limits of Knowledge," wrote (p. 121):

> The limits of human knowledge are at the root of Alfarabis claim that there can be a multiplicity of virtuous religions (*Political Regime*, Hydrabad ed. P. 56) . . . the inadequacy of our knowledge would make the imposition of one religion on all of humanity a great injustice. No philosopher-king exists whose knowledge of final causes or prudent grasp of particulars can match the variety of human experience.

And cf. p. 149 note 15, that "the absence of adequate knowledge of decisive and human purpose accounts for [the acknowledgment of] the ultimate superiority of the rule of law over the rule of the best human being. And law, in turn, is a kind of mixture of reason . . . and consent (democracy) necessitated, at least in part, by the Limitations of our knowledge."
This leads him on to his notion of the multiplicity of Religions.
And in chapter five, entitled "The Multiplicity Argument," Parens writes that:

> Alfarabi claims that religion is inherently multiple. Religions must be adapted to the time and place for which they are given (*AH* secs. 24, 33, 46). (AH= Alfarabi, *Attainment of Happiness*, transl. Muhsin Mahdi, New York, 1962.)

Parens continues (ibid. pp. 76–79):

> Of course, we should not be surprised that he holds that there are not only certain opinions but also certain acts that "all or most nations" may share in common (44, 34. 3–5 and 45, 34.II–13). Alfarabi goes on to argue that the basis of these shared acts and opinions is human beings' shared "human nature" (*al-tab ah al-insaniyyah*) (45, 34.14; Yasin, 83). (Jasin – *Tahsil al sa'adah*, ed. Jafar al Yasim, Beirut, 1981.) Yet it should be obvious that the view that we share some acts and opinions in common need not entail the view that all of our religions should be the same, or that Alfarabi aims at a relatively homogeneous

virtuous regime of the inhabited world. On the contrary, he immediately follows up his references to such a shared nature and its entailed shared acts
and opinions with references to the ruler's need to attend to the differences
between "every group in every nation" (*kull ta'ifatin min kulli 'ummah*) (45,
34.15; Yasin, 84). What he says about the things that human beings share is
characteristically schematic. He could mean that all or most have common
beliefs, such as in one God. He could mean that all or most share the view that
justice and mercy need to be practiced at least within one's own community,
if not toward the enemies of one's faith. Of course, the beliefs and actions
that monotheistic religions share are quite extensive, indeed, so extensive that
at times each faith must search for ways of distinguishing its own teaching.

This, of course, is not yet the "Perrenial Philosophy" or "World Religion," but, I
believe, a step in that direction; but resulting out of our inadequacy of knowledge
and the ultimate element of uncertainty.

Incidentally, let me quote a very witty criticism of this notion of a universal
religion. It is brought by R.J. Zwi Werblowsky, at the end of his *Beyond Tradition
and Modernity: Changing Religious in a Changing World*, London, 1976, p. 115:

> And having quoted, in this chapter, both Dogen Zenji and Martin Buber, I
> would conclude with a story that brings the two together in Jerusalem and
> which I heard from one of our generation's great Zen masters. It is the story
> of a fruitful misunderstanding, and of an encounter in which one participant
> did all the talking, the second participant did all the listening, and the third
> participant did nothing at all.
>
> The Zen master was invited on a tour around the world by an ardent
> American admirer. When the two came to Jerusalem they called on Buber. The
> American talked, Buber listened, and the Zen master sat in silence. With great
> verve the American held forth that all religions were basically one, different
> variations of an identical theme, manifold manifestations of one and the same
> essence. Buber gave him one of his long, piercing looks, and then shot at him
> the question: "And what is the essence?" At this point the Zen master could
> not contain himself: he jumped from his seat and with both hands shook the
> hands of Buber.

See also his essay, "Universal Religion and Universalist Religion," in *International
Journal for Philosophy of Religion* 2, 1971, pp. 1–13.

21. See *De Roma*, apud *Suda* s.v. Alexandros of Milesios, apud M. Stern, *Greek and
Latin Authors on Jews and Judaism*, vol. 1, Jerusalem, 1976, no. 52, p. 163.

Stern, in his commentary ad loc. suggests that Alexander Polyhistor may have
recounted the tradition of the female Jewish lawgiver in connection with King

Numa and the Nymph Egeria. For Pompilius Numa, the legendary second King of Roma (traditionally 715–673 B.C.E.), according to Ennius received instruction from Egeria, in the formulation of the alleged "Laws of Numa" (Cicero, *Rep.* 2.26, etc.), which, of course, have not survived. Egeria, the water goddess, received her name etymologically from the Latin root *egerere*, to deliver, to draw out to extract. And for this reason pregnant women sacrificed to her for an easy delivery. The Hebrew name Mosheh (Moses) was given him by Pharoah's daughter because she "drew him out of the water" (Exodus 2:10) – "drew out" in Hebrew being *meshitihu* – hence *Mosheh*. On one of the strange mistakenly associative connections of the Polyhistor text was a faulty Jewish tradition that Moses appeared in the form of a woman, see M.M. Kasher, *Torah Shelemah* vol. 8 (part 9), New York, 1954, p. 246, (to Exodus 2:2), an amusing tale of multiple errors.

22. This has been argued from a totally different standpoint but with a similar conclusion by Robert Erlewine, in his *Monotheism and Tolerance: Recovering of Religion of Reason*, Bloomington and Indianapolis, 2010, following the lead taken by John Hick, in his *God has Many Names*, Philadelphia, 1980, and in Jürgen Habermas' many publications, listed in Erlewine ibid., thought, I must admit, I have not really followed their line of reasoning.

CHAPTER 9

Limits of Toleration

Now in the area of religion, tolerance[1] can perhaps be accepted, so long as one person's faith does not *harm* the other.[2] But when an extreme ideological position impacts negatively upon those who do not accept it,[3] then tolerance is no longer seen as an option.[4] Or as John Stuart Mill wrote in his essay *On Liberty* in 1859 (ed. H.B. Acton, [1972] p. 73):

> The only purpose for which power can be rightfully exercised over any number of a civilized community against his will is to prevent harm to others.

Indeed, the famous "Dutch Catachism," which was formulated in the wake of the Second Vatican-Council, attempting fully to render its message to adult Catholics, deals with this issue at some length. We cite the English translation entitled *A New Catachism: Catholic Faith for Adults*, West Germany, 1965 (being a translation of *De Nieuwe Katechismus* by Kevin Smyth), pp. 353–354, section entitled "Tolerance":

> Here we may insert a few words on tolerance. This does not merely mean that we respect the Christian element in the opinions of those whose beliefs are different. It also means that *we respect the convictions of others even where their tendency is away from Christianity*, when, therefore, we find that they impoverish men instead of enriching them. The question of tolerance is not an easy one which can be dismissed with a few catch-words or slogans.
>
> The difficulty is not so much that another possesses such convictions in his own mind. *The Church recognizes that faith is a free act and hence that force or pressure may never be used to bring men to believe.*

Thus the inner freedom of others is clearly recognized as a principle. And the Church emphasizes just as strongly that each man must follow his conscience. *The difficulty begins when a conviction becomes the subject of propaganda and tries to impose itself with all the means it can dispose of.* Take for instance the typically non-Christian racialism of the Nazis. No amount of respect for the opinions of others should prevent us from airing our distaste and disagreement.

May we also call in the law of the land? If the conviction which is being put about is not merely unchristian but inhuman, criminal, then this may be done. But who is to decide ultimately that an opinion is such? The law of the land? But if so, no revolution would ever be possible or permissible. Then who decides? It is impossible to define this clearly, and hence tolerance must always be something which must be worked out in each particular case by society.

The Church has the Ten Commandments, which therefore provide a help. But one cannot use these without more … as the norms for what human society should regard as inhuman. (For instance, it would not do to impose the first commandment on atheists.) The Church must defend these commandments with all its might. But what we are concerned with now is whether society may impose them as the norm to decide what is criminal and what is not and hence upholds them by its laws and sanctions.

Hence it is obviously difficult to describe in theory the limits of tolerance and define them sharply. But this should not make us underestimate the value of this virtue. We must make the greatest possible tolerance of the convictions of others an ideal after which we strive. Love, the gentleness of the gospel and reverence for the uniqueness and freedom of the other demand this of us. We must be proud to see responsible functions in a practically fully Catholic society placed in the hands of those of different beliefs. We should be proud of the fact that in such a society other convictions can freely exist and exercise their attraction and find nothing opposed to them except the clear light of truth and the patience which comes from the Spirit.

[My emphasis. D.S.]

So while the Church recognizes the fact that it is difficult to formulate definitive guide-lines delineating the limits of tolerance, it is also clear that when religion then turns to being divisive and inextricably confused and entwined with negative political policies, then this is a clear recipe for violence and bloodshed. Thus, for example, when rituals clash in a single location of holiness, philosophical theology is forgotten in the heat of the moment, and an eruption occurs, which serves as the basis of a new ideology, creating new narratives,[5] and once again positions of intolerance gain ascendency. Add to that the fact that the general public as a norm is not trained in sophisticated thinking, and finds difficulty in accepting the legitimacy of "multiple truths," or even to be "condescending" to the views of the other. Hence, it is easily led on by charismatic preachers to a fundamentalist position, with all which that implies. Furthermore, liberalism is then explained as an ideology of compromise, and hence, one of weakness that must never be exposed. And so a complete reversal of thought may cancel the achievements of a century of progressive thinking.

Undoubtedly the publication of *Nostra Aetate* constituted for Jews a watershed event, and indeed for Christians it was a "theological break-through," (as stated in the 2015 Declaration, sect. 39).

Endnotes to Chapter 9

1. Wilhelm Halbfass, in his important book *India and Europe: An Essay on Understanding*, New York, 1981, chapter 22, pp. 403–418, entitled "'Inclusivism' and 'Tolerance' in the Encounter between India and the West," discusses the extensive writings of Paul Hacker (193–1979) at various stages of his thinking on the relationship and difference between inclusivism and tolerance. Interalia, the distinction is made between "practical tolerance," which is a way of human interaction with members of different religious groups, and "doctrinal tolerance . . . which is a manner of recognizing other religious teachings" (ibid. pp. 403–404). The discussion is primarily within the content of Hindu thought. Thus, for instance, we read (ibid.):

> Hacker discussed examples often cited as evidence for the "doctrinal tolerance" of Hinduism, such as the identification of the highest principles of different religious and philosophical traditions with the absolute of Vedāntic monism, or the recognition of foreign traditions as preliminary stages. Again, this should not be called "tolerance." Instead, it is "a peculiar mixture of doctrinal tolerance and intolerance" and a "form of religious self-assertion" which seems to be particularly appropriate to the Indian way of thinking.

However, the categorization of different kinds of tolerance, even though at times the distinctions are blurred, are surely revealing, and should be taken into account in such discussions.

Hacker also introduced another category "inclusivism" which also needs to be considered, not only in relation to "tolerance" but also to "pluralism." But, once again, a fuller examination of these terms and their implications is beyond the scope of this study.

See further R. Panikkar, *Myth, Faith and Hermeneutics*, New York, Toronto 1979, pp. 22–25 on his four categories of tolerance, and pp. 25–30 on the limits of tolerance.

2. As, indeed, Benjamin Constant expressed it in the early 19th century:

> . . . everything which does not interfere with order; everything which belongs only to the inward nature of man, such as opinion; everything which, in the expression of opinion, does not harm others . . . everything which, in regard to industry, allows the free exercise of rival industry – is individual and cannot legitimately be subjected to the power of society (*Mélanges de literature et de*

politique [Paris 1829] Preface; apud *Dictionary of the History of Ideas: Studies of Selected Pivotal Ideas*, vol. 2, ed. P.P. Wiener, New York, 1973, p. 599 [in Steven Lukas' entry "Individualism: Types of"].)

Or as James A. Froude (1818–1894) said:

> Toleration is a good thing in its place; but you cannot tolerate what will not tolerate you, and is trying to cut your throat (T. Edwards, *The New Dictionary of Thought*, U.S.A. 1986, p. 676a).

This too was clearly fomulated in *Dignitatis Humanae*, in the words (cited above) "within due limits," and further explicated in paragraph 4:

> Provided the just demands of public order are observed, religious communities rightfully claim freedom in order that they may govern themselves according to their own norms. . . .

And again in paragraph 7:

> The right to religious freedom is exercised in human society; hence its exercise is *subject to certain regulatory norms*. [My emphasis, D.S.]

And it continues:

> Furthermore, society has the right to defend itself against possible abuses committed on the pretext of freedom of religion. It is the special right of government to provide this protection.
> These norms arise out of the need for effective safeguard of the rights of all citizens and for peaceful settlement of conflicts of rights. They flow from the need for an adequate care of genuine public peace, which comes about when men live together in good order and in true justice. They come, finally, out of the need for a proper guardianship of public morality. These matters constitute the basic component of the common welfare: they are what is meant by public order.
> For the rest, the usages of society are to be the usages of freedom in their full range. These require that the freedom of man be respected as far as possible, *and curtailed only when and in so far as necessary*. [My emphasis, D.S.]

The commentator in *The Documents of Vatican II*, edd. W.M. Abbott and J. Gallagher, America Press 1966, pp. 686 (notes 20, 21) has lengthy comments on this section which are of considerable importance and hence cited here at length:

> It is a matter of common sense that the exercise of all freedoms in society must be subject to certain regulatory norms. The Declaration states first the moral norm – the principle of personal and social responsibility. Its juridical norm which should control the action of government in limiting or inhibiting the

exercise of the right to religious freedom. (Note that the right itself is always inalienable, never to be denied; only the exercise of the right is subject to control in particular instances.) The norm cannot be the common welfare, since the common welfare requires that human rights should be protected, not limited, in their exercise. Hence the Declaration adopts the concept of public order. The concept has good warrant in constitutional law. However, it is more frequently used than defined. The Declaration undertakes to define it. In doing so, it makes a contribution to the science of law and jurisprudence.

First, the requirements of public order are not subject to arbitrary definition – at the hands, say, of tyrannical governments, which might abuse the concept for their own ends. The public order of society is a part of the universal moral order; its requirements must be rooted in moral law. Second, public order exhibits a threefold content. First, the order of society is essentially an order of justice, in which the rights of all citizens are effectively safe-guarded, and provision is made for peaceful settlements of conflicts of rights. Second, the order of society is a political order, an order of peace ("domestic tranquility" is the American constitutional phrase). Public peace, however, is not the result of repressive action by the police. It is, in the classic concept, the work of justice; it comes about, of itself, when the demands of justice are met, and when orderly processes exist for airing and setting grievances. Third, the order of society is a moral order, at least in the sense that certain minimal standards of public morality are enforced at all.

Public order herefore is constituted by these three values – juridical, polit-ical, moral. They are the basic elements in the common welfare, which is a wider concept than public order. And so necessary are these three values that the coercive force of government may be enlisted to protect and vindicate them. Together they furnish a reasonable juridical criterion for coercive restriction of freedom. The free exercise of religion may not be inhibited unless proof is given that it entails some violation of the rights of others, or of the public peace, or of public morality. In these cases, in other words a public action ceases to be a religious exercise and becomes a penal offense.

And on the last passage he writes:

Secular experts may well consider this to be the most significant sentence in the Declaration. It is a statement of the basic principle of the "free society." The principle has important origins in the medieval tradition of kingship, law, and jurisprudence. But its statement by the Church has an accent of blessed newness – the newness of a renewal of the tradition. The renewal, already hesitantly begun by Pius XII, was strongly furthered by John XXIII. Catholic thought had consistently held that society is to be based upon truth (the truth of the human person), directed toward justice, and animated by charity. In "Pacem in Terris," John XXIII added the missing fourth term, freedom. Freedom is an end or purpose of society, which looks to the liberation of the human person. Freedom is the political method par excellence, whereby the other goals of society are reached. Freedom, finally, is the prevailing social usage, which sets the style of society. This progress in doctrine is sanctioned and made secure by "Dignitatis Humanae Personae."

The Council calls attention to the paradox of the moment. Freedom today is threatened; freedom today is itself a threat. Hence the Council calls for education both in the uses of freedom and in the ways of obedience. When freedom is truly responsible, it implies a rightful response to legitimate authority.

This is also stressed in *A New Catechism: Catholic Faith for Adults*, West Germany 1967, (being a translation of the Dutch *De Nieuwe Katechismus*, pp. 353–354, section entitled "tolerance").

This is already indicated in John Paul XXIII's *Pacem in Terris*, promulgated on April 11, 1963, paragraph 12. See further, D. Edwards, "The Limits of Toleration," apud S. Mendes, ed., *On Toleration*, Oxford 1987, pp. 125–126; Yossi Nehushtan, "Limits of Tolerance, A Substantive-Liberal Perspective," *Ratio Juris* 20/2, 2007, p. 230, etc.

Although this might not seem to be completely "politically correct" in contemporary thinking, I would like to present this notion in the context of Jewish legal thought. In Deuteronomy 19:11–13 we read:

> But if any man hate his neighbour, and lie in wait for him, and rise up against him, and smite him mortally that he die, and fleeth into one of these cites [i.e. of refuge]. Then the elders of his city shall send and fetch him thence, and deliver him into the hand of the overger of blood that he may die.
>
> Thine eye shall not pity him, but thou shall put away the guilt of innocent blood from Israel, that it may go well with thee.

On which the Rabbis of old commented:

> *Sifrei ad loc* (second century C.E.): "This eye shall not pity him" – What does this teach us? Perhaps you might argue: Since he murder so and so, why should we take vengeance of the blood of that person? For this we are told: "Thine eye shall not pity him."

And this is followed up by Nachmanides (1194–1270) in his commentary to Deuteronomy ad loc. that this statement should be listed among the negative commandments (i.e. it is not *advice*, but a mandated *command*), and so too Maimonides (1135–1204) in his *Hilchot Sanhedrin* 4:4, and Hilchot *Hovel u-Mazik* 1:4, and his *Sefer ha-Mitzvot* no. 279, etc. Nonetheless, in practice the Rabbis were very reticent to actually carry out executions (even in Temple times), so much so that R.

The "Judensau." Badly weathered sandstone relief outside the choir of the city church in Wittenberg, c. 1305.

The "Judensau." Anonymous woodcut from south Germany c. 1470, Germanisches National Museum.

Eliezer ben Azaria (early 2nd century C.E.) stated that a *Sanhedrin* (supreme court of law) that executes once in seventy years is regarded negatively (*nikreit hovlanit,* literally: is called injurious), and the contemporary R. Akiva stated that if he were to serve in those courts there would never be an execution. (*M. Makkot* ad fin). To this end the Rabbis put numerous structures upon the legal procedure, demanding that the "criminal" be warned in advance close to the criminal event by the same witnesses who give testimony, and who are not related to the accused, nor known to have prior bad relations with him, etc. So the law existed in the codes, but was very rarely actually executed, and only in unique situations where no possible doubt existed and where there were no extenuating circumstances. Similarly, the State of Israel does not exercise capital punishment, and only did so in the single solitary and unique case of Eichmann. I shall not further expand on this very complex theme, which, however, should be related to the case of the Nuremberg trials, and other international cases such as that of Idi Amin and other massacres in Africa, Paul Pott in East Asia, and those involved in Bosnian tragedy, etc.

See further R. Aharon Lichtenstein, "The Parameters of Tolerance" apud Moshe Sokol, ed. *Tolerance, Dissent, and Democracy: Philosophical Historical, and Halakhic Perspectives,* Northvale, 2002, pp. 137–174.

3. See e.g., Karl Jaspers, *The Perennial Scope of Philosophy,* New York, 1949, pp. 92–95, referred to above chapter 2.

This has been termed the "paradox of toleration," and is resolved by recognizing the difference between "first-order judgements" and "second-order moral judgements." The first is an emotional reaction and/or a practical judgement, while the second is beyond emotion. Thus when there is a genuine conflict between "second-order" commitments, that is, when the total commitment to autonomy runs against an intolerant rejection of autonomy was against an intolerant rejection of autonomy, then there is no need to tolerate. In other words, the paradox is resolved when one realizes that toleration is not a commitment to relativism, but rather that it is a commitment to the value of autonomy and to the distinction between "first order judgements" and "second-order moral commitments."

4. Herbert Marcuse, in his essay entitled "Repressive Tolerance," apud *A Critique of Pure Tolerance,* Boston 1965, writes (pp. 84–85):

> Generally, the function and value of tolerance depends on the equality prevalent in the society in which tolerance is practiced. Tolerance itself stands subject to overriding criteria: its range and its limits cannot be defined in terms of the respective society. In other words, tolerance is an end in itself only when it is truly universal, practiced by the rulers as well as by the ruled, by the lords as well as by the peasants, by the sheriffs as well as by their victims. And such

241

universal tolerance is possible only when no real or alleged enemy requires in the national interest the education and training of people in military violence and destruction. As long as these conditions do not prevail, the conditions of tolerance are "loaded": they are determined and defined by the institutionalized in-equality (which is certainly compatible with constitutional equality), i.e., by the class structure of society. In such a society, tolerance is *de facto* limited on the dual ground of legalized violence or suppression (police, armed forces, guards of all sorts) and of the privileged position held by the predominant interests and their "connections."

These background limitations of tolerance are normally prior to the explicit and judicial limitations as defined by the courts, custom, governments, etc. (for example, "clear and present danger," threat to national security, heresy). Within the framework of such a social structure, tolerance can be safely practiced and proclaimed. It is of two kinds: (1) the passive toleration of entrenched and established attitudes and ideas even if their damaging effect on man and nature is evident; and (2) the active, official tolerance granted to the Right as well as to the Left, to movements of aggression as well as to movements of peace, to the party of hate as well as to that of humanity. I call this non-partisan tolerance "abstract" or "pure" inasmuch as it refrains from taking sides – but in doing so it actually protects the already established machinery of discrimination.

The tolerance which enlarged the range and content of freedom was always partisan – intolerant toward the protagonists of the repressive status quo. The issue was only the degree and extent of intolerance. . . .

5. See G. Langmuir, *Towards a Definition of Antisemitism*, Oakland, 1990, who calls these irrational fantasies and beliefs about Jews "chimerical assertions."

The "chimerical" nature of the "Adversus Judaeos" expresses itself more overtly in the development of the Judensau motif, in which the Jew suckles from the teet of a sow. See the classic study of Isiah Sachar, *The Judensau: A Mediaeval Anti-Jewish Motif and its History*, London, 1974.

We may add that in these horrific illustrations there is also a Jew sucking from the posterior of the pig. This reminds us of the other sign of the black cat discussed by Sara Lipton in her *Images of Intolerance: The Representation of Jews and Judaism in the Bible Moralisée*, Berkeley, Los Angeles, London, 1999, chapter 4. On p. 89 she refers to the image included by Walter Map, in his *De Nugis Curialium*, c. 1185 (Dist.1, chapter 30):

> There is, too, another old heresy who recently has increased beyond all mea-
> sure . . . They are called Publicans or Paterenes . . . about the first watch
> of the night each group of these, closing all gates and windows, sitteth in
> expectant silence in their synagogues. Then cometh down by a rope a black

cat of marvelous size. [The heretics] approach, feeling their way to the spot where they have seen their lord, and . . . they kiss him, some his feet, *many under the tail, and very many his private parts.*

See also Lipton ibid. pp. 191–192 note 74, and the Cathars being called after the cat, "because they kiss the posterior of a cat in whose shape, it is said, Lucifer appears to them" (ibid. p. 89). See her continued analysis ibid. See also Irina Metzler, "Heretical Cats: Animal Symbolism in Religious Discourse," *Mediam Aevum* 59, 2009.

It is somewhat ironic that the image of the Jew suckling from a sow, iconographically goes back to the legend of Romulus and Remus who were suckled by a wolf. See, e.g., the Capitoline Wolf (Lupa Capitolina), a bronze sculpture probably from the 12 or 13 centuries, to be found in the Palazzo dei Conservatore on the Campidolglio at Rome, where two human infants are being suckled by a wolf. This, then, is the foundational myth of the founding of Rome. (On the dating see Francis Haskell and Nicholas Penny, *Taste and the Antiquite: The Lure of Classical Sculpture, 1500–1900*, Yale, 1981, p. 241; Adriano La Regina, "Roma, l'ingarnno della Lupa e' 'nata del Mideoeva:" *La Republica* 17, 2006.) Furthermore, this image was favoured by Benito Mussollini, who in 1929 sent several copies of it to American cities, such as Cincinnati, Ohio, etc., representing, in his opinion, the "New Rome." It was also used as an emblem for the summer Olympics at Rome in 1960.

As to the pig representing Rome in Jewish sources – it was the symbol of the *Legio XX Fretensis* which destroyed the Temple at Jerusalem on 70 C.E., this was seen as a symbol of hypocrisy. See, e.g., *Genesis Rabba* 65:1 ed. Albeck, p. 713 and parallels, and commentary. Further on the pig see Misgav Har-Peled's doctoral dissertation, Baltimore, Maryland, 2013, entitled *The Dialogical Beast: The Identification of Rome with the Pig in Early Rabbinic Literature*; Claudine Fabre-Vacsas, *The Singular Beast: Jews, Christians and the Pig*, New York, 1997, pass.

(Incidentally, sometimes it is the Jew himself who is depicted as a pig, as, for example, in V. Lenepreu's caricature in his *Musée des Horreurs*, 1900, "Le Roi des Porcs," where Emile Zola, archenemy of the Dreyfusards is portrayed as a pig, besmirching France with excrement, while sitting atop his own obscene novels. See *The Dreyfus Affair: Art, Truth and Justice*, ed. Norman L. Keablatt. [Berkeley, Los Angeles, London, 1987], p. 244, plate 169.) See also Heinz Schreckenberg, *The Jews in Christian Art: An Illustrated History*, SCM Press. London, 1996, pp. 331–338. A different artistic expression of this Judaeophobia has been uncovered in Ruth Mellinkoff's *Antisemitic Hate Signs in Hebrew Illuminated Manuscripts from Mediaeval Germany*, Jerusalem, 1999, where she shows that the illustrations in many early Jewish manuscripts were carried out by Christian artists who inserted signs of their loathing of the Jews, of what, much later came to be called anti-Semitism. See further in her magisterial two volumes of *Outcasts: Signs of Otherness in European Art of the Late Middle Ages*, Berkeley, Los Angeles, Oxford, 1993. Of course, the imposition of special dress codes for Jews further encouraged this hatred. See, for example, Henry N. Claman, *Jewish Images in the Christian Church: Art as the Mirror of the Jewish Christian Conflict* 200–1250 C.E. Macom Sergia, 2000, pp. 121–124. Raphael Straus, "The 'Jewish Hat' as an Aspect of Social History," *Journal of Social Studies* 4, 1942, pp. 59–71; Guido Kisch, "The Yellow Badge in History," *Historica Judaica* 19, 1957, pp. 89–146; Judith A. Kidd, *Behind the Image: Understanding the Old Testament in Mediaeval Art*, Germany, n.d., (but c. 2010), pp. 201–228, etc.

CHAPTER 10

The Role of Christianity
in the Development of Anti-Semitism

The full extent to which *Nostra Aetate* was truly revolutionary can only be fully appreciated when we pause to contemplate in lurid detail the horrendous nature of Christian Judaeophobia[1] throughout the generations.[2] Let us recall, for example one of the most popular German mystery-plays the *Alsfelder Passionspeel* ("Das Drama des Mittelatters," *Deutsche Nationaliteratur* ed. Fronig, vol. 14, pp. 767ff; cited in Leon Poliakov, *The History of Antisemitism*, vol. 1, New York, 1974, pp. 130–131). There the crucifixion plotted by twenty devils, who assign the crime to Jesus, is described in meticulous and exquisitely excruciating detail, thus:

> CAIAPHAS. Jesus, take off your clothes.
>> They shall go to the soldiers.
>> Lie down on the Cross
>> And stretch out your feet and arms!
>> (He is stretched on the Cross and the second executioner says)
> SECOND EXECUTIONER. Give my three heavy nails
>> And a hammer and tongs!
>> Bind his hands and feet fast
>> And lay him out along the Cross
>> To the notch that is marked.
>> Let his legs and feet go so far,
>> And let the nails pass through.
>> Thus he cannot escape.
>> This nail I shall drive through your right hand.
>> You shall suffer pain and grief!
> FIRST EXECUTIONER. Helper, the hands and the feet

> Do not reach to the notches!
> THIRD EXECUTIONER. I shall give good counsel:
>   Bring a rope;
>   We shall stretch his arms;
>   We shall draw out his body
>   So as to pull it to pieces!

And if in the *Alsfelder Passionspiel* the Jews are merely *provocateurs*, in the famous French mystery-play attributed to Jehan Michel, it is the Jews who actually carry out the torture. Beginning in Pilate's palace, they strike him on the shoulders and head with reeds:

> ROULLART. See the blood streaming
>   And how his whole face is covered.
> MALCHUS. Here, false and bloody man,
>   I pity not your pain
>   More than that of a vile trickster
>   That nothing avails, he is so Low.
> BRUYANT. Let us play at pulling out his beard
>   That is too long anyway.
> DENTART. He will be the bravest
>   Who gets the biggest handful.
> GRIFFON. I have torn at him so hard
>   That the flesh has come away too.
> DILLART. I would take my turn at tearing
>   So as to have my share as well.
> DRAGON. See what a clump this is
>   That I pull away as if it were lard
> BRUYANT. But see how I go about it now.
>   Behold he has not one left.

And this until Pilate's indignant intervention puts an end to the bloody scene. However, the actual scene of the crucifixion is even more intense, with details such as how:

He is all covered
With spittle high and low ...
(*Mistère de la Resurrection de Notre-Seigneur Jésus Christ* ..., ed. Anton Verard, Paris [classification Res. Y. f.15, of the Bibliothèque

Nationale]; Poliakov ibid. pp. 131–133. And further on the *Passionssplielen*, see John D. Martin, *Representation of the Jews in the Late Medieval and Early Modern Literature*, Bern 2004, chapter 2 on the *Passionspiel der St. Galler*, and *Der Frankfurter Dirigierrelle*.)

The accusation was repeatedly stressed and underscored by the Church in a variety of manners. Such, for example the "celebrated catechism of Abbé Fleury, which in two centuries went through one hundred and seventy-two editions, is more explicit:

> "Did Jesus have enemies? – Yes, the carnal Jews. – To what point did the hatred of Jesus' enemies go? – To the point of causing his death. – Who was it who promised to hand him over? – Judas Iscariot. – Why was this city [Jerusalem] treated in this way? – For having caused the death of Jesus. – What became of the Jews? – They were reduced to servitude and scattered throughout the world. – What has become of them since? – They are still in the same state. – For how long? – For seventeen hundred years" [*Catéchisme historique*, by M. Fleury, Paris 1766; Lesson 19, "Des enemies du Christ," and 27, "De la ruine de Jérusalem," Poliakov p. 180.]

Let us imagine, in space and time, the millions of young voices gaily and faithfully repeating their well-learned lesson. Imagine, too, the commentaries that the teacher or curé may have made, according to his own views and fancy ...

More laconic, but still more devastating, is the catechism of Adrien Gambart, which, its author expressly tells us, was intended "for the simple-minded," for those who are not capable of understanding long speeches or reasoning.

> "Is it a great sin to take communion unworthily? It is the greatest of all sins, because one makes oneself guilty of the body and blood of Jesus Christ, as Judas and the Jews were; and one becomes the object of His judgment and condemnation." [Adrien Gambart, *Le Bon Partage des Peuvres et la doctrine chrétienne et la connaissance de salut*, Paris 1652, p. 72, Poliakov p. 181.]

Such texts are to be found in multiple numbers throughout almost all

Europe spanning the generations (as so powerfully shown by Poliakov ibid.).

Indeed even as late as 1962, in the first session of *Complotto contra la Chiesa* (Conspiracy against the Church) which was circulated with an *Acta* attributed to Maurice Pinay – a collective pseudonym – we read of the "Synagogue of Satan" and the Jewish-Masonic connections. (See Gavir D'Costa, *Vatican II: Catholic Doctrines on Jews and Muslims*, Oxford 2014, p. 120 noite 32.) This was an attempt to sabotage, as it were, the formulation of the *Nostra Aetate* section on Jews and Judaism.

Thus, the total repudiation of a deeply embedded and vastly popular and widely prejudicial belief vilifying the Jews and the explicit exoneration of the change of deicide was indeed a truly momentous move[3] on the part of the Catholic Church. As one observer put it in 1964:

> We are witnessing something that has been all but unknown in almost 2000 years of Christianity.[4]

And exchanging the description of the Jews from "infamous murderers, detestable nation, abhorred by men, everywhere rejected," or "demons escaped from hell, race of Jews, detestable men, more accused than Lucifer, and more wicked than all the devils ..."[5] to *Nostra Aetate's* "God holds the Jews most dear for the sake of her Fathers ..." served to change the image of the Jews among the Christian faithful.

It created a new relationship between Judaism and the Catholic Church, and consequently with Christianity in general (see Appendix 1).[6] It paved the way to a more meaningful and open dialogue in which problems facing both religions could be discussed suggesting possible approaches, joint or specific. Undoubtedly it took great courage and honesty on the part of the Papal authorities to reach such a radical statement.[7] And indeed anyone who peruses the preliminary drafts will see the great tension and struggle to find just the right formulation.[8] Needless to say, this encyclical, to the extent it was known to the Jewish world, was greatly welcomed (though by some with reservations).[9]

Endnotes to Chapter 10

1. On the terms "anti-Semitism" and "Judaeophobia," see Zeev Yaavetz, *Sinat Yisrael bi-Yemei Kedem*, Lod, 2002, p. 97 et seq., and in his article "Judaeophobia in Classsical Antiquity: A Different Approach," *JJS*, 44, 1993.

   And, of course, there is a very considerable bibliography on the Crusades, and the Inquisition, which we cannot encompass. But see, e.g., L.E. Halkin, *De l'Inquisition à la tolerance*, Bruxelles, 1939. Idem, *Intolérance et inquisition*, Paris, 1950, etc.

2. See, for example Robert Michael, *A History of Catholic Antisemitism: The Dark Side of the Church*, New York, 2011, and, of course, the first history of anti-Semitism by a Catholic priest, Edward H. Flannery, *The Anguish of the Jews*, New York and London, 1965. See further David Nirenberg, *Anti-Judaism: The Western Tradition*, New York-London, 2014, pass. Jocelyn Hallig, *The Holocaust and Antisemitism: A Short History*, Oxford, 2003, especially Part III, entitled "Inter-religious Rivalry and Antisemitism," pp. 157–221, with a rich survey and evaluation of earlier literature on the subject.

3. See Egal Feldman, *Catholics and Jews in Twentieth Century America*, Urban and Chicago, 2001, who writes in chapter 7, entitled "Revolt of the Bishops, 1960–75," pp. 102–103:

   > It is rare in religious history for a great ecclesiastical establishment, such as the Church of Rome, to acknowledge publicly its need to review and reevaluate long-held cherished beliefs and practices. Yet this revolutionary event occurred during the four sessions of the Second Vatican Council (which came to be known also as Vatican II), convened in the years 1962–65. More than many of their European colleagues, American bishops, archbishops, and cardinals welcomed these changes, viewed them as arriving at a most propitious time, and were eager to implement them. Looking back, one cannot help but rank the achievement, at least with respect to Jewish-Catholic relations, as one of the most remarkable in the long centuries of Christian history.

   As to the deliberation in America, Feldman (ibid. p. 103) writes:

   > However, as a part of a universal Church with religious directions emanating from the papal throne, the American Catholic Church was at this very moment

about to embark upon an *earth-shattering theological reassessment* which
would alter radically its view of itself and the and the world around it.
[My emphasis, D.S.]

Here we may add (from ibid. p. 105):

Unlike the prelates who preceded him, Pope John maintained friendly although
unofficial contacts with the leaders of the state of Israel. Jewish leaders were
well aware of the aid he had offered numerous Jews during World War II. He
also maintained a warm relationship with the leaders of the American Jewish
community, with whom he had met shortly after he assumed the papal office. In
1960, an American Jewish delegation visiting Rome presented Pope John with a
Torah scroll as a token of appreciation for the Jewish lives he had saved during
the Shoah [Pinchas Lapid, *The Last Three Popes*, Hawthorn .... p. 322].

An indication of John's sensitivity toward Jews occurred in 1959. He ordered
that the phrase "unbelieving Jews," employed in the Good Friday service,
be completely removed, both in its Latin and vernacular forms, [Augustin
Cardinal Bea, *The Church and the Jewish People*, transl. Philip Lavetz, New
York, 1966, p. 22.]. When a few weeks later, a group of bishops celebrating the
Good Friday service in Rome, which Pope John attended, ignored his directive
and recited the old text, the pope quietly halted the service and requested that it
be repeated properly. The event served notice to all Catholics of his seriousness
about this matter. In the following months, the new Catholic leader deleted
other phrases and passages offensive to Jews from a number of other prayers
[ibid. p. 320–321; Eugene C. Blanchi, "A Talk with Cardinal Bea, *America
Council and the Jews*," August 11, 1962, pp. 584–590; Arthur Gilbert, The
Vatican World Publishing Co. 1968, p. 41].

See also Helga Croner, *Stepping Stones to Further Jewish-Christian Relations: An
unabridged collection of Christian Documents*, London, New York, 1977, p. 87,
citing:

The House of Bishops of the Episcopal Church issued a statement on "Deicide
and the Jews." St. Louis, Mo., 1964.

The poison of anti-Semitism has causes of a political, national, psychological, social, and economic nature. It has often sought religious justification in
the events springing from the crucifixion of Jesus. Anti-Semitism is a direct
contradiction of Christian doctrine. Jesus was a Jew, and, since the Christian
Church is rooted in Israel, spiritually we are Semites.

The charge of deicide against the Jews is a tragic misunderstanding of
the inner significance of the crucifixion. To be sure, Jesus was crucified by
some soldiers at the instigation of *some* Jews. But, this cannot be construed
as imputing corporate guilt to every Jew in Jesus' day, much less the Jewish

250

people in subsequent generations. Simple justice alone proclaims the charge of a corporate or inherited curse on the Jewish people to be false.

Furthermore, in the dimension of faith the Christian understands that all men are guilty of the death of Christ, for all have in some manner denied Him; and since the sins that crucified Christ were common human sins, the Christian knows that he himself is guilty. But he rejoices in the words and spirit of his Lord who said for the Roman soldiers and for all responsible for His crucifixion, "Father, forgive them, for they know not what they do."

Again, we note the date of this statement, 1964, a year before the publication of *Nostra Aetate*.

4. See Ronald B. Sobel, "To Anglicum Colloquium on *Nostra Aetate*," April 19, 1985, apud Pope *John Paul II on Jews and Judaism 1978–1986*, ed. Eugene J. Fisher and Leon Klenicki, Washington D.C. and New York, 1987, pp. 68–73.

However, we should take notice of Cardinal Bea's comment in his *The Church and the Jewish People*, New York, 1966, p. 71 note 1, that:

Although it [i.e. the term "deicide"] was employed in earlier redactions, the expression "guilty of deicide" no longer appears in the final draft of the Declaration. The reason for this omission was officially explained at the Council by the President of the Secretariat for Christian Unity before the voting: "A comparison of the present text with the draft which you approved last year shows that the Secretariat proposes to remove the term "guilty of deicide" from the text. Why? It is known that most of the difficulties and controversies arose from the use of this expression, so that it almost seemed as if the schema was at variance with the Gospel. On the other hand, it will be clear to anyone who reads the text, which you have just heard and examined, that *the ideas which we wished to express in the former text by means of this term are fully and accurately set out in the new text which is now being put to the vote.*" The omission is simply due to practical reasons of pastoral prudence and provides no grounds for doubting the teaching proposed above.

In some quarters this prudence has been regarded as a cowardly capitulation to political pressure. This view, however, loses sight of two things:

(a) It was in every sense an obligation in charity to avoid any expression which not only could, but in fact had, led to errors and caused distress to many.

(b) In the long run it is to the advantage of the Jewish people that the Declaration should be fully understood and well received in Arab countries.

See the whole section on "the accusation of deicide" ibid. pp. 68–71, and also pp. 160–162.

5. Poliakov pp. 192–193.

Of course, the ultimate source of these defamatory statements is in the New Testament itself.

As a somewhat random selection of such famous passages I shall quote the following:

> O Jerusalem, Jerusalem, thou that killest the prophets and stonest them that are sent unto thee, how often would I have gathered thy children together even as a hen gathereth her chickens under her wings, and ye would not! Behold your house is left unto you desolate. (Matthew 23:37, 38) Then answered all the people (Jews) and said, "His blood be on us and on our children" (Matthew 27:25).
>
> Ye are of your father the devil and the lusts of your father ye will do. He was a murderer from the beginning, and abode not in the truth, because there is no truth in him. When he speaks a lie, he speaketh of his own: for he is a liar and the father of it. And because I tell you the truth, ye believe me not. Which of you convinceth me of sin? And I say the truth, why do you not believe me? He that is of God heareth God's words: ye therefore hear them not, because ye are not of God (John 8:44–47).
>
> Stiff-necked and uncircumcised in heart and ears, ye do always resist the Holy Ghost: as your fathers did, so you do. Which of the prophets have not your fathers persecuted? And they have slain them which showed before of the coming of the Just One; of whom ye have been now the betrayers and murderers (Acts 7:51–53).
>
> For there are many unruly and vain talkers and deceivers, specially they of the circumcision: whose mouths must be stopped, who subvert whole houses, teaching things which they ought not, for filthy lucre's sake . . . (Titus 1:10–12).
>
> . . . The Jews, who both killed the Lord Jesus and their own prophets, and have persecuted us; and they please not God and are contrary to all men: forbidding us to speak to the Gentiles that they might be saved, to fill up their sins always: for the wrath is come upon them to the uttermost (I Thessalonians 2:14–16).
>
> . . . I know the blasphemy of them which say they are Jews and are not, but are the synagogue of Satan. (Revelation 2:9, 10).
>
> Behold I will make them of the synagogue of Satan, which say they are Jews and are not but do lie (Revelation 3:9).

Prof. A. Roy Eckhardt, in his *Elder and Younger Brothers: The Encounter of Jews and Christians*, New York, 1967, has shown that, using the New Testament as its authoritative source, the Church has stereotyped the Jewish people as an icon of unredeemed humanity; they became an image of a blind, stubborn, carnal and perverse people, which dehumanization formed the psychological prerequisite to the atrocities that followed. It has been shown that there are hundreds of verses in the New Testament containing defamatory anti-Jewish polemic. And many of them have been included in the Roman Catholic *Lectionary for Mass* used during the 1980s, (adapted in the *Lutheran Book of Worship*, and then found in *The Revised Common Lectionary* of 1992). Thus in Matthew 3:7, Jews (Pharasees and Sadducees) are called a "generations of vipers" (cf. Luke 3:7). And in John 8:44, Jews are "of your father the devil, and the lusts of your father ye will do. He was a murderer from the beginning, and abode not in truth, because there is no truth in him . . ., he is a liar, and the father of it." And in John 5:38, "You have not his word abiding in you . . .," and in verse 43: ". . . ye have not the Love of God in You." (But compare the 2015 declaration in sect. 34: "Israel is God's chosen and beloved people of the covenant which has never been repealed or revoked.") Professor Herman A. Beck, at Texas Lutheran University, in an article entitled *Anti-Jewish Polemic from our Christian Lectionaries: A Proposal*, (http://www.icrelation.net/en/display/tens.php.2=id=737), and others have identified the offensive passages in the New Testament and indicated which of them are included in the major testimonies. The statistical results are tabulated in Uri Yosef, *The Anti-Jewish New Testament*, 2010–2011, p. 7. There is a considerable literature on the subject, but we will only refer to three items as representative: Lilian C. Freudmann, *Antisemitism in the New Testament* University Press of America 1994; Howard Clark Kee and Irvin J. Borowsky, edd., *Removing the Anti-Judaism from the New Testament*, American Interfaith Institute, Philadelphia, PA; idem. *Removing the Anti-Judaism from the Pulpit*, 1996.

And throughout the ages, these positions have been given additional support by interpretative reference to Old Testament texts. Thus, for example, St. Augustin, in his *Against Faustus* 12:10, writes:

> Then God said to Cain, "What have you done? The voice of your brother's blood is crying out to me from the earth" (Genesis 4:10). Thus from the sacred scriptures does God's voice accuse the Jews.

And he continues (12:11):

> Thus the unbelieving people of the Jews are cursed "from the earth" (ibid. 4:11), which is to say, from the Church. In the confession of sins the Church has opened her mouth to receive the blood of Christ poured out for the remission of sins. The blood was poured out by the hand of the persecutor who chose not to be *sub gratia* but *sub lege*. And so the Church issues the curse, that is, the Church understands and declaims that curse spoken by the apostle Paul when he says, "Thou who are under the works of the Law are under the curse of the Law" (Galatians 3:10). The Church acknowledges and declares that the Jewish people are cursed "from the earth" because after killing Christ ["Abel" in this imagery] they still continue to "till the earth . . ."

(See in detail Paul Frederiksen, *Augustine and the Jews: A Christian Defense of Jews and Judaism*, New Haven and London, 2010, in the chapter entitled "The Mark of Cain," pp. 200–289.)

Such quotations could be vastly multiplied, but this may suffice to give a general impression of the homiletic tendencies throughout the many generations.

It should further be noted that this kind of scurrilous language was revived in modern anti-Semitism Arab writings, as was demonstrated by Y. Harkabi in his *Arab Attitudes to Israel*, Jerusalem, 1972, p. 345, "who collects examples of such coarse language," under the title of "Other Epithets," sic:

> *Other Epithets*. The Zionist monster; the pollution of Zionism, the Zionist plague (*waba*); the enemy of the peoples; the ally of the murderers; the occupation authorities; the purulent abscess; the illegitimate daughter of Europe; a cancer in the heart of the Arab nation, or in the Middle East; the Zionist cancer; the imperialist cancer (see below); Israel the bleeding thorn (*shawka damiya*); the gang of hypocrites and criminals; the focus of evil (*bu'rat al-sharr*); dirt, filth, sewage (*huthala, qadhura*); the Zionist gangs (*shirdhima sahyuniyya*). The comparison with cancer implies the danger of expansion. Ali Muhammad Ali, in the introduction to his book *Inside Israel*, criticizes this term as inaccurate, since cancer comes from inside the body, while Israel is a foreign element; besides, there is no cure for cancer, which puts an end to the sufferer, while in Israel's case "the effective treatment is known."
>
> *Biological Epithets*. The viper State; the adder; the Zionist adders; the octopus (*akhtabut*); the spider; the bacillus of evil (*jurthumat al-sharr*); the claws of the cat (*makhalib al-qitt*); the parasites; the claws (*barathin*) of Zionism, [etc.].

Cf. also Harkabi ibid. p. 282 that the Jews are "a chronic disease" (al-'Aqqad, 'Abbas Mahmud, *al Sahaniyya al-'Alamiyya* [*World Zionism*], Cairo, 1956, p. 15).

So while we see there is still a considerable problem, we may nonetheless underscore the great progress achieved in the last half-century.

6. Thus, in *Nostra Aetate* we read:
> Since the spiritual patrimony common to Christians and Jews is thus so great, the sacred synod wants to foster and recommend that mutual understanding and respect which is the fruit, above all, of biblical and theological studies as well as fraternal dialogues.

7. It seemed to be in conflict with the principle of papal infallibility proclaimed by the Church in 1870, when the Pope and the Council declared in the Dogmatic Constitution on the Church (Italics added):

This is the infallibility which the Roman Pontiff, the head of the college of bishops, enjoys in virtue of his office, when, as the supreme shepherd and teacher of all the faithful, who confirms his brethren in their faith (cf. Luke 22:32) by a definitive act he proclaims a doctrine of faith or morals. Therefore his definitions, *of themselves, and not from the consent of the Church, are justly styled irreformable*, for they are pronounced with the assistance of the Holy Spirit, promised to him in blessed Peter. Therefore they need no approval of others, nor do they allow an appeal to any other judgment.

See Paul Blanchard, *Paul Blanchard on Vatican II*, London, 1967, p. 72. The whole chapter (4) in that book, entitled "Collegiality to Infallibility," pp. 52–71, 351–353, is highly illuminating. On the doctrine of "papal infallibility," Blanchard gives the following bibliographic information (p. 352 note 2):

Whole libraries have been written on Peter, primacy, infallibility and the associated problems. Valuable works include: James T. Shotwell and Louise R. Loomis, *The See of Peter*, Columbia University Press, 1927; Fred-Bury, *History of the Papacy in the 19th Century* (Introduction by Frederick C. Grant), Schocken Books, New York, 1964; George Salmon, *The Infallibility of the Church*, Searcy, Kansas, 1948; Abbot Basil Christopher Butler, *The Church and Infallibility*, Sheed and Ward, 1954; Monsignor Charles Journet, *The Primacy of Peter from the Protestant and from the Catholic Point of View*, Newman Press, Westminster, Md., 1954; Oscar Cullmann, *Peter, Disciple, Apostle, Martyr*, S.C.M. Press, London, 1962; Geddes Mac-Gregor, *The Vatican Revolution*, Beacon Press, 1957; C. J. Cadoux, *Catholicism and Christianity*, Allen and Unwin, 1928; Kirsopp Lake, *An Introduction to the New Testament*, Christophers, London, 1938; Vittorio Subilia, *The Problem of Catholicism*, Westminster Press, 1964; Lord Acton, *Essays on Freedom and Power*, Beacon Press, 1948. MacGregor, in Appendix I, has the texts of Vatican I's decrees in both Latin and English.

8. See this Oesterreicher, ibid. pp. 103–295.

9. See, for Example Paul Blanchard's critical reservations in *Paul Blanchard on Vatican II*, London, 1967, though written primarily from an American viewpoint. (See his Preface).

CHAPTER 11

The Dominant Component of the Holocaust and Feelings of Christian Guilt

This encyclical, on the other hand, was also seen as a tragically belated act of contrition,[1] coming after the horrific public disclosures of the full extent of the holocaust.[2] By no means did these public disclosures have an immediate effect.[3] But there was ever-growing feelings of guilt and a sense of shame on the part of prominent Catholic thinkers. (Perhaps we should recall that Julius Streicher (1885–1946), editor of the infamous *Der Stürmer* (1923–1945), came from a devoutly Catholic family, as indeed did Hitler himself.) Thus, The World Council of Churches in 1948 proclaimed:

> We have failed to fight with all our strength the age-old disorder which anti-Semitism represents. The Churches in the past have helped to foster an image of the Jews as the sole enemies of Christ which has contributed to anti-Semitism in the secular world.[4]

It is not by chance that the first history of anti-Semitism was written by a Catholic priest, Edward H. Flannery in 1964, and published under the title, *The Anguish of the Jews* in New York and London in 1965.[5] And a year earlier, in March, 1964, Guenter Lowy's book *The Catholic Church and Nazi Germany* appeared, revealing the Catholic Church's congeniality towards some of the aims of National Socialism, and its gradual entrapment into Nazi policies and programs, and the episcopate's support of Hitler's expansionist policies and failures to speak out on the persecution of the Jews. Only gradually did the facts become known through the publication of photographs[6] of the camps, personal testimonies, reports from soldiers returning from "liberating" the survivors, etc. And what played significant roles, of varying character, in bringing the full impact

256

to the general public were the Nuremberg and Eichman trials. The former (called the Nurnberger Prozesse) took place in 1945 and 1946, at an International Military Tribunal (IMT), and were followed subsequently by the Nuremberg Military Trials (NMT).[7] Their legacies were in the formation of a number of very important international bodies set up by the United Nations' General Assembly, such as *The Genocide Convention* of 1949, *The International Declaration of Human Rights* of 1948, *The Geneva Convention* of 1949, and *The International Law Commission* of 1950. The extent to which they impacted upon the general public is somewhat less evident.

We may add that André Schwarzbart's *Les Dernier des Justes*, first appeared in 1959; and was subsequently translated into sixteen languages!

However, the Eichman Trial, which took place in Jerusalem in 1961 was given highly prominent media coverage with major journalists from all over the world, resulting in an increase not only in publications of memoirs and scholarly studies, but also undoubtedly triggered off heightened awareness and active interest in the horrors of the Holocaust. For the Eichman trial, which began on 11 April 1961, and ended on the 12 December that year had a vast media coverage. Gideon Hausner, the prosecutor, opened his leading statement by declaring that:

> ... it is not as an individual that is in the dock at this historic trial, and not the Nazi regime alone, but anti-Semitism throughout history (Tim Cole, *Images of the Holocaust*, London, 1999, p. 50).

And undoubtedly this statement, which became a central theme in the whole trial had a remarkable impact and resonated throughout much of the Christian world.[8]

At the time of the trial, the German bishops asked all German Catholics to recite the following prayer:

> Lord God of our fathers! God of Abraham, of Isaac, and of Jacob! ...
> We confess before you: Countless men were murdered in our midst because they belonged to the people from which comes the Messiah, according to the flesh. We pray: Lead all of those among us who became guilty through deed, omission, or silence that they may see their wrong and turn from it. Lead them so that they examine themselves, be converted, and atone for their sins. In your limitless mercy forgive,

for the sake of your Son, that limitless guilt no human atonement can wipe out.[9]

And Pope John Paul II, when visiting the Wailing Wall on March 26, 2000, inserted into a crack between the stones of the Wailing Wall the following prayer, which he had composed for a Liturgy of Repentence that had been held in St. Peter's some weeks earlier.

> God of our father,
> You chose Abraham and his descendants
> To bring your Name to the Nations:
> We are deeply saddened
> By the behaviour of those
> Who in the course of history
> Have caused these children of yours to suffer,
> And asking your forgiveness
> We wish to commit ourselves to
> Genuine brotherhood
> With the people of the Covenant.

This prayer very poignantly expresses the feeling of guilt and contrition. And it was the bishops of Germany who were to declaim this admission of culpability, as did the Pope himself. And so it is understandable that the declaration of *Nostra Aetate* a few years later was seen as a reflection of the guilt of the Church, a sense of an attempt at some sort of atonement, and ever more so in view of the position of the Holy See during the holocaust itself.[10]

And, perhaps in partial parenthesis, we should add the significant component of Italian Fascism, so well described and documented in E.R. Tannenbaum, *The Fascist Experience: Italian Society and Culture 1922–1945*, New York, 1972, and in a clear and condenced fashion in Roger Griffin, *The Nature of Fascism*, chapter 3, "Italian Fascism," pp. 56–84 (with a rich bibliography). And see also Leni Yahil, *The Holocaust: The Fate of European Jewry*, New York, Oxford, 1990, pp. 422–427, on the Jews in Fascist Italy. And though the relationship between Fascism and Catholicism was a complex one, with some clergy who were implacably hostile to it, nonetheless, in February 1937 Cardinal Schuster delivered a major speech at the *Scuola di mistica fascista*, established in 1930, justifying Fascism's occupation of Ethiopia as "the synthesis of Italy's Roman and Catholic heritage which was Mussolini's greatest achievement – after all, as he assured readers of *Il Popolo d'Italia* on Feb. 27, 1937. "(Christ) is Roma" (D. Marchesini, *La Scuola dei gerardhi*, Milan, 1976, p. 208; see Griffin pp. 69–70). One may, therefore, fairly assume that many members of the Church, especially those in Rome, felt both guilty and relieved at the demise of post-war Fascism.

But returning to our main theme, *Nostra Aetate* was seen as a final admittance to what had been, from a Jewish viewpoint, a totally irrational accusation against the Jews (but one based on Matthew 27:25, "His blood be on us, and on our children," and cf. Thessalonians 2:15, "who both killed the Lord Jesus and their own prophets, and have persecuted ....."), and which had engendered almost two millennia of hatred, suffering, bloodshed, and inquisition, to mention but a few of the many expressions of this hatred.[11]

Endnotes to Chapter 11

1. See, for example, what Robert Louis Wilken (1936–) wrote in his book, *The Myth of Christian Beginnings: History, Impact on Belief*, New York, 1972, p. 197:
   Christian anti-semitism did not arise by the importation of ideas foreign to Christianity through some historical accident. Christian anti-Semitism grew out of the Christian Bible, i.e. the New Testament as it was understood and integrated by Christians over the countries. The roots of anti-Semitism need be traced no further than Christians itself; Christians have been antisemites because they have been Christians. They thought of themselves as the people of God, the true Israel, who had been faithful to the inheritance of ancient Israel. Judaism, in the Christian view, had no reason to exist once Christianity came on the scene. We must learn, I think, to live with the unpleasant fact that anti-Semitism is part of what it has meant historically to be – Christian, and is still part of what it means to be Christian.

2. See Father John T. Pawlikowski OSM, *The Challenge of the Holocaust for Christian Theology*, New York, 1972, pass., but especially pp. 25–26. There he refers to Alice Eckhardt's article, "The Holocaust: Christian and Jewish Responses," *Journal of the American Academy of Religion*, 42/3, 1974, p. 454, who wrote:

> Those Christians who have grappled with the reality and implications of the Holocaust see a church in vast apostasy, involved not only in the murder of Jews but also of God through his people, still linked to the supersessionist theology that bears the genocidal germ, in danger of repeating its complicity in criminal actions, and without credibility because of its failure to understand that everything has been changed by Auschwitz.

See also the interesting reflections of Marc Supperstein, in his *Moments of Crisis in Jewish-Christian Relations*, London, Philadelphia, 1989, pp. 38–50.
   See further Eugene J. Fisher, *Faith Without Prejudice: Rebuilding Christian Attitudes*, New York, 1977, p. 9, quoting Cardinal Eichinger of Strasbourg as saying:

> We cannot deny that not only during this century but also during past centuries crimes have been committed against the Jews by the Sons and Daughters of the Church . . . We cannot ignore that during the course of history, there have been persecutions and outrages against the Jews; there have been violations of conscience as well as forced conversions. Lastly, we cannot deny that up until

recently, errors have insinuated themselves, too frequently, into preaching and into certain catechetical books in opposition to the spirit of the New Testament. In going back to the sources of the Gospels, why not draw sufficient greatness of soul to ask forgiveness in the name of numerous Christians for so many misdeeds and injustices?

And this was affirmed in Pope John Paul II famous statement in his meeting in Rome in 1982, to Catholic representatives of the Episcopal Conference, (apud *Contemporary of the Documents of Vatican II*, ed. H. Vorgrimler, vol. 2, New York and London, 1967, pp. 76–77):

> Certainly, since a new bough appeared from the common root 2,000 years ago, we know that relations between our two communities have been marked by resentments and a lack of understanding. If there have been misunderstandings, errors and even insults since the day of separation, it is now a question of overcoming them with understanding, peace and mutual esteem. The terrible persecutions suffered by the Jews in various periods of history have finally opened many eyes and disturbed many hearts.

3. Michael Phayer, in his article "The German Catholic Church After the Holocaust," in *Holocaust and Genocide Studies* 10/2, 1966, pp. 151–167, talks of three periods of adjustment that the Catholic Church went through vis-à-vis the Holocaust. During the first church, leaders suppressed a debate on the subject regarding collective guilt, but recognized the obligation of restitution. In the 1950s, the Triumphal Church disregarded the Holocaust and problems such as anti-Semitism. However, around 1959 a new generation of Church leaders called attention to the Church's lapses regarding the Jews during the Nazi era, the reawakening being largely due to the Freiburg circle, under the leadership of Gertrud Luckner, a Yad Vashem Righteous Gentile. (See especially pp. 161–163.)

We should further point out that already early in April 1945, when Buchenwald was first discovered by the Allied forces, this discovery was given wide publicity. On April 13 of that year, Eisenhower, Bradley and Patton toured Buchenwald, and on April 19, Churchill made a statement on this in Parliament, and on the 25 April, 18 prominent newspaper publishers from around the world were invited to view Buchenwald. So the world knew about the genocide. See David A. Hakkett, *The Buchenwald Report*, Boulder San Francisco, Oxford 1995, (introduction pp. 9–13), being a translation of the first edition of Eugen Kogon report. (He was the author of *The Theological Practice of Hell*, English ed. 1950.)

See also Franklin Littell, "Essay: Reinhold Niebuhr and the Jewish People," *Holocaust and Genocide Studies* 6/1, 1992, pp. 45–61.

In point of fact British intelligence already decoded dozens of open reports of mass killings directed by the Higher SS and Police Leaders and carried out by the

Order Police and Waffen SS. Boch-Zelewski boasted on August 7 that a total of over 30,000 executions had been carried out in his region. And by January 1942 the British knew that "the Germans clearly persue a policy of extermination against the Jews." And by November 1942 the truth about Auschwitz was known but the British were hesitant to reveal their knowledge for various reasons. A similar situation is to be found in the American response to information they received. See Richard Breitman, *Official Secrets: What the Nazis Planned, what the British and Americans Knew*, New York, 1999, pp. 110–136. Breitman writes (p. 136):

> In retrospect, both governments limited their coverage to the stories they believed would work against the Nazi regime in the occupied countries, in Germany itself, and with the neutrals . . . They were not much concerned with reporting what was happening to the Jews, they also failed to display effectively the values of Western democratic societies.

And in his concluding chapter he remarks (p. 228):

> Both Churchill and Roosevelt, but particularly Churchill, deserve great credit for recognizing the evils of Nazism at an early date; and both men, especially Churchill, took tremendous risks to oppose Nazi Germany, but during the war they inevitably dealt far more with larger questions of military and diplomatic strategy and of Allied partnership than with specific decisions about rescue of Jews.

See also Arthur D. Morse's classic, *While Six Million Died: A Chronicle of American Apathy*, New York, 1968, pass.

4. W.A. Visser 't Hooft, ed., *The First Assembly of the World Council of Churches: The Official Report*, New York, 1949, p. 161.

5. And already in the Third Assembly of the World Council of Churches in New Delhi (November 19 to December 14, 1961), there was a recommendation of the Policy Reference to the assembly, which resulted in a final resolution stating:

> We call upon all the churches we represent to denounce anti-Semitism, no matter what its origin, as absolutely irreconcilable with the profession and practice of the Christian faith. Antisemitism is sin against God and man. Only as we give convincing evidence to our Jewish neighbours that we seek for them the common rights and dignities which God wills for his children, can we come to such a meeting with them as would make it possible to share with them the best which God has given us in Christ.

And they went as far as to say concerning the corporate guilt of Jews for the crucifixion that "the historic events which led to the crucifixion should not be so presented as to fasten upon the Jewish people of today, responsibility that belongs to our corporate humanity and not to one race or community," (*The New Delhi Report: Third Assembly of the World Council of Churches*, New York, 1962, p. 148).

See further Gerhard Falk, *The Jews in Christian Theology*, Jefferson, North Carolina and London, 1993, p. 117. And on p. 119, he writes:

> In September of 1964, Richard Cardinal Cushing of Boston spoke to the Vatican Council before the Declaration on the Jews was passed. Said Cushing: "In this Declaration in clear and evident words we must deny that the Jews are guilty of the death of our Savior, except insofar as all men have sinned and on that account crucified Him, and, indeed, still crucify Him. And especially we must condemn any who would attempt to justify inequities, hatred, or even persecution of the Jews as Christian actions. . . ."
>
> Another American proponent of a strong Declaration on the Jews was Albert Cardinal Meyer of Chicago. "Justice demands," said Cardinal Meyer, "that we give explicit attention to the enormous impact of the wrongs done through centuries to the Jews." To which Joseph Cardinal Ritter of St. Louis added, "Therefore all should be careful lest they represent the Jewish people as a rejected people, cursed, or in any way as deicides; lest they impute to the whole Jewish people then living, nor a *fortiori* to the Jews of our time, what was perpetrated in the passion of Christ. . . ." [Vincent A. Yzermans, ed., *American Participation in the Second Vatican Council*, New York, 1967, pp. 586–593].
>
> The contribution of the American Catholic theologian Thomas Merton should not be overlooked in this connection. Before the Declaration on the Jews Merton corresponded extensively with Rabbi Abraham Heschel and Rabbi Zalman Schacter, both important Jewish theologians. In that correspondence he expressed the desire "to be a true Jew under my Catholic skin," and in *Conjectures of a Guilty Bystander* he says, "One has either got to be a Jew or stop reading the Bible. The Bible cannot make sense to anyone who is not spiritually a semite," [Thomas Merton, *Conjectures of a Guilty Bystander*, Garden City, New York, 1966, pp. 5–6].

In his preface to the book, John M. Oestereicher, of the Institute of Judaeo-Christian Studies at Seton Hall University, discussing Flannery's book, wrote as follows:

> This is a book that is filled with pain: the pain of events and the pain of their narrator. To the best of my knowledge it presents the first history of anti-Semitism written by a priest. As priest and as writer, Father Flannery has combined the patience of a historian with the impatience of a prophet. With untiring labor he has searched, sifted, weighed the facts and ordered them into a chronicle of woe. He has done so not because he wants to inhabit the past but because he wishes to join the builders of a new future. In stirring hearts he does not look

for an indignation that turns into self-righteousness but for one that leads to discernment and gives birth to resolve.

In the pages that follow, Father Flannery seeks to unmask the wrongs done not to his own but to the Jewish people. It is this devotion to the cause of others that gives his work its character. No doubt, to cry out against an injustice we ourselves endure is fully legitimate; by itself, however, it remains an instinctive reaction and is not yet a moral stance. A moral attitude comes to life only where *all* loose thought and speech, *all* ready-made opinions, *all* judgments shrunk to the size of nutshells, *all* forms of bigotry are shunned and fought.

If this sounds like an exhortation or plea, I gladly admit to a breach of etiquette. As one committed to that brotherhood which is the burden of everyone, I have no choice but to plead with the reader that he give the right response to the cruel things related here – indeed, to all the cruelty of this world. Nothing, after all, seems more consistent with bitter reality than to meet it with bitterness, nothing more realistic to the sufferer than to let sorrow become his tomb. Absurd though it may sound, history's bitterness and sorrow call rather for wisdom, for goodness, for a lasting openness of heart. There is, I think, no truer answer to the anguish Jews have suffered through the centuries than such grace, no better way to honor the victims of what Maurice Samuel has called "the great hatred."

Flannery ends his book albeit with a nuanced assessment of the Christian contribution to anti-Semitism. Nonetheless his final paragraph reads as follows:

For the believing Christian this tale of horror ends in the deepest chambers of the spirit. The sin of anti-Semitism is many things, but, in the end it is a denial of the Christian faith, a failure of Christian hope and a malady of Christian love. Nor is it the least of the sins. The agony of the Jews is one, Jacques Maritain has pointed out, in which Christ participates, [From the Preface of *Racisme, Antisemitisme, Antichristianism*, by John Oestereicher, New York, 1942, p. 19.]. And was not this the supreme defection: that the most severely and persistently persecuted of Christian history were not those to whom persecution was promised by the Master (John 16:2–4) but rather the people from which He came? Maritain saw this clearly when he wrote: "The passion of Israel is more and more clearly taking the shape of the Cross" [ibid. p. 20].

6. See, for example, the Soviet film *Colour of Darkness*, etc.

7. On the implications and effect of these trials in Germany, see Rolf Vogel, *Der deutsche-israelitische dialogue: Documentation eines erregenden Kapitals deutscher Aussenpolitik*, vol. 1, München, New York, London, Paris, 1987, pp. 171–197.

Mrs. Shamir: "Why are you throwing out the girl's blood before you use it to bake matzoth?" *Al-Bian*, Bahrain, March 18, 1990.

The Zionist Devil, *A-Dastur*, Jordan, September 30, 1994.

8. It is all the more shocking to learn of the reactions in the Arab world to the Eichman trial. Y. Harkabi, in his *Arab Attitudes to Israel*, Jerusalem 1972, pp. 278–279, writes as follows:

> In the Lebanese paper *al-Anwār* of June 9, 1960, there was a caricature showing Ben-Gurion and Eichmann shouting at each other. The text below the drawing is as follows:
> Ben-Gurion: "You deserve the death penalty for killing six million Jews."

Eichmann: "There are many who argue that I deserve the death penalty for not finishing the job."

The Jordanian English language daily, *Jerusalem Times*, published the following "Open Letter to Eichmann" on April 24, 1961:

Dear Eichmann,

I address you in your glass cell to extend a word of sympathy in your present plight. German genius that has invented sputniks and missiles and all sorts of things has failed to inspire you to avert the disaster that has befallen you.

What a pity Eichmann that you allowed those swine to arrest you and stage their drama. But don't worry Eichmann it will in the end fall on their heads.

Listen Eichmann you are accused of dissimating [*sic*] six million of his breed. Whether this is correct or not it is not our object to debate this issue but what we like to say is this if you actually managed to liquidate six million of them and if the remaining six million have been instrumental in inflicting so much havoc and suffering on the Arabs and disgorging them from their homes we wonder what would have been the result if the dissimated [*sic*] six million would have been allowed to survive.

It is likely that a similar drama would have been staged in another part of the Arab countries. So that by liquidating six millions you have minimized the extent of the calamity and conferred a real blessing on humanity you can imagine dear Eichmann the feelings of the million or so of Arab refugees at this drama . . .

The object of this trial is simply to attract more tourists to the occupied section and to exploit it for fund raising and for skinning the rest of mankind.

But be brave Eichmann find solace in the fact that this trial will one day culminate in the liquidation of the remaining six million to avenge your blood and the manner in which you have been kidnapped and brought to trial by the very same people who tortured and ejected a million or so from their homes.

Abdallah Tall [*The Danger of World Jewry to Islam and Christianity*, Cairo 1964] writes of Eichmann as one "who fell in the Holy War" (*shahid*):

We have not forgotten the abduction of the martyre Eichmann, whom the Jewish gangs brought over from Argentina to the gangster Government in Palestine and put him to death in order to make of his fate a terrorist. sword to be brandished over the head of anyone in the West who might dare to deviate from the line laid down by criminal World Jewry." (p. 282)

Indeed the Arabs were infuriated when the Catholic Church considered exonerating the Jews from collective guilt for the crucifixion of Jesus. (See Harkabi ibid. pp. 288–292.)

9. See Edward Flannery, *The Anguish of the Jews: Twenty-Three Centuries of Antisemitism*, 2004, p. 342. Fleanary Eran – 1998) was a Catholic priest, who served as pastor and chaplain to the Diocese of Providence, and throughout his whole career was active in fostering Judeo-Christian dialogue. From 1967 till 1976 he served as the first director of Catholic-Jewish Relations at the National Conference of Catholic Bishops. He also became Associate Director of the Institute of Judeo-Christian Studies at Seton Hall University, and Director of the Continuing Education for the Clergy for the Diocese of Rhode Island, Providence.

See further John Rousmaniere, *A Bridge to Dialogue: The Story of Jewish-Christian Relations*, 1991; Edward Kessler, *An Introduction to Jewish Christian Relations*, Cambridge, 2010; Egal Feldman, *Catholics and Jews in Twentieth Century America*, University of Illinois Press, 2001. On the Impact of Eichman Trial, see David Caesarani, *Eichman: His Life and Crimes*, London, 2005, pp. 325–332, (published in the U.S.A. under the title: *Becoming Eichman: Rethinking the Life and Trial of a "Desk Murderer,"* DeCapo Press, 2006.

10. See for example the statement of Archbishop John Carmel Heenan of Westminster, in the "debate" (Oesterreicher ibid. p. 21) who said:

> I humbly ask that our declaration publically acknowledge that the Jewish people, as such, is not guilty of the Lord's death. *It would undoubtedly be unjust were one to blame all Christians of Europe for the number of six million Jews in Germany and Poland in our day.* In the same way, I maintain that it is unjust to condemn the whole Jewish people for the death of Christ [My emphasis, D.S.]

This is echoed in a letter of 12 March 1998, addressed to Edward Idris Cassidy, president of the Commission for Religious Relations with the Jews, by Pope John Paul II, in which he describes his "deep sense of sorrow [regarding] the sufferings of the Jewish people during the Second World War," and how the "Shoah remains an indelible stain on the history of the century." With his hopes that the document – i.e. the document entitled "We Remember: A Reflection on the Shoah," published in 1998 under his authority – would "help to heal the wounds of the past misunderstandings and the injustices," and help create a "future in which the unspeakable iniquity of the *Shoah* will never again be possible. May the Lord of history guide the efforts of Catholics and Jews and all men and women of good will as they work together for a world of true respect for the life and dignity of every human being, for all have been created in the image and likeness of God" (Staff, "The Vatican and the Holocaust: John Paul's Plea: Never Again," 14 March 1998).

The influence of the holocaust on Christian theology may be clearly seen (albeit much later) in S.G. Hall's *Christian Anti-Semitism*, New York, 1983, pass. See David

Rokeah's comments in his *Sugyot be-Inyanei de-Yoma ve-Shaar Yerakot*, Jerusalem, 2016, pp. 134 et seq.

We should not disregard the problematic nature of Pope Pius XII's attitude to the Shoah.

For the Vatican already in 1942 was well-informed on what was happening to European Jewry, as Gerhart M. Riegner, in his autobiographical, *Ne Jamais Désespérer,* Paris, 1998, pp. 169–180 gives clear testimony.

Further detailed information on the knowledge of what was happening to the Jews already in 1942, may be found in David S. Wyman, *The Abandonment of the Jews: America and the Holocaust 1941–1945*, New York, 1984 Part II pp. 19–58, sections entitled "The News Filters Out" and "The Worst is Confirmed." Indeed, already earlier, in the spring of 1941, Eduard Schulte was passing on to the Allies valuable information about the Eastern front. He, Benjamin Sagalowitz and Gerhart Riegner were active in getting information out on what was happening in Germany and Eastern Europe. Indeed Schulte was involved in the famous Riegner telegram. See, in detail, Walter Laquer and Richard Breitman, *Breaking the Silence: The Story of Eduard Schulte, the German industrialist who risked everything to oppose the Nazis and was the first to tell the world of the fate of the Jews in Hitler's Europe*, New York, 1986, pass. And especially pp. 99–177.

That the Holy See was kept cognizant of what was happening throughout Europe from 1942 onwards, and even what was being done to the Jews of Italy, and Rome itself, has been convincingly demonstrated by John Morley, in his carefully documented study *Vatican Diplomacy and the Jews During the Holocaust* 1939–1943, New York, 1980. See, most especially, the various appendices containing letters written to Cardinal Maglione, the Secretary of State at the Vatican, from the year 1942, describing in detail the deportations and harsh treatment of Jews in several different European countries (pp. 216–262). (On Maglione, his character, the degree of control exercised over him by the Pope, see pp. 14–16.)

And already in October 1941 Maglione was informed that Jewish prisoners had been shot by Germans (ibid. p. 135), and even in April 1940 the Vatican had been informed about Pogroms against the Jews in Poland, (p. 134), and so forth.

Morley's concluding paragraph (p. 201) states that:

> It must be concluded that Vatican diplomacy failed the Jews during the Holocaust by not doing all that was possible for it to do on their behalf. It also failed itself because in neglecting the needs of the Jews, and persuing a goal of reserve rather than humanitarian concern, it betrayed the ideals that it had set itself. The nuncios, the secretary of State, and, most of all, the Pope share the responsibility for this dual failure.

There has been a sharp controversy on this whole issue, some scholars criticizing the Pope's position very severely, other justifying (apologetically?) his position. See,

Encyclopaedia Brittanica, "Reflections on the Holocaust: Pope Pius XII, Additional Reading," by Frank J. Coppa. There we may find a bibliography of studies in both directions. Among the denigrators are: Guenter Lewi, *The Catholic Church and Nazi Germany*, 1964, p. 200; Saul Friedländer, *Piux XII and the Third Reich: A Documentation*, 1966, 1980; Carlo Falconi, *The Silence of Pius XII*, 1965, 1970; John Cornwell, *Hitler's Pope: The Secret History of Pope Pius XII*, 1999, etc. These critical accounts have been countered by a number of favourable volumes, listed in the *Brittanica* article ibid. On this debate see the bibliographic survey on José M. Sanchez, *Pius XII and the Holocaust: Understanding the Controversy*, 2001.

To the above we may add the following references: *Pius XII and the Holocaust*, edd. David Bankier, Dan Michman, Lael Nidam-Orvieto, Yad Vashem, Jerusalem, 2012; Meir Michaelis, "The Current Debate over Fascist Racial Policy," apud *Fascist Antisemitism and the Italian Jews*, Jerusalem, 1995, pp. 77–78. And on the Pope's relationship to the Jesuits, known for their anti-Semitism, see R.A. Webster, *The Cross and the Fasces: Christian Democracy and Fascism in Italy*, Stanford, 1960, pp. 55–56; *Il manguello e 'l'aspersoris*, Florence, 1958, pp. 351–393; Guenter Lewy, ibid. pp. 296–298; Arthur D. Morse, *While Six Million Died: A Chronicle of American Apathy*, New York, 1968, index s.v. Pope Pius XII, p. 418a.

The main axis of this bitter controversy is highlighted in the two polar studies, that of David I. Kerzer, *The Popes Against the Jews*: published in New York, 2001, and the counterattack by Justus George Lawlor (and see his *Pope and Politics: Reform, Resentment and the Holocaust*, 2002), *Were the Popes Against the Jews*: Grand Rapids, Michigan and Cambridge U.K., 2012. See also Kerzner's most recent *The Pope and Mussolini: The Secret History of Pius XI and the Rise of Fascism in Europe*, New York, 2014. We should also add Jose M. Sanches, *Pope Pius XII and the Holocaust: Understanding the Controversy*, Washington D.C., 2002; Kevin P. Spicer's review of Lawler in *Commonweal*, May 2012, "Blind Spots"; and David G. Dalin, summarizing comments in *"First-Things,"* August 1, 2002, who also lists the dramatis personae on both sides of the controversy. And see Joseph Boltum and David G. Dalin, edd., *The* Pius *war: Responses to the Critics of Pius XII*, Lanham, Md., 2004. It should further be noted that even before Kertzer's critique, John Cornwell in 1999 wrote a book entitled *Hitler's Pope*, in which he asserted that as early as the 1940s Eugenio Pacelli, later Pius XII, had anti-Semitic tendencies, associating the Jews with the Bolshevik revolution, while Frank J. Coppa, writing in the *Encyclopedia Britannica* argues that the accusation lacks credible substantiation. And see further his book *The Pope, the Jews, and the Holocaust*, Washington, D.C., 2000, pp. 180–218; idem, *The Policies of Pope Pius XI: Between Diplomacy and Morality*, 2011, and *The Life and Pontificate of Pope Pius XII, Between History and Controversy*, 2013.More recently Dan O'Shea, published a book entitled *A Cross Too Heavy: Pope Piux XII and the Jews of Europe*, Palgrave MacMillan, 2011, in which he gives a nuanced assessment of Pius XII, concluding that he was neither an anti-Semitic villain nor a "lamb without blemish." Already his policy was complex and controversial, and the final authoritative and conclusive assessment must be left to others.

Susan Zuccotti, in her meticulously documented study, *Under His Very Windows*, New Haven and London, 2002, and earlier in his *The Italians and the Holocaust: Persecution, Rescue, Survival*, New York, 1987, shows that Pope Pius XII, though frequently expressing in general terms his sorrow for the sufferings of innocent civilians, never directly mentioned the Jews, nor did he protest the deportations and destructions of European Jewry at the hands of the Nazis, though it remains unclear whether such protestations would have had any real effect. And, on the contrary, it has been argued that it may have further endangered Jews and Christians alike – though this argument is puzzling, in view of the fate of European Jewry. On the other hand, she has demonstrated the paradoxical situation that the "fascist anti-semitic" Italians were far more helpful towards Italian Jews, and that many Catholic priests did much to alleviate their situation. And the fact remains that out of some 45,200 Jews known to have been in Italy around September 1943, only some 6,800 of them perished at the hands of the Nazis. And while this may still be a horrifying statistic, it is nonetheless far less than what happened in any other European country under Nazi (or Fascist) occupation.

Incidentally, the title "Under His Very Windows" is based on a statement of Ernst von Weizäker, German ambassador to the Holy See, from October 17, 1943, one day after the German rounding of 1,259 Jews in Rome and one day before most of them were deported to Auschwitz. He said:

> I can confirm the reaction of the Vatican to the removal of Jews from Rome. The curia is dumbfounded, particularly as the action took place under the very windows of the pope, as it were.

Zuccotti stresses in both books, the earlier one on pp. 127–130, and the later one on pp. 156–160, that the Pope remained silent during those fateful days around October 16, 1943, when 1,259 Jewish men, women and children were rounded up in Rome, 195 of them eventually perishing in Auschwitz. She also argued most convincingly that the Pope must have known about this, and nonetheless was silent. We shall not persue this issue which has been the subject of so much controversial discussion. But even the above will explain the serious doubts and reservations that many Jews have as to the behaviour of Pope Pius XII.

However, Rabbi David Rosen called my attention to some interesting new approaches to this whole somewhat distressing subject. For, most recently, in 2016, Mark Riebling published a book entitled *La Spie del Vaticano* which seeks to reveal Pope Pius XII's attempts at covert activities against Hitler. This was already suggested in 1968, in Harold Deutsch's *The Conspiracy against Hitler* in the *Twilight War*, University of Minnesota Press, and later in Dominico Bernabei's *L'Orchestra*

Neva: Militari, Civili, Preti Cattolici, Pastori Protestanti, Una Rete Contra Hitler, Torino, 1991.

Here again it is way beyond the scope of this study and my competence, to draw definite conclusions on this issue.

We should also note the explosive controversy that was triggered off by Rolf Hochuth's 1963 drama *"Die Stellvertreter: Ein Christliches Trauerspiel,"* ("The Deputy: A Christian Tragedy"), which was first performed in Berlin on 20th February 1963, and then in London on that same year where it ran for 314 performances, and abridged on Broadway in 1964, where it had 316 performances. It discussed very critically Pius XII role in World War 2, creating a stormy debate. See, e.g., Eric Benttey, ed., *The Storm Over the Deputy: Essays and Articles about Hochuth's Explosive Drama*, New York, 1964. Hochuth's play has been lauded and lambasted by the various sides of the Pius XII debate. See, e.g., Pinhas E. Lapide, *Three Popes and the Jews*, New York, 1967, index s.v. Hochuth, Rolf (p. 378b), and Justus George Lawlor, *Were The Popes Against the Jews?* Grand Rapids, Michigan and Cambridge U.K., 2012, index s.v. Hochuth Rolf, (p. 379a).

We may further add that the unedited version would have run to eight or nine hours. Consequently, each production adapted it in its own way. No audience saw it in the original form. (See Christopher Bigsby, *Remembering and Imagining the Holocaust: The Chain of Memory*, Cambridge, 2006, p. 117). In 2002, it was made into a film entitled Amen by Costa Gavras.

And in this connection we call attention to the fact that the document that Pope Pius XI requested to be formulated by the American Jesuit John La Farge on fascism and racism, and which was completed by September 1938, shortly before the Pope died on February 9, 1939, was shelved, probably by Father Ledochowski, the Superior General of the Jesuit Order. The story of the so-called "hidden encyclical" became publicized only at the end of 1972, when the story appeared in the Kansas City-based lay-edited *National Catholic Reporter* (*NCR*), in an article by Jim Castells. And Gordon Zahn, in *NCR* December 15, 1972, wrote that "the heart of [the draft] encyclical, its whole reason for being written in the first place, was the explicit condemnation of racism and anti-Semitism." Whether the publications of the encyclical would have had a dramatic effect, or perhaps at least might have slowed down the process of planned extermination, remains a matter of controversy. Conor Creise O'Brian, in his article "A Lost Chance to Save the Jews?" *The New York Review of Books*, April 27, 1989, pp. 28, 35, thought that this encyclical, entitled *Humani Generis Unitas* (The Unity of the Human Race) was a "lost chance to save the Jews," and puts much of the blame on Ledochowski negative view shared by Pius XII, while Frederick Brown, "The Hidden Encyclical," *The New Republic*, 15 April 1996, p. 31, also included Catholic teaching, of contempt for Jews, and would have been of little help to the Jews. (See the summarizing article of Michael R. Marcus, "The Vatican on Racism and Antisemitism, 1938–39: A New Look at a Might-Have-Been," *Holocaust and Genocide Studies* 11/3, 1997, pp. 378–395). This long interpolation is just to point yet another finger of accusation at the head of the Jesuit Order.

A very detailed and penetrating study of Pope Pius XII and the Jewish Question may be found in David Jonah Goldhagen, *A Moral Reckoning: The Role of the Catholic Church in the Holocaust and its Unfulfilled Duty of Repair*, London, 2002. For a critique on Goldhagen's thesis, see Mitchell G. Ash, "American and German Respectives on the Goldhagen Debate: History, Identity and the Media," *Holocaust and Genocide Studies* 11/3, 1997, pp. 396–411.

See further Pinhas E. Lapide, *Three Popes and the Jews*, New York, 1967, pp. 92–116 on Pope Pius XI, and pp. 125–305 on Pope Pius XII.

11. In all due fairness, it should be noted that hatred of the Jews long outdates Christianity.

See, for example, Joseph Mélèze-Modrzejewski, "Sur l'antisémitisme paien," apud *Pour Léon Poliakov: Le Racisme: Mythes et Sciences*, ed. Maurice Olender, Bruxelles, 1981, pp. 411–439; Robert Wistrich, *A lethal Obsession: Antisemitism from Antiquity to the Global Jihad*, New York, 2010, pp. 79–84. See also David Nirenberg, *Anti-Judaism: The Western Tradition*, New York-London, 2014, pp. 13–47.

(This is one of the "excuses" of the Church itself, as stated in the Holy See's Commission for Religious Relations with Jews, "We Remember: A Reflection on the Shoah" [March 1998]: The *Shoah* was the work of a toughly modern neopagan regime. Its anti-Semitism had its roots outside of Christianity.)

However, an admission of a measure of guilt may be found in the United States Catholic Conference, *Catholic Teaching on the Shoah: Implementing the Holy See's "We Remember"* (2001), where we read:

> Christian anti-Judaism did lay the ground work for racial, genocidal anti-sem-
> itism by stigmatizing not only Judaism but Jews themselves for opprobrium
> and contempt. So the Nazi theories tragically found fertile soil in which to
> plant the horror of an unprecedented attempt at genocide.

(See Goldhagen ibid. p. 1.)

See further Michael R. Marrus, "The Vatican on Racism and Antisemitism, 1938–1939: A New Look at a Might-Have-Been," *Holocaust and Genocide Studies* 11/3, 1997, pp. 378–395.

See, for example, Peter Schäfer, *Judaeophobia: Attitudes towards the Jews in the Ancient World*, Cambridge Mass., 1997, (with full bibliography, pp. 287–299); Bezalel Bar-Kochva, *The Image of the Jews in Greek Literature: The Helllenistic Period*, Berkeley, Los Angeles, London, 2010; John G. Gager, *The Origins of Antisemitism in Pagan and Christian Antiquity*. Oxford 1983; J.V. Stevenster, *The Roots of Pagan Anti-Semitism in the Ancient World*, Leiden 1975. And David

Nirenberg, in his book *Anti-Judaism in the Western Tradition,* New York, 2013 which traces in minute detail this phenomenon from Hellenistic Egypt onwards. He also shows how the notion of "the Jew" came, at times, to be applied to non-Jews who were, for one reason or another, hated personalities, and thus they were seen to have the characteristics of Jews, and were accorded that identification. He amassed a vast and very varied amount of data demonstrating this phenomenon.

See also Bezalel Bar-Kochva's important article "An Ass in the Jerusalem Temple – *The Origin and Development of the Slander,"* apud *Josephus' contra Apionem's Studies in its Character and Context – with a Latin Concordance to the Portion Missing in the Greek,* edd. L.H. Feldman and John Treviso, Leiden, New York, London, 1996 pp. 310–326; and also cf. E. Bickerman, "Ritualmord und Eselkant," *MGWJ* LXX, 1927, pp. 245–255.

We should also add here Gavin I. Langmuir's very thought-provoking study, *Towards a Definition of Antisemitism,* Berkeley, Los Angeles, Oxford, 1990. Antisemitism is a vast field of study, with a huge bibliography, which is beyond the scope of this study.

Nonetheless, it is fascinating and significant to see how certain pre-Christian "chimeric" myths somehow or other appear to reappear in a different guise in the mediaeval period and even in relatively modern times. Thus, we read in a passage of Apollonius Molon of Rhodes of the first century C.E. (apud Menachem Stern, *Greek and Latin Authors of Jews and Judaism,* vol. 1, Jerusalem, 1976, pp. 153–154, 48) as follows:

> (91.) He asserts that Antiochus found in the temple a couch, on which a man was reclining, with a table before him laden with a banquet of fish of the sea, beasts of the earth, and birds of the air, at which the poor fellow was gazing in stupefaction. (92) The King's entry was instantly hailed by him with adoration, as about to procure him profound relief; falling at the king's knees, he stretched out his right hand and implored him to set him free. The king reassured him and bade him tell who he was, why he was living there, what was the meaning of his abundant fare. Thereupon, with sighs and tears, the man, in a pitiful tone, told the tale of his distress. (93) He said, Apion continues, that he was a Greek and that, while travelling about the province for a livelihood, he was suddenly kidnapped by men of a foreign race and conveyed to the temple; there he was shut up and seen by nobody, but was fattened on feasts of the most lavish description. (94) At first these unlooked for attentions deceived him and caused him pleasure; suspicion followed, then consternation. Finally, on consulting the attendants who waited upon him, he heard of the unutterable law of the Jews, for the sake of which he was being fed. The practice was repeated annually at a fixed season. (95) They would kidnap a Greek foreigner, fatten him for a year, and then convey him to a wood, where they slew him, sacrificed his body with

their customary ritual, partook of his flesh, and, while immolating the Greek, swore an oath of hostility to the Greeks. The remains of their victim were then thrown into a pit. (96) The man (Apion continues) stated that he had now but a few days left to live, and implored the king, out of respect for the gods of Greece, to defeat this Jewish plot upon his life-blood and to deliver him from his miserable predicament.

(Josephus, *Contra Apion*, trans. H. St. J. Thackeray, LCL.)

Compare the mediaeval legend of Simon of Trent below note 177.

And see further Gavin I. Langmuir, *Towards a Definition of Antisemitism*, Berkeley, Los Angelesew, London, 1966, chapter 11 (pp. 262–281), entitled "Ritual Cannibalism."

Or again, in the writings of the Greco-Egyptian Lysimachus, of the second or first century B.C.E., (apud Stern ibid. pp. 385–386):

(304) I will next introduce Lysimachus. He brings up the same theme as the writers just mentioned, the mendacious story of the lepers and cripples, but surpasses both in the incredibility of his fictions, obviously composed with bitter animus. (305) His account is this: In the reign of Bocchoris, king of Egypt, the Jewish people, who were afflicted with leprosy, scurvy, and other maladies, took refuge in the temples and lived a mendicant existence. The victims of disease being very numerous, a dearth ensued throughout Egypt. (306) King Bocchoris thereupon sent to consult the oracle of Ammon about the failure of the crops. The god told him to purge the temples of impure and impious persons, to drive them out of these sanctuaries into the wilderness, to drown those afflicted with leprosy and scurvy, as the sun was indignant that such persons should live, and to purify the temples; then the land would yield her increase. (307) On receiving these oracular instructions, Bocchoris summoned the priests and servitors at the altars, and ordered them to draw up a list of the unclean persons and to deliver them into military charge to be conducted into the wilderness, and to pack the lepers into sheets of lead and sink them in the ocean. (308) The lepers and victims of scurvy having been drowned, the others were collected and exposed in the desert to perish. There they assembled and deliberated on their situation. At nightfall they lit up a bonfire and torches, and mounted guard, and on the following night kept a fast and implored the gods to save them. (309) On the next day a certain Moses advised them to take their courage in their hands and make a straight track until they reached inhabited country, instructing them to show goodwill to no man, to offer not the best but the worst advice, and to overthrow any temples and altars of the gods which they found. (310) The rest assenting, they proceeded to put these decisions into practice. They traversed the desert, and after great hardships reached inhabited country: there they maltreated the population, and

plundered and set fire to the temples, until they came to the country now called Judaea, where they built a city in which they settled. (311) This town was called Hierosyla because of their sacrilegious propensities. [*Hiero syleo* in Greek means "rob of temple, commit sacrilege," D.S.] At a later date, when they had risen to power, they altered the name, to avoid the disgraceful imputation, and called the city Hierosolyma and themselves Hierosolymites. (Josephus ibid.)

Here we see how the biblical tradition was distorted almost beyond recognition. And, compare the passage in a letter written by Marx to Engels, 3 October 1866, (apud Poliakov, *The Aryan Myth*, p. 246):

> I now see clearly that he [i.e. his rival Ferdinand Lassale] is descended, as the shape of his head and his hair clearly indicate, from the Negroes who were joined to the Jews at the time of the exodus from Egypt (unless it was his mother or paternal grandmother who mated with a Negro). But this mixture of Judaism and Germanism with a Negro substance as a base was bound to yield a most curious product. The importunity of the man also is negroid. . . . One of the great discoveries of this Negro, which he confided to me, is that the Pelasgians are descended from the Semites. His main proof is that, according to the Book of Maccabees, the Jews sent messengers to Greece to ask for help and appealed to their tribal relationship. . . .

This is not a direct comparison, but here again the biblical source is "elaborated upon" for his purposes. For the fuller context of this passage, see Poliakov, ibid. and p. 364 note 99.

Incidentally, we may note that in the twelfth century Europe witnessed an upsurge of cases of Hansen's disease, which was commonly taken to be the same as the Biblical *tzaraat* – leprosy– and Jews were accused of speading this leprosy. See M. Barber, "Lepers, Jews and Moslems: The Plot to Overthrow Christendom in 1321," *History* 66, 1981, pp. 1–17. See also Jeffrey R. Woolf, *The Fabric of Life in Medieval Ashkenaz* (1000–1300): *Creating Sacred Communities*, Leiden, Boston, 2015, p. 96 note 72.

For an additional aspect of this leprosy myth, see Louis Ginzberg, *The Legends of the Jews*, vol. 2, Philadelphia, 1946, 296, and Ginzberg's comments in vol. 5. Philadelphia, 1955, pp. 412–413, notes 101–104. And cf. Saul David Brody, *Disease of the Soul: Leprosy in Mediaeval Literature*, New York, 1974.

The connection between Jews and lepers, was already noted by Carlo Ginzburg, in his brilliant study *Ecstasies: Deciphering the Witches' Sabbath*, transl. Raymond Rosenthal, London, New York, 1991, p. 38. There he also notes that "the diffusion of Against Apion in the Middle Ages circulated this damaging legend in the West, together with others (donkey worship, ritual murder) likewise refuted by Josephus, that were destined to become more or less enduring items in anti-Jewish propaganda." And on p. 55 note 20, he gives the relevant bibliographic references, which for the reader's convenience I shall cite in full:

> Cf. Flavius Josephus, *Against Apion*, I, 26ff.; on which see A. Momigliano, *Quinto contributo alla storia degli studi classici e del mondo antico*, I, Rome, 1975, pp. 179–84; and the same author's *Sagezza Straniera*, Turin, 1980, pp. 78–9. See also J.Y. Yoyotte, "L'Egypte ancienne et les origins de l'antijuda-isme," *Revue de l'histoire de religions*, 163 (1963), pp. 133–43; L. Troiani, *Commento storico al 'Contro Apione' di Giuseppe*, Pisa 1977, pp. 46–8. On the fortunes of Flavius Josephus, see H. Schreckenberg, *Bibliographie zu Flavius Josephus*, Leiden, 1968 and 1979; idem, *Die Flavius-Josephus-Tradition in Antike und Mittelalter*, Leiden, 1972; idem, *Rezeptionsgeschichtliche und textkritische Untersuchungen zu Flavius Josephus*, Leiden, 1977.

In that chapter, entitled "Lepers, Jews, Muslims" (pp. 33–62), he traces in minute detail the development of this calumny, namely how the Jews paid the lepers to spread the disease by poisoning fountains and wells with a compound whose ingredients were "human blood, urine, three unspecified herbs and a consecrated host [!] – all of this dried, reduced to powder and placed in small bags weighted down so as to sink to the bottom [of the wells] more easily" (ibid. p. 35). [My additions, D.S.] He further shows how the (Moslem) King of Granada, "unable to defeat the Christians by force . . . decided to do so by coming . . . [and] turned to the Jews, offering them an enormous amount of money to hatch a criminal scheme to destroy Christianity. The Jews accepted . . . but could not act directly because they were under too much suspicion. . . . [So they] assembled a number of lepers' leaders, and, with the devil's help . . . induced them to adjure their faith and grind the consecrated host into the pestilential potions" (ibid. and cf. ibid. p. 36). And cf. ibid. pp. 65–68, on Jewish poisons spreading the Black Death. See further on Jews as lepers R.I. Moore, *The Formation of a Persecuting Society*, Oxford, 1987, pp. 73–80.

On the accusation of Jews poisoning wells, and this as the cause of the Black Death, see Joshua Trachtenberg, *The Devil and the Jews: The Mediaeval Conception of the Jew and its Relations to Modern Antisemitism*, Yale University Press, 1943. (Reprinted New York, 1966, chapter seven, "The Poisoners," pp. 97–108). See especially pp. 101–103, which I quote in full:

> Popular belief in the possibility of wholesale poisoning was so strong that the rumors of Jewish plots to murder a large part of Christendom, which began to circulate widely early in the fourteenth century, won immediate acceptance. The charge of well poisoning was not altogether unprecedented; it had already cropped up in three places (1308 in the Vaud; 1316 in the Eulenburg region; and 1319 in Franconia) prior to the first really serious incident. In 1321 the lepers of France were accused of harboring the same design and suffered widespread

persecution, but it shortly appeared that they were little more than agents and that the Jews had been the responsible entrepreneurs behind the scheme. One report has it that a Hebrew letter found in Parthenay in 1321 and "translated" by a converted Jew was said to reveal a huge plot of the Jews, the lepers, and the Saracens of Spain to destroy the whole Christian population of Europe by poisoning the wells. In Teruel (Aragon) a Christian, arrested and tortured for having thrown poison into the local wells, at first placed the responsibility upon a Breton, but when this evidently did not satisfy his interrogators, who continued the torture, he recalled that it was really the Jews who had put him up to it.

The chronicler of St. Denis recounts that "a great and rich Jew" had hired the lepers to do this and had given them the recipe for the poison, which contained "human blood and urine, three kinds of herbs the names of which he did not know or did not wish to disclose," and also "the body of Jesus Christ." This purports to be the confession of a leper "of great renown." Another account would have the poison include "adders' heads, toads' legs, and women's hair."

Many lepers were cross-examined and abundant testimony elicited as to the complicity of the Jews. According to this testimony the plot had originated with the King of Granada, who sought the aid of the Jews; they declined to carry out his plan themselves but with the help of the devil induced the lepers to betray their Christian faith and to procure consecrated hosts for the manufacture of the poison. Some of the lepers went even further in their confessions and told of four meetings attended by delegates from the various leproseries, at which, following the counsel of the devil supported by the promise of the Jews to apportion the land among the lepers after they had taken it over, this nefarious scheme was agreed upon.

Evidently little credence was placed in these tales, for an edict issued June 21, 1321, directed the arrest and punishment of the lepers involved, without mentioning Jews. However, the incident could not be left wholly unexploited: it would appear that the Parliament of Paris, the King's highest court, exacted a large fine from the Jews of France in consequence of these reports, and the following year Charles IV, having mulcted them of most of their possessions, expelled them from France for their alleged complicity in the plot. This incident became a popular theme for later poets and chroniclers and thus developed into a recurrent motif in European folklore.

If the accusations of 1321 passed without bloody repercussions, it was perhaps only because the immediate resentment of the masses spent itself upon the doubly unfortunate lepers. Apparently the implication of the Jews in the plot came after these wretches had already been victimized by popular credulity, and the Jews escaped comparatively unscathed. But the Black Death which broke out in 1348 – in April it had reached Florence; by August it was devastating France and Germany, and a short while later it attacked England; during this and the next year all of Europe was ravaged, from one-half to two-thirds of the population in many places perishing from the scourge – revived the rumors of well poisoning by Jews. This time these rumors did not fail to evoke a swift reaction. To the horrors of the plague itself were added the wholesale massacre of thousands of Jews and the expulsion of thousands more from their homes.

The impression that Jews were intent on the destruction of Christendom was deeply rooted. The leper incident in France had brought it out into the open and Europe could now entertain itself with speculating on the form the plot would next assume. That it was a real conspiracy few doubted, then or later. A sixteenth-century chronicler, Johannes Aventin, records that in 1337 the Jews had planned to poison the entire Christian population of Germany but their plan had miscarried. Another sixteenth-century tradition has it that the Jews of Provence, in revenge for the edict of the Second Council of St. Ruf, in 1337, forbidding intermarriage and the use of Jewish physicians and apothecaries, had brought the pest from India and caused it to destroy entire villages in that region, whence it spread through Europe. Still another sixteenth-century report has it that in 1348 the Jews held a meeting at Benfeld in Alsace, "as they later confessed," and there hatched a plot to poison all the wells in Germany "from the German Sea to the Italian (*welsch*) mountains. Whether these identical stories were current during the Black Death is immaterial. They testify to the undiminished belief of Europe in the nefarious plans of the Jews, a belief which is amply documented at the time in the widely circulated reports holding Jews responsible for the plague.

Rumors of Jewish well poisoning began to circulate in Southern France, where, as early as May, 1348, the Jews of a Provençal town were burned on this charge. From there the wave of persecutions moved southward over the Pyrenees. Pope Clement VI sought to stem the tide with a renewal, on July 4 of that year, of the old bull forbidding violence against Jews, and again, on September 26, with a bull denying that the Jews were guilty of spreading the disease. But his solicitude hardly made an impression outside Avignon, the seat of the Papacy, where the Jews suffered no harm (there the plague was ascribed to astrological causes, or to the wrath of God, or to natural causes – but not to the Jews). Elsewhere the rumors received ready credence. In the Dauphiné large numbers of Jews were imprisoned, their property seized – and only thereafter was an investigation instituted which evidently exonerated the suspects, for there is no report of any further punishment being meted out to them. In Savoy not a few Christians suffered along with Jews, who supposedly had dragged them into the plot. . . .

See the continuation of Trachtenberg's description.

278

CHAPTER 12

The Mediaeval Calumnies

Without entering into the question of the historicity of the Gospel narrative describing the role of the Jews leading to the crucifixion of Jesus, a historicity which in recent times has been called into considerable doubt by numerous scholars,[1] and the fact that those identified in the narrative as having been involved in that event were, as is well known from near contemporary rabbinic sources, accursed and hated by most Jews of that period as being corrupt temple authorities manipulated by their Roman overlords, the mere concept that subsequent generations, completely disconnected from that event and any ideology that may have led up to it, should be regarded as continuously bearing guilt, was seen as totally irrational. Not only generations divided them for the early 1st century C.E., but also geographic location, language and cultural characteristics etc., all of which constituted a total disconnect in the eyes of Jewry from that vicious culumny that was so virulently directed against them.[2]

Disputation between Christian and Jewish scholars. Woodcut by Johann von Armssheim in *Der Seelen Wurzgarten*, a German collection of examples orientated on salvation history, which was made in 1466/67 in the monastic foundation of Komburg (near Schwabisch Hall), printed by Konrad Dinckmut, Ulm 1483. Illustration after Liebe 1903, no. 42.

In the wake of this culumny, in order to preserve the smouldering hatred of the Jews, the myth of the wandering Jew was engendered,[3] the fictional story of Simon of Trent was invented,[4] so too William of Norwitch,[5] the desecration of the host,[6] and so forth.[7] Here we should note that the establishment of the State of Israel in 1948 was a serious theological blow to the "doctrine" of the wandering Jew.[8]

Malmö, 1832, 1833.

Стоскполм, Элмёнс оф Огаибетдв Сгрёссг, 1823

Stockholm, 1823; Jönköp-
ing, 1826, 1833.

Lund, 1833, 1834.

Stockholm, 1829.

Jönköping, 1833-57.

Norrköping, 1845.

The Wandering Jew.

Sweden, 18th century, after 17th-century German illustration.

Anti-Semitic broadsheet, 1734.

Nyköping, Sweden, 1774, 1787.

Norrköping, 1776.

Örebro, 1787.

Gefle, 1793, 1798.

The Wandering Jew.

282

"The Errant Jew." A large picture in colors of the Jew in transit throughout the world.
Epinal (France), printed by Pellerina, c. 1870.

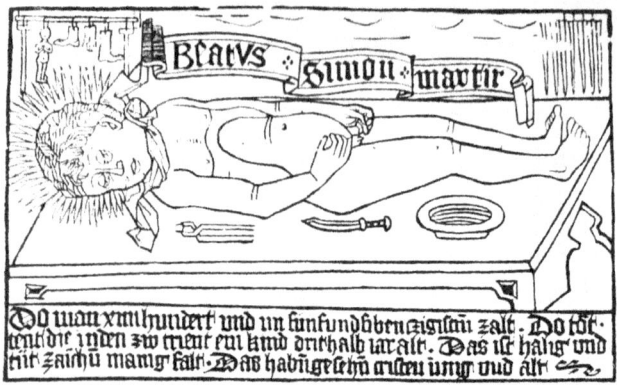

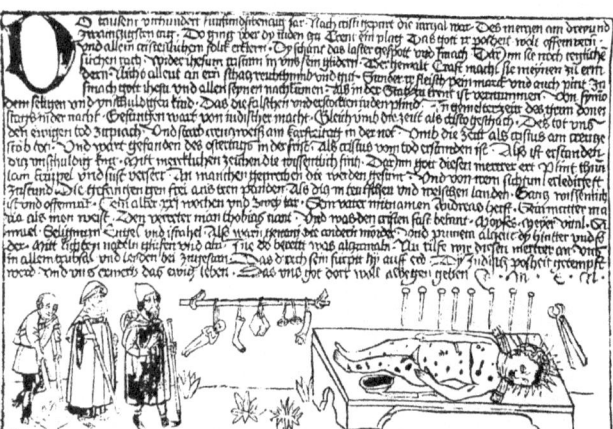

Simon of Trent. Woodcut in an edition in German of the Latin account of the events in Trent by J.M. Tiberinus, the most influential source, Nuremberg [nd], by Friedrich Creussner (active as printer in Nuremberg 1470–1500). Illustration after Schramm 1920, XVIII, no. 343.

Desecration of the Host. Woodcut in *La rappresentazione d'uno miracolo del corpo di Christo* (miracle play) printed in Florence around 1500. Illustration after Kristeller 1968, no.48.

Desecration of the Host. The trial for profanation of a host in Berlin, 1510. Wooduct: Burning of the Jews.

And as part of this process of vilification, in the post-Crusade period the Jew became the personification of evil and nothing less than an agent of the Devil.[9] Jews and the Devil were thought of as allied in opposition to Christ, and thereby to contemporary Christian civilization, and from this vilification, there grew an actuality in the minds of the uncritical.[10] So much so, that in a superscription on the Forest Roll of Essex from 1277, Aaron is described as the son of the Devil![11] It is thus easy to understand how it came about that in the words of Mellinkoff:[12]

The Jew was thought to have certain physical characteristics, setting him apart from human beings, and identifying him with the Devil – and horns were an integral part of this image, [Trachtenberg ibid. pp. 44–53]. The firmly rooted popular belief that Jews had horns has even persisted into the present. Joshua Trachtenberg reported that on a trip through Kansas a farmer refused to believe that he was Jewish because he lacked horns on his head. [Ibid. p. 227 note 5. See also Norman Cohn, "The Horns of Moses," *Commentary Magazine* 26/3, 1958, p. 220.] Others have testified to similar beliefs.

Artistic evidence for this incredible fantasy can be found in later documents. For example, Lucas Cranach executed a woodcut for the title page of Luther's *Von den Jüden und Iren Lügen* in 1543; it features a Jew with a horned headdress (fig. 126). And in a satirical caricature, "Der Jüden Ehrbarkeit," of 1571, horned devil figures are identified as Jews by means of the best known of the Jewish badges, the *rouelle*, also known as the circular or wheel badge (fig. 127). Jews depicted with horns occur in a scurrilous seventeenth-century print, [see Georg, *Das Judentum in der Deutschen Vergangenheit*, Leipzig 1903, p. 55], and in an almost completely similar picture at the beginning of the eighteenth century, where the artist has added, with what seems to be gratuitous literalness, "Dieses ist der Juden Teuffel" (fig. 128). It is pertinent to recall in this context that the pointed Jew's hat, discussed above, was often referred to as a horned hat (*pileum corunutum*); and there is evidence that Philip III required the Jews of France to attach a horn-shaped figure to the customary Jew-badge [Felix Singermann, *Die Keunzeichnung der Juden in Mittelalter*, Berlin 1915, p. 20].

Is it possible that the preposterous fantasy that Jews had horns influenced the interpretation of horned Moses among those who held such attitudes? Perhaps the horned image of Moses, who in some circles was thought of as the Jew par excellence, even served as confirmation for the belief that all Jews had horns.[13]

This theme was further augmented by Mellinkoff, in her *Antisemitic Hate Signs in Hebrew Manuscripts from Mediaeval Germany*, Jerusalem 1999, especially pp. 53–54.

In this way vilification turned into demonization, an easier and more effective vehicle for generating racial hatred among the masses. And, of course, as a sort of corollary to this process of developing distorted visual stereotypes of the "Jew," with his hooked nose, enlarged mouth, fleshy protruding or puffing lips and enlarged eyes (see Mellinkoff's *Antisemitic Hate Signs* pp. 23–29),[14] the Nazis, under the monsterous Julius Streicher (publisher of Der Stürmer), "fine tuned their racist propaganda machine with books, posters, and educational manuals for 'recognizing' Jews by those facial characteristics." Thus, for example, in a children's book published by Streicher in 1938, written by Ernst Hiemler and illustrated by Phillip Rupprecht, entitled *Die Giftpilz* ("The Poisonous Mushroom), we read:

> How to tell a Jew:
>   The Jewish nose is bent. It looks like the number six ... We call it the Jewish nose. One can recognize a Jew by his lips. His lips are usually puffy. The lower lip protrudes. The eyes are different too. The eyelids are mostly thicker and more fleshy than ours. The Jewish look is wary and piercing. One can tell from his eyes that he is a deceitful person.[15]

One can hardly understand Goebbles' success[16] without this backcloth of malevolent prejudicial animosity.[17] Add to that, Pope Pius XII's silence,[18] in full knowledge of what was happening to European Jewry,[19] which is all the less understandable bearing in mind his predecessor, Pope John XXIII (1958–1963), formerly Cardinal Angelo Guiseppe Roncalli's activity on behalf of refugee Jews and camp survivors in Slovakia, Bulgaria, Romania, Italy and Hungary during the holocaust era.[20] And in 1938, when he received a group of Belgians for an audience, and when he accepted a prayer book they had brought him, he told them:

> Anti-Semitism is not compatible with the thinking and sublime reality that is expressed in this text. It is a hateful movement, a movement that we cannot, as Christians, take any part in.

Through his tears, as he thought about the plight of the Jews, he said:

> Anti-Semitism is inadmissible. We are all spiritually Semites.[21]

Also bearing in mind Pius XII's close relationship with the Jesuit leadership, with the checkered history which included notable elements of

288

anti-Judaism,[22] one sees the holocaust in a different light, namely an admittedly Nazi atrocity, but, shall we say tacitly, supported (perhaps covertly) by the Catholic Church.

At a totally different level, deicide, i.e. the phrase "guilty of deicide" (deicidii rea) – was seen as an oxymoron, for how could God be killed![23] The formulaters of *Nostra Aetate* were acutely aware of this issue, as is evidenced from the earlier drafts, and consequently omitted this term from the final text.[24] However, it was this accusation that continuously ignited the fires of hatred and acts of inconceivable cruelty.

Hence, *Nostra Aetate* was seen by many thinking Jews, especially the "survivors" of the holocaust, as a totally belated admission of a terrible historical injustice which plagued two millennia of Jewish life in Christian society with its attendant horrors.

The Poisonous Mushroom or Der Giftpilz. Julius Streicher, publisher.

Endnotes to Chapter 12

1. And not merely modern scholarship. For already Celsus and his Jew, in the second century C.E., while not doubting the narrative of the cross, sees Jesus' passion "as being an example of an infamous life and a miserable death," and the story of resurrection as unconvincing. See, in detail, John Granger Cook, *The Interpretations of the New Testament in Greco-Roman Paganism*, Peabody Mass., 2002, pp. 26, 50–54, 338.

Furthermore, the council of Trent (1545–1563), under the direction of Paul III (1545–1547), Julius III (1551–552) and Pius IV (1562–1567), would appear to (at least partially) exonerate Jews – certainly contemporary Jews – from the sin of deicide. For in the Catechism to the Council of Trent it is stated that:

> In this guilt (i.e. the crucifixion) are involved *all* those who fall frequently into sin. . . . This guilt seems more enormous in us than in the Jews since according to the apostle, if they had known it, they would never have crucified the Lord of Glory . . .

So the Catechism of 1566 underscores that we cannot lay responsibility for the trial of Jesus as a whole upon the Jews of that period. Still less can we extend responsibility to other Jews of different times and places (no. 597).

Furthermore, the Second Vatican Ecumenical Council stated that the crucifixion was of Christ's free will, therefore, "Not all that happened in Jesus passion can be charged against all Jews then alive nor Jews today. Jews should not be presented as rejected or accused" (*Biblical Studies*, ed. L. Boadt, H. Kroner and L. Klenicki, 1980).

Indeed this was explicitly stressed in *Notes on the Correct way to present the Jews and Judaism in preaching and catechesis in the Roman Catholic Church* (1982):

> IV F: There is no putting the Jews who knew Jesus and did not believe in him, or those who opposed the preachings of the apostles on the same plain with the Jews who come after or those of today.

But even more remarkable is the continuation:

> IV F2: The catechism of the Council of Trent teaches that Christian sinners are more to blame for the death of Christ than the Jews who brought it about. [!]

This conciliar document was signed by Cardinal Willebrands as President, Pierre Duprey as Vice President, and Jorge Meija as secretary.

2. Already in 1944 Aloisius Cardinal Muench (1899–1962), who later on from 1951–1959 was the Vatican nuncio to Germany, but already from 1946–1947 was Pope Pius XII's apostolic visitor to Germany, wrote:

> The Church does not blame the Jews of today, but rather sees the sins of men through old time as responsible. (Aloisius Muench and Vincent Ryan, *The Church, Fascism and Peace*, Huntington IN, *Our Sunday Press*, 1944, pp. 42–43.)

Cardinal Ritter of St. Louis stated in the debate (Oestereicher ibid. p. 197) that: . . .

> For this reason, all must take care that they in no way present the Jewish people as rejected or decidal, or throw blame for all the crimes committed during the Passion of Christ upon the, a fortiori, upon the Jews of our days. . . .

And in the second draft of Nov. 1963, (supplementary to the fourth chapter) it was stated that:

> The death of Christ is not to be attributed to an entire people then alive, even less to a people today.

This was frequently expressed by Christian thinkers of various denominations over the generations. A fine example of this is the statement of the American clergyman, John Haynes Holmes (1879–1964), in his *Through Gentile Eyes*, New York, 1938, ff p. 76:

> To hold any grudge, or to cherish any prejudice and hate, against Jews as a group because Jesus was slain in Jerusalem would be as foolish, as incredible, as to despise and persecute Greeks today because Socrates was made to drink the hemlock in Athens, or modern Englishmen and Frenchmen because Joan was burned at Rouen, or to assert my own countrymen because the fathers of men now living hanged John Brown at Charlestown. . . .

And the American baptist church historian Conrad Henry Moelman (1879–1961), in his *The Christian-Jewish Tragedy: A Study in Religious Prejudice*, Rochester and New York, 1933, p. 3, writes:

> The Christian accusation against Israel has been that it participated in the events of Passion Week nineteen centuries ago. Suppose that participation were superlatively exaggerated. Even then it would be difficult to understand why twentieth century Judaism should be held responsible for a first century sin!

And the Polish born German novelist, Carl Spindler (1796–1855), in his historical romance *The Jew*, New York, 1844, p. 38, puts in the mouth of Ben David the Jew, the following:

. . . The Duke looking at him [Ben David] with some surprise, asked, "Why should I or the emperor reward you for the good deeds which your father may have done?" Ben David smiled, then bowing with the profoundest humility, replied: "If your eminence will not recompense me for the *good* my father did fifty years ago, why force me to pay for the *evil* my forefathers did upward of fifteen hundred years ago?"

Since this is a very central issue, I think it important to cite at length part of Augustin Cardinal Bea's *Relatio on the schema*, from 25 October 1964, (apud his *The Church and the Jewish People*, New York, 1966, section b, No. 4, pp. 160, 161.), this being a highly significant statement:

The central issue which caused the more important changes was the question of "deicide." We all know how widely this question was discussed in the press – without the slightest intervention of co-operation by the Secretariat. Consequently, I must now point out the major issues. The question is if and how the condemnation and death of Christ the Lord is to be laid to the charge of the Jews *as such*. Now many modern Jews claim that the principal reason for anti-semitism stems from the conviction of general Jewish guilt, and that this conviction is the source of the flood of evils and persecutions which the Jews have suffered through the centuries. This cannot be sustained. In my address given in this "Aula" a year ago on this schema, I clearly stated: "We are all well aware that there are many reasons for anti-semitism which are not religious at all but are political, national, psychological, social and economic." And yet it is still true that not a few instances can be found in the history of different peoples where conviction of general Jewish guilt led Christians to consider and designate the Jews with whom they lived as members of a race rejected and cursed by God for "deicide" and so to despise or even persecute them. It is for this reason that the Jews today are most anxious that the Council should show itself opposed to this conviction of general Jewish guilt and should publicly and solemnly declare that our Lord's death is in no way to be laid to the charge of the Jewish people *as such*. We must now decide whether such a declaration by the council is possible and if so, how should it be made, what should be its tenor?

I need scarcely say that there is not and cannot be any question of denying or attenuating anything affirmed in the Gospels. The issue must be carefully defined and it is this: The leaders of the Jerusalem Sanhedrin, although not democratically elected, yet, according to the ordinary understanding of those days, accepted by the scriptures, were regarded and must be regarded as the embodiment of legitimate authority among the people. Here lie the gravity and the tragedy of their action – the exercise of their authority in the condemnation and death of Christ. Yet how grievous was their guilt? Did those "rulers" of the people in Jerusalem fully understand the divinity of Christ and so become formally guilty of deicide? Our Lord on the cross said in his prayer to the Father: "Father, forgive them: for they know not what they do" (Luke 23:34). If this reason for forgiveness is no mere empty formula – God forbid – it surely shows that the Jews were far from full understanding of the crime they were committing. St. Peter also, addressing the Jewish people on the crucifixion of Christ, repeated: "And now, brethren, I know that you acted in ignorance, as did also your rulers" (Acts 3:17). So St. Peter finds an excuse even for the very rulers! So likewise does St. Paul (Acts 13:27). Furthermore, whatever may have been the knowledge possessed by the leaders in Jerusalem, the case of the people is quite different: *can the whole Jewish people of that time, generally and without distinction, be held answerable for the proceedings of their leaders in Jerusalem*, which led to the death of Christ? Statistics show that in the apostolic age the Jews dispersed throughout the Roman Empire numbered about 4,500,000: are all of them to be accused of the deeds done by the Sanhedrists on that first sad Good Friday? And even granting – which we do not grant – that the people of that time were as a whole responsible, by what right can their descendants today be held in any sense as guilty? Can any other case be found anywhere in which we blame a nation for the actions of its ancestors over 1900 years ago?

The significance of this statement is not only in that it exonerates world Jewry of the historic crime of deicide, but also reveals how the Church in general, and Cardinal Bea in particular, deals – or perhaps struggles somewhat apologetically – with a reinterpretation of canonic sources and hitherto accepted doctrinal norms. We are given a glimpse of the inner workings of the Church in making "the enormous strides . . . into a relatively new field" (ibid. p. 12).

On "relatively new," he notes (ibid. note 1) that there were earlier occasions on which the Church stated her position vis-à-vis the Jewish People, such as in the declaration of the congregation of Holy office of 25 March 1928, condemning anti-Semitism (cf. *A.A.S.* 20, 1928, p. 104).

However, he readily admits that:

> For Catholics, one of the chief difficulties will be the task of correctly integrating the teaching of the Declaration with what they have already been more or less explicitly taught. For them, both the general principles of the Declaration and their application as presented therein will be somewhat new. We believe, notwithstanding, that taken as a whole the present study will serve to embrace all that and to demonstrate the biblical foundation of this teaching (ibid. p. 13).

His heroic efforts in the complex process of the promulgation of *Nostra Aetate* are all the more to be admired.

A further glimpse may be found in note to the passage in Romans 5:18 et seq., where we read (on p. 107):

> As one man's trespass led to condemnation for all men, so one man's act of righteousness leads to acquittal and life for all men. For as by one man's disobedience many were made sinners, so by one man's obedience many were made righteous.

On which passage he comments (in note 1 ibid.):

> The reference in our text to the basic Christian truth that Christ died for the sins of all men, might be used by some in the present context to exonerate the authorities in Jerusalem from the responsibility which we have maintained is attributable to them. It is well known that a somewhat similar passage in the catechism of the Council of Trent, composed by order of the Holy See for the use of parish priests, has in fact been interpreted in this sense at times (cf. *Catechismus Romanus ex Decreto Sacros. Conc. Trid. iussu S. Pii V, Pont. Max.*, Rome, 1726, pars. 1. cap. V. spec. murn 11.13; French transl., Paris, 1936).
>
> What can be said of such an interpretation? (a) The catechism states that the guilt of Christians who commit grave sins is in a *certain sense* greater than that of the Jewish leaders, because the former have a far clearer knowledge of Jesus than the Jews. But the very use of the word "greater" does not exclude but confirms the existence of guilt on the part of the Jews which is described as "lesser."
>
> As far as the text of the tridentine catechism is concerned, two points are noteworthy:
>
> (b) Later on in the same context the guilt of the Jews is explicitly affirmed.
>
> With regard to the present Council document, it must be said:
>
> (a) Here we are no longer in the context of the guilt of the Jewish people for the condemnation and death of Jesus.
>
> (b) Our text follows immediately upon a repudiation of anti-semitism. There is therefore good reason to suppose that it too is in opposition to the manifestations of anti-semitism from the facts of the passion, that the Church does not look upon the passion in this way, but takes a very different view. This opposing view is then explained. It is not legitimate, therefore, to draw conclusions from our text as to the existence or otherwise of the guilt of the leaders at Jerusalem.

And on pp. 86–87, notes 1 and 2, he further confronts this issue as follows:

As is known, the text of the Declaration which was approved at its first reading in November 1964 differs from the final text in that it speaks more indirectly of the part of the Sanhedrin in the passion. This explains why the present version surprised and somewhat disturbed some of the Jewish people and also those who espoused the cause of Israel within the Council. Which of the two texts is better in itself and better suited to its purpose is naturally a question open to discussion and, in fact, was very widely discussed at the sittings of the competent Commission. The final choice and promulgation of the present text obliges Catholics to accept it as true, but not necessarily as the best of all possible texts. Personally I regard it as better than the previous text. It is true that the latter shows more consideration for the sensibilities of the Jewish people by only speaking indirectly of the part played by the Sanhedrin. It did not, however, convey sufficiently clearly to the minds of Christians what was to be affirmed and what was to be denied. In this sense also it was less effective in serving the Jewish cause. Moreover, in view of the atmosphere created by the demythologizing school of exegesis, and the consequent tendency to take a relativistic view of historical facts, the previous text could all too easily foster in certain minds the delusion that, to avoid any appearance of anti-semitism, the Church had occasionally at least soft-pedalled these distressing historical facts in her preaching. The subsequent disillusionment would have been all the greater and more painful. It must never be forgotten that anti-semitism does not consist in the recognition of undeniable historical facts but in misinterpreting the facts and in drawing erroneous conclusions from them. The present text begins by establishing the facts as they are reported in the New Testament and constantly read by Christians. By clearly proclaiming the facts and at the same time denouncing erroneous interpretations of them from which the collective culpability of the whole Jewish people is deduced, the Council was performing once and for all an indispensable work of clarification and was doing it in the only way psychologically effective for Christians.

Furthermore, consideration of the question of the responsibility of the Jewish people for the events of Christ's passion may well lead us to a more abstract consideration of the general role played in human affairs by the solidarity which exists between the governmental and party leaders of a nation and its rank and file. Everyone finds it quite natural, for example, to benefit from the advantages obtained through leaders, to boast of the glories of illustrious men and distinguished ancestors. Likewise, one often has to suffer through their fault. All this is considered natural up to a certain point and no one would be so bold as absolutely to exclude it. In the same way one is ashamed of the misdeeds committed by one's fellow citizens or nationals. It is to be noted, however, that this is only valid within certain limits of intensity and duration. Often enough, with the passing of generations and a little luck, the consequences of blunders and reprehensible behaviour are cancelled out, otherwise coexistence between groups and nations would become impossible. In addition, common sense reminds us that, in all fairness, other nations could make legitimate complaints about our own nation. Above all, however, justice demands respect and esteem for the dignity of the human person, and in particular the right of every man in the last analysis to be judged according to his *own* free decisions and his own actions. In the general sense outlined above, it would be natural to think that some discredit would fall upon the Jewish people as a whole in consequence of the action of the Sanhedrin which was the recognized legitimate, religious authority of the Jews. It is not this point of view which is suggested by the New Testament. As we have seen above, to cite only one example, the apostles blamed only the Sanhedrin and the inhabitants of Jerusalem for the crucifixion of Jesus; they never extended the blame to the Jews in other cities, unless they too showed the same spirit of violence and opposition to God and to his works (cf. I Thessalonians 2:14ff).

And on p. 83 note 1 we stress the rebuttle of the accusation of collective responsibility, as follows:

In support of the theory of the Jewish people's collective responsibility for the events of the passion, a recent author takes his stand on *the general principle* of "collective responsibility" for good or for evil and explains it as follows: "The entire people is held responsible, and therefore punished, for the crimes committed by their leaders in an official capacity, even when a large proportion of the people has had no part in them." He then maintains that this principle is also valid in the New Testament (in spite of the fact that its validity is denied as far back as the time of the exile in Ezekiel 18), and he attempts to prove this from our Lord's words addressed to the entire cities of Chorazain, Bethsaida and Capernaum (cf. Matthew 11:21–24); he also makes use of the texts we have already quoted in which Jesus imputes the murder of the prophets in former times to the Scribes and Pharisees and in which the destruction of Jerusalem is presented as punishment for these murders.

We have already given a general explanation of these texts and we would like here to add an explanation of the principle involved. In actual fact it is necessary to distinguish between collective social solidarity on one hand, and collective responsibility in the strict sense on the other. Social and collective *solidarity* in good or in evil is manifested when a body of people collectively experience the good or the evil consequences of the acts of their own leaders (e.g., the consequences of the census of David described in 2 Kings 24). Collective *responsibility*, on the other hand, for good or for evil, exists when a whole people acquires merit or demerit as the result of the actions of its leaders and shares in the consequent reward or punishment. Hence in order to prove that the principle of collective responsibility in the strict sense is valid in the New Testament it is not sufficient to adduce instances in which the whole people has suffered the consequences of the actions of their leaders; it must be also shown that these consequences constitute a punishment for the guilt collectively contracted as a result of those acts. It must be said at once that the author does not provide any such proof.

We have treated of this subject rather extensively because of its crucial centrality to the *Declaration*. Cardinal Bea's arguments reveal both his honest transparency as well as his theological courage.

Other aspects of the problem of deicide are discussed in a very interesting note in David Berger's ed. of *Sefer Nitzahon Yashan*, a late 13th or early 14th century Jewish polemic against Christianity. (See his *The Jewish-Christian Debate in the High Middle Ages*, Philadelphia, 1979.) On p. 293 (note to p. 136 lines 10–11) he wrote as follows:

> **Those who killed him fulfilled his will.** The problem of Jewish culpability for the crucifixion was frequently discussed. Its most common context, however, was the dilemma of foreknowledge and free will; indeed, in light of the belief that the purpose of the incarnation was the passion, it was almost a problem of predestination versus free will. In this formulation, of course, it would be insoluble by definition, and the point of various Christian statements on the subject was to deny the validity of this formulation. The Jews were not predestined to kill Jesus; God simply knew that they would do so of their own accord. See Eucher of Lyon, [*Instructions, PL* 50, 773–882, *CSEL* 31. 65–161], cited in B. Blumenkranz, *Les Auteurs Chrétiens Latin du Moyen Age Sur les Juifs et la Judaism*, Paris, 1963, p. 23, and cf. Leo the Great, PL 54.369: "Impios furentium manus non immisit in se dominus, sed admisit, nec praesciendo quod faciendum esset coegit ut fieret . . ."
>
> However, the question in *Nitzahon Yashan* (*Vetus*), which is also found in *Nestor HaKomer*, [ed. A. Berliner, Altona 1874–1875.], p. 2, is somewhat different. The author argues that the deed itself was not blame-worthy but meritorious, and the elimination of predestination would therefore be of no use to a Christian polemicist. Augustine's response to this problem was that the intention of the Jews was evil even though God made the effect good (see *Judenpredigt*, p. 190; cf. Genesis 50:20 and Isaiah 10:5–7); in fact, it was probably this sort of response which impelled one Jewish polemicist to remark, "We can even say that the intention of the Jews was good when they killed him, inasmuch as they had heard him say that the salvation of the world depends upon his death" (the additions to *Sefer HaBerit, Mil. Hovah*, by Joseph Kimhi, p. 36b = Talmage's ed. Jerusalem, 1974, p. 64). The problem of Jewish culpability even led to the view that the cause of the punishment of the Jews

was their cruel persecution of the apostles after the crucifixion (Gregory I in PL 75.862, cited in Blumenkranz ibid. p. 86, and Bede [pseudo.] in PL 93.460, cited in Blumenkranz, p. 138). Cf. also Lanfranc's enthusiastic description of the marvelous effects of the sin of the Jews (PL 150.141). In general, see Blumenkranz, *Juifs et Chrétiens dans le Monde Occidental*, Paris, 1960, pp. 269–72. See also below, p. 216, [sect. 226] for the argument that the crucifixion ought to be commemorated by a joyous festival in light of Christian belief.

On the history of Judaeo-Christian disputation, see James Parkes, *The Conflict of the Church and the Synagogue*, London, 1934; J.D.l Eisenstein, *Otzar Vikuhim*, New York, 1922; Daniel Lasker, *Jewish Philosophical Polemic against Christianity in the Middle Ages*, New York, 1977; Hyam Maccoby, *Judaism on Trial: Jewish-Christian Disputation in the Middle Ages*, East Brunswick N.J., 1982; Oliver S. Rankin, *Jewish Religious Polemic*, Edinburg, 1956; Frank E. Talmage ed., *Disputation and Dialogue: Readings in Jewish-Christian Encounter*, New York, 1975; Jeremy Cohen, *The Friars and the Jews*, Ithaca, NY, 1982; Two fine summarizing articles are in : *The Jewish Encyclopaedia*, London & New York, 1902 vol. 4, pp. 615–618, by Kaufmann Kohler, and *Encyclopaedic Judaica*, Jerusalem, 1970, vol. 6, 79–103, by Haim Hillel Ben-Sasson.

This, of course is only a partial bibliography, and there is much literature on individual disputations.

The remarkable thing is that what in the past were *Judae-Christian disputations*, have now become *intra-filial dialogues*.

3. The history of the Legend of "The Wandering Jew" has been discussed in a number of major monographs. We might mention:

> *The Wandering Jew*, by Moncure Daniel Conway, London, 1881.
> *The Legend of the Wandering Jew*, by Georg K. Anderson, Providence, 1965.
> *The Wandering Jew: Essays in the Interpretation of a Christian Legend*, by Hason-Rokem and Alan Dundes, Bloomington, 1986, with a number of illustrations, pp. 166–168.
> Richard I. Cohen, "The 'Wandering Jew,' from Mediaeval Legend to Modern Metaphor," apud *The Art of Being Jewish in Modern Times*, edd. Barbara Kirshenblatt and Jonathan Karp, Philadelphia, 2008, pp. 147–175.

This motif is also the subject of numerous visual portrayals, perhaps the most famous of which are those of Gustave Doré, a series of twelve designs, with explanations, published by Gabbie in 1873. A much publicized image was published in France in 1852, and shown in a Nazi exhibition both in Germany and Austria throughout the years 1937–1938. Yet another well-known illustration is that of Samuel Hirszenberg, *Le Juif Errant,* 1899.

We should also call attention to Sabine Baring-Gould's essay, in his *Curious Myths of the Middle Ages*, London, 1884, pp. 1–31, and also his brief note in his *Legends of the Patriarchs and Prophets*, New York, 1872, p. 296, on El Khoudr.

The legend seems to be based on the Gospel statement, "Verily I say unto you, there be some standing here, which shall not taste death till they see the Son of Man coming into His kingdom" (Matthew 16:28; Mark 9:1; Luke 9:27). The legend itself first appeared around the 13th century, in the chronicles of the Abbey of St. Albans, which was copied and continued by Mathew Paris, recording a certain event in 1228. However, it has perhaps its antecedents in a passage in Prudentius' (348–413) *Apotheosis* (c. 400), which states that:

> From place to place the homeless Jew wanders in an ever-shifting exile, since the time when he was torn from the abode of his fathers, and has been suffering the penalty for murder, and having stained his hands with the blood of Christ whom he denied, paying the price of sin.

The theme reminds us of the curse of Cain in Genesis 4:11, as scholars have pointed out. But I wish to point to yet another expression of this basic theme, brought in S. Baring-Gould, *Legends of the Patriarchs and Prophets*, New York, 1872, p. 289:

> Another version of the story is as follows. Samiri (Micah), who had fashioned the golden calf, was of the tribe of Levi. When Moses came down from the Mount, he would have beaten Aaron, but his brother said, "It is not I, it is Samiri who made the calf." Then Moses would have slain Samiri, but God forbade him, and ordered him instead to place him under ban.
>
> From that time till now, the man wanders, like a wild beast, from one end of the earth to the other; every man avoids him, and cleanses the earth of which his feet have rested; and when he comes near any man, he cries out, "Touch me not!"

Cf. *Quran, Surah Ta-Ha* (20), 85: See Cyril Glassé, *The Concise Encyclopaedia of Islam*, 3rd edition, London, 2008, p. 461b, s.v. as-Samire. This parallel was already noted by Haim Schwartzbaum, in his *Biblical and Extra-Biblical Legends in Islamic Folk-Literature*, Waldorf-Hessen, 1982, pp. 14–18, 129 notes 42–43, 167–168 note 215; and for rich bibliographic information of the Wandering Jew, see idem *Studies in Jewish and World Literature*, Berlin, 1968, pp. 399–401, 482.

And for yet another example of how these myths develop, we may relate what was said to have happened in Brussels in 1370, where local Jews were accused of stealing and desecrating the Blessed Sacrament from St. Catherine's church. A Jew was said to have stolen them, taken them to the synagogue where the congregants engaged in stabbing them and mutilating them; and miraculously the wafers bled. In 1402 Petrus de Alliaco investigated the desecration, and in 1453 the building that housed the synagogue where the desecration was said to have taken place was appropriated for a chapel dedicated to the Blessed Sacrament. Shortly afterwards a second church constituted yet another chapel dedicated to the "Miraculous Sacrament." The tale was subsequently embellished, and even represented in a stained glass window in the church of St. Gudule, and also in tapes in the Cathedral of St. Michael and St. Gudule.

In 1968, in the wake of the Second Vatican Council, a bronze tablet was erected in the chapel of the Blessed Sacrament that sought to make historical amends. It reads as follows:

> In 1370 the Jewish community of Brussels was accused of the profanation of the Holy Sacrament and punished for this act. On Good Friday 1370 the Jews were supposed to have used daggers to stab the communion wafers stolen from the chapel. These wafers were supposed to have bled.
>
> In 1968, in the spirit of the Second Vatican Council, the authorities of the archdiocese of Mechelen – Brussels, in the light of historical research on this subject, drew attention to the tendentious character of these accusations and to the legendary nature of the miracle.

We have stated above that the legendary myth of the "wandering Jew"" was engendered in order to preserve the smoldering hatred of the Jews.

A thematically similar phenomenon may be found in what we read in Socrates, *Historia Ecclesiastica* 5:16, and Cassiodorus, Historia tripartite 9:27 (apud Th. Hopfner, *Fontes historiae* religionis aegyptiacae, Bonnae, 1922–1925, pp. 656, 721 et seq.), that in 391 C.E., in Alexandria of Egypt, there were anti-pagan riots. The Christians, led by Bishop Theophilus, drove away the pagan priests and destroyed pagan temples and idols, with one exception: Theophilus commanded them to preserve a statue of an ape and to set it up in a public place, as a monument to heathen depravity. Something visual-physical had to be preserved to ensure the continuity of the hatred. (See H. W. Janson, *Apes and Ape Lore in the Middle Ages and the Renaissance*, London, 1952, pp. 17, 24 note 29, where he writes "the eloquent defence of idols in the Hermetic Books" [of Hermes Trismegistus], referring to Louis Ménard, *Hermès Trismégiste*, Paris, 1867, pp. 146 et seq.)

4. The story of Simon of Trent, a small child who was murdered in 1475, and Jews were accused of slaughtering him for his blood to be used in the baking of *matzot* for the Passover, is one of the three most famous mediaeval blood libels, along with that of William of Norwich and Little St. Hugh of Lincoln, (the latter mentioned in Geoffrey Chauser's *The Prioress Tale* 182, written around 1386. (See John M. McCulloh, "Jewish Ritual Murder: William of Norwitch, Thomas of Momonth and the Early Dissemination of the Myth." *Speculum* 72:3, 1997, pp. 698–740.) On Little St. Hugh of Lincoln, see the Studies of Joseph Jacobs and Brian Babbington, in *The Blood Libel Legend: A Casebook in Antisemitic Folklore*, ed. Alan Dundes, Madison,

Wisconsin, London, 1991, pp. 41–90; Gavin I. Langmuir, *Towards a Definition of Antisemitism*, Berkeley, Los Angeles, London, 1996, pp. 237–262. Simon was declared a martyr and canonized in 1588, but in 1758 Cardinal Ganganelli, later Pope Clement XIV, (1769–1774) prepared a report clearing the Jews of Trent of the murder of Simon. This report (headed "Non Solis accusatoribus credentum") was published with an introduction and translation from the Italian by Cecil Roth, in his *The Ritual Murder Libel and the Jew: The Report by Cardinal Lorenzo Ganganelli (Pope Clement XIV)*, London [1934]. (The book was dedicated to the memory of Ganganelli on the 160th anniversary of his death in 1774.) See R. Po-chia Hsia, *Trent 1475: Stories of a Ritual Murder*, New Haven, 1992; idem, *The Myth of Ritual Murder: Jews and Magic in Reformation Germany*, New Haven, 1988; idem, *Trent, 1475*, New Haven Conn., 1992; Walter Laqueur, *The Changing Face of Antisemitism: From Ancient Times to the Present Day*, Oxford, 2006.

More recently, Daniel Baraz has analyzed the account of the event by the doctor who, allegedly, examined Simon's body soon after his martyrdom. He was Giovanni Mattia Tiberino, whose description was published in Frumenzio Ghelta. *Fra Bernadino Tomitano de Feltre e gli ebrei di Trento nel 1475*, Trent, 1986, pp. 40–45. Baraz, in his *Mediaeval Cruelty: Changing Perceptions, Late Antiquity to the Early Modern Period*, Cornell University Press, Ithaca and London, 2003, pp. 146–148, writes as follows:

> Tiberino's account was one of the influential factors in launching the fury against the Jews, as his account benefited from the invention of the printing press and achieved wide circulation. Tiberino's account, in the form of a letter to the people of his native city Brescia, is written in a florid style. At the outset, Tiberino claims that he is writing of "a matter of the utmost importance, which no age from the passion of the Lord until these times has heard." He urges his audience to "hear . . . of the unheard of crime," and proceeds to his subject. The Jews, writes Tiberino, are like vipers nurtured at the breasts of the Christians. And from implicit connotations of cruelty evoked by the animal imagery, Tiberino passes at once, in the same sentence, to explicit accusations: The Jews are cruel (*crudels iudei*) not only because they are usurers but because "they feed of the live blood of our sons," whom they atrociously torture in their synagogues and kill as they killed Christ. The danger posed by the Jews is driven home by the use of the first person ("our sons") [*filiorum nostrorum*].
>
> In this short prologue, before any fact of the case has been disclosed, Tiberino has established the cruelty of the Jews, their animal qualities, and their cannibalistic characteristics. Concerning this last issue, it is to be noted, Tiberino exceeds even the alleged facts of the specific case, because he presents the Jews as feeding on blood as a dietary habit (which was attributed in the past to the Mongols), not just making ritual use of it. In the following narrative,

Tiberino switches between these three strands of imagery – human cruelty, animal-like characteristics, and cannibalism. The tone of narration varies as well, from affective descriptions of the suffering of Simon to a purportedly factual tone in the references to the Jews.

Tiberino develops the cannibalistic imagery, vividly describing the Jews of Trent sitting at their Passover dinner, one of them declaring, "We have an abundance of meats and fish, only one thing is missing." According to Tiberino, all the Jews present understood the "missing thing" as referring to a Christian child, whom "they kill atrociously in contempt of our Lord Jesus Christ." Thus Tiberino again insinuates that dead Christians are a dietary preference for the Jews, and only then does he mention the ritual use of blood for the Passover bread. Thus in fact, Tiberino establishes three motives for the killing of Christian children: dietary cannibalism, ritual cannibalism, and hatred of Christians. When Simon arrives, Tiberino describes the Jews as wild animals howling in anticipation of Christian blood. The narrative switches to the affective mode whenever Tiberino moves from the Jews to Simon. Describing Simon's abduction, for instance, Tiberino writes: "The child, looking back, started, with tears, to raise childish cries, and to invoke the sweet name of mother."

These elements combine in the culminating scene of Simon's martyrdom. The diabolical character of the Jews is insinuated implicitly in the statement that the deed was done at a time when both men and animals slept. The torture is depicted vividly, a task probably facilitated by Tiberino's profession. Twice during this scene he refers explicitly to the cruelty of the Jews. Tiberino relates affectively how the Jews continue to torture the already half-dead child (*semimortuum infantem*). Describing the moment of death, Tiberino gathers up all his literary talents, showing Simon dying as he inclines his bloody head like a poppy falling under heavy rain. Tiberino later sums up by referring sentimentally to Simon as "the glorious Simon, virgin, martyr and innocent, hardly weaned, and whose tongue did not yet unravel human speech."

As mentioned earlier, the successful portrayal of the cruelty of the Jews was aided by the technological innovation of the printing press. It assured wide circulation of Tiberino's text and, perhaps more significantly for the actual impact of the story, a pictorial representation of Simon's martyrdom appeared as an engraving in the Chronicle of Hartmann Schedel, published in 1493. The picture shows Simon tortured by a group of Jews while he stands on a table. One Jew inflicts a cut on his penis, probably intended to represent a circumcision, while another collects the blood in a bowl. All of the Jews in the image are named, thus increasing the verisimilitude of the illustration.

The alleged cruelty of the Jews supplied an implicit justification for excessive judicial violence against them, which later caused Pope Sixtus IV to order

Simon of Trent. Engraving made in 1475–1485, probably in Florence. Illustration after Hind 1938, II, pl. 74.

a thorough review of the investigation itself. This combination was probably a major factor in the unprecedented canonization of Simon in 1588.

Schedel's illustration is to be found in his *Liber Cronicarum Cum figures et ymaginibus ab initio mundi*, Nuremberg, 1493, fol. 254 v.

Blood-Libel accusations continued in the twentieth century. On the day "The Declaration on the Relationship of the Church to Non-Christian Religions" (Oct. 28, 1965), – part of *Nostra Aetate* – was promulgated, the Congregation of Rites issued a decree banning further veneration of Simon of Trent, investigation having shown that Simon was probably killed by non-Jews (*The Documents of Vatican II*, edd. Walter M. Abbott S.J. and Very Rev. Msgr. Joseph Gallagher, The America Press, 1966, p. 665 note 20).

The material of the investigation is to be found in the work of W.P. Eckert, "Il beato Simonino negli 'ATTI' del processo di Trento contra gli Ebrei," in *Studi di Scienze Storiche* 44, 1915, pp. 193–221, and his articles in W.P. Eckert and E.L. Ehrlich, *Judenhass-Schuld der Christen*, Essen, 1964.

5. The story of William of Norwitch is described in detail by Daniel Baraz, in his *Mediaeval Cruelty: Changing Perceptions, Late Antiquity to the Early Modern Period*, Ithaca and London, 2003, pp. 79–80. Because of its importance I quote it at length:

> The *vita* tells that William, a twelve-year-old boy living in the vicinity of Norwich, was taken to the city by a mysterious stranger who convinced his mother that he was going to work in the archdeacon's kitchen. On the next day, the stranger visited William's aunt together with the boy. The aunt suspected the stranger and sent her daughter to follow them. She saw them entering the house of a Jew. Then, according to Thomas's narrative, William spent the next day with the Jews. The following day, at the table, they seized him, tortured him, and finally murdered him. The body was thrown in Thorpe wood and was discovered by the forester, who immediately suspected the Jews of the deed.
>
> The account of William's torture and martyrdom is unsettling in the amount of detail it supplies, especially concerning the torture instrument used by the Jews (*teseillun* [teazle]). This instrument was forcibly introduced into William's mouth and was fastened to both jaws and then to the back of the neck. Another rope was fastened with knots applying pressure to the forehead and temples, and then it was tied around the back of the head and the neck. This intricate torture instrument presumably applied increasing pressure to the most sensitive parts of the head. The mention of the torture instrument is important in establishing systematic cruelty as a basic trait of the Jews. It emphasizes that this was not an outburst of violence and hatred against Christians but an established procedure that the Jews were well equipped to implement. Thomas

does not neglect, however, the other aspect of cruelty – that is, that of excess which is motivated by pleasure – and it is in this context that Thomas refers explicitly and elaborately to the cruelty of the Jews:

But not even yet could the *cruelty* [*crudelitas*] of the torturers by satisfied without adding even more severe pains. . . . And *cruel* [*crudeles*] were they and so eager to inflict pain that it was difficult to say whether they were more *cruel* [*cruaeliores*] or more prompt in their tortures. For their skill in torturing kept up the strength of their *cruelty* [*crudelitati*] and ministered arms thereto. . . . But while in doing these things they were adding pang to pang and wound to wound, and yet were not able to quench the madness of their *cruelty* [*crudelitatis*], and satisfy their inborn hatred of the Christian name. [*Vita et passio Sancti Willelmi Martyris Norwicensis* 1.5, in *The Life and Miracles of St. William of Norwich*, ed. and trans. Augustus Jessopp and Montague R. James (Cambridge, 1896), 20–22 (translation modified)].

The density of references to cruelty is in itself a novel feature not encountered to this extent in martyrdom accounts of the early Middle Ages. References to the cruelty of the Jews recur on the occasion of the finding of the body. Henry of Sprowston, the forester, notices the wooden torture instrument in the boy's mouth, and it is the *unusual* character of the torments (*inusitatis penis*) suffered by the boy that leads him to conclude it is the work of a Jew. He then notifies a priest that he has found the body of a boy who was "most cruelly treated" ["Crudelissimis attrectatus modis" (ibid. 1.6, 34–35)].

The cruelty of the Jews is an issue in the case of other child martyrs as well. Hugh of Lincoln, who died in 1255, achieved even greater fame than William and is commemorated in a number of chronicles and popular songs.

[For an analysis of this case, see Langmuir, *Towards a Definition of Antisemitism*, California, 1990, 237–62.]

His death is presented, much more so than that of William, as a reenactment of the crucifixion of Christ. In the most famous account of his martyrdom, from Matthew Paris's *Chronica majora*, the Jews put up a perverted "mystery play," with a Jew assuming the role of Pilate. [This version, via the mediation of John Capgrave, was the one incorporated later into the *Acta Sanctorum*.] Most of the sources refer explicitly to the cruelty of the Jews in this episode. The most outspoken and affective are the *Burton Annals*, which are also the earliest. They refer to the "cruelty [of the Jews], which should be detested and abhorred."

[*Annales monastici*, ed. Henry R. Luard (RS 36) (London, 1864), 1:340–44.] On this source, see Langmuir, *Towards a Definition of Antisemitism*, 239. See also the *Waverly annals* in *Annales monastici*, ed. Henry R. Luard (RS 36) (London, 1865), 2:346–48. Matthew Paris does not refer explicitly to the cruelty of the Jews but mentions the testimony of a Jew to the effect that they crucified

Hugh "without pity" ("immisericorditer crucifixerunt," *Chronica majora*, ed. Henry R. Luard [RS 57] [London, 1880], 5:518)].

Nevertheless, in none of these sources is the cruelty of the Jews as important an issue as it is in the *vita* of William of Norwich.

6. Add to what we have noted above, the charge of "Host-desecration" which triggered off pogroms in mediaeval Europe; See Joshua Trachtenberg: *The Devil and the Jews: The Mediaeval Conception of the Jew and its Relation to Modern Antisemitism*, New Haven & London, 1943, pp. 109 et seq.; Cecil Roth, "Desecration of the Host," *Encyclopaedia Judaica*, Jerusalem, 1971, vol. 8, 1040–1043; Miri Rubin, "Desecration of the Host: The Birth of an Accusation," apud *Christianity and Judaism*, ed. Diana Wood, Oxford, 1992, pp. 165–185.

On "ritual murder," or "the blood libel," see H.L. Strack, *The Jew and Human Sacrifice: Blood and Ritual Murder*, New York, 1909, especially pp. 247 et seq., and 274–286; Alan Dundes, *The Blood Libel Legend: A Casebook in Anti-Semitic Folklore*, University of Wisconsin Press, 1991; Shlomo Simonsohn, *The Apostolic See and the Jews: History*, Toronto, Ontario, 1991, pp. 82–85, and ibid. p. 58–60, on the Desecration of the Host; Israel Y. Yuval, "Vengeance and Damnation, Blood and Defamation: From Jewish Martyrdom to Blood Libel Accusations," *Zion* 58:1, 1992, pp. 32–90 (Hebrew).

See *Antisemitism: Myth and Hate from Antiquity to the Present*, edd. Marvin Perry and Frederick M. Schweitzer, New York, 2002, pp. 54–55.

7. Thus, for instance, "The Pig Libel: A Ritual Crime Legend from the Era of the Spanish Expulsion of the Jews (15th–16th centuries)," *Revue des études juives*, 175 (1–2), Jan–June, 2016, pp. 107–133, etc. See further Marvine Perry and Frederick M. Schweitzer, *Antisemitism: Myth and Hate from Antiquity to the Present,* New York, 2002, chapter 3, pp. 73–117, "The Diabolization of Jews: Demons, Conspirators, and Race Defilers."

8. See, e.g., James Parkes, *End of An Exile: Israel, The Jews and the Gentile World*, London, 1954; idem *Jews and Christians and the World of Tomorrow*, from 1969 (Already in 1929, in his book *The Jew and his Neighbour*, he created the foundations for a Christian reevaluation of Judaism.) And see the statement of David Brickner, (a prominent member of "Jews for Jesus"), from March 13, 2013):

> But the good news is that God has forever changed the consolation of the wandering Jew, I believe, by establishing the modern State of Israel. . . .

This, again, is too large and complex a subject to be treated in the context. In fact it is a serious threat to Catholic theology in general. The State of Israel was not mentioned in *Nostra Aetate*, nor in the *Guidelines and Suggestions for Implementing the Conciliar Document "Nostra Aetate,"* of 1974. It is first mentioned in *Notes on the Correct Way to Present Jews and Judaism in Preaching and Catechesis in the Roman Catholic Church,* from June 24, 1985.

The questions rightly raised are:

Why did it take the Holy See twenty years to mention the State of Israel, and why is *Notes* so cautious about religious interpretations of Israel?

These questions and others have been carefully examined by Anthony Kenny, in his *Catholics, Jews and the State of Israel*, New York, 1993. See his conclusion on pp. 114–119.

9. This was not really new. Already John Chrysostom (c. 345–407) wrote in his *Homilies*:

> How can Christians dare "have the slightest converse with Jews, "Most miserable of all men" [*Homily* 4:1], men who are ". . . lustful, rapacious, greedy, perfidious bandits." Are they not "inveterate murderers, destroyers, men possessed by the devil," whom "debauchery and drunkenness have given them the manners of the pig and the lusty goat. They know only one thing, to satisfy their gullets, get drunk, to kill and maim one another . . ." [1:4]. Indeed, "they have surpassed the ferocity of wild beasts, for they murder their offspring and immolate them to the devil" [1:6]. "They are impure and impious . . ." [1:4].
>
> Their Synagogue? Not only is it a theatre and a house of prostitution, but a caravan of brigands, a "repair of wild beasts" [6:5], a place of "shame and ridicule" [1:3], "the domicile of the devil [1:6], as is also the souls of the Jews" [1:4, 6]. Indeed, Jews worship the devil; their rites are "criminal and impure," their religion is "a disease" [3:1]. Their synagogue, again, is "an assembly of criminals . . . den of thieves . . . a cavern of devils, and an abyss of perdition" [1:2; 6:6].
>
> God hates the Jews and always hated the Jews [6:4; 1:7], and on Judgment Day He will say to Judaizers, "Depart from Me, for you have had intercourse with My murderers." It is the duty of Christians to hate the Jews; "He who can never love Christ enough will never have done fighting against those [Jews] who hate Him" [7:11]. "Flee then, their assemblies, flee their houses, and keep far from venerating the synagogue because of the books it contains in it" [1:5]. ". . . I hate the Synagogue precisely because it has the law and prophets . . ." [6:6]. ". . . I hate the Jews also because they outrage against the law . . ."

(I quote from Harry James Cargas' essay, "Revisionism and Theology: Two Sides of the Same Coin?" apud *Contemporary Christian Religious Responses to the Shoah,* ed. Steven L. Jacobs, [*Studies in the Shoah* VI], London, New York, London, 1993, p. 5.)

And a generation later Gelasius I (492–496) had seen the destruction of a synagogue or its conversion into a church as a victory over the Synagogue of Satan. And this was echoed in the highly inflammatory statements of Martin Luther (1483–1546) more than a millennium later, such as:

> First, their Synagogue or school is to be set on fire and what won't burn is to be heaped over with dirt and dumped on, so that no one can see a stone or chunk of it forever. . . . Second, their houses are to be torn down and destroyed in the same way. . . . Third, they are to have all their prayerbooks and Talmudics taken from them. . . . Fourth, their rabbis are to be forbidden publicly to praise God, to thank [God], to pray [to God], to teach [of God] among us and ours. . . . And furthermore, they shall be forbidden to utter the name of God in our hearing; no value shall be accorded the Jewish mouth [Maul] by us Christians, so that he may utter the name of God in our hearing, but whoever hears it from a Jew shall report him to the authorities. . . . Fifth, the Jews are to be deprived totally of walkways and streets. . . . Sixth, they are to be forbidden the lending of interest and all cash and hold of silver and gold are to be taken from them and put to one side for safe keeping. . . . Seventh, the young, strong Jews and Jewesses are to have flail, axe, and spade put into their hands.

(Cargus ibid. p. 10.)

Indeed, a special prayer was composed in honour of such an occasion, attributed to Galasius I and included in the *Sacramentary* named after him. It runs thus:

> Orationes et preces in dedicatione loci illius ubi prius fuit synagoga. Deus qui absque ulla temporis mutabilitate cuncta disponis, et ad meliorandium perducis quae eligis esse mutanda, respice super hanc basilicam in honore beate illius nomini tuo dicatam; ut vestutate Iudaica erroris expulse, huic loco sancti spiritus novitatem ecclesiae conferas veritatem etc. (See Nenry Austin Wilson, *Gelasian Sacramentary*, Oxford, 1894, pp. 141f.)

And, indeed, in 1182, French Jews were expelled and their synagogues converted into churches. (See Simonsohn, *History*, pp. 124–130.) And in that same *Sacramentary* we read the following prayer:

> We pray also for the unbelieving (*perfidies*) Jews that our God and Lord should remove the veil from their hearts and they should themselves recognize our Lord Jesus Christ.

(See S.W. Baron, *A Social and Religious History of the Jews*, 2nd edition, New York, 1952, pp. 169, 395 note 52. This is the *Pro Judaeis* in the Gelasian Sacramentary, *PL* 74, 1005, analyzed by Z. Caret, *REJ* 61, pp. 213–221, and J.M. Oesterreicher in *Theological Studies* 8, pp. 80–86. See further Jean Juster, *Les Juifs dans l'Empire*

Romain, Leur Condition Jurisdique Economique et Social, vol. 1, 1914 [republished New York, n.d.], pp. 81–82, 290–291.)

The *Gelasian Sacramentary*, also called *Decretum Gelasianum*, was probably composed in Paris c. 750, and is found in a number of early manuscripts, the earliest being Vatican Library Reg. lat. 316, and Paris National Library, ms. lat. 7193, fol. 41–56, from the 8th century. See further F.C. Burkitt, for his review of the *Decretum Gelasianum*, in the *Journal of Theological Studies* 14, 1913, pp. 460–471.

10. See Joshua Trachtenberg, *The Devil and the Jews*, Cleveland and New York, 1961. But cf. Berger ibid. p. 336, that some Jews thought of Christians as being consciously allied with the devil.

11. See Ruth Mellinkoff, *The Horns Moses in Mediaeval Art and Thought*, Berkeley, Los Angeles, London, 1970, p. 135, and fig. 125.

12. Ibid. pp. 135–136.

13. The concept of the "Horned Moses" – the subject of Mellinkoff's book – is the result of a mistranslation (?) of the verses in Exodus 34:29, 30, 35) where Moses, coming down from Mt. Sinai, is described as *karan or penav*, his face having become radiant. The Hebrew *Karan*, is a verbal form from the noun *keren*, which can be understood either as "a horn" or a "ray of light."

14. See also Mellinkoff's *Outcasts: Signs of Otherness in Northern European Art of the Late Middle Ages*, Berkeley, Los Angeles, Oxford, 1923, pp. 123–124, 128–129, 133–135, 141–144.

See also Bernard Glassman, *Anti-Semitic Stereotypes without Jews: Images of the Jews in England 1290–1700*, De Moit 1975; Eric Myles Zafran, *The Iconography of Antisemitism: A Study of the Representation of Jews in the visual Arts of Europe 1400–1600*, P.h.d. diss. New York University, 1973. Pamela Berger, "The Depiction of the Jews in Early Passion Iconography," apud *Pondering the Passion: What's at Stake for Christians and Jews*? ed. Philip A. Cunningham, Lanham, Boulder, New York, Toronto, Oxford.

15. See the invention of the Jewish monster, by Sara Lipton, *New York Review of Books*, Nov. 14, 2014; and idem, *Dark Mirror: The Mediaeval Origins of Anti-Jewish Iconography*, Macmillan, 2014; and cf. her *Images of Intolerance: The Representation of Jews in the Bible moralisée*, University of California Press, 1999.

Here we should take account of Gavin I. Langmuir's concluding remarks in his *Towards a Definition of Antisemitism*, Berkeley, Los Angeles, London, 1996, pp. 349–352:

Finally, in addition to the already socially significant xenophobia and the chimerical rumors, both kinds of chimerical accusations come to be used in literature, art, and other cultural media, where their function of symbolizing social and psychic menaces makes them peculiarly valuable. Thereby, they become deeply rooted in the culture, an almost unavoidable element in social indoctrination, and an influence on social policy. The essential inferiority produced by the self-fulfilling prophecy has acquired monstrous lineaments. The monster may in fact be a combination of the chinks in the social armor protecting the members of the ingroup and of the psychic cleavages within individual members, but for many in the ingroup those threatening fissures leading from cosmos to chaos will have been reassuringly located, localized, externalized, and concretized so that they may be attacked directly, immediately, and brutally. . . .

Yet if we continue to use that literally most misleading term, we, as social scientists, should free "anti-Semitism" from its racist, ethnocentric, or religious implications and use it only for what can be distinguished empirically as an unusual kind of human hostility directed at Jews. If we do so, we may then be able to distinguish more accurately between two very different kinds of threats to Jews.

On the one hand, there are situations in which Jews, like any other major group, are confronted with realistic hostility, or with that well-nigh universal xenophobic hostility which uses the real conduct of some members of an outgroup to symbolize a social menace. On the other hand, there may still be situations in which Jewish existence is much more seriously endangered because real Jews have been irrationally converted in the minds of many into a symbol, "the Jews," a symbol whose meaning does not depend on the empirical characteristics of Jews yet justifies their total elimination from the earth.

Further on the image of the Jew in mediaeval times, see John D. Martin, *Representations of Jews in Late Medieval and Early Modern N. German Literature*, Bern 2004; P. Schöner, *Sudenbilder in deutchen Einblattdruck der Renaissance: Ein Beitrag zur Imagalogia*, Baden Baden, 2002; O. Frank C. *Der Jude in der deutschen Dichtung des 15,16,17 Jahrhunderts*, Leipzig, 1905, etc.

16. As a random but characteristic example of how the early Christian culumnies were adopted and used by the Nazis, see Hym Maccoby, *Judas Iscariot and the Myth of Jewish Evil*, London, 1992. On pp. 82–83 he quotes a passage from the fragmentary apocryphal *Exposition of the Lord's Sayings* by Papias (died c. 140 C.E.) who was the Bishop of Hierepolis in Phrygia (Avia Minor), which reads as follows:

> As a great example of impiety, Judas walked about in this world. He was so swollen in his body, that where a wagon could go through easily, he could not

go through; nay, he could not even insert the mass of his head. His eyelids were so swollen, it is said, that he could not see the light at all, nor could his eyes by seen even with an optical instrument; so deep did they lie from the surface.

His genitals were repellent and huge beyond all shamelessness. From his whole body flowed blood mixed with worms, which exuded particularly during his natural needs.

After many trials and sufferings, they say, he died in his own place, which, because of the stench, has remained deserted and uninhabitable to the present day. Until today, no one can pass by that place without holding his nose. So great was the exudation from his body that spread over the ground.

(The first two sentences are found in Oecumenius. The rest in Theophylact, who begins by quoting the sentences from Oecumenius and completes the remarks of Papias from some other sources. For a discussion of the text see J. Kürzinger, *Papia von Hieropolis und die Evangelium des Neuen Testaments*, Regensburg 1983, pp. 104 et seq.; U.H.J. Körtner, *Papius von Hieropolis: Ein Beitrag zur Geschichte des frühen Christentums*, Göttingen, 1983, pp. 59–61; H.-J. Klauk, *Judas – Ein Jünger des Herrn*, Freiburg, Basel, Wien, 1987, pp. 110–111. Maccoby ibid. p. 180 note 3.)
And on p. 84 he writes:

The inclusion of genital symptoms is especially interesting here. This may simply be a transfer from the death of Herod I, whose "privy member was putrefied and produced worms." But Papias also introduces a monstrous swelling of Judas's member, which makes a grotesque picture of pathological lasciviousness. Judas in his final illness thus becomes a kind of gross priapic figure. One cannot help seeing here a forerunner of the priapic Jew, who in medieval and Nazi propaganda, threatened the pure virgins of Christendom or the Aryan race with his enormous and repulsive appetites. Equally prophetic is the ghastly stench affecting Judas both in his life and death, which may be seen as a forerunner of the *foetor Judaicus* (Jewish stench). It was believed by many generations of medieval Christians that this adhered to Jews, who only become free of it if they became converted to Christianity. The fantasies that clustered round the figure of Judas were always liable to be transferred to the Jews as a whole.

On the "stinking Jews" and "Jewish stench," only to be removed by baptism, see ibid. pp. 112–113.

Descriptions such as that above made it easy for the Nazis to invest the Jews with images of contamination, polluted blood, and making them a sort of transmitting bacillus, as has been convincingly shown by Janes M. Glass, in his *"Life Unworthy of Life:" Racial Phobia and Mass Murder in Hitler's Germany*, New York, 1997.

17. Edward H. Flannery, in his revised and updated version of his *The Anguish of the Jews: Twenty-Three Centuries of Antisemitism*, New York, 1985 (the first edition was in 1965), writes on p. 293:

> Poliakov, interestingly, has extended this interpretation to include Nazi antisemites, several of the most vicious of whom – Himmler, Goebbels, Hoess, and others – he finds, were products of families of a "rigid Catholic piety" (Poliakov, Brériair, p. 350).

Flannery modifies this theory in his footnote on p. 350, no.15 as follows:

> The theory of a rigorist origin of anti-Semitism seems to break down in face of the near universality of anti-Semitism among Christians. Most Christians are not rigorists. An adjustment and reformulation of the theory is necessary: To the extent that a Christian finds his/her Christianity a burden, he/she will tend to be anti-Semitic. Christianity, obviously, is not a yoke found easy, a burden found light, by many Christians.

Flannery's second edition reflects a serious change in his assessment of the degree to which the Catholic Church was a very significant component in the development of anti-Semitism. In the first edition (p. 275) his position is "nuanced" (as I indicated earlier), where he writes that:

> To posit the causality of anti-Semitism either in Christian or in gentile reaction partaken of the scapegoat theory of anti-Semitism. Are Jews, therefore, to be absolved of all responsibility or complicity in their fate?

This passage is omitted in the revised edition; there he writes, inter alia, (on p. 290):

> Modern racist anti-Semitism, historically, is doubly rooted. The longer *but thinner* root [my emphasis, D.S.], Christian anti-Judaism and anti-Semitism, supplied a necessary historical preparation. Its proper development began as the process of secularization emerged with the breakdown of the mediaeval theocentric synthesis.

Here is not the place to persue this critical discussion.

18. See Leon Poliakov, "The Vatican and the 'Jewish Question:' The Record of the Hitler Period – and After," *Commentary*, Nov. 1950. Pius XII's role in the holocaust has been examined in great detail in Daniel Jonah Goldhagen's book *A Moral Reckoning: The Role of the Catholic Church in the Holocaust and its unfulfilled Duty of Repair*, London, 2002, index p. 358, s.v. Pius XII. That the Church, and the Pope, knew what was happening in the extermination camps is known from many sources, among them from a document of May 5, 1943, in which an official of the Vatican Secretariat summarized the Church's extensive knowledge about the genocide in Poland.

> In Poland, there were, before the war, about 4,500,000 Jews; it is calculated now that there remain (including all those who came there from other countries occupied by the Germans) only 100,000.
>
> In Warsaw a ghetto containing about 650,000 was created: now there are only 20–25,000 Jews there.
>
> Naturally many Jews have gotten away; but there is no doubt that the majority has been killed. After months and months of transport of thousands and thousands of people, they have made nothing more known of themselves: something that can only be explained by their deaths. . . .
>
> Special death camps at Lublin (Treblinka) and near Brest Litovsk. It is said that several hundred at a time are jammed into large rooms, where they die by gassing. (Goldhagen, p. 151, referring, on p. 320 note 74, to SW. Zuccotti, *Under His Very Windows: The Vatican and the Holocaust*, New Haven, 2000, pp. 109–110.) Goldhagen further notes that the report has some mistakes in the details; Madjanek was actually in Lublin and Treblinka near Warsaw.

Goldhagen (ibid.) continues:

> The knowledge that the Germans and their helpers were slaughtering Jews by the millions – making it easily foreseeable that they would also want to murder the Jews of Italy – did not deter the Pope and his Church from conveying their approval of Italy's criminal anti-Jewish laws (described ibid. pp. 145–151). For Pius XII and his Church, expressing their own anti-Semitism and conveying their solidarity with many of the murderers' nonlethal policies was closer to their hearts than was speaking for the lives of the victims.

(See David I. Kerzer, *The Pope and Mussolini: The Secret History of Pius XI and the Rise of Fascism in Europe*, New York, 2014.)

It may be difficult for us nowadays to comprehend how such an untenable position be held by the head of the Catholic Church. Goldhagen has an interesting suggestion to cast light upon this perplexing problem. He writes as follows (p. 148):

> There was a symbiosis between the Nazis' anti-Semitism and the Church's conception and teachings about Jews. The significant differences between the racial foundation of the first and the religious foundation of the second notwithstanding, they shared a common foundational feature that marked them as being of the most dangerous kind of antisemitisms, distinguishing them from all lesser varieties of this prejudice. Unlike most forms of anti-semitism, and most forms of prejudice, each conceived of Jews in terms of the fundamental moral order of the world. In this view, Jews are more than grave transgressors

of moral norms. They are beings whose very existence constitutes a violation of the moral fabric of society. For the Nazis the Jews were genetically evil, an inveterate and powerful force for harm. For the Church they were the ontological enemies of God, inflicting great injuries on his earthly flock. Antisemitisms of this ilk are more tenacious than other kinds of anti-Semitism, arouse more passion, usually provoke and support a wider variety of more serious and inflammatory charges against the Jews, and inhere within them a greater potential for violent and deadly anti-Jewish action.

The Nazis and the Church could therefore conclude in common that the Jews were so threatening that the danger they putatively posed could not be neutralized so long as they mixed freely among the nations. In light of this, the silence of national church after national church, of bishops and priests in country after country, as they watched, sometimes with mixed emotions, others implementing eliminationist anti-Jewish policies becomes more understandable. As I have already discussed, the absence of protest on the part of an institution and people who are all but professional critics, commentators on the immorality of policies, deeds, and ideas that they oppose confirms this obvious conclusion. Furthermore, the testimony of the leading churchmen themselves makes it clear that the Church was in sync with the intellectual and nonlethal programmatic core of the Germans' eliminationist enterprise.

(He has expanded on this issue in his *Hitler's Willing Executioners: Ordinary Germans and the Holocaust*, New York, 1996, pp. 37–38, and pass.) And indeed, already in 1941, after the killing of 18,999 Jews in Kovno, Margarite Summer filed an accurate report which was circulated among German Bishops. See Michael Phayer, *The Catholic Church and the Holocaust*, 1930–1945, Bloomington, Indianapolis, 2000, pp. 43–51. And on the Pope's silence, see ibid. pp. 51–66. And on October 17, 1943, and also October of that year Van Weizäcker, the Third Reich's ambassador to the Holy See reported on Nazi anti-Jewish activities, and Bishop Hudel sent a telegram on October 16 of that year to the Secretary of State Kepler, Rome (Vatican) on the situation. See Leon Poliakov, *Harvest of Hate: The Nazi Program for the Destruction of the Jews of Europe*, Westfort, Connecticut, 1951, pp. 296–305, and especially note 16. Poliakov has a rather weak attempt to find some kind of justification for the Holy See's silence.

This whole subject is one of considerable debate, with a very lengthy bibliography, some of the items of which are indicated in Goldhagen's *A Moral Reckoning* pp. 12, 293 note 3. See, e.g., John Marley, *Vatican Diplomacy and the Jews during the Holocaust*, New York, 1980, pp. 207–209; S. Friedlander, *Pius XII and the Third Reich*, London, 1966; G. Lewy, *The Catholic Church and Nazi Germany*, New York, 1964. See also Walter Laqueur: *The Terrible Secret: Suppression of the Truth About*

Hitler's "Final Solution," Harmondsworth, 1980; Martin Gilbert, *Auschwitz and the Allies*, London, 1981.

On the other hand, see Justus George Lawlor, *Popes and Politics: Reform, Resentment and the Holocaust*, 2002, and idem, *Were the Popes against the Jews: Tracking the Myths and Confronting the Ideologies*, 2012.

The subject of Pius XII's silence has been discussed in a richly documented book by George Pascelecq and Bernard Suchecky, entitled *The Hidden Encyclical of Pius XI*, New York, San Diego, London, 1997, translated from the French edition of 1995 by Steven Randall. The book contains a fascinating introduction by Garry Wills (pp. IX–XXIV) on the history of the document, which "is the stuff of spy novels" (ibid. p. IX). This 1937 encyclical, entitled *Mit Brennender Sorge*, "With Burning Dismay," written by Father John LaFarge, was conceded by the Pope's order, called *non expedit* – "It does no good." The abridged French Version from late 1938 was entitled *Humani Generis Unitas*, "The Unity of the Human Race," and constitutes an attack on totalitarianism and racism, and mentions specifically persecutions against the Jews (5:131–134,144,149 etc., pp. 246–249, 253–254, 257–258 etc.). See further Pinchas E. Lapide, *Three Popes and the Jews*, New York, 1967, pp. 97–113, on "Mit Brenneder Sorge." But see, more recently, Pius XII, *The Holocaust and the Revisionists: Essays*, ed. Patrick J. Gallo, Jefferson, North Carolina and London, 2006.

19. See *Jews under The Italian Occupation*, by Leon Poliakov and Jacques Sabille, Paris 1955, with copious documentation on Italian knowledge of Nazi activities, and the Italian response.

We should note that already in 1942 there was ample evidence in the international media on the murder of over one million Jews by the Nazi regime. This has been revealed in minute detail by Deborah E. Lipstadt in the *Beyond Belief: The American Press and the Coming of the Holocaust 1933–1945*, New York, 1986, especially in Chapter 8, entitled "Official Confirmation," pp. 159–196. It is true that the American press tended to downgrade the information by relegating it to back-pages, or adding "cautionary" words, such as "allegedly." But the British press coverage was far more direct and forceful, having boldface headlines like "Germans murder 700,000 Jews in Poland –Travelling Gas Chambers" (*Daily Telegraph* and *Morning Post*), or "Massacre of Jews – Over 1,000,000 died since the War Began" (*London Times*), "Greater Pogrom – One Million Jews Die" (*Daily Mail*), etc., (Lipstadt, pp. 163–164). Furthermore in December 8, 1942, a delegation of Jewish leaders went to the White House to present President Roosevelt with a memorandum on the massacres of Jews in Europe, and the President "did not express shock or surprise," but rather acknowledged that:

The Government of the United States is very well acquainted with most of the facts you are now bringing to our attention. Unfortunately we have received confirmation from many sources. Representatives of the United States government in Switzerland and other neutral countries have given us proof that confirms the horrors discussed by you" (Lipstadt, pp. 185–186, 331 note 61).

Furthermore, William Temple the Archbishop of Canterbury, in the *London Times* issued a call for immediate action, "to receive here any Jews who are able to escape the clutches of the Nazis" (ibid. pp. 190, 332 note 70, December 4, 1942 etc., and cf. p. 195), and he was later joined by the archbishop of York and Wales, in the "name of the whole Anglican Episcopate" that the British government provide a sanctuary (ibid. p. 204).

And already in June 1942 Polish authorities in London released a report from Poland that had already been transmitted to London by the Jewish socialist organization, the Bund, in May of that year, describing how the massacres were committed:

"Men, fourteen to sixty years old, were driven to a single place – a square or a cemetery, where they were slaughtered or shot by machine guns or killed by hand-grenades. They had to dig their own graves. Children in orphanages, inmates in old-age houses, the sick in hospitals were shot, women were killed in the streets. In many towns the Jews were carried off to 'an unknown destination' and killed in adjacent woods" (ibid. pp. 162, 327 note 9).

Lipstadt's book presents a wealth of additional information, but the above should suffice to make the point. And though her study is directed primarily to the role of the American press during this period, it is surely abundantly clear that the Catholic Church, and most especially the Vatican, must have been keenly aware of what was going on even at this early stage.

This is also the conclusion of Walter Laqueur, in his *The Terrible Secret: Suppression of the Truth about Hitler's "Final Solution,"* London, 1980, that already from early 1942 a stream of information was reaching the West from a variety of sources, describing the horrors of Jewish extermination. See, e.g., pp. 129, 137, 177, especially 201–202 where he writes:

Millions of Germans knew by late 1942 that the Jews had disappeared. . . . Neutral and international organizations *such as the Vatican* and the Red Cross knew the truth at an early stage. Not perhaps the whole truth, but enough to understand that few, if any, Jews would survive the war. *The Vatican had an unrivalled net of informants all over Europe.* It tried to intervene on some occasions on behalf of the Jews, but had no wish to give publicity to the issue. For this would have exposed it to German attacks on the one hand and pressure to do more from the Jews and the Aliens. Jews after all were not Catholics. . . . [My emphasis, D.S.]

And cf. pp. 223–228 for further documentation etc.
There is much literature on this subject. But the above should suffice.

20. See *Humanitarian actions of Monsignor Angelo Roncalli, The International Raoul Wallenberg Foundation,* 28 April 2014.

21. David I. Kertzer, *The Pope Against the Jews: The Vatican's Role in the Rise of Anti-Semitism,* New York, 2002, pp. 279–280. See p. 325 notes 30–31: "A propos de l'antisemitisme Pélegrimage de la Radio Catholique Belge," *Documentation Catholique* 39, 1938, pp. 1459–1462's "Un discourse de pape – l'antisemitism est inadmissible. Nous sommes spirituellement des sémites," *La Croix* 17, Septembre 1938, p. 1. Kertzer points out that "the Pope's statement to the Belgian pilgrims was never reported in the Vatican's own newspaper, although other Catholic papers in Europe carried the story. His remarks were informal and spontaneous, and so they were not recorded in any official document. They were heartfelt and sincere, the cry of a man who saw a dark shadow growing ever darker across Europe." On p. 325 note 32, he writes:

> Miccoli (I dilemmie ei silenzi di Pio XII, Milan 2000, pp. 308–10) speculates that the decision of both *Civilta cattolica and L'Osservatore Romano* not to publish Pius XI's comments on the Jews reflects the changing center of Vatican power at this juncture. With Pius XI ailing, others in the Vatican – presumably the secretary of state, Eugenio Pacelli, who would soon succeed him as Pope, above all – held sway, and they did not approve of Pius XI's remarks on behalf of the Jews. Although earlier the Pope had brooked no such internal opposition, by this point, just a few months before his death, he was no longer the powerful figure he had previously been. The German ambassador to the Holy See, Ernst von Weizsäcker, contrasting Pius XI with his successor, Pius XII, later wrote: "If Pius XI, so impulsive and energetic, had lived a little longer he would in all likelihood have brought about a rupture in the relations between the Reich and the Curia" (quoted in Miccoli 2000, p. 163).

22. On the influence of the Jesuits on Eugenio Pacelli, Pope Pius XII (1939–1958), see, for example, John Cornwell, *Hitler's Pope: The Secret History of Pius XII,* New York, 1999, pp. 23–24, where he writes as follows:

> Pacelli had completed his education in "Sacred Theology" with a doctoral degree (by today's standards, the degree was more accurately a licentiate) awarded on the basis of a short dissertation, now lost to posterity, and an oral examination in Latin. In the autumn he registered again at the St. Apollinaris Institute to study canon law. This marked the beginning of serious postgraduate research, during which he probably came under the influence of the Jesuit

canonist Franz Xavier Wernz, an expert on questions of ecclesiastical authority in canon law.

But the influence of Rome's Jesuits, whom Pacelli regarded as his special mentors while he was a seminarian and throughout his life, is notable for other reasons. In 1898, as Pacelli was completing his studies for the priesthood, *Civiltà Cattolica*, the Rome-based Jesuit journal, was arguing the guilt of Alfred Dreyfus, the Jewish army officer accused of treason in France. The journal continued to proclaim his guilt the following year, even after he had been pardoned. The editor, Father Raffaele Ballerini, charged that the Jews "had bought all the newspapers and consciences in Europe" in order to acquit Dreyfus. In a chilling conclusion, he asserted that "wherever Jews had been granted citizenship" the outcome had been the "ruination" of Christians or the massacre of the "alien race," (see P.E. Lapide, *The Last Three Popes*, New York, 1967, p. 83).

How Pacelli was affected by these opinions, published in a highly influential periodical in Rome, we do not know. But Catholic ordinands at the end of the nineteenth century were bound to be influenced by the long history of Christian attitudes toward Judaism.

And cf. ibid. pp. 45, 192, 227, etc. See most recently David I. Kerzer, *The Pope and Mussolini: The Secret History of Pope Pius XI and the Rise of Fascism in Europe*, New York, 2014, and on the Jesuits ibid., index p. 527 s.v. Jesuits, especially pp. 127–129, where we read that Italy's chargé d'affaires, Carlo Fecia di Cossato said that "the recent racial laws have not, as a whole, found unfavorable reaction in the Vatican," and that "the Jesuits have always been convinced anti-Semites – albeit for doctrinal reasons different from ours," and that "the Jesuits are still clearly and fundamentally anti-Jewish." (Cf. ibid. p. 484 note 38 for sources.)

See further D. Goldhagen, *A Moral Reckoning*, St. Ives, Great Britain 2002, pp. 154–155; Pinchas Lapide, *Three Popes and Jews*, New York, 1967, pp. 282–283, and cf. ibid. p. 108, etc. On Jesuit anti-Semitism in general, see, for example, David I. Kertzer, *The Popes Against the Jews*, New York, 2002, p. 207:

> It was in the sixteenth century that a Spaniard, Ignatius Loyola, founded the Jesuit order. Although initially some of its most important recruits came from among the descendants of Jews who had been forcibly converted in Spain, the Jesuits soon put an end to this. In 1592 they introduced a rule forbidding the admission of men of Jewish origin, calculating ancestry to the fifth generation. The rule was only expunged in 1946, having been often cited by both the Nazis and the Italian Fascists to demonstrate that their own racial policies merely echoed those of the Church's most respected religious order. [See Lionel .... Steiman, *Paths to Genocide: Antisemitism in Western History*, New York, 1998, p. 154.]

In this they were more strict than the Nazis themselves.

See further Pinchas E. Lapide, ibid. p. 283:

> And on June 19, 1948, the Jesuits solemnly exhumed a libel as old and despicable as Ritual Murder: "In Gaza two Zionist emissaries were arrested who were charged with the poisoning of the city's wells. According to written evidence, they have also thrown typhoid and dysentery germs into several watering places. Rumour has it, in fact, that the Jews rely for their victory upon the sanitary havoc of the Arab states. Such facts [*sic*] would certainly not enhance their good name . . ." (*Civilta Cattolica*, June 19, 1948, p. 670).

On the culumny of well-poisoning in Mediaeval Europe, see Joshua Trachtenberg, *The Devil and the Jews: The Medieval Conception of the Jew and its Relation to Modern Antisemitism*, New York, 1943, pp. 101–106, and indeed the whole of chapter seven, entitled "The Poisoners," pp. 97–108. (Cf. above note 90.)

And see Lapide's continuing remarks (ibid.) on the joint sentiments between the Jesuits and Haj Aamin El-Husseini, "the Mufti of Jerusalem."

We might add that the Catholic periodical *La Civilta Cattolica*, which was regarded as a "Semi-official organ of the Holy See" (Roger Anbert, *Le Pontificat de Pie IX* (1846–1878), Tourmay, 1963, p. 40), founded by Italian Jesuits in 1850, gave extensive coverage to the causes, effects and remedies of the "Jewish Question in Europe," also designated as the "Jewish Danger" (*La Civilta Cattolica,* 1928, pp. 335–344), which posed a "threat" to all the world, and especially to Christian nations with their "adverse interference" (*ingerenze nefasten*) and "harmful infiltration" (*perniciose infitrazioni*) into society (ibid. p. 341). There are repeated references of a pejorative nature to Jews from a variety of different viewpoints. (See on this in Ronald Modras, *The Catholic Church and Antisemitism in Poland*, 1932–1939, Herwood Academic publishers, 1994, pp. 334–340.)

This again is too broad a subject to be discussed here, and would require a detailed history of Jesuitism and its anti-Jewish elements. However, clearly not all Jesuits were anti-Semites, and significantly Cardinal Augustin Bea, who was a German Jesuit priest, was highly influential in the drafting of Vatican II. He had also held secret talks with Heschel.

23. Cf. Cook ibid. p. 54: For Celsus it is impossible to believe that God's son could suffer, (Origen, *Contra Celsum* 7:15, ed. Paul Koetshau, *GCS.* 2,3. Leipzig 1899, 166, 9–10).

It is worthwhile recalling the words of the important American Reform Rabbi, Issac Mayer Weiss (1819–1900), in his *The Martyrdom of Jesus of Nazareth* (written in 1874), seventy years before the Holocaust, pp. 129–131:

One of the falsehoods to be erased from the memory of Christendom, for the sake of truth and humanity, is the horrid and shocking mad-dog cry – the Jews crucified Jesus. What hell could invent of fiendish torments and diabolic scorns was employed in Christendom, to make the Jew miserable with Christian love. Every fanatic, imbecile, or robber assumed the right to trample and spit upon the Jew. Every crazy priest has a doctrine on hand to justify those barbarous outrages as the special work of Providence. Every smooth-faced hypocrite or sorrowful bigot in our days has something harsh in his heart against the Jew who killed Christ . . . So tenacious, however, and unreasoning is fanaticism, that it must be burnt out of the soul to be overcome. As long as that source of hatred exists in Christendom, Christianity is no religion: it is a misfortune for weeping humanity. . . .

The pack of howling fanatics who still cry at the heels of the Jew, "Christ Killer," have yet to learn to read and understand the gospels correctly. Cunning wickedness and furious fanaticism, for centuries of ghostly darkness, raised the bloody cry, the Jews crucified Jesus; blind ignorance and servile obedience re-echoed the unreasoning howl at carnivals of madness, to oppress, exile, persecute, plunder and slaughter. Shame, burning shame, on priests and mobs of the past who used this barbarous war-cry in defiance of humanity; thousand-fold shame on modern priests and preachers who still unblushingly proclaim this infamous lie, not only in defiance of the Gospel, but also of truth, humanity, and religion. They ought to be driven from the pulpits of every civilized community, and sent to savages whose conception of religion are as narrow as their own (*"The Martyrdom of Jesus of Nazareth"*).

24. The final text of *Nostra Aetate* was preceded by four drafts, first entitled *Decretum de Judeais*, presented between 11 October 1962, and 28 September 1964, and also debates on the draft on 28 September 1964. The third draft, (also called *Decretum ad Iudaeis*) appendix to *Schema on Ecumenism* (*De Ecclesia unitate*, "*Ut omnes Unium Sint*" which was the second draft), deleted the word "deicide" from chapter IV of the second draft (of 8 November 1963).

In the "debate" Auxiliary Bishop Stephen Leven of San Antonio stated that:

In chapter IV of the draft on Ecumenism, presented to us last year, it was said that the Jews were not guilty of deicide. Now, in the present text, this statement is missing. Some say it has been suppressed because the word "deicidal" is philosophically and theologically absurd, self-contradictory and therefore unworthy of a Conciliar document. [*sic*, D.S.] Fathers of the Council, we have to deal here, not with a philosophical entity, but with an infamous abuse that was invented by the Christians for the sole purpose of bringing shame and disgrace on the Jews.

> For hundreds of years and even in our own century, Christians have thrown the word "deicide" into the face of Jews in order to justify all kinds of excesses, even murder. . . . We must remove this word from the vocabulary of Christians, so that it can never be turned against the Jews.

See Oesterreicher ibid. pp. 198–199; and *The Documents of Vatican II*, edd. W.M. Abott and J. Gallagher, America Press, 1966, p. 666 note 23.

The controversy within the Council, and the resistance to absolving Jews from the crime of deicide is evident from the voting results. Gary Wills, *Papal Sin: Structures of Deceit*, New York, 2000, pp. 19–26 (cited by Goldhagen, p. 205) writes:

> In an item-by-item vote of the whole Council, the vote against the sentence that opposed blaming Jews for the death of Christ was 188, and that against opposition to calling the Jews cursed was 245. Admittedly, this is a small minority – the votes for the statements were 1,875 and 1,821 respectively. But it is astounding that even the weakened form of the statement, unaccompanied by any recognition of past persecution or any expression of sorrow and repentance, could still be rejected by hundreds of Catholic bishops.

And when we speak of "the Church," we mean not only the Catholic Church. For the Protestant Church in many countries was also compliant with Nazi policy during the war. See Doris L. Bergen, *Twisted Cross: The German Christian Movement in the Third Reich*, University of North Carolina Press, Chapel Hill, 1996, for "j'accuse" of German Christians, who already in 1932 welcomed Hitler's rise to power, remained aligned to his regime until its end, adopted National Socialist policy without reservation, "out of real conviction [rather] than opportunism." See Maria Mitell's review in *Holocaust and Genocide Studies* 11/3, 1997, pp. 434–437, who ends her review with the following disturbing statement:

> Bergen's question about the value of Christianity in the face of such evil is, in the case of German Christians difficult to answer indeed.

CHAPTER 13

Prof. Jules Isaac's Role in the Process Resulting in *Nostra Aetate*

Here we should pay homage to the significant role played by the French Jewish scholar Prof. Jules Isaac (1887–1963), towards the forming of the "subcommission of the secretariat for Promoting Christian Unity," under the leadership of Cardinal Augustin Bea. This has been succinctly and very clearly delineated by Claire Huchet Bishop in her "Biographical Introduction" to Isaac's *The Teaching of Contempt*, New York, Chicago, San Francisco, 1964.[1] His activities in this direction begin as early as 1943, and by 1947 he submitted his six-hundred page manuscript, *Jésus et Israel* to his publisher. In 1947 he met in Paris with a group of distinguished Jewish and Christian intellectuals, submitting his Eighteen Points for the purification of Christian teachings regarding the Jews, which formed the basis of the Ten Points of Seelisberg, elaborated later that same year in Switzerland. (This was called *The International Conference of Christians and Jews*, and took place in Seelisberg on 30 July till the 5 August 1947.)[2] In 1948, together with Edmund Fleg, he created *L'Amitié Judéo-Chrétienne*, an interfaith group working towards eradicating false notions as to the beliefs of Jews and Christians, and also towards a positive appreciation of each other's heritage. In 1949 he had an audience with Pope Pius XII, arguing that the Good Friday prayer for Jews, *pro perfidiis judaeis*, which had now used the milder translation "unfaithful" or "unbelieving," arguing that this change was insufficient, especially since priests continued to use the Latin word with its damaging psychological associations. In 1956 he published his *Genèse de l'antisémitisme*, and in 1958, with one stroke of the pen, Pope John XXIII eliminated the word *perfidiis*, both in the Latin and the vernacular. And in 1959 the Pope did away with two other prejudicial sentences, one in the *Act of Consecratius to the Sacred Heart*, recited every Friday, and the other to the ritual of baptism for converts.

In 1960 a private audience was granted him with Pope John XXIII,[3] in which he presented his practical suggestion, for the creation of a subcommission in the Council, empowered to study the questions raised in his books. The Pope listened alternatively and sympathetically, and declared spontaneously, "I have been thinking about that ever since you began to speak."[4]

The *subcommission of the Secretariat for Promoting Christian Unity* was subsequently created under the leadership of Cardinal Augustin Bea. In this dramatic atmosphere of expectancy at the age of eighty-five, Isaac wrote his *The Teaching of Contempt* (his first book to appear in English, published in 1964),[5] which ends with the following paragraph (pp. 146–147):

> God be thanked, a purifying stream exists in Christianity and grows stronger every day. This book is fresh evidence, however, that this new attitude is still far from having prevailed. Evil habits persist; they are too old to be uprooted overnight. All the more reason to persevere in our efforts, to strive without ceasing to attain the desired end – the necessary reappraisal of Christian education regarding Israel, a reappraisal which will also be an atonement; a work of truth, but also of justice, and one which I am convinced is of the greatest significance and will have infinitely beneficial consequences for Christianity as well as for Judaism.[6]

And in January 5 1964, Pope Paul VI visited the Holy Land. (Already on the 4 December 1963, he had surprised his audience during the Second Vatican Council by declaring his intention to make this pilgrimage, which was to be the first of a series of Papal Journeys during the following decades to various regions of the Catholic world.)[7]

And in 1965 *Nostra Aetate* was published, and even if we think it was late, it was undoubtedly a watershed event in the history of Judaeo-Christian relations.[8]

Echoes of this document reverberate in subsequent Christian statements. Thus, for example, the first point which is directed against the supersessionist view that the Old Covenant has been replaced and abrogated by the New Covenant, which is now the only valid one, was taken up by

Pope Paul John II, who in a speech delivered on November 17, 1980 to the Jews of Berlin, stated that the Jewish people are the "people of the Old Covenant, which was never revoked." In this statement he explicitly rejected the superessionist position, as exemplified, for instance, in Pope Eugene IV's papal bull, published at the Council of Florence in 1441:

> The Holy Roman Church ... firmly believes and teaches that the matter pertaining to the law of the Old Testament, of the Mosaic Law ... after our Lord's coming [and] after the promulgation of the Gospel it asserts that they cannot be observed without the loss of eternal salvation.

The opposite of the supersessionist position usually called "dual-covenant theology"[9] has been criticized by many prominent Catholic theologians, such as the Jesuit Cardinal Avery Dulles (1918–2008), in his "Evangelization and Mission," *Covenant and Mission* Oct.21, 2002,[10] and others. However this is beyond the scope of this study.

If we wish to evaluate Isaac's contribution to *Nostra Aetate*, we can do no better than by quoting what John T. Pawlikowski (Professor and Acting President of the Catholic Theological Union in Chicago) stated in his article, "The Teaching of Contempt: Judaism in Christian Education and Liturgy," published in *Auschwitz: Beginning of a New Era: Reflections on the Holocaust*, ed. Eva Fleischer, New York, 1974, p. 155.[11]

He opened his essay as follows:

> The title of this presentation, this paper itself, is a personal tribute to a man who has made a great difference in the Christian community's understanding of the anti-Judaism inherent in its theological traditions, its catechetics, its biblical interpretation, and its liturgy. That man is Jules Isaac. *It may be said that no one person was more influential in preparing the way for the Declaration on the Church and the Jewish People adopted at the Second Vatican Council.* And it was through a reading of Isaac's *The Teaching of Contempt: Christian Roots of Anti-Semitism* while in the seminary that I first became alerted to the very serious distortion of Judaism central to Christian theology. In short, I probably would not be making this presentation today if it were not for Jules Isaac.

He succinctly summarizes Isaac's explanation for Christian anti-Semitism thus:

> Jules Isaac zeroes in on three main themes in *The Teaching of Contempt*, amplified more fully in his other major volume on the subject, *Jesus and Israel*, New York, 1971, but first published in French, in Paris, 1948, under the title *Jésus et Israèl*: (1) the dispersion of the Jews, seen by Christian writers as a providential punishment for the crucifixion; (2) the Christian portrait of Judaism as degenerate at the time of Jesus; and (3) the deicide charge.

Claire Fluchet-Bishop, who was a close collaborator with Isaac, and responsible for the English editions of the two above-mentioned books, writes in her response to Pawlikowski thus (ibid. pp. 179–180):

> Auschwitz: the beginning of a new era? Yes, to a certain extent; and this we owe to a Jew, Professor Jules Isaac, who in 1948 sounded the alarm in his book *Jesus et Israel*, which rocked the complacency of European Christians and pointed to their blindness. The Ten Points of Seelisberg came out of that, as did also the first analysis of French catechisms.
>
> Would we have had the beginning of a new era without the decisive meeting of Professor Isaac with John XXIII in 1960? It was my privilege to hear about that memorable private audience from Jules Isaac himself, as we sat in his lovely garden at Aix-en Provence. He told me: "As I waited in the anteroom of the pope's private library, where the audience was to be held, I felt weighed down by my responsibility. How to convey to the pope, within a few minutes, nearly two thousand years of Jewish suffering at Christian hands? I felt all the martyrs of the past ages present in that room, and also the six million victims of Hitler." The victims, as we know, included Isaac's wife, daughter, and son-in-law.
>
> Out of that audience came the creation of a committee within the Second Vatican Council for the reevaluation of Christian teaching regarding the Jews. Out of it too, eventually, came the council's Declaration on the Jews, which, though unsatisfactory in many ways, yet gave us Catholics an opening toward a new attitude regarding the Jewish people. I am particularly grateful to John Pawlikowski for his moving personal tribute to Jules Isaac, distinguished scholar, gallant

Jewish fighter for truth (Isaac's own motto: *pro veritate pugnator*) and noble human being.

As is glaringly apparent throughout John Pawlikowski's report, eleven years after Jules Isaac's death we are still plodding along, not even quite sure sometimes whether the few points gained are for the good. "What Christian teaching has done, it has to undo; and it will take a long time," Jules Isaac used to tell me. How true!

Now some forty-two years later we can affirm that many points were indeed for the good.

Endnotes to Chapter 13

1. See also Egal Feldman, *Catholics and Jews in Twentieth Century America*, Urbana and Chicago, 2001, pp. 106–108; Katherine T. Hargrove, "A Burning Love of Truth: Jules Isaac, 1877–1963," apud *The Star and the Cross: Essays on Jewish Christian Relations*, ed. Katherine T. Hargrove, Milwakee, 1966, pp. 127–et seq.

See also Msgr. Jorge Mejia's comment in his essay in *More Stepping Stones to Jewish-Christian Relations*, ed. Helga Croner, New York, 1985 – this is "An Unabridged Collection of Christian Document," 1975–1983, on p. 6:

When Jules Isaac came to Rome to see Pope John XXIII, and even before, when he met Pope Pius XII, he found a ground already prepared. I can hardly imagine that a corresponding gentleman of Jewish extraction would have been received in the preceding century by Leo XII, Gregory XVII, Pius IX (at least during the second part of his reign), and even Leo XIII. But Pius X had already received Theodor Herzl, and if what happened between them, according to Herzl's diary, was not particularly promising, the very fact that he was received in a private audience is not without significance, especially if one considers the then rather rigid Vatican protocol. Besides this, always according to Herzl's testimony, Cardinal Merry del Val, then Secretary of State, was not at all closed to his ideas, and one may conclude that this could have been a way, even from the Pope itself, to manifest more openness than Herzl got from his actual audience with the Pontiff.

2. The Seelisberg conference was of cardinal importance for the subsequent development of Jewish-Christian dialogue. It brought together some seventy participants from seventeen countries, 28 Jews, 23 Protestants and 9 Catholics. Among the Jews were: Jules Isaac, Jacob Kaplan, acting chief rabbi of France, Alexandar Safran, chief rabbi of Romania, Prof. Selig Brodetsky, president of the Representative Council of the Jews of England. Among the Catholics were: Pere Marie-Benoit, Abbot Charles Journet, Father Jean de Menasce, Father Paul Deman.

At this conference the Christians undertook a re-examination of Christian teaching with regard Jews and Judaism. The result was a document listing ten points, largely inspired by the eighteen proposals of Jules Isaac, all aimed at eradicating prejudices against Jews.

Because of the undoubted importance of this document I shall list the ten points.

They were published in "An address to the Churches" in 1947, by the ICCJU – International Council of Christians and Jews. They are as follows:

1. Remember that one God speaks to us all through the Old and the New Testament.

2. Remember that Jesus was born of a Jewish mother of the seed of David and the people of Israel, and that His everlasting love and forgiveness embraces His own people and the whole world.

3. Remember the first disciples, the apostles and the first martyrs were Jews.

4. Remember the fundamental commandment of Christianity, to love God and one's neighbour, proclaimed already in the Old Testament and confirmed by Jesus, is binding on both Christians and Jews in all human relationship, without any exception.

5. Avoid distorting or misrepresenting biblical or post-biblical Judaism with the object of extolling Christianity.

6. Avoid using the word Jews in the exclusive sense of the enemies of Jesus, and the words the enemies of Jesus to designate the whole Jewish people.

7. Avoid presenting the Passion in such a way as to bring the odium of the killing of Jesus upon all Jews or upon Jews alone. It was only a section of the Jews in Jerusalem who demanded the death of Jesus, and the Christian message has always been that it was the sins of mankind which were exemplified by those Jews and the sins in which all men share that brought Christ to the Cross.

8. Avoid referring to scriptural curses, or the cry of a raging mob: His blood be Upon Us and Our Children, without remembering that this cry should not count against the infinity more weighty words of Our Lord: Father Forgive Them, for They Know not What they Do.

9. Avoid promoting the superstitious notion that the Jewish people are reprobate, accused, reserved for a destiny of suffering.

10. Avoid speaking of the Jews as if the first members of the Church had not been Jews.

The significance of this document has been discussed in depth by Christian M. Rutishauser, in his "The 1947 Seelisberg Conference: The Foundations of the Jewish Christian Dialogue," *Studies in Christian Jewish Relations*, 2, 2008.

3. See Thomas F. Stransky, "Holy Diplomacy: Making the Impossible Possible," apud *Unanswered Questions: Theological Views of Jewish Catholic Relations*, ed. Roger Brooks, Notre Dame 1988, p. 54.

4. See Johannes Cardinal Willebrands, *Church and Jewish People: New Considerations*, New York, 1992, pp. 257–258.

5. See Joseph L. Lichlen, "Jules Isaac: The Teaching of Contempt," apud *The Star and the Cross: Essays on Jewish-Christian Relations*, ed. Katherine T. Hargrove,

Milwaukee 1966, pp. 133–136. He also published in 1960 *L'Antisemitisme: A-t- il des Racines, Chrétienne*, translated into English as *The Christian Roots of Antisemitism*, New York, 1961.

6. See André Kaspi, *Jules Isaac ou le Passion de la Liberté*, Paris 2002.

7. For a detailed examination of the Israeli perspective of this journey, see, most recently, the article (in Hebrew) by Doron Bary, "Fifty Years after the Visit of Pope Paul VI to the Holy Land" (January 1964); "The Israeli Context," *Cathedra*, 160, 2016, pp. 123–152, 211. And for a study of the various reactions and positions within the Vatican, see Th. Stransky, "Paul VI's Pilgrimage in the Holy Land," apud *I Viaggi Apostolici di Paolo VI*, ed. R. Rossi, Brescia 2004, pp. 341–373.

8. See, for instance, D.G. Schultenover (ed.) *Did Anything Happen?*, New York, 2007; M.L. Lamb, *Vatican II: Renewal within Tradition*, Oxford 2008.

And for a brief history of the document and its implications, see Augustin Cardinal Bea, S.J., *The Church and the Jewish People: A Commentary on the Second Vatican Council's Declaration on the Relation of the Church to Non-Christian Religions*, transl. Philip Coretz S.J., New York, 1986, pp. 22–50, and 154–172.

9. For a fine history of super-sessionary theology and its sources, and the new dual covenant theology and the story of its development, on the book by John T. Pawlikowski, OSM. *Restating the Catholic Church's Relationship with the Jewish People: The Challenge of Super Sessionary Theology*, Lampeter, Ceredigion, Wales, 2013. He traces the development of the new theological position from *Nostra Aetate's* origins, through the various attempts and approaches of Catholic theologians, such as Hellwig, Dubois, Martin, Remund, van Buren, and Musser, Thoma and Metz, with an analysis of each stage and comprehensive bibliography.

10. In parenthesis we may add that his father, John Foster Dulles, was hardly a friend of Israel. See, e.g., Warren Bass, *Support Any Friend: Kennedy's Middle East and the Making of the U.S.-Israel Alliance*, Oxford, 2003, pp. 35, 39, 41, 48, 114, 150–153, 163. But it could be argued that perhaps I am not being objective.

11. This was one of the papers given at the International Symposium on the Holocaust held at the Cathedral of Saint John the Divine, New York, June 31, 1974.

CHAPTER 14

Heschel's Contribution

We should not overlook other important contributors to the dialogical process which gave birth to *Nostra Aetate*. Egal Feldman, in his *Catholics and Jews in Twentieth Century America*, Urbana and Chicago, 2001, pp. 113–114, pays a deserving tribute to Abraham Joshua Heschel, for his heroic efforts in their direction (I cite him in full):

> Abraham Joshua Heschel, the prominent Jewish theologian and professor at the Jewish Theological Seminary of New York, was, like Jules Isaac, present at the council whenever the occasion called for it, communicating with council leaders before the entire body convened. When asked why he became involved in Vatican II, Heschel replied, "The issues at stake were profoundly theological. To refuse contact with Christian theologians, to my mind, was barbarous. There is a great expectation among Christians today that Judaism has something unique to offer." Heschel, therefore, working tirelessly "to the point of exhaustion," became involved with Vatican II. [Eva Fleischer, "Heschel's Significance for Jewish-Christian Relations," *Quarterly Review* 4, 1984, p. 75.] During the council's preparatory stages, Heschel acted as a consultant to the American Jewish Committee and other Jewish agencies. In 1962, Heschel requested of Cardinal Bea that the council in its declaration repudiate the deicide charge against the Jews. When Cardinal Bea visited the United States in 1963, Heschel chaired a meeting between him and a group of Jewish leaders [ibid. pp. 75–76].
>
> In 1963, Heschel became concerned when he realized that efforts were being made to introduce the issue of conversion of the Jews into a revised version of the text of the "Declaration on the Jews." Heschel wrote to Bea about his concerns, strongly condemning the new version

of *Nostra Aetate*, No. 4. He met with Pope Paul VI over this matter on the eve of Yom Kippur, September 14, 1965. Such a meeting at such a time stands as evidence of Heschel's deep concerns about the outcome of the inclusion of the statement [ibid. p. 76]. Few American religious leaders were better able than Heschel to articulate Jewish concerns to Pope Paul VI. According to a Jewish observer, Heschel is credited with the changing of "the thinking of ... many of the Council Fathers and affecting the final outcome of the declaration" [David Polish, "A Very Small Lever Can Move the Entire World," apud *Unanswered Questions: The Theological Views of Jewish Christian Relations*, ed. Roger Brooks, Notre Dame, 1988, p. 86]. Of all the American rabbinical scholars and writers, Abraham Joshua Heschel was the best known and most respected in the American Catholic community.[1]

Endnotes to Chapter 14

1. Feldman (pp. 113–114) also pays credit to yet another Jewish individual whose work influenced the council's deliberations:

> [He] was Joseph Lichten of the B'nai B'rith's Anti-Defamation League. Lichten also spent considerable time in Rome, distributing memos to the council fathers about Christian anti-Semitism in Catholic teaching. Lichten calculated results of sociological surveys which indicated that the majority of American Catholics continued to believe that all the Jews shared in the guilt of Christ's crucifixion and that nearly half believed that Jews would never be forgiven for this sin. Lichten explained to American Catholics shortly before the opening of the third session of Vatican II why a strongly worded statement on behalf of the Jews was so important. He offered these reasons:
>
> First, we are persuaded that anti-Semitism is partly rooted in Christian traditions.
>
> Second, we know that our sufferings are too often looked upon, even today, as God's righteous punishment for the alleged guilt of the Jewish people for the death of Christ.
>
> Third: We see our beliefs and our solidarity as a people used against us, persistently and harmfully to exclude us not only from the respect of other religious groups, but also from civil and social benefits.

(See Vincent A. Yzermans, "Declaration on the Relationship of the Church to Non-Christian Religions: Historical Introduction," apud *American Participation in the Second Vatican Council*, ed. Vincent A. Yzermans, New York, 1967, p. 573.) Feldman adds (ibid.):

> None of this is to suggest that Jews, uninvited, insinuated themselves into the work of the council. On the contrary, Cardinal Bea and his staff welcomed suggestions from Jewish leaders. Bea was eager to fashion a declaration which, although designed for Catholics, Jews would also be comfortable with, and he turned to Jewish organizations for help. Unofficially, when needed, Jewish advice was solicited. Jewish views were sought by the secretariat from Reform, Conservative, and Orthodox authorities. There was considerable Catholic confusion about Jewish thinking on theological matters. This was not surprising, given the long history of Catholicism's misconceptions of Judaism.

There were, of course, other oft-unsung heroes in this terrible saga. We should recall the heroic efforts of Johannes (John) M. Oesterreicher (1904–1993) born a Jew, but converted to Catholicism, and was appointed a Papal Chamberlain with the title of Monsignor in 1961, who played a crucial role in the development of *Nostra Aetate*, as has been brilliantly documented by John Connelly, in his *From Enemy to Brother: The Revolution in Catholic Teaching on the Jews* 1993–1965, Cambridge Mass. and London, 2012. See index s.v. Oesterreicher, Johannes M. ((John), p. 373b. Thus Maurice Perlzweig, (1895–1985), one of the founders of the World Jewish Congress, and first chairman of the British section, headed the delegation to the United Nations in 1945, and was active in the formulation of the "Commission of Human Rights and Sub-Commission as Prevention of Discrimination" to the U.N.

Gerhart M.G. Rigner's *Ne jamais désespérer: Soixante années au service du people juif et des droits de l'homme*, Paris 1998 – "Never despair," puts the roles of the various players in the *Nostra Aetate* saga in context, (albeit with his reservations) and others who get little mention in the histories of the process. (Rabbi David Rosen's comment.) Gerhart Riegner (1911–2011) was the secretary to the World Jewish Congress 1965–1983. On August 8, 1942, he sent from Geneva the famous so-called "Riegner telegram" through diplomatic channels to Rabbi Stephen Wise. The "telegram" ran as follows:

> Received alarming report that in the Fuehrer's Headquarters, a plan has been discussed, and is under consideration, according to which all Jews in countries occupied or controlled by Germany numbering 3.5 to 4 million should, after deportation and concentration in the East, be at one blow exterminated, in order to resolve, at once and for all the Jewish question in Europe. Action is reported to be planned for the autumn. Ways of execution are being discussed including the use of prussic acid. We transmit this information with all the necessary reservations, as exactitude cannot be confirmed by us. Our informant is reported to have close connections with the highest German authorities, and his reports are generally reliable. Please inform and consult New York. (*The National Archives*, UK copy of the Riegner telegram.) See Riegner, ibid. pp. 55–75.

Similarly, in March 17, 1942, Riegner and Richard Lichthein were received by Monsignor Filippe Bernadini, the apostolic nuncio in Bern, and following that meeting a lengthy memorandum about the fate of European Jewry was submitted to the Nuncio, who undoubtedly sent it on to the Vatican. (See Saul Friedlander, *Pius XII and the Third Reich: A Documentation*, New York, 1966, pp. 104 et seq.; idem, *Nazi Germany and the Jews 1939–1945: The Years of Extermination*, New York, 2007, p. 463.)

In May of that year, the Italian abbot Piero Scavizzi, who frequently travelled to Poland, sent the following report to Pius XII:

The struggle against the Jews is implacable and constantly intensifying, with deportations and mass executions. The massacre of the Jews in the Ukraine is by now nearly complete. In Poland and Germany they want to complete it also, with a system of murders. (Friedlander ibid., citing Pierre Blet, Angelo Martini and Burkhart Schneider, edd., *Actes et documents de saint Siège relatifs á la Seconde Guerre modiale*, Vatican City, vol. 8, 434; and cf. S. Zuccotti: *Under His Very Window: The Vatican and the Holocaust in Italy*, New Haven, 1993, p. 102.)

On September 26, 1942, the American minister to the Holy See, Myron C. Taylor, delivered a note to Secretary of Slate Maglione, reporting events in the Warsaw ghetto, camps in Belzek etc., deportations from many European countries, requesting that the information be passed on to the Holy Father, and the answer sent by the cardinal's secretary to the American chargé d'affaires, Harold Tittman, the gist of which was cabled to Washington on October 10, was that (inter alia) the Holy See was taking advantage of every opportunity offered in order to mitigate the suffering on *non-Aryans*, [my emphasis D.S.]. (Friedlander ibid. pp. 464–465, 763 notes 267–268.) And the British minister to the Vatican, Francis d'Arcy Osborne, confided his bitterness about the Pope's obstinate silence in private letters and in his diary. (Friedlander ibid. p. 465, 783).

In England and the United States it was met with disbelief and considered by the US State Dept. to be "a wild rumour, fueled by Jewish anxieties," while the British Foreign Office did not forward it for some time, and not till 28 August 1942 did it reach Stephen Wise, President of the World Jewish Congress. (See Yehuda Bauer, "The Holocaust, America, and American Jewry," *Israel Journal of Foreign Affairs* VI (1), 2012.) In early 1944, Treasury Secretary Henry Morgenthau Jr. stated before President Roosevelt that "certain officials in our State Dept. had failed while it would have been commanded by duty to prevent the extermination of the Jews in German-controlled Europe."

CHAPTER 15

The Role of the "Sisters of Our Lady of Sion"

There were other largely unsung heroes in this remarkable process of theological development. Among them we should take note of the special role played by members of the "Sisters of Our Lady of Sion." This has recently been documented in detail by Celia Deutsch (one of the Sisters) in her article in *SCJR* 11/1, 2016, pp. 1–6, entitled "Journey to Dialogue: Sisters of Our Lady of Sion and the Writing of *Nostra Aetate.*"[1]

Prominent among them, and central to their influence, was St. Bénédicte Salmon, who together with other sisters and collaborative activities with colleagues, laid the foundations for the final formulation on Jews and Judaism, and strengthened the legitimacy of the "tournant apostoliqus" – the apostolic ministerial revolution from conversion of Jews to dialogue. Sisters Magda and Marie-Dominique, both members of the general council, became close collaborators in Fr. Bruno Hussar and others in writing draft material for what would become *Nostra Aetate* 4.

Moreover, their role did not end with the approval of the document. For a few days after the approval of the document's promulgation, in November …, a group of Council Fathers led by Bishops Léon-Arthur Elchinger of Strasburg and a number of theologians who had been involved in the production of the document, met to consider ways of its implementations. At the initiative of Fr. Bruno Hussar, three sisters from Sion's general council, Sisters Edward, Magda and Marie-Dominique, were invited to participate, and then asked to take charge of the project. Sister Edward accepted the responsibility and under the direction of Fr. Cornelius Rijk, founded SIDIC (Service Internationale de Documentation Judéo-Chrétienne/International Service for Jewish-Christians Documentation), which was first in the new generalate and later in 1970 in a large apartment on the Piazza Venezia.

As mentioned above Celia Deutsche's article gives a full description of the whole historic role played by the Sisters with its major dramatis personae, its ideological sources and forces motivating it, and its pivotal contributions. In doing so she seeks to rectify what in her opinion was the former incomplete narrative focused primarily on men's part in the process, by now shining a new spotlight on the important component of women's role in the development of *Nostra Aetate* and its subsequent implementations.[2]

Here, then, is yet another thread in the complex interwoven skein of constituents which led to the formulation of the Declaration.

Endnotes to Chapter 15

1. Note 1 ibid. gives copious bibliographic information on previous discussions and publications in their role in the writing of *Nostra Aetate*, which need not be duplicated here.

2. I am most grateful to Rabbi Rosen for calling my attention to this article.

CHAPTER 16

The Revolutionary Nature of *Nostra Aetate*

Nostra Aetate, however belated it might be,[1] ultimately it was, and must be, most warmly welcomed. As stated above, it forged the way to a new relationship between the two religions, in which the common and the similar would bear greater stress than the different.[2] Ironically, Christianity, despite its problematic beliefs in the trinity,[3] in virgin birth,[4] in transubstantiation, (based on *John* 6:54)[5] which to a Jew are difficult to comprehend, became closer to Judaism than that which was regarded as the purer form of Monotheism, i.e. Islam. And whereas historically Jews had fared better in most Islamic lands than they had in Christian ones, more recently Christianity has become a greater friend and ally in the wake of fanatic fundamentalist Islam.[6]

Radical tectonic upheavals have necessitated a realignment of forces.[7] Thus politics bolstered by ideology has brought about a remarkable change in the complex relationship between the three great monotheistic religions. And as alliances changed, so, as it were, ideologies were mutating. The forces ranged against one another were no longer Church versus Synagogue,[8] but the geopolitical divide between "East" and "West;" Judaism and Christianity became more clearly aligned against the fundamentalist elements in Islam,[9] with their terrible atrocities. Isis and Al-Kaida have become the enemies of western society which include Judaism, and possibly Israel, in its ranks. Of course, there are also moderate liberal elements in Islam, but their voice is smothered by the extremist elements, and they currently do not constitute a counterbalance to very vocal fundamentalist movements. The sources of this new alliance, while primarily political and sociological, have intensified the recognition of the very special relationship between Judaism and Christianity, between the Old and New Testament, i.e. the Hebrew Bible and the Christian Bible.

No longer an accursed nation,[10] John Paul II could speak of the Jews in glowing terms, declaring, ". . . this extraordinary people continues to bear signs of its divine election."[11]

And in *Notes on the correct way to present the Jews and Judaism in preaching and teaching in the Roman Catholic Church*, from 1982, superssionism was explicitly rejected, thus:

> VI The permanence of Israel (while so many ancient peoples have disappeared without trace) is a historic fact and a sign to be interpreted within God's design. We must in any case rid ourselves of the traditional idea of a people punished, preserved as a living argument for Christian apologetic. It remains a chosen people, "the pure olive on which were grafted the branches of the wild olive which are the gentiles" (John Paul II, 6 March 1962, alluding to Rom, 11: 17–24). . . .

(This, of course, is also a rejection of the "wandering Jew" theme.)

And in August 31, 1985, in the *Theses for Evanston*, being the Second Assembly of the World Council of Churches, (published in *Freiburger Rundbrief* 25–28 August 1984, pp. 26–28), Karl Thieme argued (II:2) that:

> They [i.e. the Jews] can never be definitely rejected because God keeps his word (Hos. II:8f; Rom. 9:11). . . .

340

Endnotes to Chapter 16

1. Or in the words of Arthur Gilbert, in his *Vatican Council and the Jews*, Cleveland and New York, 1968, concerning not only the Vatican Council, but also the Resolutions adopted by the Protestant World Council of Churches and by the Lutherans at an international consultation of the Church and Jews at Logumkloster, Denmark (see ibid. pp. 258–259 notes 1 and 2), where on p. 219 he writes:

> However inadequate, theologically, the statements may seem from a Jewish perspective, there is no gainsaying their profound contribution to a more open atmosphere in the relations between Jews and Christians. The fact that each Church had to travel a labored course in order to achieve its statement reflects accurately on the actual depth of anti-Semitism in our culture. But the fact that such statements were *eventually* issued [my emphasis D.S.] ought to be reassuring. A good will is at work attempting to undo a bitter past.

See further Egal Feldman, *Catholics and Jews in Twentieth-Century America*, Urbana and Chicago, 2001, p. 116, and the whole chapter (pp. 103–125), entitled "Revolt of the Bishops, 1960–1975."

2. So much so that Gilbert could write in 1968 (!), at the end of his book (p. 242):

> God's spirit certainly was present in the Council's deliberations. Protestants and Orthodox Christians and Jews and men of good will everywhere were touched by its achievement. They were moved to explore, each in their own way, their relation to God's purpose and their understanding of His will.
>
> Now, God willing, by the quality of our associations with each other and the courage with which we shall seek to repair the world, we may increase the experience of godliness among men. To be a blessing unto people and a light unto nations is to be Israel. Toward that vocation both Christians and Jews feel themselves called. May we be worthy of our name.

3. We should also bear in mind that there were those who, perhaps mistakenly, identified trinitarianism with tritheism. There were admittedly in early Christianity some "tritheismists," such as John Philipon, John Askunages (mid-6th century), and others, but generally they were regarded as heretics. (See, e.g., Timothy, *The*

341

Reception Haereticorum, (*PG* LXXXVI, col. 61); John of Damascus, *De Fide Orthodoxa*; and cf. A. Harnack, *History of Dogma*, English transl., London, 1894–59, vol. 4, p. 126; James Hastings, *Encyclopaedia of Religion and Ethics*, vol. 9, New York, 1928, s.v. Tritheism, pp. 462b–464a.) We cannot here expand on this complex issue. On the Jewish arguments on the insuperable philosophical difficulties in the notion of trinitarianism, see for example, David Berger, *The Jewish-Christian Debate in the High Middle Ages: A critical Edition of Nizzahon Vetus*, Philadelphia, 1979, pp. 13–14, 49, 51–52, 366–369.

There, in a review article on R. Shlomo Riskin's book *The Living Tree: Studies in Modern Orthodoxy*, which he published in *Jewish Action*, 2016, pp. 56–58, and in his essay in "Jews, Gentiles and the Modern Egalitarian Ethos: Some Tentative Thoughts," apud the Orthodox Forum volume, *Formulating Responses in an Egalitarian Age*, ed. Marc Stern, London, MD, 2005, pp. 83–108, Berger suggested that from *his* perspective, "Christianity can best be characterised as *avodah zarah* [idolatry] in a monotheistic mode," adding that "it is of great importance to recognize that although it is *avodah zarah*, certainly for Jews, there is a chasm separating it from paganism" (*Jewish Actions* ibid. p. 58). He cautions us (ibid.) that:

> It is deeply objectionable to blur, trivialize and even erase the theological dimension of *avodah zarah*, which is the most grievous theological sin in Judaism. Mediaeval Jews did not give up their lives to avoid "illegitimate theology," and it is not at all the case that the majority, let alone the overwhelming majority, of mediaeval decisors did not believe Christianity to be *avodah zara* for born Christians [as Riskin would propose], though many modern ones did take this position. . . .

(See also his article in *Makor Rishon, Musaf Shabbat*, Nov.16, 2012, entitled "*Emunah bi-Reshut ha-Yahid*.")

Though this is undoubtedly a pivotal issue, it is certainly beyond the scope of this study. I myself have delved into it in my forthcoming book on the *Halachic Status of Hinduism*. And as to the argument that "Mediaeval Jews did not give up their lives to avoid illegitimate theology," this touches upon yet another very important ongoing controversy between Avraham Grossman (see in *Kedushat ha-Hayyim ve-Heiruf ha-Nefesh*, ed. Y. Gafni and A. Ravitsky, Jerusalem, 1993, pp. 99–130, article entitled "Shorshav *Shel Kiddush ha-Shem be-Ashkenaz ha-Kedumah,*") and Haym Soloveitchik (see his "Religious Law and Change: The Mediaeval Ashkenazi Example," *AJS Review* 12/2, 1987, pp. 209–210) who wrote:

> Whether one is permitted to suffer voluntary martyrdom is highly questionable, suicide is forbidden beyond question, and the permissibility of murder needs no discussion. Thus if the law were to be followed, the scholars of these communities would have to rule that all martyrs – *qedoshim*, or "holy ones,"

as they were called – were not only not "holy," but were "self killers," and murderers. . . .

As mentioned above, this is an extremely complex issue with a very considerable body of discussion both in the early sources and the later ones. But just to give an inkling of the parameters of the discussion/controversy, I should like to quote parts of the discussion of Rabbi J.D. Bleich, in his recent book *The Philosophic Question of Philosophy, Ethics, Law and Halakhah*, Jerusalem, 1993. In his chapter 3, "Divine Unity in Maimonides, the Tosafists, and the Meiri," he writes as follows: (The discussion relates, of course, to Christianity, but is relevant for one purpose in defining attitude to gentile religious and determining whether they be idolatrous or not.)

> A somewhat different view of Christianity [i.e. that it is not idolatrous] is ascribed to the Tosafists (12th–13th centuries) in their comments on Sanhedrin 63b and Bekhorot 25, (with parallel statements in Rosh Sanhedrin 7:3: Rabbenu Yerucham, Sefer Adam Ve-Havah 17:5). A literal reading indicates that they hold that acceptance of a doctrine of *shittuf* (association) is permitted to non-Jews. The doctrine involves a belief in the "Creator of the heavens," but links a belief in the Creator with a belief in some other being or entity. The term *shittuf* is not uncommon in medieval philosophical literature and connotes plurality in the Godhead, (see David Kaufmann, *Geschichte der Attributen Lehre*, Gotha 1877, p. 460 note 148). *Tosafot* refer explicitly to the gentiles of their day, and the most obvious example of *shittuf*, clearly the doctrine which *Tosafot* seek to legitimize for non-Jews, is Trinitarianism.

He continues to say that "this interpretation of the *Tosafot* is by not means universally accepted," citing the *Noda bi-Yehudah* (*Tinyana, Yoreh Deah* no.148), but concludes that

> It is probably correct to say that the majority of latter-day authorities interpret Tosafot more broadly as declaring that *shittuf* does not constitute idolatry for Noahides. (*Sha'ar Efraim*, no. 24; *Me'il Tzedakah*, no. 22; *Teshuvot ve-Shav ha-Kohen*, no. 38; *Teshuvot Hadashot le-Rabbeinu Akiva Eger* [Jerusalem, 5738], pp. 164–66; *Pri Megadim, Yoreh De'ah, Siftei Da'at* 65:11; idem, *Orah Hayyim, Eshel Avraham* 156:2; and Mahatzit ha-Shekel, Orah Hayyim 156:2.)

(Here we may add the following references to be examined: M.M. Kasher, *Torah Shelemah, Yitro*, vol. 16, New York, 1955, pp. 230–233; David Tzvi Mecklenburg, *Ha-Ktav ve-ha-Kabbalah*, New York, 1946 [ed. Princ. Leipzig 1839], Deut. pp. 7–8.)

See continuation of his discussion (pp. 38–39), which I shall not quote, but leave to the reader to persue with interest, for here again we have strayed far beyond the parameters of this study.

But returning to the subject of trinitarianism, it was argued, for example, if the

Son alone was incarnated, this contradicts the Christian assertion that the persons are inseperable, and if they were all incarnated, "then who was in heaven all that time in as much as they are inseparable?" (ibid. p. 366).

However, we should also note a notion in Kabbalistic Judaism that has striking similarity to the Christian mystery of the triune Godhead, i.e. trinity, namely the "tripatilte soul." Thus, Rabbi Mosheh de Leon, in his *Sefer ha-Nefesh ha-Hachamah*, Basel 1708, cited in Y. Tishby, *Wisdom of the Zohar*, vol. 2, p. 711 note 202, writes:

> The Mystery of the Soul is that it is divided into three parts, but joined together in a single unity. Even though they appear to be separated from one another because of their separate names, they really form one mystery: *nefesh*, *ruah* and *neshamah*. . . . They are indeed a single mystery without division.

See further Antony F. Buzzard and Charles F. Hunting, *The Doctrine of the Trinity: Christianity's Self-Inflicted Wound*, London, 1998; Patric Navas, *Divine Truth or Human Tradition, A Reconsideration of the Roman Catholic Protestant Doctrine of the Trinity in the Light of the Hebrew and Christian Scriptures*, Bloomington, 2007.

An attempt to find a "logical" solution to the trinity conundrum was made by Antti Laato, *Monotheism*, the *Trinity and Mysticism: A Semiotic Approach to Jewish-Christian Encounter*, Frankfurt am Main, 1999.

4. For Roman-pagan criticisms of the doctrine of Virgin birth, see John Granyer Cook, *The Interpretation of the New Testament in Greco-Roman Paganism*, Peabody Mass. 2002, pp. 28–31 (Celsus); 137–138 (Porphyry, Philosabbatios), 238–239 (Mecarius), etc. And on trinitarianism (see below), p. 330 (Julian). It is interesting to read what the Jewish apostate Johannes Pfefferkorn (1469–1529) wrote in his *Der Juden* Spiegel (first German ed. Cologne 1507), English translation *The Jews' Mirror*, by Ruth I. Cape, Temple Arizona 2011, sect. 1.2.4, p. 49:

> Fourthly, there are some Jews who would agree that Christ was God and man, but by no means do they want to believe in Mary's virginity or even hear anything about it. Moreover, they assert that it is not natural to give birth to a child as a virgin. And secretly they say among themselves that Mary was outlawed with other such abominable words they revile the noble and blessed Mother and Queen of Heaven, Mary, from whom arises all our blessedness. . . .

The translator adds (ibid. note 25):

> In anti-Jewish sermons and pamphlets, offending Mary was held to be a worse crime than desecrating the sacred host, ritual murder of Christians, or well poisoning. (Cf. Heike A. Oberman, "Zwischen Agitation Und Reformation: Die Flugschriften als Judenspiegel," apud *Flugschriften also Massenmedium der Reformationzeit*, ed. M.J. Köhler, Stuttgart 1981, p. 282.) Her virginity

played an important role in Christian disputes with the Jews. In just about every discussion the Jews would point out that the "Vulgate" text of Isaiah 7:14, which says that a woman interpreted as Mary will conceive and give birth to a son, was translated into Latin wrongly, since while the word "virgo" indeed means virgin, the original Hebrew term "*alma*" has only the connotation of "young woman." Usually, the Christian side would curse such objections and suggest that Jews ought to know about Mary's virginity from the Old Testament. Cf. Oberman ibid. p. 281.

On Pfefferkorn's battle against Judaism, see Erica Rammel, *The Case Against Johann Reuchlin: Religions and Social Controversy in Sixteenth-Century Germany*. Toronto, Buffalo, London, 2002, pp. 3–13, 63–67. In Pfefferkorn's *The Enemy of the Jews* Augsburg 1509, he again refers to the Mary issue. There too he accuses the "faithless Jews" of calling Jesus *mamzer ben ha-nidah*, "an illegitimate son of an unclean women," and Mary as *zonah* and *temeiah*, "prostitute" and "an unclean woman" (Rammel ibid. p. 54).

This, of course, was also the view of the Unitarians, an anti-Trinitarian movement which emerged in the 16th century. This movement sometimes called Socianism, after Faustus Socianus, who with Loelius in the sixteenth century developed this new form of anti-Trinitarianism. At that time people were being burned for this heresy, (e.g., George van Paris in 1551, and Jhon Bocher, the "Maid Of Kent," etc.). Erasmus in his publication of the Greek text of the New Testament (1516) omitted the famous Trinitarian verse in John 5:37. In the 18th century this process of theological change was further promoted by John Priestley (1733–1804), and Thomas Belsham (1750–1829), and in 1791 the "Unitarian Society for Promoting Christian Knowledge and Practice by Distribution of Books" was founded; its leaders were the aforementioned and Theophilus Lindsey (1723–1808). The basis of the movement was the belief in the proper unity of God, and of the simple humanity of Jesus Christ, in opposition to the Trinitarian doctrine of Three Persons in the Diety, and to the Arian hypothesis of a created Maker and Preserver of the world. They argued at length that Trinitarianism has no biblical foundation, is inconsistent with its clear teaching, is contradictory or unintelligible, or even idolatrous, having been, as it were, illegally imported from Platonic philosophy.

Indeed, minister Stephan Nye (1648–1719), in his *A Brief History of the Unitarians, Called also Socinians, In Four Letters, Written to a Friend* (1691) p. 9, arguing polemically against mainstream trinitarian views, wrote:

> But we would not, say they, trouble ourselves at the Non-sense of this Doctrine, if it did not impose false Gods on us; by advancing two to be Gods, who are not so: and rob also the One true God of the Honour due to him, and of which he is jealous.

(Cited from *Stanford Encyclopedia of Philosophy, Unitarianism* 2:3.)

In the 19th century, American Unitarianism morphed into Transcedentalism and Universalism, even accepting theism as an option for its congregants. By the 20th century, American Unitarianism was largely viewed as a version of theological liberalism or simply not a form of Christianity, and it is now, in its various forms, mainly rejected by main-stream Christian theologists.

Returning to Virgin birth, see ibid. 15, 44, 301–302, 350–354, and especially on "The Jewish revulsion at the notion of God in a woman's stomach" (p. 350), these are but two of the many examples from one book out of the very many on Jewish-Christian polemics literature. But not only the Jews found these notions unacceptable.

Even in this orthodox Christianity a more "modernist" approach has occasionally be voiced. Thus, in the Introduction to the Report of the Commission on Christian Doctrine, entitled *Doctrine In the Church of England* from 1938, the Archbishop of York writes (ibid. p. 12):

> In view of my own responsibility in the Church I think it right here to affirm that I wholeheartedly accept as historical facts the Birth of our Lord from a Virgin Mother and the Resurrection of his physical body from death and the tomb. But I fully recognise the position of those who sincerely affirm the reality of our Lord's Incarnation without accepting one or both of these two events as actual historical occurrences, regarding the records rather as parables than as history, a presentation of spiritual truth in narrative form.

Cf. Cook ibid. pp. 28–29: The claims about Jesus' virgin birth were simply incredible to Celsus. . . . Celsus summarizes the charges: "He made up . . . the story of virgin birth. . . ." (ibid. 1.28, ed. Koetschau 79, 21–28).

The passage in Origen's *Contra Celsum* 1:28 is as follows:

> He [Celsus] accuses him [Jesus] of having "invented his birth from a virgin," and upbraids him with being "born in a certain Jewish village, of a poor woman of the country, who gained her subsistence by spinning, and who was turned out of doors by her husband, a carpenter by trade, because she was convicted of adultery; that after being driven away by her husband, and wandering about for a time, she disgracefully gave birth to Jesus, an illegitimate child, who having hired himself out as a servant in Egypt on account of his poverty, and having there acquired some miraculous powers, on which the Egyptians greatly pride themselves, returned to his own country, highly elated on account of them, and by means of these proclaimed himself a God."

And cf. ibid. 1:32. Origen died in 251. See further M. Niehoff, "A Jewish Critique of Christianity from Second-Century Alexandria: Revisiting the Jews in Contra Celsum," *Journal of Early Christian Studies* 21/2, 2013, pp. 151–175. Similarly

Macarius Apocriticus 4.22, Cook ibid. pp. 338. And Tertullian, in his *On Spectacles* 305–306, speaks of "the carpenter's son, the son of prostitution" (*quaesetuaria*). . . . And similar such terms were used in mediaeval Jewish sources, such as *ben-ha-niddah, ben ha-zimah*, child of a menstruant, child of licentiousness, (A.M. Haberman, *Sefer Gezerot Ashkenaz ve-Tzorfat*, Jerusalem, 1945, pp. 24, 31, 101, 104 etc.) ; J.R. Woolf, *The Fabric of Religious Life in Mediaeval Ashkenaz*, Leiden, Boston, 2015, p. 193). And, of course, this is elaborated upon in *Toldot Yeshu*. See John G. Gager, ibid. pp. 121–122, 178–179, and 117–138 on *Toldot Yeshu*.

It may further be noted that in mediaeval ecclesiastical dramas it is the Jew who makes such arguments. Thus, for example, in the German *Christmas Play of Benediktheuren*, dating from about 1225, in Latin, we read how:

> The Jews are led by the high priest, the *arch-synagogus*, and stand facing the prophets under the leadership of St. Augustine. The subject of the controversy is Jesus's virgin birth, the possibility of which is strongly disputed by the *arch-synagogus* who makes use of derisive words, forced humor, grimaces, and crude jokes. According to the stage directions in the text, the Jews employ primarily derision and witticisms, whereas Augustine replies "in a cautious and polite tone. . . ."
>
> The high priest and his Jews are to shout loudly when they hear the prophecies. The high priest shall then imitate the behavior of a Jew by the manner in which he holds his cane, nudges his companions, moves his head and entire body, and stamps his foot on the ground, while angrily saying to his companions:
>
> "Tell me what the hypocrite says
> This whitewashed wall
> Tell me what the scoundrel declares
> Who is a stranger to truth. . . .
> As I hear, those people
> Come to this conclusion:
> A son must be born by
> A maiden without a man.
> Such great foolishness makes
> Those people void of wisdom;
> They proclaim that the camel
> Is descended from the ox. . . ."
> Later, the high priest says to St. Augustine:
> "The fact that this virgin
> Gives birth to a child without a man
> Is a dishonor to nature
> So that it becomes irrational."

The controversy remains undecided. The Jews insist on *res neganda*, the prophets on *res Miranda*. Then Augustine proclaims the birth of Christ, and the actual Christmas play begins.

(Cited from Wolfgang S. Seiferth, *Synagogue and Church in the Middle Ages: Two Symbols in Art and Literature*, [transl. from the *German, Synagoge und Kirche im Mittelalter*, Munich 1959], New York, 1970, pp. 92–93; referring to K. Langosch, *Geistliche Spiele*, Darmstadt 1954, and W. Creizenach, *Geschichte des neueren Dramas*, 2nd edition, vol. 1, Halle 1911, p. 90.)

Even contemporary Catholic theologians have struggled with the historicity of virginal birth. Thus, the very highly respected Father Raymond Brown, a member of the recently newly constituted Roman Pontifical Biblical Commission set up by Pope Paul VI, published a book in 1973, entitled "The Virginal Conception and Bodily resurrection of Jesus," (Paulist Press, New York, Paranius, Toronto), listing the "Scriptural Arguments Against Historicity" (of the Virginal Conception of Jesus, pp. 53–61 – as indeed he did with the issue of Resurrection (ibid. pp. 69 et seq.). In his conclusion he writes (pp. 66–67):

> My Judgement in conclusion, is that the totality of *scientifically controllable* evidence leaves an unresolved problem a conclusion that should not disappoint since I used the word problem in my title – and that is why I want to induce an honest, ecumenical discussion of it. Part of the difficulty is that past discussions have often been conducted by people who were interpreting ambiguous evidence to favor positions already taken.

But he also writes there:

> I would urge, however, that this discussion be persued in an atmosphere of pastoral responsibility.

And ibid. in note 117, he reveals his personal feeling with greatly commendable transparent honesty as follows:

> In particular, as a Roman Catholic whose biblical studies have led him to appreciate all the more the importance of a teaching Church, I cannot resolve the problem independently of the question of authority raised in Section II. I am not afraid that an honest discussion of the virginal conception will lead to a traumatic choice between fidelity to modern exegesis and fidelity to a teaching Church, provided that both the Bible and tradition are subjected to intelligent historical criticism to find out exactly what was meant and the degree to which it was affirmed. Inevitably, however, openness to discussion will be misrepresented as denial of tradition.

The virginity of Mary was a target for derision towards which the barbs of Jewish criticism were aimed. In the considerable *Toldot Yeshu* literature, the earliest versions of which probably go back to even before the 8th century, a complete normative episode was created, which includes lust for an innocent maiden, seduction, deception, a cuckolded husband, and a pregnancy conceded by an adulteress through great cunning. There Jesus was reborn as a "bastard son of a menstruant," an epittet that has stuck for many a generation in the Jewish world. See the summarizing article by Eli Yassif, "The Jewish Jesus Story," *Tablet Magazine*, December 23, 2016, pp. 1–6.

Martin Luther in his pamphlet, *The Jews and their Lies* first published in 1543, and republished by the Christian Nationalist Crusade, St. Louis, Missouri, (n.d.)., pp. 35–36, repeats this accusations:

> Thus they call Him (Jesus) the child of a whore and His mother Mary, a whore, whom she had in adultery with a smith. Sebastianus Muenster also points out in his Biblia, that there is said to be a poisonous Rabbi who does not call dear mother "Maria" but "Haria," a heap of mud. And who knows what more they have among themselves of which we know nothing.
>
> And cf. ibid. p. 64: . . . They call our Blessed Virgin Mary a harlot, and her Holy son a bastard. . . .

In 1937 the Nazis displayed this pamphlet during their Nuremberg rallies, and the city of Nuremberg presented a first edition to Julius Streicher, the Catholic editor of Der Stürmer. The newspaper called it the most anti-Semitic tract ever published.

It is interesting to read a rationalist in philosophical "refutation" of the notion of virgin birth by Hasdai Crescas (c. 1340–c. 1410–1411). In his *The Refutation of the Christian Principles* (*Bittul Ikarei ha-Notzrim*, probably written c. 1390), transl. Daniel J. Lasker, New York, 1992, chapter 6, pp. 57–58, we read as follows:

> We have already explained clearly in the Preface the Christian belief, namely that the virginity was neither rent nor destroyed at any time, neither before the birth, nor during the birth, nor after the birth.
>
> The argument which contradicts this is very evident and follows from an obviously clear presupposition, namely that it is impossible for a body to be without dimensions. This is so since dimensions are part of the definition [of body]. A body is that which has three dimensions, namely, length, width, and depth; the definition is congruent with the thing defined. We then say: The sides of a virgin's womb adhere to each other and have no dimensions between them. If a body were to pass between these sides, there would be dimensions, namely the dimensions of the passing body, and it would follow, therefore, that there were dimensions between [the sides]. But it has already been posited that there were no dimensions between [the sides]. This is an impossible inconsistency. . . .

Endnotes to Chapter 16

(See continuation and translator's notes, pp. 116–117. The following chapter deals with transubstantiation.)
Needless to say, such criticisms would make little impression on his Christian counterparts, who saw Virgin Birth as a mystery, not to be analyzed logically. Here we may also cite, en passant, A.K. Coomaraswamy's note in his *Elements of Buddhist Iconography*, Cambridge Mass., 1935, p. 72 note 46:

> In Buddhist legend, the Nativity has been so far rationalized that no great stress is laid on virgin birth, though both conception and birth are in other respects miraculous. As to the virgin birth, "on n'a jamais cru que Çâkyamouni fût né des oeuvres de Çuddhodana," [Louis] de la Vallée-Poussin, [1869–1938], *Le Dogme et la Philosophie du Bouddhisme*, [Paris 1930], p. 57, and his notes. Indian tradition, however, knows a virginity of the Mother, Aditi, calling her *anarvā, apravitā, kumārī, mātā yuvatī, kanyā, yosā*, etc. An ultimate "virginity" of both parents is indeed a metaphysical necessity, for the twin poles of being, the unmoving centres of the Principal and World Wheels, act only by their presence and not by local movement: "He" is undiminished by his largesse, "She" by her parturition.

For other forms of "magical fertilization," see earlier on the same note, as follows:

> In *Rg Veda*, I, 164, 8, if we accept the interpretation of Sāyana, we have "the germ (*garbha*) was in the cloud (*vrjanī*); but it would be more natural to take *vrjanī* as "holy site," hortus inclusus (cf. *vrajah . . . sapariśrayah, Brhadāranyaka Up.*, VI. 4, 23, where cosmic analogies are applied to human generation). In any case, the Mother (Earth) is here associated (*yukta*) with the Father (Heaven) and it is made quite clear that she is fertilized by an essence that can only have fallen from Heaven as rain; "she the shy one was penetrated by the tincture (*rasa*)," cf. *Rg Veda*, VII, 101, 3, "The Father's juices (*payah*) grasped (*prati-grbhnāti*) the Mother, thereby are increased both Father and Son," *Rg Veda*, I, 164, 51, "the rain-clouds (*parjanyāh*) animate (*jinvanti*) the Earth," and similar passages. It is the descent of the *rasa*-bearing rains that is represented in the Gaja-Laksmī composition, which is rather a Conception than a Nativity. But that Conception, being of Life universally, may well have been thought of as Siddhârtha's, whose name signifies "Accomplishment of Purpose." The notion of impregnation by a cloud or rain is present even in the more familiar Buddhist Conceptions, where the Bodhisattva descends in the form of a white elephant, though this is rationalized by calling it a "dream." Cf. the elephant Paccaya, of sky-faring descent, connatural rain-giving talisman of the Bodhisattva in the *Vessantara Jātaka*, which is certainly not a tale of human happenings (incidentally, *vessa* = *viśva* rather than *vaiśya*; the "*vessa*-street" is not the merchant's street, but "Everyman's Way").

And see further Julius Morgenstern, *Some Significant Antecedents of Christianity*, Leiden 1966, pp. 85–90. And we may also call attention to this same theme in Chinese Mythology, where in *The Classic of Poetry* from c. 600 B.C.E., poem 245, we read how Chiang Yuan gave miraculous birth to "Our People." See Anne Birrell, *Chinese Mythology: An Introduction*, Baltimore and London, 1993, chapter 5, entitled "Miraculous Birth," pp. –129.

5. On the traditional understanding of this transubstantiation, see Michael O'Carroll, *Corpus Christi*, Collegeville Minnesota, 1988, pp. 185–200, s.v. Transubstantiation. Rejected by the Lutherans, see Cook, ibid. pp. 202–205, citing Macarius Magnus' *Apocriticus*, probably from Asia Minor during the last quarter of the fourth century (ibid. pp. 170–171). The pagan questioner in that work finds Jesus' teaching in John 6:54, namely that "Unless you eat of my flesh and drink my blood, you have no life in you," utterly repellent. He states in very lucid terms that:

> . . . this statement is not merely beast-like and absurd, but is more absurd than any absurdity, and more beast-like than any fashion of a beast, that a man should taste human flesh, and drink the blood of members of the same tribe and race, and that by doing this he should have eternal life. For tell me, if you do this, what excess of savagery do you introduce into life? What kind of evil more under curse than this defilement could you invent? Ears cannot bear it. . . . (*Apocritias* 3:15; Cook ibid. p. 203).

See continuation ibid. Jews did not necessarily see the act of communion as a form of cannibalism, but rather disbelieved the notion of transubstantiation.

It is interesting to see how an Eastern thinker understands the notion of transubstantiation. For so writes Ananda Kentish Coomaraswamy in his article "Immitation, Expression, and Participation," (first published in *Journal of Aesthetics and Art Criticism*, III 1945, reprinted in *The Door in the Sky: Coomaraswamy on Myth and Meaning*, ed. Rama P. Coomaraswamy, Princeton New Jersey, 1997, p. 69):

> We are still familiar with the notion of a transubstantiation only in the case of the Eucharistic meal in its Christian form; here, by ritual acts, i.e., by the sacerdotal art, with the priest as officiating artist, the bread is made to be the body of the God; yet no one maintains that the carbohydrates are turned into proteins, or denies that they are digested like any other carbohydrates, for that would mean that we thought of the mystical body as a thing actually cut up into pieces of flesh; and yet the bread is changed in that it is no longer mere bread, but now bread with a meaning, with which meaning or quality we can therefore communicate by assimilation, the bread now feeding both body and soul at one and the same time.

Finally, it should be noted that the concept of transubstantiation is first mentioned by Hildebert de Lavardin, Archbishop of Tours, in the 9th century, although the concept is already brought foreward in the 9th century by Pascharius Robertus. It was ecclesiastically established on November 11, 1215, at the Fourth Lateran Synod. (See Charles Habermann, "Fourth Lateran Council (1215)," in the *Catholic Encyclopedia* [1913].)

6. See, for example, Arieh Stav, *Peace: The Arabian Caricature: A Study of Anti-Semitic Imagery*, New York, Jerusalem, 1999, especially chapter 7, pp. 113–129, entitled "There is a Definite Similarity between Islam and Nazism," and cf. ibid. p. 134. He writes:

> By Western esthetic standards, the imagery conveyed in Arab caricature is, above all, perceived as little more than primitive scribbling that evokes revulsion; the observer is disgusted by the spectacle of a low-grade imitation of *Der Stürmer* serving as the message of an entire culture in the latter part of the twentieth century.

Indeed, what is particularly striking is the extent to which the earlier Christian/Nazi stereotype of the Jew has been wholly adopted by the Arab-Muslim judeo-phobe. Not only do we see in their caricatures the same physiognomic characteristics described earlier on, the hooked nose, the thick lips, the bulging eyes, but even certain Christian themes have been recast in a new political context. See, e.g., p. 236, fig. 4, entitled "The Blood of a Palestinian Child, A Gift for Mother's Day" (*A Dastur*, Jordan, March 22, 1994), which had echoes of Simon of Trent, and perhaps even more p. 234, fig. 2, entitled "Mrs. Shamir: 'Why are you throwing out the girl's blood before you use it to bake matzoth,'" (*Al-Bian*, Bahrain, March 18, 1990), a "reincarnation" of the "Blood Libel." And on p. 203, fig. 4, entitled "The Zionist Devil," (*A-Dastur*, Jordan, September 30, 1994), the "Zionist Devil" Jew has all the requisite physiognomic characteristics, plus the Devil's horns.

For a similar study relating to the Nazi and Soviet period, see Yaakov Guri, *Jewish Hatred as Reflected in Caricature*, Tel Aviv, 1986. And see also the basic study on anti-Semitic caricature by Edward Fuchs, *Die Juden in der Karikatur*, München, 1921. This book appeared before the publication of *Der Stürmer*, so the Nazi caricature as developed in Julius Streicher's publication could not appear in Fuch's classic study. Had it been published a year or so later, it would have been greatly "enriched!"

But, not only in pictorial sources do we find the resurgence of mediaeval Christian/Nazi anti-Jewish themes, but also, of course, in literary sources. See, for instance, what Fatma Abdullah Mamud, one of *Al-Akhbar* regular columnists writes of the Jews, that they:

The Blood of a Palestinian Child, A Gift for Mothers' Day. *A-Dastur*, Jordan, March 22, 1994.

. . . are accursed in heaven and on earth. They are accursed from the day the human race was created and from the day their mothers bore them. . . .

These accursed ones are a catastrophe for the human race. They are the virus of the generation, doomed to a life of humiliation and wretchedness until Judgment Day. . . .

Finally, they are accursed, fundamentally, because they are the plague of the generation and the bacterium of all time. Their history always was and always will be stained with treachery, falseness, and lying. ("Accursed Forever and Ever," *Al-Akhbar*, April 29, 2002, cited by Gabriel Sohoenfeld, in his *The Return of Anti-Semitism*, San Francisco, 2004, p. 13.)

And yet another columnist, in the same newspaper, Mohamet Kasanein Heikal, after stating that Jews are the "most vile criminals on the face of the earth," gives "thanks to Hitler, of blessed memory" for what he did to the Jews; however, Muslims "do have a complaint against him [Hitler], for his revenge on them was not enough." (Schoenfeld ibid. citing Foreward to the Arabic editions of Garandy's *The Founding Myths of Modern Israel*, Cairo, 1998, translated by Abdullah M. Sindi, and printed in *Journal for Historical Review* 19/6, Nov. / Dec. 2000.)

This from two of Egypt's columnists. While in Saudi Arabia's major outlet *Al-Riyadh* we find a variation on the old blood-libel motif, but not, as usually relating to making the Passover *matzah*, but here to making pastry for the annual Purim celebration! Thus:

The Jewish people must obtain human blood so that their clerics can prepare the holiday pastries. In other words, the practice cannot be carried out as required if human blood is not spilled!!

. . . For this holiday, the victim must be a mature adolescent who is, of course, a non-Jew – that is, a Christian or a Muslim. His blood is taken and dried into granules. The cleric blends these granules into the pastry dough; they can also be saved for the next holiday. . . .

Let us now examine how the victims' blood is spilled. For this, a needle-studded barrel is used; this is a kind of barrel, about the size of the human body, with extremely sharp needles set in it on all sides. [These needles] pierce the victim's body, from the moment he is placed in the barrel.

These needles do the job, and the victim's blood drips from him very slowly. Thus, the victim suffers dreadful torment – torment that affords the Jewish vampires great delight as they carefully monitor every detail of the bloodshedding with pleasure and love that are difficult to comprehend.

After this barbaric display, the Jews take the spilled blood, in the bottle set in the bottom [of the needle-studded barrel], and the Jewish cleric makes his coreligionists completely happy on their holiday when he serves them the pastries in which human blood is mixed.

There is another way to spill the blood: The victim can be slaughtered as a sheep is slaughtered, and his blood collected in a container. Or, the victim's veins can be slit in several places, letting his blood drain from his body. (Schoenfeld ibid. pp. 17–18, citing Dr. Umayna Ahmad al-Jalahma, "The Jewish Holiday of Purim," *Al-Ridadh* March 10, 2002.)

Incidentally in *Al-Akhbar* of March 25, 2001, Dr. Mahmoud al-Said al-Kurdi tells us that Jews made the *matzos* of Atonement Day (!) kneaded with blood from a non-Jew (Schoenfeld ibid. p. 14).

Further evidence of the revival of the "blood libel" in modern Islam has been collected by Y. Harkabi, in his *Arab Attitudes to Israel*, Jerusalem, 1972, pp. 270–276, in a section (8) entitled "The Blood Libel." On pp. 270–275 he writes:

A book entirely devoted to this question has been published in Egypt, and it might be regarded as a curiosity it if were the only one of its kind and were it not for the auspices under which it was published. It was issued in a series of information pamphlets, "National Books" No.184, 1962, 164pp. In the list of books published by the UAR Ministry of Education, *al-Nashra al-Misriyya lil-Maiba'at*, it is given the number 3931. On its cover, the book bears the symbol of the Egyptian institute for Publications, with a line above: "Selections from Radio and Television." The book, which is called Human Sacrifices in the Talmud (*al-Dhaba ih al-Bashariyya al-Talmudiya*), is a reprint of an old work issued by Habib Faris in Cairo in 1890. The fact that such a book should be found suitable for "national guidance" is shocking. It was seen through the press by 'Abd al-'Ati Jalāl, who checked the text and added linguistic notes on the differences between Arabic idiom in 1890 and today. . . .

This is not the only, or the last, review of the blood libel by the Arabs. 'Abd al-Mun'im Shamis, in pp. 96–103 of his book *Secrets of Zionism*, published in Cairo in 1957 as No.1 of the Policy Books, deals with the subject, going into greater detail on the two Damascus cases, quoting Jewish confessions and so forth. He regards the use of blood for ritual purposes as part of the crimes of Zionism.

In a book called *The End of Israel*, published in 1960 in Cairo by the Arab Printing and Publicity Company, affiliated to the Voice of the Arabs (the director of which, Ahmad Sa'īd, wrote an introduction to the book), Abu-al-Majd quotes the alleged evidence of a "Rabbi Taunitus," a convert to Christianity, who testified:

"The Zionists believe that Christian blood is essential for the performance of several religious rites:"

Surprising statements are made by Tall in his book *The Danger of World Jewry to Islam and Christianity*, published by Dār al-Qalam, and affiliate of the National Publishing Institute in 1964. He returns to the blood libel repeatedly, devoting a 28-page chapter (pp. 77–105) to the subject. In the introduction he explains:

"The God of the Jews is not content with animal sacrifices; he must be appeased with human sacrifices. Hence the Jewish custom of slaughtering children and extracting their blood to mix it with their *matzot* on Passover" (p. 20).

In his summary he writes that thousands of children disappear every year, and:

"These are mostly the victims of Jewish religious rites and their blood sinks into the bellies of the Jews together with the *matzot* of their four festivals" (p. 104).

Na'nā'a also uses the blood libel in his *Zionism in the Sixties. The Vatican and the Jews*, published by the official Egyptian Institute for Publications in 1964, and bearing its symbol. After discussing the prohibition of the baking of *matzot* in the Soviet Union, he continues:

The kneading of Passover *matzot* with Gentile blood is not a groundless charge against the Jews. We have in our possession hundreds of proofs (*sha-wahid*), from East and West, in ancient history and modern times, of this barbaric traditional Jewish custom. The subject of this book does not permit me to expatiate on this matter, therefore I shall be content with the confirmation (*uhbat*) of the case published by the news agencies and referred to in The Jewish Chronicle of May 17, 1963 (p. 113).

> *The Jewish Chronicle* indeed refers to a Russian case in which a Jew was accused of sucking the blood of a child, but Na'na'a, despite his enthusiasm for facts, deliberately ignores the continuation of the episode and actions taken by the Soviet Government to counter the blood libel, including the allegations in the case in question.
>
> The list of Arab books dealing with this charge has not been closed. Nuwayhid devotes a section of his book *The Protocols of the Elders of Zion*, Beirut, 1967, affirming that this is indeed a custom among the Jews.
>
> Another book dealing with the blood libel is Iliyā al-Rus: *World Judaism and its Continuous War Against Christianity*, Beirut, 1964.

In a particularly horrific passage, under the heading "Israel Blood Bank Equipped with Arab blood" Na'nā'a tells a story:

> Of a young Arab who reached a certain Arab country from Israel and collapsed in a faint as soon as he arrived. The youth told how he had been held in an Israeli prison and compelled to give frequent blood donations in larger quantities than those medically permissible. This, he said, was a regular routine in the Israeli prisons for Arab offenders, for Israel did not care if they died or fell dangerously ill when they left prison as a result of loss of blood. Na'nā'a appealed to Bishop Hakīm, head of the Greek Catholic Church in Israel, to investigate and to submit his conclusions to the Vatican (pp. 282–286; Harkabi p. 346).

See further *NGOS, Antisemitism and Government Funding: NGO Monitor's Report to the 2015 Global Forum on Antisemitism, NGO Monitor*, Jerusalem, 2015, pass. Does all this not sound familiar? They resonate and reverberate of the ancient culumnies. And these are but the minimum samplings of what is a great body of virulent literature, as demonstrated by Schoenfeld in his chapter on "The Islamic Strain," in his book *The Return of Anti-Semitism*, pp. 7–56. And in *The Legacy of Islamic Antisemitism*, edited by Andrew C. Bostom, Amherst, New York, 2008, there is an extensive collection of documentation testifying to the long history of Muslim anti-Semitism, demolishing the myth that it is a twentieth century European import. However, in our times it does make ample use of European Judaeophobic motifs, adding apparently some ones of their own, such as Jews descending from becoming apes and swine etc. (based on *Quran* 5:60–65; see Bostom p. 223, and p. 225 note 13, citing *Tabari* 4, p. 293; also Aluma Solnick's article on "Descendants of Apes, Pigs and Other Animals," ibid. pp. 663–640). And see further in Harkabi ibid. pp. 263 et seq. section (7) entitled "'Islamization of Jew-Hatred;" Yossef Bodansky: Islamic Anti-Semitism as a *Political Instrument*, Houston, Texas and Shaarei Tikva, 1999.

On the lowly and devilish status of apes in medieval times, see H. W. Janson, *Apes and Ape Lore in the Middle Ages and the Renaissance*, London, 1952, chapter

1, pp. 13–21, entitled "Figura Diaboli"; chapter 2, entitled "The Ape as the Sinner," pp. 24–72; chapter 4, "The Ape and the Fall of Man," pp. 107–144.

I think that this is the place to point to at least some of the roots of what we would call radical Islam. For classical Moslem sources quite unequivocably mandate punishment of death for apostasy: death by the sword, by burning or by maiming and mutilating to death, such as chopping off hands and feet. See, for example II 217, as interpreted by Al-Shafii, (died 820 C.E.), Al-Thalabi, Al-Khazan and Al-Razi. Even more explicit is *Sura* IV.89, again explicated by Baydawi (died c. 1315–1316), and Ibn Kathin quoting al-Suddi (died 745). (See S. Zwemer, *The Law of Apostacy in Islam*, New York, 1924, pp. 34–35; Ibn Warraq, *Virgins? What Virgins? And other Essays*, Amherst, New York, 2009, pp. 322–325, 503–504.) According to the Shafiites also apostacy from other religions is punishable by death, such as if a Jew became a Christian, or vice-versa (see T.W. Junyboll "Apostacy," apud *Encyclopaedia of Ethics and Religion*, ed. Hastings, vol. 1, New York, 1928, p. 626). This is, of course, contrary to the *Universal Declaration of Human Rights* of 1948, which explicitly states that:

> Everyone has the right to freedom of thought, conscience and religion; this right includes freedom to change his religion or belief, and freedom either alone or in community with others and in public or private, to manifest his religion or belief in teaching practice, worship and observance.

Many Muslim countries objected strongly to the clause regarding the right to change one's religion, and various Islamic human rights declarations are purposely vague on this issue (Ibn Warraq ibid. pp. 326–327).

Furthermore, according to Islamic thought humankind is divided into two categories – Muslims and non-Muslims. Muslims are members of the Islamic community, the *umma*, who possess territories in the *Dar-al-Islam*, the Land of Islam. Non-Muslims are the *Harbi*, people of *Dar al-Harb*, the Land of Warfare – any country belonging to the infidels that has not been subdued by Islam. Nonetheless, it is destined to pass into Islamic jurisdiction either through conversion or by war (*harb*). All acts of war are permitted in the *Dar al-Harb*, and after it has been subjugated the *Harbi* became prisoners of war. This is part of the doctrine of *jihad*, which R. Peters, in his *Jihad in Classical and Modern Islam: A Reader*, Princeton, 1996, p. 3, summarizes as follows (rejecting modern apologists who interpret the term as only referring to *defensive* war, etc.):

> The doctrine of Jihad, as laid down in the works on Islamic Law, developed out of the Koranic prescriptions and the example of the Prophet and the first caliphs, which is recorded in the *Hadith*. The crux of the doctrine is the existence of one single Islamic state, ruling the entire *umma* [Muslim community]. It is the duty of the *umma* to expand the territory of this state in order to bring

357

as many people under its rule as possible. The ultimate aim is to bring the whole earth under the sway of Islam and to extirpate unbelief: "Fight them until there is no persecution and the religion is God's entirely." (*Sura* II:193; VIII:39). Expansionist jihad is a collective duty (*fard ala al-kifaya*), which is fulfilled if a sufficient number of people take part in it. If this is not the case, the whole *umma* [Muslim community] is sinning.

Furthermore, Peters (ibid. pp. 29–43), quotes Averroes (*al-Bidayat*) as saying:

According to the majority of scholars, the compulsory nature of the jihad is founded on *Sura* II:216: "Prescribed for you is fighting, though it is hateful to you." The obligation to participate in the jihad applies to adult, free men who have the means at their disposal to go to war and who are healthy. Scholars agree that all polytheists should be fought. This is founded on *Sura* VIII:39: "Fight them until there is no persecution and the religion is God's entirely." Most scholars agree that, in his dealing with captives, various policies are open to the Imam. He may pardon them, enslave them, kill them, or release them either on ransom or as dhimmi [non-Muslim, second class subject of the Islamic state], in which latter case the released captive is obliged to pay poll-tax (*jizya*). *Sura* VIII:67: "It is not for any Prophet to have prisoners until he make wide slaughter in the land," as well as the occasion when this verse was revealed [viz. the captives of Badr] would prove that it is better to kill captives than to enslave them. The Prophet himself would in some cases kill captives outside the field of battle, while he would pardon them in others. Women he used to enslave. The Muslims are agreed that the aim of warfare against the People of the Book is two-fold: either conversion to Islam or payment of poll-tax (jizya).

And Ibn Khaldun, in *The Muqaddimah*, transl. F. Rosenthal, ed. N. Dawood, Princeton, 1967, p. 160, says clearly:

In the Muslim community, the holy war is religious duty, because of the universalism of the Muslim mission and [the obligation to] convert everybody to Islam either by persuasion or by force.

(Cf. Ibn Warraq ibid. pp. 276–278, 495.)

It is all too clear from this brief, and by no means comprehensive description of classical Muslim doctrines that intolerant fundamentalist extremism has its very "respectable" canonic sources. Human rights, as described (above) in the *Declaration* of 1948, are, thus, hardly compatible with such doctrines. (See, in detail in Ibn Warraq, *Why I am not a Muslim*, Amherst, New York, chapter 7, entitled "Is Islam Compatible with Democracy and Human Rights," pp. 172–197, and cf. ibid. chapter 9, "The Arab Conquests and the Position of Non-Muslim Peoples," pp. 214–240.) It requires innovative (apologetic?) interpretations of these classical sources in order to accommodate tolerance and a pluralistic approach to heterodox views in contemporary Islam.

7. It is somewhat ironical that in rabbinic literature the traditional iconic enemy of Israel is the biblical Esau (*Sifrei Numbers*, ed. H.S. Horowitz, 2nd edition, Jerusalem, 1966, no. 69, p. 65) – Edom who was identified first with Rome and subsequently in the Byzantine period and onwards with continuation of the Roman Empire). But now "Esau" has become our friend and partner, and while the (fundamentalist Arab) Moslem world, children, as it were of Ismael – whose daughter Mahalat married Esau! – has become our bitter enemy. But here is not the place to expand on this theme.

(Suffice it to refer to the following as to the identification of Esau with Rome: *Y. Avodah Zara* 1:2, *Genesis Rabba* 65:1, ed. Theodor Albeck? Jerusalem, 1965, vol. 2, p. 713 etc. And cf. *Genesis Rabba* 63:12, pp. 696–697, and for an understanding of that enigmatic text see Graham Sumner, *Roman Military Clothing* 1, and with Reffaele D'Armato, vol. 3, Osprey Publ. 2005, p. 12. And for a fine study of the identifications of Esau with Rome/Christendum, see Gerson D. Cohen, "Esau as Symbol in Early Mediaeval Thought," apud *Jewish Mediaeval Renaissance Studies*, ed. Alexander Altman, Cambridge, Mass., 1967, pp. 19–48, reprinted in Gerson D. Cohen, *Studies in the Variety of Rabbinic Cultures*, Philadelphia, New York, 1991, pp. 243–269.)

8. In the language of Christian anti-Judaism, Leonard Rutgers, (in his *Making Myths: Jews in Early Christian Identity Formation*, Leuven 2009, pp. 104–105) has noted that behind the rhetorical and physical attacks on Jews and Synagogues there stood a dramatic shift in the Christian use of the term "synagogue" itself . . . "It ceased to be an actual place and was abstracted into the very Essence of evil." See John Gager *Who Made Early Christianity? The Jewish Lives of the Apostle Paul*, New York, 2015, p. 85.

For the images of *Ecclesia* and *Synagoga* in mediaeval Christian art, see *Ecclesia und Synagoga: Das Judentum in der christlischen Kunst*, Ausstellungskatalog: Alte Synagogen Essen Regional-geschichtliche Museum Saarbrüken, 1993. Further on the personification of the synagogue in Berhard Blumenkranz, *La Juif medieval au miroir de l'art chrétien, Études Augustiniennes*, Paris, 1966, pp. 105–115; Wolfgang S. Saiferth, *Synagogue and Church in the Middle Ages: Two Symbols in Art and Literature*, transl. from German by Lee Chadeayne and Paul Gottwald, New York, 1970. The fullest discussion, with numerous illustrations, is in Heinz Schreckenberg's magnificent *The Jews in Christian Art: An Illustrated History*, London, 1996, pp. 31–74.

9. This has been described in great detail in Daniel Goldhagen's recent book *The Devil that Never Dies: The Rise and Threat of Global Antisemitism*, New York, Boston, London, 2013, chapter 9 et seq. (pp. 163 et seq.). Thus, for instance, the infamous *Protocols of the Elders of Zion* is explicitly cited in Hamas' charter:

> Today it is Palestine and tomorrow it may be another country or countries. For Zionist scheming has no end, and after Palestine they will covet expansion from the Nile to the Euphrates. Only when they have completed digesting the area on which they will have laid their hand, they will look forward to more expansion, etc. Their scheme has been laid out in the Protocols of the Elders of Zion, and their present [conduct] is the best proof of what is said there [ibid. pp. 211, 465 note 25].

And on p. 213 he writes:

> In 2013, the Palestinian Ma'an news agency carried a piece by the director of the Palestinian Center for Research and Cultural Dialogue that explained that the depravity laid out in the *Protocols* extends well beyond its local catastrophic effects for Palestinians and Arabs:
>
> The Protocols of the Elders of Zion are a kind of plan formulated by the Jews to infiltrate the world and take it over. While many Jewish leaders claim that they (the Protocols) are a forgery and one of the greatest political fabrications of the modern era, others confirm that they are true and that they are the most dangerous plot of global domination that history has ever known. The first protocol calls for the spread of anarchy and wars. The second protocol calls for a takeover of government, education, and the press. The fourth protocol calls for a takeover of trade and the destruction of religion – especially Christianity. While the seventh protocol calls to instigate global wars, the ninth lays out plans to destroy moral values and dispatch agents.
>
> Now, after this quick review of a few of these protocols, one wonders if the Jews belong to some other kind of human species, different from other nations. From where does all this evil and destructive energy derive? Do all the other nations deserve all this evil and hostility, just so that Jews may control them? Do all nations other than Jews really have clouded minds? Have most of the things that appear in the Protocols been implemented in the West and in the East? Did the idea of a Jewish world government begin to be carried out towards the end of the last century? And does the US rule the world today in the name of the new world order for the benefit of the Jews, in accordance with these Protocols? Are we on the brink of the establishment of an evident Jewish world government? Until we have answers to these questions and ponderings – as well as others – we say, "May Allah help us, we the children of Palestine."

Dehumanization ("some other kind of human species"), demonization, unmatched power and threat, all woven into a discussion of the *Protocols,* which is "true."

The whole book is a masterly, and profoundly disturbing analysis of the massive resurgence of anti-Semitism, anti-Zionism and Judaeo-phobia, not only throughout the Arab and Islamic world, but also radiating globally, affecting, or perhaps more correctly infecting, numerous non-Islamic and international organizations.

10. Goldhagen (ibid. p. 203) points out that even in the post-war period examples abound of Catholic instruction to the young inspiring enmity and hatred of the Jews. Thus:

> An Italian Catholic textbook declared about Jews: "This people will be torn from their land . . . scattered through the world . . . under the burden of a divine curse which will accompany them through the course of their history." A French Catholic textbook: "The Jews remain those who reject Christ, and the people whose ancestors solemnly asked that his blood fall upon them." A Spanish Catholic textbook: "The wretched Jews could not imagine the accumulation of calamities that would befall them and their descendants for having taken upon themselves the responsibility for the blood of the Just One, the Son of God." Given these teachings, read by the children of Catholic Europe during the postwar period, how could the Holocaust *not* be in some senses understood as just punishment?
> (Judith Hershcopf Banki, "Religious Education Before and After Vatican II," apud Eugene J. Fisher, A. James Rudin, and Marc H. Tanenbaum eds. *Twenty Years of Jewish-Catholic Relations*, Mahwah N.J. 1986, pp. 126–127; Goldhagen ibid. p. 330 note 48.)

And he adds (pp. 203–204):

It took the Church twenty years after the Holocaust before it produced the reforms of the Second Vatican Council. Twenty more years of explicitly teaching the most damaging anti-Semitism to hundreds of millions of people.

11. *John Paul II, Crossing the Threshold of Hope*, New York, 1994, p. 99. However see Goldhagen ibid. p. 199, that this same book also further confirmed supersessionism in a statement (ibid. pp. 99–100) that, "The time will come when the peoples of the Old Covenant will be able to see themselves as part of the New, is naturally a question to be left to the Holy Spirit."

CHAPTER 17

Towards the Future

Undoubtedly, in its time it was a great and courageous revolution,[1] despite the fact that I personally think that *Nostra Aetate* came a thousand years too late.[2]

It had the effect of paving the way to a new religious and theological position vis-à-vis Judaism and indeed other world religions,[3] and, of course, Catholic relations with Protestantism.[4] Indeed, I believe that it is only this new theological position that enabled, for example Mauro Gambatti, most recently to declare when describing the message of St. Francis of Assisi, at the closing ceremony of "Thirst For Peace: Religions and Cultures in Dialogue," on 20 September 2016, before Pope Francis himself that:

> At this point, it is just simple prophecy. The world will experience a phase of development if those who here do not search for glory, do not regard themselves as better than others, and *do not consider their own religions*, their own group or their own culture as *superior to others*, [my emphasis, D.S.]. (Text of *Final Ceremony*, Community of Sant' Egidio, Diocese of Assisi, Franciscan Families-Assisi, p. 3.)

Others continued to tread this new path, notably Pope John Paul II, who in his 2000 visit to Israel, declared on arriving at Ben Gurion airport

> L'établissement des relations diplomatiques entre le Saint-Siège et Israel en 1994 [...] a ouvert une ère de dialogue et de *liberté religieuse* [...] ce voyage est un homage aux trois traditions religieuses qui co-existent sur cette terre ...
>
> Que ma visite serve à l'approfondissement du dialogue interreli-gieux qui conduira les Juifs, le chrétiens et les musulmans à rechercher

dans leurs origines respectives et dans la fraternité universelle qui unit tous les members de la famille humaine, la normalization et l'espérance d'oeuvrer pour la paix et la justice que les populations de Terre sainte n'ont pas encore et auxquelles elles aspirant si profondément. [My emphasis, D.S.][5]

Indeed, we can hardly overestimate his contribution to the fostering of this new relationship to the Jewish people and the State of Israel. Thus, it was under his reign that:

On December 30, 1993, representatives of the Holy See and the State of Israel signed in Jerusalem the Fundamental Agreement that would lead the way to full diplomatic "normalization" of relations between the two. On August 16, 1994, the Apostolic Pro-Nuncio, Archbishop Montezemolo, presented his credentials to President Chaim Weizman of the State of Israel as the first Ambassador of the Holy See to the Jewish State.

As the Fundamental Agreement acknowledges, this was not just a moment of international diplomacy between two tiny Mediterranean states. It was a theologically significant moment in the nearly two-millennia-long history of the relationship between the Jewish people and the Catholic Church. The preamble defines the significance with precision:

The Holy See and the State of Israel,

Mindful of the singular character and universal significance of the Holy Land;

Aware of the unique nature of the relationship between the Catholic Church and the Jewish people, and the historic process of reconciliation and growth in mutual understanding and friendship between Catholics and Jews. . . .

Realizing that such Agreement will provide a sound and lasting basis for the continued development of their present and future relations. . . .

Agree upon the following Articles. (December 30, 1993 / 16 Tevet 5754)

363

(*Spiritual Pilgrimage: Texts on Jews and Judaism 1979–1989; Pope John Paul II*, ed. Eugene J. Fisher and Leon Klenicki, New York, 1995, pp. XXXII–XXXIII.)

And almost a decade earlier in his apostolic letter, *Redemptionis Anno*, he stated (*Spiritual Pilgrimage* ibid. p. XXXIII):

> For the Jewish people who live in the State of Israel and who preserve in that land such precious testimonies of their history and faith, we must ask for the desired security and the due tranquility that is the prerogative of every nation and of progress for society. (April 20, 1984)

And on May 14, 1982, in an address to religious leaders in Portugal he stated (ibid. p. 21):

> We are united in some way by faith and by a commitment, similar in many ways, to demonstrate by good works the consistency of our respective religious positions; and also the desire that, honoring as Lord the Creator of all things, our example may serve to help others in the search for God, in the opening toward transcendence, in recognition of the spiritual value of the human person, and, at times, in the identification of the foundation and permanent source of man's rights.
>
> This – we well know – is the condition in which criteria of esteem for the human being may exist, which are not limited to "practical usefulness," but which may safeguard his intangible dignity.

Indeed the whole volume is replete with statements which reflect his warmth and also his horror at the advent of the holocaust, as even the most cursory perusal will clearly testify.

Other Church leaders continued in his steps, so much so that this has become a trodden pathway.

It should further be noted that in Otranto in Italy he had declared

> "Poussé pas l'angoisse de la sécurité, le people juif a donné vie à l'État d'Israël."

And this was the first time the Vatican pronounced the name Israel.[6]

Similarly great changes are taking place on the Jewish position as to the nature of interreligious dialogue. Thus, in an important statement by one of the great twentieth century orthodox Jewish thinkers, Rabbi Joseph B. Soloveitchik, published in his article "Confrontation," in *Tradition* 6/2, 1964 pp. 5–29, he stated:

> We are not ready for a meeting with another faith community in which we shall become an object of observation, judgment and evaluation, even though the community of the many may then condescendingly display a sense of compassion with the community of the few and advise the many not to harm or persecute the few. Such an encounter would convert the personal Adam-Eve meeting into a hostile con-frontation between a subject-knower and a knowable object. We do not intend to play the part of the object encountered by dominating man. Soliciting commiseration is incongruous with the character of a democratic confrontation. There should rather be insistence upon one's inalienable rights as a human being, created by God.

While in 2005, in an article published in *CCAR Journal* 1/2 – a Reform Jewish Quarterly – p. 24, Leon Klenicki,[7] director of Interfaith Affairs for the Anti-Defamation League, a self-acknowledged disciple of Rabbi Soloveitichik, (though he was never actually a student of R. Soloveitchik and was a graduate of the Reform seminar, Hebrew Union College) reflects:

> Our teacher reflects a social condition typical of his time and his European background. We can affirm today that dialogue is not con-frontation, making the other an object of clinical observation. This attitude belongs to the time of monologues in encounter, part of the non-democratic reality of Europe in the '30s and '40s. A real encounter of dialogue entails, as it is experienced today, "one's inalienable rights as a human being, created by God."

He concludes his essay (p. 28) saying:

> The interfaith Christian-Jewish dialogue is a search for the essence of a new dimension: the possibility to witness God together, not unified, but standing together in a time of general unbelief and ideological triumphalism. Ours is a search for God's presence and call, a search that includes other religious commitments.

Our dialogue is hope as described by Martin Buber:

We live in an unredeemed world. But out of each human life that is unarbitrary and bound to the world, a seed of redemption falls into the world, and the harvest is God's. (Martin Buber, *The Origin and Meaning of Hassidism*, New York, 1960, pp. 109–110.)

Let us hope that we, *Ecclesia et Synagoga*, Christians and Jews and other religious people, are that seed of redemption. [8]

Ecclesia and Synagoga. Miniature in a manuscript of the French translation of the *Rationale divinorum officiorum* (i.e. handbook of liturgy) of William Durandus the Elder (died 1296), made in the fourteenth century. Paris, BA, Ms 2002, folio 2. Literature: Martin 1924, fig CVIII; cf. Rabel 1992, fig. 3. Illustration after Martin-Lauer 1929, pl.XXXV.

Ecclesia and Synagoga. The latter, bowed, blinded (to Christ) by a blindfold over her eyes, with a falling crown, is piercing the lamb of God with a lance, and Ecclesia is receiving his blood in a chalice. Ecclesia is putting her right foot on the serpent. Spenstrup (Denmark), church, mural in the arch ofo apse, c.1200. Schreckenberg II, 615f. Illustration after de Boor 1934, no. 4, and Schubert 1978, no. 48.

In 1993 the *International Council of Christians and Jews* (*ICCJ*), an umbrella organization combining thirty-eight Jewish-Christian dialogue-organs, published "Jews and Christians in Search of a Commom Religious Basis for Contributing Towards a Better World." This document presented both Jewish and Christian ideas on mutual cooperation, and joint activities, and was intended, not as an official document of the *ICCJ*, but rather as a vehicle for further thinking and philosophical-theological examination of the relevant issues.

And on September 10, 2000, the New York Times and other major American newspapers and internet news sites published a document entitled *Dabru Emet* – "Speak the Truth" – which was signed by over 220 rabbis and intellectuals from all branches of Judaism, concerning the relationship between Judaism and Christianity.[9]

While affirming that there are theological differences between the two religions, it stressed the common ground and legitimacy of Christianity for non-Jews from a Jewish perspective. The main points of the document are that:

1. Jews and Christians worship the same God.

2. Jews and Christians seek authority from the same book.

3. Jews and Christians together accept the moral principles of the Torah (Pentateuch).

4. A new relationship between Jews and Christians will not weaken Jewish practice.

5. Jews and Christians must work together for justice and peace.

To a certain extent *Dabru Emet* came as a kind of response to the document published by the Holy See on March 1998, entitled "We Remember: *A Reflection on the Shoah*,"[10] signed by Cardinal Edward Idris Cassidy, President, Bishop Pierre Duprey, Vice President, Rev. Remi Hoekman, OP, Secretary.

We shall quote sections of this remarkable document which begins (more or less) as follows:

> This reflection concerns one of the main areas in which Catholics can seriously take to heart the summons which Pope John Paul II has addressed to them in his apostolic letter *Tertio Millennio Adveniente*:
>
> It is appropriate that as the second millennium of Christianity draws to a close the Church should become more fully conscious of the sinfulness of her children, recalling all those times in history when they departed from the spirit of Christ and his Gospel and, instead of offering to the world the witness of a life inspired by the values of faith, indulged in ways of thinking and acting which were truly forms of counter-witness and scandal. [*Tertio Millenio Adveniente. Acta Apostolicoe Sedis* (*AAS*) 87, 1995:25, no. 33.]
>
> This century has witnessed an unspeakable tragedy which can never be forgotten: the attempt by the Nazi regime to exterminate the Jewish people, with the consequent killing of millions of Jews. Women and men, old and young, children and infants, for the sole reason of their Jewish origin, were persecuted and deported. Some were killed immediately, while others were degraded, ill-treated, tortured, and utterly robbed of their human dignity, and then murdered. Very few of those who entered the camps survived, and those who did remained scarred for life. This was the Shoah. It is a major fact of the history of this century, a fact which still concerns us today.
>
> Before this horrible genocide, which the leaders of nations and Jewish communities themselves found hard to believe at the very

moment when it was being mercilessly put into effect, no one can remain indifferent, least of all the Church, by reason of her very close bonds of spiritual kinship with the Jewish people and her remembrance of the injustices of the past. The Church's relationship to the Jewish people is unlike the one she shares with any other religion. [Cf. John Paul II, speech given at the Rome synagogue on April 13, 1986, *AAS* 78, 1986, 1120, No. 4.] However, it is not only a question of recalling the past. The common future of Jews and Christians demands that we remember, for "there is no future without memory." [John Paul II, Angelis prayer, June II, 1995, *Insegmanenti* 18/1, 1995:1712.] History itself is *memoria future....*

We deeply regret the errors and failures of those sons and daughters of the Church. We make our own what is said in the Second Vatican Council's declaration *Nostra Aetate*, which unequivocally affirms: "The Church ... mindful of her common patrimony with the Jews, and motivated by the gospel's spiritual love and by no political considerations, deplores the hatred, persecutions, and displays of anti-Semitism directed against the Jews at any time and from any source...." [*Nostra Aetate* No. 4].

Looking to the future of relations between Jews and Christians, in the first place we appeal to our Catholic brothers and sisters to renew the awareness of the Hebrew roots of their faith. We ask them to keep in mind that Jesus was a descendant of David; that the Virgin Mary and the apostles belonged to the Jewish people; that the Church draws sustenance from the root of that good olive tree on to which have been grafted the wild olive branches of the gentiles (cf. Rom 11:17–24); that the Jews are our dearly beloved brothers, indeed in a certain sense they are "our elder brothers" [Rome speech at Synagogue No. 4].

We pray that our sorrow for the tragedy which the Jewish people has suffered in our century will lead to a new relationship with the Jewish people. We wish to turn awareness of past sins into a firm resolve to build a new future in which there will be no more anti-Judaism among Christians or anti-Christian sentiment among Jews, but rather a shared mutual respect as befits those who adore the one Creator and Lord and have a common father in faith, Abraham.

It ends:

> Finally, we invite all men and women of good will to reflect deeply on the significance of the *Shoah*. The victims in their graves and the survivors through the vivid testimony of what they have suffered have become a loud voice calling the attention of all humanity. To remember this terrible experience is to become fully conscious of the salutary warning it entails: The spoiled seeds of anti-Judaism and anti-Semitism must never again be allowed to take root in any human heart.

In this rather extensive document, which also includes a kind of brief history of anti-Semitism we have echoes of *Nostra Aetate* and of the many declarations of Pope John Paul II.[11]

This document by the Catholic Commission for Religious Relations with the Jews, crafted under the papalship of John Paul II, condemned Nazi genocide, called for repentance on the part of Catholics who failed to intercede to stop it, to repeat "past errors and infidelities" and "renew the awareness of the Hebrew roots of their faith."

In a letter included in it from the Pope to Edward Idris Cardinal Cassidy, the Pope describes:

> A sense of deep sorrow [regarding] the sufferings of the Jewish people during the Second World War. Shoah remains an indelible stain on the history of the century. . . . Let us head the wounds of past misunderstandings and injustices . . . [and help create] a future in which the unspeakable iniquity of the Shoah will never again be possible.

And earlier on, in 1982 the Commission for Religious Relations with the Jews published their "Notes on the correct way to present the Jews and Judaism in preaching and catechesis in the Roman Catholic Church."

This long and detailed document, which is based on *Nostra Aetate*, contains a number of very remarkable statements, such as, for example:

> II 6: It is true then, and should be stressed, that the Church and Christians read the Old Testament in the light of the event of the dead and risen Christ and that on their ground there is a Christian reading of the Old Testament which does not necessarily coincide with the Jewish reading. The Christian identity and Jewish identity should be carefully distinguished in their respective reading of the Bible.

But this detracts nothing from the value of the Old Testament in the Church and does nothing to hinder Christians from profiting discerningly from the traditions of Jewish reading.

III 8: It is noteworthy too that the Pharisees are not mentioned in accounts of the Passion. Gamaliel (Acts 5:34–39) defends the apostles in a meeting of the Sanhedrin. An exclusively negative picture of the Pharisees is likely to be inaccurate and unjust (cf. Guidelines [in the Implementation of *Nostra Aetate*, 1995] Note 1; cf. AAS *loc. cit.* p. 76).

IV 1. F: There is no putting the Jews who knew Jesus and did not believe in him, or those who opposed the preaching of the apostles, on the same plane with Jews who came after or those of today. If the responsibility of the former remains a mystery hidden with God (cf. Rom 11:25), the latter are in an entirely different situation.... [also cited above in note 171].

IV 2: The delicate question of responsibility for the death of Christ must be looked at from the standpoint of the conciliar declaration *Nostra Aetate* 4 and of *Guidelines and Suggestions* III): "What happened in (Christ's) passion cannot be blamed upon all the Jews then living without distinction, nor upon the Jews of today, Christ in his boundless love freely underwent his passion and death because of the sins of all men, so that all might attain salvation." (*Nostra Aetate* 4). The Catechism of the Council of Trent teaches that Christian sinners are more to blame for the death of Christ than those Jews who brought it about – they indeed "know not what they did ..." (cf. Luke 23:24). "The Jews should not be represented as repudiated or cursed by God, as if such views followed from the Holy Scriptures." (*Nostra Aetate* 4)[12]

VI 1: The permanence of Israel (which so many peoples have disappeared without trace) is a historic fact and a sign to be interpreted within God's design. We must rid ourselves of the traditional idea of a people *punished*, preserved as a *living argument* for Christian apologetics. It remains a chosen people, "the pure olive on which were grafted the branches of the wild olive which are the gentiles" (John Paul II, 6th March 1982, alluding to Rom. 11:17–24). We much remember how much the balance of relations between Jews and Christians over two thousand years has been negative. We must remind ourselves how the permanence of Israel is accompanied by a continuous spiritual fecundity, in the rabbinic period, in the Middle Ages and in modern times, taking its start from the patrimony which we long shared so much so that "faith and religious life of the Jewish people as they are professed and practiced still today, can greatly help us to understand better certain aspects of the Church" (John Paul II, March 6th 1982).

VI 2: The Council presented it thus: "Moreover, (the Church) mindful of her common patrimony with the Jews and motivated by the Gospel's spiritual love and by no political considerations, deplores the hatred, persecutions and displays of anti-Semitism directed against the Jews at any time and from any source" (*Nostra Aetate* 4). The *Guidelines* comment: "The spiritual bonds and historical links binding the Church to Judaism condemn ... all forms of anti-Semitism and discrimination, which in any case the dignity of the human person alone would suffice to condemn" (*Guidelines*, Preamble).

This document was signed by Johannes Cardinal Willebrands (President), Pierre Duprey (Vice President), Jorge Meija (Secretary).

We see in this document too the constant references to *Nostra Aetate* and the deep influence of its formulations.

And already in 2002, many of these themes, drawing upon the text of *Nostra Aetate* were voiced in the very long, complex and detailed document published by the Pontifical Biblical Commission, entitled "The Jewish People and their Sacred Scriptures in the Christian Bible." This document was crafted under the imprimatur of Joseph Cardinal Ratzinger.[13]

But what I find to be particularly significant, in this very rich document, is what is expressed in section 7, paragraph 22:

> Christians can and ought to admit that the Jewish reading of the Bible is a possible one, in continuity with the Sacred Scriptures of the Second Temple period, and a reading analogous to the Christian reading which developed in a parallel fashion. Both readings are bound up with the vision of their respective faiths, of which the readings are the result and expression.
>
> Consequently, both are irreducible.

This, I believe, is a very sophisticated formulation of the "multiple truth" doctrine, and constituted a radical departure from early Christian thinking.

Indeed we find evidence that this view, expressed in a variety of different formulations, permeated Catholic thinking. Thus Leonard Swidler,

Catholic theologian and Professor of Catholic Thought and Interreligious Dialogue at Temple University, writes in *Towards a Universal Theory of Religion*, Maryknoll, N.Y., 1987:

> Why, indeed, should one pursue the truth in the area of religion and ideology by way of dialogue? A fundamental answer to these questions lies in the even more dramatic shift in the understanding of truth that has taken place first in Western civilization, and now beyond it, throughout the nineteenth and twentieth centuries, making dialogue not only possible but necessary.
>
> Whereas the notion of truth was largely absolute, static and exclusive up to the last century, it has subsequently become deabsolutized, dynamic and dialogic – in a word, "relational." This new view of truth came about in at least four different but closely related, ways:
>
> 1. Historicization of truth: truth is deabsolutized and dynamized in terms of time, both past and future, with intentionality and action playing a major role in the latter.
>
> 2. Sociology of knowledge: truth is deabsolutized in terms of geography, culture and social standing.
>
> 3. Limits of language: truth as the meaning of something, and especially as talk about the transcendent, is deabsolutized by the nature of human language.
>
> 4. Hermeneutics: all truth, all knowledge, is seen as interpreted truth and knowledge, and hence is deabsolutized by the observer, who always is also interpreter.

And, of course, as a sort of high point of this theological odyssey, though by no means the end of the journey, comes the conciliar document of 2015, the fiftieth anniversary of *Nostra Aetate*. It has the (somewhat lengthy) title "The Gifts of God are Irrevocable" (Rom 11:29), with a subtitle "A Reflection on Theological Questions Pertaining to Catholic-Jewish Relations on the Occasion of the 50th Anniversary of *Nostra Aetate* (No. 4;)" and was published by the Commission for Religious Relations with the Jews. (Collana Document; Vatican), and is dated 10 December 2015, and signed by Cardinal Kurt Koch (President). The Most Reverend Brian Farnell (Vice-President) and the Reverend Norbert J. Hofmann, SDB (Secretary). The *Preface* clearly defines the aim of the document as follows (p. 3):

Fifty years ago, the declaration "Nostra Aetate" of the Second Vatican Council was promulgated. Its fourth article presents the relationship between the Catholic Church and the Jewish people in a new theological framework. The following reflections aim at looking back with gratitude on all that has been achieved over the last decades in the Jewish-Catholic relationship, providing at the same time a new stimulus for the future. Stressing once again the unique status of this relationship within the wider ambit of interreligious dialogue, theological questions are further discussed, such as the relevance of revelation, the relationship between the Old and the New Covenant, the relationship between the universality of salvation in Jesus Christ and the affirmation that the covenant of God with Israel has never been revoked, and the Church's mandate to evangelize in relation to Judaism. This document presents Catholic reflections on these questions, placing them in a theological context, in order that their significance may be deepened for members of both faith traditions. The text is not a magisterial document or doctrinal teaching of the Catholic Church, but is a reflection prepared by the Commission for Religious Relations with the Jews on current theological questions that have developed since the Second Vatican Council. It is intended to be a starting point for further theological thought with a view to enriching and intensifying the theological dimension of Jewish-Catholic dialogue.

It begins with "a brief history of the impact of *Nostra Aetate* (No. 4) over the last 50 years," (pp. 4–13); it continues with "the special theological status of the Jewish-Catholic dialogue" (pp. 13–22).

And there, after the "replacement" or "supersessionist" Doctrine, paragraph 20 (pp. 21–22) states the following:

Nevertheless, from the theological perspective the dialogue with Judaism has a completely different character and is on a different level in comparison with the other world religions. The faith of the Jews testified to in the Bible, found in the Old Testament, is not for Christians another religion but the foundation of their own faith, although clearly the figure of Jesus is the sole key for the Christian interpretation of the Scriptures of the Old Testament. The cornerstone of the Christian faith is Jesus (cf. Acts 4:11; 1 Pt 2:4–8). However, the dialogue with Judaism occupies a unique position for Christians;

Christianity is by its roots connected with Judaism as with no other religion. Therefore the Jewish-Christian dialogue can only with reservations be termed "interreligious dialogue" in the true sense of the expression; one could however speak of a kind of "intra-religious" or "intra-familial" dialogue *sui generis*. In his address in the Roman Synagogue on 13 April 1986 Saint Pope John Paul II expressed this situation in these words: "The Jewish religion is not 'extrinsic' to us but in a certain way is 'intrinsic' to our own religion. With Judaism therefore we have a relationship which we do not have with any other religion. You are our dearly beloved brothers and, in a certain way, it could be said that you are our elder brothers."

So no longer is the Jew the "wandering Jew,"[14] faithless[15] rejected and accursed, but one who has been welcomed into the family with an honoured status. This in itself is the acknowledgment and "ratification," as it were, of a radical change in Catholic theology. It continues (in paragraph 25 on p. 25) reiterating what we noted above, namely:

Judaism and the Christian faith as seen in the New Testament are two ways by which God's people can make the Sacred Scriptures of Israel their own. The Scriptures which Christians call the Old Testament is open therefore to both ways.... [My emphasis D.S.]

Although it continues in a sophisticated manner to state that:

A response to God's word of salvation that accords with one or the other tradition can thus open up access to God, even if it is left up to his counsel of salvation to determine in what way he may intend to save mankind in each instance. That his will for salvation is universally directed is testified by the Scriptures (cf. eg. Gen 12:1–3; Is 2:2–5; 1 Tim 2:4). Therefore there are not two paths to salvation according to the expression "Jews hold to the Torah, Christians hold to Christ." Christian faith proclaims that Christ's work of salvation is universal and involves all mankind. God's word is one single and undivided reality which takes concrete form in each respective historical context.

Two paths to one truth?! The document struggles with this issue,[16] on the one hand denying that there can be different paths to God's salvation, a theory that would endanger the foundations of Christian belief, (p. 38). How then can Jews also be in a salvatic state?

> From the Christian confession that there can be only one path to salvation, however, it does not in any way follow that the Jews are excluded from God's salvation because they do not believe in Jesus Christ as the Messiah of Israel and the Son of God. Such a claim would find no support in the soteriological understanding of Saint Paul, who in the Letter to the Romans not only gives expression to his conviction that there can be no breach in the history of salvation, but that salvation comes from the Jews (cf. also John 4:22). God entrusted Israel with a unique mission, and He does not bring his mysterious plan of salvation for all peoples (cf. 1 Tim 2:4) to fulfillment without drawing into it his "first-born son" (Ex 4:22). From this it is self-evident that Paul in the Letter to the Romans definitively negates the question he himself has posed, whether God has repudiated his own people. Just as decisively he asserts: "For the gifts and the call of God are irrevocable" (Rom 11:29). That the Jews are participants in God's salvation is theologically unquestionable, but how that can be possible without confessing Christ explicitly, is and remains an unfathomable divine mystery (p. 36).

And on p. 37 we read:

> Another focus for Catholics must continue to be the highly complex theological question of how Christian belief in the universal salvitic significance of Jesus Christ can be combined in a coherent way with the equally clear statement of faith in the never-revoked covenant of God with Israel. It is the belief of the Church that Christ is the Saviour for all. There cannot be two ways of salvation, therefore, since Christ is also the Redeemer of the Jews in addition to the Gentiles. Here we confront the mystery of God's work, which is not a matter of missionary efforts to convert Jews, but rather the expectation that the Lord will bring about the hour when we will all be united, "when all peoples will call on God with one voice and 'serve him shoulder to shoulder'" ("Nostra Aetate," No. 4).

So the solution to the "contradiction," to the *conincidentia oppositorum*, is in the realm of "unfathomed divine mystery" – "the mystery of God's work."[17] "Mystery" admits the legitimacy of contradiction, and the document states clearly (p. 38) that not "all theological questions which arise in the relationship of Christianity and Judaism have been revolved in the text (of *Nostra Aetate*).

These questions require further theological reflection." And this is what I meant when I indicated that this was by no means the end of the journey.[18]

And now to return to the Jewish responses, on 9 December 2015, 28 Orthodox Rabbis released a statement through the *Center for Jewish-Christian Understanding and Cooperation* in Israel, declaring praise for *Nostra Aetate*, stating:

> Now that the Catholic Church has acknowledged the eternal Covenant between God and Israel, we Jews can acknowledge the ongoing constructive validity of Christianity as our partner in World redemption, without any fear that this will be exploited for missionary purposes.

We see, then, the remarkable effect *Nostra Aetate* has had both on Christian theology vis-à-vis Judaism, as well as a radically new perception of Christianity on the part of Jews.[19]

Despite the great progress, nonetheless, the voices of progressive liberalism and the philosophy legitimizing tolerance for different opposing views must be much more forcefully and proactively proclaimed. We must confront our joint challenges, be they societal, such as secularization, theological, such as concepts of life, afterlife, etc., with their attendant implications, abortion, birth-control, euthanasia, or ethical, such as the sanctity of the family unit, homo-lesbianism and so forth. Such problems confront all of us, as do the grave challenges of ecology and conservation, which have most recently been addressed by the Holy See.[20]

So too, globalization with its far-reaching implications, societal inequalities, be they societal, legal, economic or political, and any number of additional issues must be resolutely faced.[21] Joining forces openly, and non-apologetically, utilizing our joint traditions and our accumulated wisdom[22] and the overall similarities in our moral codes, drawing upon our common heritage,[23] we may perhaps lead the way to a rectification of the many misconceptions that plague us.[24] Furthermore, we must counter the hysterical outcries of uncompromising fanaticism, so that the call for reason, mutual respect and understanding may prevail.[25] That, in my opinion, is the most urgent existential challenge of our day, one that can only be achieved by joining forces in this crucial combat of ideologies. This indeed, will be our *tikkun olam*,[26] to use the Hebrew term,[27] meaning to repair the rampant ills of our contemporary global society.[28]

Endnotes to Chapter 17

1. As Lorenzo Cremmesi, Jerusalem correspondent for the Italian newspaper *Corriere della Sera*, wrote (in *Haaretz*, March 26, 2000):

> It is one of the most radical and complex processes of ideological and doctrinal revisions of this century, but one of the least known, especially among Jews in Israel.

John Connely, in his *From Enemy to Brother*, Cambridge, Mass., 2012, pp. 241–242, notes that this was a process beginning with Cardinal Bea's initiation of the Apaldrom Initiative of August 1960. It aimed at setting out a guide to Catholic-Jewish dialogue, the "high-point of [the] pre-Vatican II deliberation forming the prophetic element that over the years prepared a place in the church, intellectually and spiritually, emotionally and theologically for the Council declaration of which as yet they knew nothing. . . . This was a controversial process among practitioners of "la nouvelle theologie" as *ressourcement*, a return to the sources in which "the past was taken as a lens to understand the present."

Here I should also like to quote partially the closing paragraphs of Owen Chadwick's *The Secularization of the European Mind in the Nineteenth Century*, Cambridge, 1975, pp. 265–266, in relation to my use of the term "revolution:"

> The historian knows how powerless are revolutions. Men chop off the king's head and remake the constitution and declare that it is the year one; and at the end the historian sees how like new is to old, and how Stalin's political police are but the Tsar's political police with an equal tyranny, secrecy and inefficiency. The historian's vocation is to see continuity, and he therefore meets temptation to underestimate change. . . .
>
> And therefore he might [indeed] underestimate change and fail to mention that something irreversible happened to the past; that though the instinct of religion might be as powerful as ever, and men use hallowed words to express it, yet they begin to understand those words in a new way, often a radically different way. . . .

And what happened, and why, must still be matter for much enquiry by students of history and religion and society.

2. As Lorenco Cremmesi wrote (ibid.):

In this sense, *Nostra Aetate* came too late. From the Middle Ages until the modern era, it would have been extremely useful, since Christian anti-semitism was in fact the root of the persecutions of Jews in Europe. Undoubtedly, had it been pronounced before the Holocaust, Hitler would have been far more limited in his implementation of the "Final Solution."

3. See, for example, *A New Catechism: Catholic Faith for Adults*, West Germany, 1967, being an English translation of *De Nieuwe Katechismus*, commissioned by the Heirarchy of the Netherlands and produced by the Higher Catechetical Institute at Nijnegen, while attempts "to render faithfully the renewal which found expression in the Second Vatican Council" (ibid. p.v). See pp. 38 et seq. on Israel, and pp. 353–354 on tolerance, on Hinduism, Buddhism and Islam, pp. 271–272, etc.

See further Gavin D'Costa, *Vatican II: Catholic Doctrines on Jews and Muslims*, Oxford 2014.

4. Protestants heralded the *Declaration on Religious Liberty*. Indeed, one observer wrote:

> The passing of the "Declaration on Religious Liberty" marked one of the most significant milestones, not only for the Council, but the whole history of the Church . . . to the great joy of all Christians and men of good will throughout the World. (Frank Cuttris, "Observer Reports on Council," *Advocate*, February 10, 1966, p. 5; cited by Melissa J. Wilde, *Vatican II: A Sociological Analysis of Religious Change*, Princeton and Oxford, 2007, p. 100.)

And Robert MacAfee Brown, *Observer in Rome*, New York, 1964, p. 174, had written:

> I do not think there is a single direct thing the Council can do that will have more immediate effect in bettering Catholic-Protestant relations than a forthright unambiguous statement favoring a full religious liberty for all. . . . The Catholic Church is not fully trusted on this point. Whether rightly or wrongly, non-Catholics. . . . are fearful that the Church may still espouse a position of intolerance, persecution and penalty for the exercise of a faith not Roman Catholic (Wilde, ibid. p. 85).

The *Declaration* has to a large extent served to banish, or at least assuage, those fears.

5. See Jean-Bernard Raimond, *Jean-Paul II: Un pope au coeur de l'histoire*, 2nd edition, Paris, 2005, p. 292.

6. Ibid. p. 207, of course, as the name of the "State of Israel." In comparison, when Paul VI came to the Holy Land in 1964, he entered Israel from Jordan, then visiting Jerusalem. But

> Il a en secours à des circumlocutions on des images, mois jamais *ni le mot Juif ni le mot Israël n'a été prononcé*. [My emphasis, D.S.]

(Raimond ibid.)

Here we should parenthetically take into account the explanatory comment of Augustin Cardinal Bea in a note in his *The Church and the Jewish People*, New York, 1966, p. 10 (note 1), where he writes as follows:

> In passing, we may take note of a *terminological* question. A writer has recently made the following distinctions: "From the *ethnological* aspect, the Jewish people, or better still the Jewish race, comprise all those individuals who are descendants of the twelve tribes of Israel, no matter what their religion or their nationality may be. From the *political* standpoint, however, the Jewish 'people' cannot mean only those Jews who are citizens of the Republic of Israel since this would exclude large numbers of the Jews of the diaspora who have not chosen to return to Palestine." The author concludes that the Council has no reason to concern itself with the Jews from an ethnological or a political point of view but solely from a religious standpoint. As a consequence he speaks only of the "*Jewish religion*," or if one prefers, of "*Judaism*," this term being taken to indicate the community of those who, irrespective of time or place, profess the mosaic religion and therefore regard themselves as "God's chosen people."
>
> Apart from any other remarks which might have to be made on the question of terminology, the crucial point lies for us in the fact that holy scripture still speaks of the people of Israel in St Paul's time (cf. Romans 9–11) when there was a very wide dispersal of the Jews all over the Roman Empire and when, in addition, the new people of God, "Israel according to the Spirit," the Church, had been constituted. As has been seen above, the same language was also used in the text of the Constitution on the Church. It is true that the Declaration on the Relation of the Church to Non-Christian Religions does not employ the term "Jewish people" (although it did occur in the earlier redactions). The reason for this, however, is not that this expression is illegitimate in itself but that it might give rise to misunderstanding from a political point of view or to false theological interpretations, as though the Jewish people were still the people of God in the sense of an institution for the salvation of mankind.

And cf. ibid. pp. 102–114.

And returning to Raimond ibid. pp. 208–209, he cites further statements of Pope John-Paul II in which he emphasizes his aim of rapproachment with the Jews. Thus, at Mainz, Germany he declared:

Il ne s'agit pas seulement de la rectification d'une fausse vision du people juif, mais avant tout d'un dialogue entre les deux religions qui, avec l'islam, ont pu donner au monde la foi en un Dieu unique et ineffable que nous voulons server au nom du monde entire. (*Documentation Catholique* 1980, 1148.)

And on April 13, 1986 he visited the great synagogue in Rome for a joint prayer session, a symbolic gesture of great impact (subsequently followed by next popes). For the full text of his address, see *Spiritual Pilgrimage* pp. 60–66, and cf. ibid. p. 87. And a very significant statement of his at Mainz was:

La religion juive ne nous est pas extrinsèque, mais, dans une certaine mesure, est intrinsèque à notre proper religion chrétinne. Avec le judaisme, nous avons une relation que nous n'avons avec aucune autre religion. Vous êtes nos frère prefers et, d'une certaine manière, on peut dire que vous êtes nos frères ainés. (Documentation Catholique, 1986, 437)

Here it is well worth quoting in full the very moving description of that event in Carl Bernstein and Marco Politis *His Holiness: John Paul II and the Hidden History of Our Time,* New York, 1996, pp. 442–444:

If dialogue with the Muslims was a necessity, John Paul II saw dialogue with the Jews as a duty, particularly because of the Holocaust. Two of the Vatican Council's premises had been that the Jewish roots of Christianity had to be acknowledged and that anti-Semitism was intolerable. John Paul II brought these ideas to fulfillment with a grand gesture on April 13, 1986.

On that day Wojtyla crossed the Tiber to enter the Synagogue of Rome on the Lungotevere dei Cenci, something no pope had ever done before. As Roman Jews know, their community is older than the oldest Christian church. When Sts. Peter (as tradition has it) and Paul came to Rome, the Torah was already being read and the Sabbath observed in the capital of the Roman Empire. When Christians went from suffering persecution to instigating it, among their principal victims were the Jews. During Easter Week Jews were forced to listen to sermons (they plugged their ears) and were jeered for having "assassinated Christ." It was only thanks to the unification of Italy, carried out by the king of Savoy Victor Emmanuel II (whom Pius IX excommunicated because the king's armies had invaded the Papal States), that Italian Jews acquired full freedom and civil rights. The imposing synagogues built in Turin, Florence, and Rome near the turn of the twentieth century thus bore double witness to the faith of the Jews and the defeat of the pope.

In June 1963, the chief rabbi of Rome had gone to St. Peter's Square to pray for the dying Pope John XXIII. John was revered as the man who had expunged from the Catholic liturgy for Holy Saturday the insulting reference to the Jews as "perfidious."

Now in April 1986, John Paul II arrived in the old Roman ghetto, seeking to ease painful memories. The largo from Handel's *Xerxes* played plangently as he stepped out of his limousine. But when he walked inside – the first Roman pontiff ever to enter a synagogue – a curtain of silence descended. A humble and respectful John Paul II exchanged an embrace with Chief Rabbi Elio Toaff. The pope wore a white zucchetto (skullcap) and his papal robes, the rabbi his eight-cornered hat and, draped over his shoulders, a white-and-blue-striped tallith. Together they walked down the Assyro-Babylonian nave of the synagogue and took their places on the teva – the platform where the cantor stands and the Torah is read.

Wojtyla listened to a speech by the leader of Rome's Jewish community, Giacomo Saban, who recalled how copies of the Talmud were burned on the Campo dei Fiori in 1553. The pope seemed pained when Saban alluded to the terrible silence of Pius XII, who never denounced Nazi atrocities against the Jews, and the deportations of Jews that were carried out in the heart of Rome: "What was happening on one bank of the Tiber [where the synagogue is located]," Saban noted, "couldn't be ignored across the river [where the Vatican is]."

That day the world saw a different Pope Wojtyla – not the master of the crowds, but a man who bore the weight of a tragic history, which the pope from Wadowice had dedicated himself to changing. Rabbi Toaff asked him to establish diplomatic relations between the Vatican and the state of Israel. (He did so in 1993, over the objections of his Secretariat of State, which was waiting for the government of Israel to reach an accord with the Palestinians first.)

When he delivered his speech in the synagogue, John Paull II's voice at times seemed close to cracking. He acknowledged the wounds endured for hundreds of years by Jews living in Christian countries, "acts of discrimination, unjustified limitations of religious freedom, and oppressive restriction of civil freedom as well. . . . Yes, once again, speaking through me the Church deplores, in the words of the [Council document] *Nostra Aetate*, the hatreds, the persecutions, and all the manifestations of anti-Semitism directed against the Jews at any time by whomever." The Pope fell silent, looked straight at his audience, and said: "I repeat, *by whomever*." Then he called the Jews the "older brothers" of Christians and, recalling the doors of convents and churches opened during World War II to Jewish victims of persecution, he pointed to future common goals: the end of all discrimination, the defense of human dignity, adhesion to individual and social ethics, peace, and coexistence between the two religions, "animated by brotherly love."

As a boy Karol Wojtyla had gone to the synagogue in Wadowice with his father to hear the celebrated cantor Moishe Savitski. Now, dressed in his satin papal robes, he sat hunched in a gilded armchair listening to a choir sing a hymn that had been chanted by condemned Jews in the death camps on their way to the gas chambers. As the voice of the choir swelled in the house of prayer, the pope bent further forward, his head bowed and his hand covering his mouth.

Further full text of his address, see *Spiritual Pilgrimage: Texts on Jews and Judaism 1979–1995*; edd. Eugene J. Fischer and Leon Klenicki, New York, 1995, pp. 60–66. (This whole volume, with its two introductions by the editors, demonstrate the Pope's progressive journey towards reconciliation with the Jews and Judaism.) In a letter dated 20 April 1984, he wrote:

> Sur le people juif qui vit dans l'État d'Israël et qui sur cette terre conserve des témoignages si précieux de son histoire et de sa foi, nous devons invoquer la sécurité désirée et la juste tranquillité, qui est la prerogative de toute nation et la condition de vie et de progress pour toute société.

And later he invited Christians "comprendre l'attachement religieux des Juifs, qui plunge ses racines dans la tradition biblique, sans pour autant faire leur une interpretation religieuse particulière de cette relation." (See further Raimond pp. 209–215.)

We cannot here document the whole unfolding process of this "rapprochement." We may note that Pope Benedict visited the great synagogue in Rome on January 17, 2010, and Pope Francis again on that same date in 2016. Pope Benedict also visited Israel in May 2009, to stress the shared roots of Judaism, Islam and Christianity. And in January 1964 Pope Paul VI visited the Holy Land. (See on this visit Doran Baer's article fifty years after that historic visit, in *Cathedra* 160, 2015, pp. 123–152, Hebrew.) Much more is to be said on this subject. But part of it is set out in *Turning the Tide of Christian-Jewish Relations*, published in 2013, by the AJC and the Konrad Adenaur *Stiftung*, which records

> The delegations of the Holy See's Commission for Religious Relations with the Jews and the Chief Rabbinate of Israel's Commission with the Catholic Church Joint Statements 2003–2013.

More than this is beyond the scope of this study.

7. Already in 1920, in the volume *In Our Times: The Flowering of Jewish-Catholic Dialogue*, edd. Eugene J. Fischer & Leon Klenicki, New York, Mahwah, N.J., 1990, pp. 77–103, in his article entitled "From Argument to Dialogus: *Nostra Aetate* Twenty-Five Years Later," he pointed to, what from a Jewish perspective, constitutes weak and problematic points in *Nostra Aetate* (see pp. 81–86).

8. See Haym Soloveitchik's response to that (polemic?) article of David Berger, "*Ha-Rav Soloveitchik, 'Imut: Ha-Du-Siah ha-Yehudi-Notzri,*" from 2012, afterwards published in *Makor Rishon – Musaf Shabbat* (16 Nov. 2012), under the title *"Emunah bi-Reshut ha-Yahid,"* in reply to Riskin on Jewish-Christian dialogue.

9. *"Dabru Emet; A Jewish Statement on Christians and Christianity"* characterizes itself as a Jewish response to the profound changes evident in Christian doctrine, especially in the aftermath of the *Shoah*. It does not have a similar status to *Nostra Aetate*, as the Jewish community is not organized hierarchically. (I have not included all the points of the document.) It was also criticized by many, and most conservative and reform rabbis did not sign it, and so too very few orthodox rabbis agreed with it. John D. Levenson wrote a critique of it in *Commentary* 112/5, 2000, entitled "How not to conduct Jewish-Christian dialogue," and again in *Commentary* 113/4, 2002 "Jewish Christian dialogue." See also *CCAR* 11/2, pp. 29–41, 2005, Jan Katzew's article, "From Other to Brother," etc.

10. On this document, see Randolph L. Braham, "Remembering and Forgetting: The Vatican, The Catholic Heirarchy, and the Holocaust." *Holocaust and Genocide Studies* 13/2, 199, pp. 222–251, for a judicious account on the nature of this declaration that was eleven years in the making.

11. In reaction to this document on the part of Jewish and non-Jewish theologians, see *The Vatican and the Holocaust: The Catholic Church and the Jews During the Nazi Era*, ed. Randolph L. Braham, Columbia University Press, 2000, pass. On the one hand Father John Pawlikowski, Prof. of Social Ethics at the Catholic Theological Union in Chicago, considers this document "as the most important document on Jewish-Catholic relations since *Nostra Aetate*," though it has its failings; while Roth-Leon Klenicki, Director of Interfaith Affairs for the Anti-Defamation League, is far less complementary, wrestling with the problem why there was such "profound disappointment" among Jews over the publication of this document. (See J.F. Morley's article, ibid. p. 51, and see A. James Rudin's article, ibid. pp. 89–98.)

12. Since this is a very central issue, I think it is important to cite at length part of Augustin Cardinal Bea's *Relatio on the schema*, from 25 October 1964 (apud his *The Church and the Jewish People*, New York, 1966, section b, nos. 4–5, pp. 161–162), this being a highly significant statement:

> The central issue which caused the more important changes was the question of "deicide." We all know how widely this question was discussed in the press – without the slightest intervention of co-operation by the Secretariat. Consequently, I must now point out the major issues. The question is if and how the condemnation and death of Christ the Lord is to be laid to the charge of the Jews *as such*. Now many modern Jews claim that the principal reason

for anti-semitism stems from the conviction of general Jewish guilt, and that this conviction is the source of the flood of evils and persecutions which the Jews have suffered through the centuries. This cannot be sustained. In my address given in this "Aula" a year ago on this schema, I clearly stated: "We are all well aware that there are many reasons for anti-semitism which are not religious at all but are political, national, psychological, social and economic." And yet it is still true that not a few instances can be found in the history of different peoples where conviction of general Jewish guilt led Christians to consider and designate the Jews with whom they lived as members of a race rejected and cursed by God for "deicide" and so to despise or even persecute them. It is for this reason that the Jews today are most anxious that the Council should show itself opposed to this conviction of general Jewish guilt and should publicly and solemnly declare that our Lord's death is in no way to be laid to the charge of the Jewish people *as such*. We must now decide whether such a declaration by the Council is possible and if so, how should it be made, what should be its tenor?

I need scarcely say that there is not and cannot be any question of denying or attenuating anything affirmed in the Gospels. The issue must be carefully defined and it is this: The leaders of the Jerusalem Sanhedrin, although not democratically elected, yet, according to the ordinary understanding of those days, accepted by the scriptures, were regarded and must be regarded as the embodiment of legitimate authority among the people. Here lie the gravity and the tragedy of their action – the exercise of their authority in the condemnation and death of Christ. Yet how grievous was their guilt? Did those "rulers" of the people in Jerusalem fully understand the divinity of Christ and so become formally guilty of deicide? Our Lord on the cross said in his prayer to the Father: "Father, forgive them: for they know not what they do" (Luke 23:34). If this reason for forgiveness is no mere empty formula – God forbid – it surely shows that the Jews were far from full understanding of the crime they were committing. St Peter also, addressing the Jewish people on the crucifixion of Christ, repeated: "And now, brethren, I know that you acted in ignorance, as did also your rulers" (Acts 3:17). So St Peter finds an excuse even for the very rulers! So likewise does St Paul (Acts 13:27). Furthermore, whatever may have been the knowledge possessed by the leaders in Jerusalem, the case of the people is quite different: *can the whole Jewish people of that time, generally and without distinction, be held answerable for the proceedings of their leaders in Jerusalem,* which led to the death of Christ? Statistics show that in the apostolic age the Jews dispersed throughout the Roman Empire numbered about 4,500,000: are all of them to be accused of the deeds done by the Sanhedrists on that first sad Good Friday? And even granting – which we do not grant – that the people of that time were as a whole responsible, by what right can their descendants today be held in any sense guilty? Can any other case be found anywhere in which we blame a nation for the actions of its ancestors over 1900 years ago?

Our Secretariat was at pains to take account of the conditions of these different classes of people, so that the schema might, on the one hand, affirm according to the Gospel narratives the guilt of those who decided upon the crucifixion of Christ, and on the other, might not ascribe any guilt to the Jewish people as a whole, much less to the Jews of today. There is no need here to appeal to the fact that Christ died for all men. For this in no way means that guilt for the death of the Lord *in the historical order* (which alone is in question here) is to be transferred to all men, or that they *were in the historical order* (which alone is in question here) is to be transferred to all men, or that they were *in the historical order* the efficient cause of his death. On the other hand the Jews as such, whether then or now, should not be charged with a crime in which they had no part. I ask you therefore to bear this in mind when you make your decision about his section of the proposed Declaration.

Because of the difficulty of the subject, it is understandable that many different formulas were tried, one after the other, in the effort, also, to satisfy the wishes and the criticisms of the Fathers. The frequent consultations that ensued became known, as many of you are aware, to the general public (how, no one knows). In consequence, both Council Fathers and others, including non-Catholics and non-Christians petitioned that the question of "deicide" should receive some treatment. It would be tiresome to describe all the deliberations in detail. Suffice it to have indicated how we arrived at the text you have before you. One thing more may be added: these deliberations took a long time. Consequently we were unable to submit this part of the Declaration for examination by the members of the Secretariat. Since the Secretariat had dealt with all its other business at its March sitting, it was decided not to recall the members to Rome to discuss this one section. All that now remains, Venerable Fathers, is to examine and discuss this schema. As you see, it is a matter of high importance and likewise of great difficulty.

For another far more critical, but nevertheless nuanced assessment of this section of *Nostra Aetate* on the Jews, see *Paul Blanchard and Vatican II*, by Paul Blanchard, London, 1967, chapter 7, "The Jews," pp. 123–146, 354–355.

13. Ratzinger, in his book *Many Religions – One Covenant: Israel, the Church, and the World*, San Francisco, 1999, basing himself on Jeremiah II, had written (pp. 63–64):

God, according to the Prophet, will *replace* the broken Sinai covenant with a New Covenant that cannot be broken: this is because it will not confront man in the form of a book or a stone tablet but will be inscribed on his heart. The *conditional* covenant, which depended on man's faithful observance of the Law, is *replaced* by the *unconditional* covenant in which God binds himself irrevocably.

He continues (ibid. pp. 70–71):

> Thus the Sinai covenant is indeed *superseded*. But once what was provisional in it has been *swept away*, we see what is truly definitive in it. So the expectation of the New Covenant, which becomes clearer and clearer as the history of Israel unfolds, does not conflict with the Sinai covenant; but rather it *fulfils* the dynamic expectation found in the very covenant.

This quote illustrates how for Ratzinger "fulfillment" of the "Old Covenant" immediately implies "replacement." He concludes (ibid. p. 106) with the paradoxical conclusion that only finds its solution in an eschatological perspective, as follows:

> It follows, therefore, that the figure of Christ both links and separates Israel and the Church. It is not within our power to overcome this separation, but it keeps both of us to the path that leads to the One who comes. To that extent the relationship between us must not be one of enmity.

His conclusion is, therefore, that "separation" and "reconciliation" among Jews and Christians are intertwined in what he calls a "virtual insolvable paradox" (p. 40), reconciling this paradox through a theological plausibility of the confusion between "replacement" and fulfillment.

I base the above on the article by Marianne Moyaert and Dilier Pollefeyt, entitled "Israel and the Church; Fulfillment beyond Supersessionism?" apud *Never Revoked: Nostra Aetate as Ongoing Challenge for Jewish-Christian Dialogue*, edd. Marianne Moyaert & Dilier Pollefeyt, Grand Rapids Michigan/Cambridge, U.K., 2010, pp. 170–172. (The italicized section in the quotations are theirs.) This important volume also contains a fine historical survey of "Vatican II and the Jews," by Mathis Lamberigt and Leo Declerck, pp. 13–56, as well as a number of other important contributions, e.g., those of David Meyer and of Mary C. Boys and others.

14. In a very fascinating article by Jerome Gellman, entitled "Jewish Chosenness and Religious Diversity – A Contemporary Approach," apud *Religious Perspectives on Religious Diversity*, ed. Robert Mckim, Leiden Boston, 2016, pp. 21–36, the theme of the "wandering Jew," is, as it were, reversed. Thus, he writes on p. 30:

> Thus do I invent the Augustian position, as ordinarily understood, according to which God keeps the Jews in existence in perpetual suffer[ing] for their rejection of Jesus, so as to be witness to what befalls his deniers. I turn Jewish

survival and suffering into a positive, rather than a negative, testimony to God's grace.

He continues:

> The controlling image here is the burning bush, which burns but never is consumed. This image has served Jewish commentators at least since the time of the ancient Jewish philosopher Philo, who wrote:
>
> For the bush was a symbol of those who suffer the flames of injustice, just as the fire symbolized those responsible for it; but that which burned did not burn up, and those who suffered injustice were not destroyed by their oppressors. (Philo, *Life of Moses,* 1:65–67.)

The Jewish role as God's chosen people implies a sacrificial existence that configures, but does not atone for, the fiery side of human existence with the promise of God's redemption. Hence, the Jews in their sacrificial mode are not the Christ figure of atonement, but are the Israelites who endure bitter enslavement only to be redeemed in an archetype of divine promico of redemption for all humankind.

15. So I translate "perfidus" (also: false, deceitful, treacherous) in the famous Good Friday Supplications on Good Friday, (in the Roman missal of Pius V. of 1570, which begins

> Oremus et pro perfidies Judaeis: Ut Deus et Dominus noster auferat valemen de cordibus corum; ut et ipsi agnoscant Jesam Christum, Dominum nostrum.

In Scholt's translation of 1913:

> Let us pray for the Faithless Jews, that God, our Lord, shall lift the veil from their hearts, so that they may also come to know our Lord Jesus Christ.

(See *Missale Ramanum ex dectreto sacrosancti Concilii Tridentini restatutum . . . ,* edition secunda juxta editionem typicam, Ratisbonne 1887, p. 152.) And in the explanators rubric it is stated that "this deacon does not alter a call for genuflection so as to avoid renewing the memory of the shame with which the Jews, by means of genuflection, mocked the Saviour at this hour." And this, indeed, is the only supplication without genuflection for the reason mentioned above.

On the history of the changes in this crucial phrase "pro perfidies Judaeis" Hubert Wolf wrote a fine comprehensive essay entitled "The Good Friday Supplication for the Jews and the Roman Caria (1928–1975): A Case Example for Research Prospects for the Twentieth Century," apud *The Roman Inquisition, the Index and the Jews: Contexts, Sources and Perspectives*, ed. Stephan Wendehorst, Leiden, Biston, 2004, pp. 235–257. He shows that this phrase was repeatedly criticized, and already in 2 January 1928, Abbot Gariador of the "*Amici Israel*" asked Pope Pius XI to eliminate

the words "perfidies" and "perfidiam," and that "Flectamus Genua," i.e. "we genu-
flect," be included in the Good Friday Supplication. But this request was rejected, as
indeed were subsequent similar such requests in the following decades. And it was
not until 1959 that Pope John XXIII eliminated the formulation "perfidis" in his first
Good Friday liturgy as Pope. And in 1970, Pope Paul VI introduced a fundamentally
new version of the text, marked by great respect for the Jewish people. (See Wilm
Sanders, "Die Karfreitagsfürbidten für die Juden von Missale Pius V. zum Missale
Pauls VI," "Ein Zeugnis Sucht Bezeugende" ibid. 23, 1973, pp. 143–158.)

On the short (!) history of the "Amici Israel," see Wolf ibid. pp. 240–257.

As mentioned above the new formulation did not come until 1970. It now reads
as follows:

> Let us also pray for the Jews to whom God, our Lord, first spoke His word. May
> He preserve them in faithfulness to His covenant and in love of His name. So
> that that may reach the goal to which His guidance would lead them. Bend your
> knees – silence – rise up. Almighty and eternal God, You gave Abraham and his
> children Your promise. Hear the prayer of Your Church for the people which
> You chose first as Your possession: give so that it might come to the fullness
> of redemption. We supplicate You through Christ, our Lord (Messbuch. Die
> Feier der heiligen Messe. Für die Bistümter der deutschen Sprachgebietes,
> Teil 1: Die Sonn – und Feiertage deutsch und lateinisch. Die Karwche deutsch,
> Ginsiedeln, 1975, p. 48.)

Wolf summarizes as follows (p. 257):

... The textual development of the Good Friday supplications from 1928 to 1970
indicates just how fundamental the change has been in the relation between the
Catholic Church and Judaism. If the Tridentine Missal had offered the "faithless
Jews" only one possibility, that of conversion, the "Amici Israel" wished for their
part to facilitate a "transpassio" from the Kingdom of the Father to the Kingdom of
the Son. The missale of 1970 goes a significant step further, according the "people
of the Old Covenant" their own independent path to salvation.

16. This is only one of its many struggles. For the document struggled with many
other issues. Paul Blanchard, in his *Paul Blanchard on Vatican II*, London, 1967, in
his concluding chapter (17), entitled "Balance Sheet" (pp. 330–347), discusses these
various "struggles," writing (p. 331) in a kind of summarizing assessment:

> In terms of its own history, the Roman Catholic Church moved rapidly and
> accomplished much during Vatican II. Hence the Council can be called a gigan-
> tic success. In terms of the movement of Western culture, however, the Council
> moved so slowly that it almost stood still. In an age when culture and science
> had moved farther in two centuries than the whole world had progressed up to

that point in time, Vatican II chose to cling to dogmas and policies that were centuries out of date, dogmas and policies that could have been abandoned without any surrender of spiritual ideals. In terms of twentieth-century velocity, the Council brought Catholicism from the thirteenth to the seventeenth century, no mean achievement, but it still left this largest segment of world Christianity three hundred years behind the times. The non-Catholic world was happy about the result, and justly so. At last Catholicism was moving in the right direction, toward the reality of modern life. But Vatican II also revealed that the Church, with all its progress, was still pre-American both in the rigidity of its dogma and the autocracy of its power structure.

Is this perhaps a little too harsh?

17. See, for example, the complex and somewhat tortuous discussion of Christoph Böttingheimer, in his "Truth and Tolerance: Opposites in the interreligious" (from *Slimmen der Zeit* II, 2007, pp. 754–766, especially pp. 759–761), and Gerd Neuhaus, "Christian and Pluralistic At Once?" Or Perry SchrireLeukel's "God without Borders" ibid. 5, 2000, pp. 348–353.

18. See, e.g., David Berger, in his article "Vatican II at 50: Assessing the Impact of 'Nostra Aetate' on Jewish-Christian relations," *Tablet* Dec.15, 2015, pp. 1–8, who wrote (p. 2):

Before proceeding to matters of greater substance and complexity, we need to ask how much of an impact these changes have exerted on ordinary Catholics and the Christian populace as a whole. With respect to what I characterized as the most focused and concrete issue addressed by "Nostra Aetate," we have a fairly extensive survey carried out by the Anti-Defamation League in 2012. Its objective was to measure attitudes toward Jews in 10 European countries (not including the former Soviet Union), and it asked respondents whether they thought a series of affirmations were probably true. The fifth and final of these was: "The Jews are responsible for the death of Jesus." (Note the present tense verb.) The average of those responding "probably true" was 22 percent, ranging from 14 percent in France and Germany to 46 percent in Poland. The percentage in Spain was only 21 percent. Since we can be certain that these numbers would have been far higher two generations ago, it almost certainly follows that even allowing for the impact of European secularization, at least a significant part of the decline can be attributed to the effect of "Nostra Aetate" and the teachings that it inspired. Nonetheless, the Polish result speaks volumes for the educational work that remains to be done.

Similarly, Rabbi David Rosen's comments in his article "Fifty Years since the

Second Vatican Council: Its significance for Christian-Jewish Relations:" apud *A Jubilee for All Time*, ed. Gilbert S. Rosenthal, Eugene, Oregon, 2014, pp. 12–17.

And already in 1966, in *The Documents of Vatican II*, edd. Walter M. Abbott S.J. and Very Reverend Msgr. Joseph Gallagher, America Press, Dr. Claud D. Nelson (the official Religious News Service correspondent at Vatican II for the National Conference of Christians and Jews) noted on pp. 669–670 that:

> One misses in both statements any satisfying expression of the warm human feeling which might in considerable measure have taken the place of the ecclesiastical kinship whose expression was found to be too difficult for formulation.
>
> One is not surprised, therefore, that Jews in general are not enthusiastic over these statements. Rabbi David Polish, for example, finds the Vatican Council Declaration condescending and lacking the spirit of reconciliation. He refers to it as "a unilateral pronouncement by one party which presumes to redress on its own terms a wrong which it does not admit."

Nonetheless, ultimately these comments cannot detract from the enormous positive value of these Declarations.

19. See also Marc H. Tannenbaum, "A Jewish Viewpoint," in *Vatican II: An Interfaith Appraisal*, ed. John H. Miller, New York, 1966, p. 349, who writes that the mass murder of Jews is "compelling us to confront the deep realities of the relationships between Christians and Jews." And ibid. p. 362, he notes that the actions of the World Council of Churches and Vatican II in labeling religious hatred as a sin was not immediately understood by everyone in the Jewish community, and that there were even Jews "who opposed the declaration and resented it." For as Tannenbaum explains, "No Jew . . . ever felt guilty for the death of Jesus. Therefore, no Jew ever felt in need of absolution." See Gerhard Falk, *The Jew in Christian Theology*, Jefferson, North Carolina and London, 1992, chapter 6, entitled "After the Holocaust: A New Christian Theology," pp. 129 et seq.

20. This was clearly formulated in the December 2015 declaration, sect. 46:

> One important goal of Jewish-Christian dialogue certainly consists in joint engagement throughout the world for justice, peace, conservation of creation, and reconciliation. In the past, it may have been that the different religions – against the background of a narrowly understood claim to truth and a corresponding intolerance – contributed to the incitement of conflict and confrontation. But today religions should not be part of the problem, but part of the solution. Only when religions engage in a successful dialogue with one another, and in that way contribute towards world peace, can this be realized also on the social and political levels.

There were, however, several reservations on the part of Jewish thinkers as to the precise formulation in the Declaration, as was readily admitted by Cardinal Bea, who, however, sought to refute them. See, for example, in his *The Church and the Jewish People*, New York, 1966, pp. 117–118 note 1:

> Anyone who has given due consideration to all the many points which we have emphasized here and which add such great force to the Church's rejection of anti-semitism, will be surprised to learn that, amongst others, it was precisely this part of the Declaration which was the object of very considerable reservation in Jewish quarters. The reason for this was the fact that the word "damnat" (condemns) used in the redaction voted upon in November, 1964 was altered to "deplorat" in the final version. These reservations were partly due to misunderstanding arising from the translation of the Latin word "deplorat" by modern, etymologically similar words, for example the English "deplores," which are much weaker and more insipid than the Latin "deplorat," which should be translated by some stronger word or phrase (e.g., the Italian *"profondamente lamentare"* or the German "tief zu bedauern.") There were also psychological reasons. Dissatisfaction was caused by the disappearance from the text of the stronger word which better expressed the execration which every honest man must feel for the recent and terrible crimes committed in the name of anti-semitism in Nazi Germany. It was also said that the reason given for the substitution, namely that the Church was "condemning" the doctrine rather than the practical attitude, was not convincing. As I have said elsewhere, even Catholics are not obliged to accept the reasons adduced by Council Commissions, but only the text promulgated by the Council. It will also be realized that in the complicated work of the Commissions it is not always easy to give in every case the precise reason which effectively determined the adoption of this or that amendment. In any case, as we have shown above, we are here concerned with a genuine "rejection" of anti-semitism which, as has been seen, is surrounded by so many reinforcing principles, rests on such a wide basis and is prompted by motives of such a character that the use of this or that word to describe it is for all practical purposes unimportant and does not detract from the force and weight of the arguments for this "rejection."

Or again on p. 119 note 1:

> Protests were raised against the omission from the schema of the formula "Let all take care that in giving catechetical instruction or in preaching the word of God they say nothing which might arouse hatred or contempt for the Jews in the minds of the faithful" and the substitution of the one we have just expounded. We may perhaps be permitted to observe that this complaint arises from an insufficient appreciation of the audience for which the Declaration was

intended. The council addresses itself primarily to Catholics and not directly to the general public. It was consequently necessary to keep in mind the psychology of these for whom the document was meant. There is no doubt that for Catholics, as for Christians in general, the rule given in the present text that teaching must in every way conform with the spirit of Christ is incomparably more compelling than any exhortation to avoid preaching hatred and contempt. For this reason the present text is of greater service to the Jewish cause.

21. See, for example, *"Guidelines and Suggestions for Implementing the Conciliar Declaration 'Nostra Aetate' (No. 4),"* presented by Johannes Cardinal Willibrands on 1 December 1974, sect. IV:

> Jewish and Christian tradition, founded on the word of God, is aware of the value of the human person, the image of God. Love of the same God must show itself in effective action for the good of mankind.
>
> In the spirit of the prophets, Jews and Christians will work willingly together, seeking social justice and peace at every level – local, national and international.
>
> At the same time, such collaboration can do much to foster mutual understanding and esteem.

This passage can be encapsulated in the Hebrew term brought at the end of this study: *Tikkun Olam*. However, see Eugene J. Fisher, "The Evolution of a Tradition: From Nostra Aetate to the Notes," *Christian-Jewish Relations* 18, 1985, pp. 32–47, on the development of churches' attitude to the Jewish People, but also showing Jewish views on the shortcomings of *"Notes."*

22. In the words of the December 2015 declaration, sect. 44:

> The first goal of the dialogues is to add depth to the reciprocal knowledge of Jews and Christians. One can only learn to love what one has gradually come to know, and one can only know truly and profoundly what one loves. This profound knowledge is accompanied by a mutual enrichment whereby the dialogue partners become the recipients of gifts. The Conciliar declaration "Nostra Aetate" (No. 4) speaks of the rich spiritual patrimony that should be further discovered step by step through biblical and theological studies and through dialogue. To that extent, from the Christian perspective, an important goal is the mining of the spiritual treasures concealed in Judaism for Christians. In this regard one must mention above all the interpretation of the Sacred Scriptures. In the foreword by Cardinal Joseph Ratzinger to the 2001 document of the Pontifical Biblical Commission "The Jewish People and their Sacred Scriptures in the Christian Bible," the respect of Christians for the Jewish

interpretation of the Old Testament is stressed. It highlights that "Christians can learn a great deal from a Jewish exegesis practiced for more than 2000 years; in return Christians may hope that Jews can profit from Christian exegetical research." In the field of exegesis many Jewish and Christian scholars now work together and find their collaboration mutually fruitful precisely because they belong to different religious traditions.

And here it is worthwhile citing the Joint Statement of the Bilateral Commission meeting of the Chief Rabbinate of Israel's Delegation for Relations with the Catholic Church and the Delegation of the Holy See's Commission for Religious Relations with the Jews, Jerusalem, April 29–30, 2013; Iyar 19–20, 5773, which includes the following paragraphs:

> The mutual respect and friendship that has been established between us over recent years, brings with it the responsibility not only to present each other the way each sees themselves; but also to defend and advance the wellbeing of each other's community. This requires us to stand up against prejudice and threats – in particular against Jews and Christians. Especially where one community is the dominant ethos of a country and the other is a vulnerable minority, the responsibility on the former is even greater.
>
> Accordingly, the Catholic delegation reaffirms the commitment of the Holy See to do its utmost to combat anti-Semitism everywhere, in keeping with the declaration *Nostra Aetate*, and especially where the dominant ethos is Catholic; and the delegation from the Chief Rabbinate reaffirms its resolve to do its utmost to promote the wellbeing of the Christian minority in the State of Israel.

(See *Turning the Tide of Christian-Jewish Relations*, Konrad Adenauer Stiftung, 2013, p. 25.)

And in the statement of March 27–29, 2012 (ibid. p. 23), section 10 states that:

> In addition to the ethical wisdom drawn from our spiritual heritages, religious communities are an integral part of civil society, which must play a central role together with politics and business, in ensuring the subsidiarity necessary for a just and economic order.

23. We are talking of the Judaeo-Christian heritage. However, I would not go so far as did Coomeraswamy in his *Sources of Wisdom* p. 46, who wrote:

> . . . using one tradition to illuminate the other [i.e. Western and Indian], and so to demonstrate even more clearly that the variety of traditional cultures, in all of which these subsisted until now a polar balance of spiritual and material values, is simply that of the dialects of what is always one and the same

language of spirit and of Perennial Philosophy to which no one people or age can have exclusive claim.

This is, of course, a formulation of the concept of "Perennial Philosophy," so popularized by Aldous Huxley in his masterful *The Perennial Philosophy*, New York, 1945, (influenced by Vivekananda's Neo-Vedanta and Universalism; see above Vivekananda's famous Chicago statement).

On this notion of a "Universal Religion," see Clement C.J. Webb, in his article "Science Christianity and Modern Civilization," apud *Science Religious Reality*, ed. Joseph Needham, New York, 1955 (first published Cambridge, 1925), pp. 337–343. On p. 341 he categorically rejects the possibility of such a phenomenon.

Note also that Irving Greenberg, in his *For the Sake of Heaven and Earth*, Philadelphia, 2004, maintains that Judaism and Christianity are different dimensions of the same covenant to work for messianic fulfillment and satisfaction of life in human history and culture.

In this connection it is interesting to read what Tetsuro Watsuji wrote in September 1959, in his "Foreword on behalf of the Japanese National Commission for Unesco," to Hajue Nakamura's *The Ways of Thinking of Eastern Peoples*, Japan, 1960, pp. ii-iii:

> Now is the time to begin to correct the mistakes of the past. The peoples of both the East and the West must begin to understand themselves and each other. By a full understanding of our own individual peculiarities, we may break down the barriers which prevent us from understanding each other. No efforts other than our own can remove restricted areas or "no man's lands" which separate us.
>
> If all the peoples of the world would only try to understand each other by forgetting for a moment apparent peculiarities which history, tradition, habits and environment have shaped and would think solely of common problems facing them as human beings since the dawn of civilization, the universal character of all peoples would appear and all causes of prejudice and misunderstanding would disappear and all mankind would unite in their efforts to enrich their lives with spiritual values and happiness.

24. See what Eugene Korn wrote in his essay "Rethinking Christianity: Rabbinic Positions and Possibilities," apud *Jewish Theology and World Religions*, edd. A. Goshen-Gottstein and Eugene Korn, Oxford, Portland, Oregon, 2012, pp. 209–215, in a section entitled "A New Theology and Different Future." He begins:

> Perhaps more important than the challenge of finding a path for neutral Jewish-Christian theological coexistence is the bolder inquiry of whether there are grounds for a new *theological* relationship and mutual appreciation between the faiths.

He continues to examine this important question.

25. We should, of course, be constantly aware of the fact that anti-Semitism has by no means been eliminated. It has taken on different forms, but, unfortunately is still very much with us. See, e.g., *Anti-Semitism in Post-Totalitarian Europe*, Franz Kafka Publishers, Prague, 1995, articles by Yehuda Bauer, Shlomo Avineri, Robert Wistrich, etc.

26. Again in the language of the December 2015 declaration sections 48 and 49:

> Justice and peace, however, should not simply be abstractions within dialogue, but should also be evidenced in tangible ways. The social-charitable sphere provides a rich field of activity, since both Jewish and Christian ethics include the imperative to support the poor, disadvantaged and sick. Thus, for example, the Holy See's Commission for Religious Relations with the Jews and the International Jewish Committee on Interreligious Consultations (IJCIC) worked together in 2004 in Argentina during the financial crisis in that country to organize joint soup kitchens for the poor and homeless, and to enable impoverished children to attend school by providing meals for them. Most Christian churches have large charitable organizations, which likewise exist within Judaism. These would be able to work together to alleviate human need. Judaism teaches that the commandment "to walk in His ways" (Deut. 11:22) requires the imitation of the Divine Attributes (Imitatio Dei) through care for the vulnerable, the poor and the suffering (Babylonian Talmud, Sotah 14a). This principle accords with Jesus's instruction to support those in need (cf. eg. Mt 25:35–46). Jews and Christians cannot simply accept poverty and human suffering; rather they must strive to overcome these problems.
>
> When Jews and Christians make a joint contribution through concrete humanitarian aid for justice and peace in the world, they bear witness to the loving care of God. No longer in confrontational opposition but cooperating side by side, Jews and Christians should seek to strive for a better world.

See also Phillip A. Cunningham, *Seeking Shalom: A Journey to a Right Relationship between Catholics and Jews*, Grand Rapids, Cambridge 2015.

27. We may note that Rabbi Mordechai Waxman, in his address to the Pope John Paul II on September 11, 1987, at Miami stressed that:

> A basic belief of our Jewish faith is the need "to mend the world under the sovereignty of God" . . . *L'takken olam b'malkut Shaddai.* To mend the world means to do God's work in the world. It is in this spirit that Catholics and Jews should continue to address the social, moral, economic, and political

problems of the world. Your presence here in the United States affords us the opportunity to reaffirm our commitment to the sacred imperative of *tikkun olam*, "the mending of the world."

(See *Spiritual Pilgrimage: Texts on Jews and Judaism 1979–1995: Pope John Paul II*, edd. Eugene J. Fisher and Leon Kleniki, New York, 1995, p. 111.)

28. Some theologians have gone even further. Thus the German Catholic theologian Hans Kung, in his book *Projekt Weltethos*, München 1990, contended that there are three requirements to be fulfilled by all religions to achieve a "world ethos." These are: the development of a "World Ethos" of the nations, peace among all nations and dialogue among all religions as a requisite for peace.

And following on Kung's (naïve?) vision, Gerhard Falk ends his *The Jews in Christian Theology*, Jefferson, North Carolina and London, 1992, p. 160, thus:

The way is set and there is no returning. Ecumenism, at one time a word referring only to Christians, now includes Jews as well. While both faiths will and should maintain a core of beliefs and practices that will be specifically and peculiarly Christian or Jewish, much that these two great faiths have in common will be and is now available to both peoples. Thereby both will be strengthened in their common hope: "Peace on Earth and Good Will to Men."

SYNOPTIC SUMMARY

This study identifies three categories of justification for the concept of "freedom of religion:"

1. My religion is the true one, so yours is not. But you still have the inalienable right to your own false faith, and I have the moral duty to permit it.
2. My religion is more correct than yours, but you have a partial degree of truth in your faith, and also positive ethical values, which require us to respect you and your beliefs and practices.
3. Different religions are, for the most part merely a variety of manifestations of the same core truth, giving equal legitimacy to (almost) all faiths.

However, in any one of these categories, when the faith of the one directly harms the person or community of the other, then tolerance becomes unacceptable.

The contributory elements of each of these positions, i.e. their philosophical, sociological, cultural and theological backgrounds, have been examined in the above study.

Finally, the past half century has revealed a new realization of the unique familial relationship between Judaism and Christianity (fitting them smoothly into the middle category), not only encouraging mutually positive attitudes, but also stimulating active efforts jointly to face concrete humanitarian challenges and to seek innovative solutions. And this has reached a truly historic zenith in the document most recently presented to Pope Francis by institutional Jewish Orthodoxy. For on August 31, 2017, a document signed by the Chief Rabbinate of Israel, the Conference of European Rabbis and the Rabbinical Council of America, entitled *"Between Jerusalem and Rome: the shared universal and the respected particular reflections on 50 years of Nostra Aetate"* was presented to the Pope. This was the first ever Jewish declaration responding to the changes in the Christian world relating to Jews and Judaism issued by the main institutions of Jewish Orthodoxy (see Appendix 1). It highlights, in the words of Rabbi David Rosen (in a paper presented to the Bilateral Commission on Jewish-Catholic relations, on 14 Nov. 2017, entitled "Reflections on Recent Orthodox Jewish Statements on Jewish-Catholic Relations):"

> The new era of normative Orthodox Jewish engagement with the Christian world reflected not least of all in this bilateral commission itself, in which there is a rapidly growing appreciation of the dramatic change that has taken place with in Christianity in relation to Jewry, Judaism and Israel; of the strategic importance of this relationship for the Jewish People and the Jewish state; and even of the theological as well as moral imperatives for deepening this mutual relationship to work together for the establishment of the Kingdom of Heaven on earth.

APPENDIX I

Some Important Roman Catholic Documents[1]

Vatican II on the Jews: Nostra Aetate (No. 4) 28 October 1965.

As this Sacred Synod searches into the mystery of the Church, it remembers the bond that spiritually ties the people of the New Covenant to Abraham's stock.

Thus the Church of Christ acknowledges that, according to God's saving design, the beginnings of her faith and her election are found already among the Patriarchs, Moses and the prophets. She professes that all who believe in Christ – Abraham's sons according to faith (cf. Galatians 3:7) – are included in the same Patriarch's call, and likewise that the salvation of the Church is mysteriously foreshadowed by the chosen people's exodus from the land of bondage. The Church, therefore, cannot forget that she received the revelation of the Old Testament through the people with whom God in His inexpressible mercy concluded the Ancient Covenant. Nor can she forget that she draws sustenance from the root of that well-cultivated olive tree onto which has been grafted the wild shoot, the Gentiles (cf. Romans 11:17–24). Indeed, the Church believes that by His cross Christ Our Peace reconciled Jews and Gentiles, making both one in Himself (cf. Ephesians 2:14–16).

The Church keeps ever in mind the words of the Apostle about his kinsmen: "Theirs is the sonship and the glory and the covenants and the law and the worship and the promises; theirs are the fathers and from them is the Christ according to the flesh" (Rom 9:4–5), the Son of the Virgin Mary. She also recalls that the Apostles, the Church's mainstay and pillars, as well as most of the early disciples who proclaimed Christ's Gospel to the world, sprang from the Jewish people.

As Holy Scripture testifies, Jerusalem did not recognize the time of

401

her visitation, (cf. Luke 9:44), nor did the Jews, in large number, accept the Gospel; indeed not a few opposed its spreading (cf. Romans 11:28). Nevertheless God holds the Jews most dear for the sake of their Fathers; He does not repent of the gifts He makes or of the calls He issues – such is the witness of the Apostle. (Cf. Romans 11:28–29, *Lumen Centinon, A.A.S.*, 57, 1965, p. 20). In company with the Prophets and the same Apostle, the Church awaits that day, known to God alone, on which all peoples will address the Lord in a single voice and "serve him shoulder to shoulder" (Zeph 3:9; cf. Isaiah 66:23; Psalm 65 (66):4, Romans 11:11–32).

Since the spiritual patrimony common to Christians and Jews is thus so great, this Sacred Synod wants to foster and recommend that mutual understanding and respect which is the fruit, above all, of biblical and theological studies as well as of fraternal dialogues. It is, however, some thirty years old, and needs serious updating.

True, the Jewish authorities and those who followed their lead pressed for the death of Christ (cf. John 19:6); still, what happened in His passion cannot be charged against all the Jews, without distinction, then alive, nor against the Jews of today. Although the Church is the new people of God, the Jews should not be presented as rejected or accursed by God, as if this followed from the Holy Scriptures. All should see to it, then, that in catechetical work or in the preaching of the word of God they do not teach anything that does not conform to the truth of the Gospel and the spirit of Christ.

Furthermore, in her rejection of every persecution against any man, the Church, mindful of the patrimony she shares with the Jews and moved not by political reasons but by the Gospel's spiritual love, decries hatred, persecutions, displays of anti-Semitism, directed against Jews at any time and by anyone.

Besides, as the Church has always held and holds now, Christ underwent His passion and death freely, because of the sins of men and out of infinite love, in order that all may reach salvation. It is, therefore, the burden of the Church's preaching to proclaim the cross of Christ as the sign of God's all-embracing love and as the fountain from which every grace flows.

*

Introduction to the discussions of the Plenary Session of bishop members of the Secretariat for Promoting Christian Unity, which demonstrates the spirit in which the work at an official level of the Church was carried out. Rome, November 1969. (Quoted from Information Service No. 9, February 1970/1, of the Secretariat for Promoting Christian Unity.)

1. It is in "searching into the mystery of the Church" itself (*Nostra Aetate*) that the Council was led to recall the bond that unites the Christian people to the descendants of Abraham. The Declaration published on that occasion, is a document that inaugurates a new era in the relations of Christians and Jews. The heritage of the past, it is true, still weighs heavily on these relations. But in the light of the clear affirmations of the Council, all Christians are called to an effort of comprehension and searching, which ought to translate itself into action in order that this document should not remain a dead letter. With a view to promoting this research and its application the following reflections and suggestions are proposed.

2. After four years it is possible to take stock of our situation. [The primary attitude to the problem of Jewish Christian relations is]:

That of those who have recognized that Christianity cannot be understood in its origin and its very nature without reference to the Jewish tradition wherein it took root and which is still very much alive in our own day. . . .

3. In order to further the concrete application of the Declaration *Nostra Aetate*, n. 4, and in the spirit that inspires it, it appears useful to us to recall the following:

(a) The problem of the relations between Jews and Christians concerns the *Church as such*, since it is in "searching into its own mystery" that it comes upon the mystery of Israel. These relations touch therefore upon the Christian conscience and Christian life in all its aspects (liturgy, catechesis, preaching, etc.) in all countries where the Church is established, and not only where it is in contact with Jews.

(b) The New Testament itself affirms the permanent value of the *Sacred Books* on which the faith of the Jewish people is founded and from which it is nourished. "Think not that I have come to abolish the law and the Prophets; I have come not to abolish them but to fulfill them"

(Mt 5:17); "to them belong the sonship, the glory, the covenants, the giving of the law, the worship and the promises; to them belong the patriarchs. ..." (Rom 9:4); the Jews "are beloved for the sake of their forefathers. For the gifts and the call of God are irrevocable" (Rom 11:28–29).

(c) The Church is not born solely of scripture but also of the living tradition of the Jewish people. Providence has not limited itself to a "simple bookish preparation of the coming of the Messiah" (L. Bouyer, La Bible et l'Evangile, 2, 248). Christ, His apostles, and the first Christians participated in this tradition. "As transforming as Christian revelation may be, it is from the Jewish tradition that it draws not only its formulas, its images, its setting, but even the marrow of its concepts" (ibid. 250). Christianity, on the other hand, is not bound directly to the Old Testament as such, but rather as it was interpreted by the ancient Jewish tradition.

Recent research by exegetes and liturgists has come to the conclusion that in order fully to understand Christian tradition and institutions it is *indispensable* to examine Jewish institutions themselves in depth. This is particularly clear in the case of the origin of the sacraments, Christians have adopted the Jewish feasts and prayers, adapting them to the Revelation brought by Christ. Their fundamental meaning, however, can be grasped only by constant reference to the original milieu. But the Jewish liturgy is still celebrated today in the same terms as in the ancient period when the first Christians participated in it. What more suggestive way is there to understand the institution of the Eucharist in the setting of the Jewish Passover meal than the Passover *Seder* in a Jewish family!

(d) This same fact has been confirmed on the plane of theological research. Every exploration of the fundamental notions of the Christian religion leads to a confrontation with analogous doctrines of inter-testamental Judaism into which they find a point of insertion. It was Providence itself which willed that the Revelation of Christ find its starting point in the doctrines we see circulating in Palestinian Judaism of the first century.

The eschatological and apocalyptical conceptions of sin and redemption, the Incarnation as a presence of the Word of God among us, and other themes again – all this cannot be studied without a profound familiarity with the world of Jewish tradition, not alone of the time of Christ, but as it was formulated at all stages and in every form of Jewish literature as well. . . .

IV. Since the problem of relations with Jews is tied to the very mystery of the Church (*Nostra Aetate*), all Christian Churches are *de facto* involved in the problem. It has therefore an *ecumenical* aspect which it is important to emphasize in the context with which we are dealing. The Christian Churches are divided and we are seeking the unity willed by the Lord. This unity cannot be built except by a return to the common sources, to the origins of faith.

Experience shows, in fact, that whenever the dialogue between Jews and Christians has developed, ecumenical dialogue has itself gained in depth and vitality. When Pope Paul VI addressed the participants of the Congress of International Organizations for the Study of the Old Testament, which brought together Jewish, Protestant, and Catholic scholars, he declared in an audience of April 19, 1968: "The three families, Jewish, Protestant, and Catholic equally hold it (Old Testament) in honor. They are therefore able to study and venerate these Sacred Books together. . . . It is fortunate that the initiative of this joint study has been taken. . . . This is an authentic and fruitful form of ecumenical work indeed" (*L'Osservatore Romano*, April 20, 1968). The deepening of ecumenical relations leads necessarily to an encounter with the Jewish people. K. Barth remarked in 1966: "There are now many good contacts between the Catholic Church and many Protestant Churches, between the Secretariat of Christian Unity and the World Council of Churches. The ecumenical movement is driven by the Spirit of the Lord. But do not forget, there is only one really important question: our relations with Israel."

Many bishops have seen this connection and have established commissions for Jewish-Christian relations in the framework of agencies in charge of ecumenical questions. This ecumenical context shows the spirit in which Jewish-Christian relations should be established and developed.

This spirit can be called ecumenical insofar as the term expresses concern to know the other as he is and as he defines himself; concern to love and respect him in his convictions and in the conceptions which rule his life.

*

Reflections and Suggestions for the Application of the Directives of Nostra Aetate (No. 4). Working Document prepared for the Holy See's Office for Catholic-Jewish Relations, by a special Commission.
December 1969.
(Quoted from Documentary Service, December 16, 1969, of the Press Department, U.S. Catholic Conference)

INTRODUCTION

At the present time the Church is attentive to those new tasks which a world in the throes of rapid cultural, social, and religious changes has thrust upon her. Vatican Council II (*Gaudium et Spes*), is cognizant of the fresh aspirations of humanity that seek to preserve the liberty and dignity of the human person and still other human values in a period of transition and searching. It is against such a background that the new encounter between the Church and Judaism is taking place.

The Declaration of Vatican Council II on Non-Christian Religions of 1965 marks an important turning point in the history of Jewish-Catholic relations. It is a considerable step forward. After two millennia, generally characterized by mutual ignorance and frequent conflict, it has presented the opportunity to engage in or pursue a dialogue aimed at better mutual understanding. In the last four years in various countries numerous initiatives have been taken in this direction, and it has been possible to ascertain better the conditions of this new relationship. The moment is apparently here to gauge with precision the directions the Council has taken and, as a fruit of the experience gained, to offer concrete suggestions that will truly help to achieve the aims of the conciliar document in the life of the Church.

Cognizance is increasingly being gained in the Church of the actual place of the Jewish people in the history of salvation and of its permanent election. This fact points toward a theological renewal and toward a new Christian reflection on the Jewish people that it is important to pursue. On the other hand, it appears that still too often Christians do not know what Jews are. They do not, in any case, see them as they are in themselves and as they define themselves in their present and living reality, as the people of the Bible living in our midst. They do not see them as that people which in its history has encountered the living and true God, the One God who established with that people a covenant, of which circumcision is the sign, the God who accomplished in its favor a miraculous exodus, which it relives each year in its Passover, both as a remembrance of its past and an expectation of the full realization of its promises. This same God has revealed Himself to His people Israel and made to it the gift of the Torah. And He has confided to it a word that "endures forever" (Is 40:8), a word that has become an unquenchable source of life and prayer, in a tradition that has not ceased to enrich itself through the centuries.

Fidelity to the covenant was linked to the gift of a land, which in the Jewish soul has endured as the object of an aspiration that Christians should strive to understand. In the wake of long generations of painful exile, all too often aggravated by persecutions and moral pressures, for which Christians ask pardon of their Jewish brothers, Jews have indicated in a thousand ways their attachment to the land promised to their ancestors from the days of Abraham's calling. It could seem that Christians, whatever the difficulties they may experience, must attempt to understand and respect the religious significance of this link between the people and the land. The existence of the State of Israel should not be separated from this perspective; which does not in itself imply any judgment on historical occurrences or on decisions of a purely political order.

But if such mutual comprehension is indispensable for dialogue between Christians and Jews, reflection on the mystery of Israel is also indispensable for Christianity to define itself, both as to its origins and in its nature as people of God. Without question, many elements from diverse civilizations have ultimately contributed to making Christianity what it is in its doctrines and its institutions; it is no less true that it was within Judaism that Christianity was born and wherein it found essential elements of its faith and cult. From the experience lived in the covenant with God emerged the Christian universe, which derived from that experience the very marrow of its concepts.

The dignity of the human person requires the condemnation of all forms of anti-Semitism (*Nostra Aetate*). In view of these relations of the Church and the Jewish people, it is easier to see how anti-Semitism is essentially opposed to the spirit of Christianity. Still more do these relations show forth the duty of better understanding and mutual esteem.

In keeping with these considerations, we propose a few suggestions that will apply to the principal areas of the life of the Church as well as to relations with Jews.

DIALOGUE

Relations between Christians and Jews have for the most part been no more than a monologue. A true dialogue must now be established. The dialogue, in effect, comprises a favored means for promoting better mutual understanding and a deepening of one's own tradition. The condition of dialogue is respect for the other as he is, for his faith and religious convictions. All intent of proselytizing and conversion is excluded. Great openness of mind, distrust of one's own prejudices, and tact, such are the indispensable qualities required if one is not, even unconsciously, to offend the other party to the dialogue. In addition to fraternal conversations and biblical studies in common, meetings of competent persons to study problems that may arise are to be fostered.

Whenever possible and mutually desirable, meeting before God in prayer and silent meditation should be encouraged. This practice can create that openness of spirit and humility of heart so necessary for understanding of self and others. It is indicated in particular when dealing with major questions, such as those of justice and peace. . . .

EDUCATION

Although much study and research remains to be done, in recent years a better understanding of Judaism and its relation to the Church has been gained through the teaching of the Church, scholarly research, and dialogue. In this respect, the following facts should be kept in mind: . . . .

(c) The Old Testament and Jewish tradition should not be opposed to the New Testament in such a way as to make it appear as a religion of justice alone, a religion of fear and of legalism, implying that only Christianity possesses the law of love and freedom.

(d) Jesus, as also His disciples, was a Jew. He presented Himself as continuing and fulfilling the anterior Revelation, the basic teachings of which He offered anew, using the same teaching method as the rabbis of His time. The points on which He took issue with the Judaism of His time are fewer than those in which He found Himself in agreement with it. Whenever He opposed it, this was always from within the Jewish people, just as did the prophets before Him.

(e) As to the trial and death of Jesus, Vatican Council II has reminded us that "what happened in Jesus' Passion cannot be blamed upon all the

Jews then living, without distinction, nor upon the Jews of today" (*Nostra Aetate*).

(f) The history of Judaism does not end with the destruction of Jerusalem, but continues to develop in a rich spiritual tradition.

(g) According to New Testament teaching, the Jewish people play an essential role in the eschatological fulfillment of history.

The teaching of these data should be extended to all levels of Christian education. Among educational media, the following hold here a particular importance: Catechetical manuals, history textbooks, social media of communication (the press, radio, films, television).

The effective use of these means, of course, presupposes a thorough training of teachers and educators in normal schools, seminaries, and universities.

Further research on problems touching upon Judaism and Jewish-Christian relations are to be urged, especially in the fields of exegesis, theology, history, and sociology. Catholic institutions of learning and individual scholars are called upon to contribute toward the elucidation of these problems. Where possible, a chair on Judaism should be established, and collaboration with Jewish scholars encouraged.

JOINT SOCIAL ACTION

Jewish and Christian tradition, founded upon the word of God, is deeply conscious of the value of the human person, made in God's image. The love of the same God ought to be translated into efficacious action in the interest of mankind. In the spirit of the prophets, Jews and Christians will collaborate willingly in the pursuit of social justice and peace. This cooperation should extend to local, national, and international levels. And joint action can also work toward a large measure of mutual knowledge and esteem.

CONCLUSION

Vatican Council II has indicated the path to follow in the rediscovery of a deepened fraternity among Christians and Jews. There remains, none-theless, a long road ahead.

The problem of Jewish-Christian relations is of concern to the Church as such by the very fact that it is in "searching into its own mystery" that it comes upon the mystery of Israel. The problem hence retains all its importance even in those places where a Jewish community does not exist.

Moreover, it includes an ecumenical aspect. Christian churches, in search of the unity willed by the Lord, will find this by a return to the sources and origins of their faith, grafted on the Jewish tradition, which is still living in our own day. In this area, the bishops are invited to take every initiative they consider opportune. They should establish, for example, on national and regional levels, commissions or secretariats, or name a competent person, charged with the responsibility of promoting implementations of the conciliar directives and the suggestions proposed herein.

The Vatican Office for Catholic-Jewish Relations has been established in order to promote and stimulate relations between Christians and Jews. It places itself at the service of all agencies devoted to this work, in order to assist them in their task and to keep them informed, in the hope that by such a collaboration the aims of the Council will be effectively carried out.

*

In October 1974, Pope Paul set up a Commission for Religious Relations with the Jews.

Guidelines and Suggestions for Implementing the Conciliar Declaration Nostra Aetate (No. 4), by the Vatican Commission for Religious Relations with the Jews. January 1975.

The Declaration *Nostra Aetate*, issued by the Second Vatican Council on October 28, 1965, "On the Relationship of the Church to Non-Christian Religions" (No. 4), marks an important milestone in the history of Jewish-Christians relations.

Moreover, the step taken by the Council finds its historical setting in circumstances deeply affected by the memory of the persecution and massacre of Jews which took place in Europe just before and during the Second World War.

Although Christianity sprang from Judaism, taking from it certain essential elements of its faith and divine cult, the gap dividing them was deepened more and more, to such an extent that Christian and Jew hardly knew each other.

After two thousand years, too often marked by mutual ignorance and frequent confrontation, the Declaration *Nostra Aetate* provides an opportunity to open or to continue a dialogue with a view to better mutual

410

understanding. Over the past nine years, many steps in this direction have been taken in various countries. As a result, it is easier to distinguish the conditions under which a new relationship between Jews and Christians may be worked out and developed. This seems the right moment to propose, following the guidelines of the Council, some concrete suggestions born of experience, hoping that they will help to bring into actual existence in the life of the Church the intentions expressed in the conciliar document.

While referring the reader back to this document, we may simply restate here that the spiritual bonds and historical links binding the Church to Judaism condemn (as opposed to the very spirit of Christianity) all forms of anti-Semitism and discrimination, which in any case the dignity of the human person alone would suffice to condemn. Further still, these links and relationships render obligatory a better mutual understanding and renewed mutual esteem. On the practical level in particular, Christians must therefore strive to acquire a better knowledge of the basic components of the religious tradition of Judaism; they must strive to learn by what essential traits the Jews define themselves in the light of their own religious experience.

With due respect for such matters of principle, we simply propose some first practical applications in different essential areas of the Church's life, with a view to launching or developing sound relations between Catholics and their Jewish brothers....

*

EUROPEAN STATEMENTS

Memorandum by the Christian-Jewish Coordination Committee of Vienna, which served as basis for the Synodal Statement. 1968 (Quoted from Christlich-Pädagogische Blätter. 1968, 2, Vienna. By kind permission. Translated from the German original.)

A legitimate catechetical representation of Judaism is a Christian problem because Christianity without the provisions of the Old Testament is unthinkable or heretical. Christians must try to understand Judaism apart from the terrible consequences of anti-Semitism in recent times. Yet, anti-Semitism frequently operates with religious arguments and it is an important task of Christian catechists to examine those arguments for their justification. Hence, general and practical proposals are herewith submitted for a new version of religious textbooks, as far as they relate to Judaism. . . .

During the Plenary Session of the Pastoral Council of the Catholic Church in the Netherlands in 1970 at Noordwijkerhout, a series of "Pastoral Recommendations" were studied from a plan for "Relations between Jews and Christians." This final document was drawn up by the Sub-Commission "The Church and Israel." According to the methods of this Pastoral Council, only the "Pastoral Recommendations" were voted on and are now official conclusions. (Quoted in SIDIC, Vol. III No. 2, 1970). With kind permission.

Plan of report: "Relations between Jews and Christians" Introduction – Motives and plan. . . .

The Jewish people have their special place in the Church's faith. They can never be simply equated with non-Christian peoples. The Church knows that she cannot be the Church for all Nations, without being connected to the living Jewish people of today. She believes that, through her Head, Jesus Christ, she remains united forever to the Jewish people, not only historically, but also in its continued existence. The unbroken and particular link between the Jewish people and the Church must be a determining factor in the Church's own mission, and her attitude towards the present-day Jewish people. This will help the Church to a better understanding of her mission in the world, and to the fostering of unity with other Churches. . . .

The close connection between Jews and Christians consists not only in the historical origin of Christianity in Judaism but, above all, despite different outlooks, they have many elements in common in the Church's daily life, and in Jewish worship, namely: the liturgy of the Word, the Lamb of God and the ministry of reconciliation.

Attention is also called to the improvement in social relations between Jews and Christians, in two paragraphs, Catechesis concerning the Jewish people, and Education and Information regarding the relations between Jews and Christians.

CHAPTER 1: ANTI-SEMITISM

Referring to the Declaration of Vatican II *Nostra Aetate*, the Pastoral Council condemns every form of anti-Semitism.

1. The Vatican Council states (*Nostra Aetate*, No. 4): "We cannot in truthfulness call upon that God who is the Father of all, if we refuse to act in a brotherly way towards all men, created as they are in God's image. A man's relationship to God the Father and his relationship with his brother men are so linked together that Scripture says: 'He who does not love, does not know God' (1 John 4:8). This is a condemnation of any theory or practice which discriminates between one man and another, between one people and another, in their human dignity, hence in their human rights."

2. This is particularly true in any sincere reflection about relations with Jews and with the Jewish people. Anti-Semitism is not only a form of unjust discrimination with regard to a human group or people, but it is also resistance to a fundamental view of life. It is directed not only against the Jews as an ethnic or sociological group but, above all, against their very existence as the result of their history and religious experience. In this context, anti-Semitism fundamentally means a misjudgment of the very nature of God's action with the Jewish people, the firstborn of all peoples. If this aspect of anti-Semitism is not recognized, we continue to risk making a wrong estimation of the qualities and behavior of the Jewish people.

3. In the past and even today, Christians and their Churches have looked upon the history of God's people too much from their own, all too human, point of view. The Church has always been predominantly considered the Church of the Gentiles, to the exclusion of the Jewish people, and a common spiritual heritage has been lost. This, among other things, has been the cause of unspeakable injustices that have been committed against the Jews. The extent of such injustice was revealed in this present century, when the vast number of Christians and their Churches hardly raised their voices against a massacre of the Jewish people which exceeds all imagining – a massacre in which all men share responsibility.

4. Religious thinking about the very existence of the Jewish people as such shows that there is a particular relationship between the Jewish people and the Promised Land. The Jews consider this relationship not only as historical, cultural, or religious phenomenon but as an indissoluble element in their expectation of the day when all nations will embrace in peace and justice. To neglect or deny this fact may be the cause of misunderstanding

413

and help to nourish prejudice about the nature of the Jewish people and its place among the nations, a misunderstanding which has already led and may lead again to discrimination. The presence of anti-Semitism requires great caution and a sound knowledge of Jewish reality.

CHAPTER II: THE RELATIONSHIP OF THE CHURCH TO THE JEWISH PEOPLE

The Declaration of the Second Vatican Council indicates the spiritual connection of the people of the New Testament with that of Abraham's race (*Nostra Aetate*, No. 4a). The Council points out the continuation of the Old Testament in the New, and how the Church was prefigured and took root in the Jewish people. In his Letters to the Ephesians and Romans, St. Paul recalled the connection which has always existed between the Church and the Jewish people; the great spiritual patrimony which they share, and how the Church, together with the prophets and the same Apostle, awaits the day, known to God alone, when all nations will invoke the Lord "and serve him with one consent" (Zeph 3:9).

The Pastoral Council of the Roman Catholic Church in the Netherlands believes that, according to the Law, the Prophets and the Psalms (Lk 24:44; Lk 13.34–35), the Jewish people has been constituted forever as a testimony of God's saving alliance with mankind (Is 43:10; Rm 9–11). God's promise *par excellence* to the Jewish people is the everlasting covenant (cf. Rm 9:4–5; 11:29; Eph 2:12). The Pastoral Council believes that Jesus Christ, born under the Law (cf. Gal 4:5), is the one whom the prophets, the righteous and kings desired to see (Mt 13:17; Lk 10:24), because in Him the revelation of God's eternal love reached its plenitude (cf. Eph 1:10; Col 1:15–23). The Pastoral Council states that in Jesus Christ, peace has been initiated, uniting the two worlds and breaking down the wall of separation between Jews and Gentiles (cf. Eph 2:14–15). He shall come to complete this peace (John 16:33; Rev 21). That is why also the as yet unfulfilled promises of God to the Jewish people are held in honor in liturgical prayer.

With gratitude the Roman Catholic Church in the Netherlands commemorates the true spiritual tradition in which the Jews have preserved the Law and the Prophets. She also recognizes the many spiritual and religious values existing among the Jewish people, which provide a permanent stimulus and the reason for an examination of the Church's conscience, being as they are of great significance for justice and peace in the whole world.

Consequently, the Roman Catholic Church in the Netherlands is doing her utmost to promote the renewal of Jewish-Christian relations through mutual knowledge and esteem, as the Second Vatican Council proposed to the whole Church. Searching the Scriptures and history together with equal readiness to learn from them will be a great contribution to this cause. Any intention or design for proselytism must be rejected as contrary to human dignity and Christian conviction. Moreover, the position of the Jewish people with regard to the universal message of Christ cannot be equated with the position of those professing other non-Christian religions. Christians are confronted today with the problem of recognizing the ways of God in human history, as well as the position of religion in a secularized society. It may be appropriate to attempt an integration of Jewish tradition into our approach to these questions....

All traces of anti-Semitism should disappear. This applies to texts in some parts of the Missal and Breviary, particularly to presentations of Christ's Passion where Jesus, Mary, and the apostles are featured as non-Jews while the other Jews are caricatured. Care must be taken that old prejudices do not unintentionally creep in again.

Texts that may give rise to misunderstanding if read out of context or without knowledge of the historical circumstances or linguistic usage of the times, should be carefully placed in their right perspective in all sermons so that they may contribute to a new attitude towards the Jewish people.

CHAPTER IV: CATECHESIS AND THE JEWISH PEOPLE

1. Catechesis should provide an important contribution to the improvement of Jewish-Christian relations, and to fruitful interaction between Judaism and Christianity. In the past, it was the way in which catechesis was presented that prejudice was fostered against the Jewish people, in succeeding generations. Even present-day catechesis frequently fails in these respects: mainly by unconscious misjudgment or disdain of the Jewish people, past or present; by lack of a positive approach to the Jewish people; by an insufficient concept of the true nature and extent of anti-Semitism.

2. Conditions to develop a correct catechesis regarding the Jewish people are:
(a) A thorough knowledge and a right understanding of the Bible as the proclamation of God's action in mankind. A correct relationship to the

Jewish people can never come about as long as the Christian feels a stranger to the Bible. Belittling ideas about the Jewish people will inevitably live on as long as the preaching of Jesus and the apostles is detached from its historical Jewish background and Christianity presented as a system of abstract truth. The history of the Jewish people before and after Christ must be considered in its particular meaning for salvation history.

(b) A sincere, faithful reflection on the relationship of the Church to the Jewish people, according to the ideas developed in the previous chapter.

(c) Respect for the full historical truth about the Jewish people and correct information on present-day Jews and Judaism.

3. Certain points that demand particular attention:

(a) The Jewish people must be seen as the people with whom God concluded His covenant for all time. The Old Testament does not exist only as a prefiguration of the New but has a significance of its own, in Jewish as in world history.

(b) The Jewish people is not collectively guilty of the Passion and the Death of Jesus Christ nor of His rejection as Messiah. Though the Jewish authorities and their followers clamored for His death, *Nostra Aetate* (No. 4) states: "... what happened in His Passion cannot be blamed upon all the Jews then living, without distinction, nor upon the Jews of today." The Jewish people is not condemned nor bereft of its election. Their sufferings, dispersion, and persecutions are not punishments for the Crucifixion or rejection of Jesus. It is unjust to accuse the Jews of "deicide."

(c) It is not self-evident at all that a complete rupture occurred between Jews and Christians since Jesus Himself – born of a Jewish mother – never severed the bonds with His people. The young Church was rooted in the Jewish people.

(d) Catechesis should truthfully represent the religious life of Jews in our day.

(e) It is incorrect and unfair to place the New Testament and the Old in opposition to one another, the New Testament as a covenant of love, the Old as one of fear. The proclamation of God's love for man and man's love for his fellow men in charity, fidelity, and injustice forms an essential part of the Old Testament.

(f) The Gospel message and apostolic preaching about the significance of the Jewish people in the ultimate unification of the world (Mt 23:37–39;

Lk 13:35; Acts 1:7; Rom 9–11; Eph 2:11–22) should be brought into more distinctive relief. . . .

8. New Testament passages on the destiny of the Jewish people refer to the tradition of the Prophets of Israel, who to the threat of rejection joined the promise of final restoration.

9. It is obvious that the Jewish people as such is not guilty of the condemnation and death of Jesus Christ in his Passion, nor of the refusal of his Messianic mission. We must not cast suspicion upon the good faith of the Jewish contemporaries of Jesus, regarding their fidelity to Judaism and their opposition to a Christianity in the making. From a theological point of view, moreover, we must underline the solidarity in sin of all mankind. "Christ underwent his passion and death freely, because of the sins of men. . . ." (*Nostra Aetate*, No. 4)

The Church and the Jewish People
10. To insist that the Church has taken the place of the Jewish people as salvific institution, is a facile interpretation according to which everything new replaces the old. In that sense, the new covenant evokes the idea of an old one, the new people of God that of an old Israel, etc. The eschatological biblical promise of a new covenant means essentially the definitive and decisive restoration of the Covenant after the rupture caused by human infidelity. According to Christian faith, that promise was realized in the Messiah Jesus. The Church may call herself "people of the covenant" only to the extent that she lives – as body of Christ – according to the message and Messianic reality of Jesus. She will not fully be that people until the end of time.

11. The fundamental Christian commandment, promulgated in the Old Testament and confirmed by Jesus Christ, to love God and neighbor, is binding for Christians and Jews in all their human relations and without exception.

12. We must avoid to disparage biblical or post-biblical Judaism, its laws, institutions, and ways of life, for the purpose of elevating Christianity, by misplaced caricaturistic opposites, e.g.: legalism-faith; flesh-spirit; fear-love; doctrine-life; earth-heaven; cult-works; institutional

417

sclerosis-prophetic élan; promise-realization. These actually are constructive tensions which exist between communities, and at the heart of any community of a religious order.

13. The Jewish people is a true relative of the Church, not her rival or a minority to be assimilated. The descendants of Abraham and the Christian people must not enter into competition in the history of salvation. In the dialectic of divine grace and human liberty Christians and Jews fulfil their specific roles and stimulate each other regarding the salvation of the nations (Rom ch. 9–11). . . . .

16. Since the relations with Jews are linked to the very mystery of the Church (*Nostra Aetate*, No. 4), all the churches and Christian communities are called upon to promote them. Christian unity cannot be realized without a return to the sources, not only by taking up the relationship at the place where it was broken, but rather by rediscovering the roots of Jesus and his message in the history and tradition of his people. To exclude Judaism as well as the Judaism of our time from Christian source material, would be a misunderstanding of the Jewish origins of Christianity. An approach to Judaism, on the other hand, from the view point of Christian sources, goes hand in hand with profound respect for Judaism's own and different character.

17. The suffering, persecution, and dispersion which Jews had to endure, must not be represented as an inevitable fate or, worse, a punishment. Anti-Semitism in all its forms, the always latent religious anti-Semitism in particular, must be denounced and combated, in order to be more true to Christian faith and divine revelation; to make possible authentic relations between Christians and Jews; and as a condition for the establishment of a more humane world.

18. To the extent that Christianity rediscovers in Judaism the roots of her own faith and no longer considers Judaism an errant or obsolete religion, the missionary witness of the Church will no more attempt a "conversion of the Jews," in the current sense of the term, that is, annexation or proselytism. Christians have a duty to witness to their faith in Jesus the Messiah, in particular by their works. This witness, however, in order to be true to the message of Christ, must be a message of love, justice, and respect

for others. With regard to Judaism in particular, Christian witness must be humble and respectful because it must take into account the common elements of Jewish and Christian Messianic hope.

Endnotes to Appendix I

1. These have been excerpted from *Stepping Stones to Further Jewish-Christian Relations*, compiled by Helga Croner, London, New York, 1977, pass. These texts document some of the early effects of *Nostra Aetate*.

This book contains many important American Catholic documents also joint Jewish-Christian ones, as well as Protestant documents from the World Council of Churches, various Church Groups, and a joint Protestant-Catholic document from 1973. They show nuanced differences, but all reflect the impact of *Nostra Aetate*.

Here I have added the references found in the version included in Augustin Cardinal Bea S.J., The Church and the Jewish People, New York, 1966, pp. 150–152 (where there is a slightly different translation of the Declaration, but not substantially so).

Between Jerusalem and Rome:
Reflections on 50 Years of *Nostra Aetate*[1]

PREAMBLE

In the biblical account of creation, God fashions a single human being as the progenitor of all humanity. Thus, the Bible's unmistakable message is that all human beings are members of a single family. And after the deluge of Noah, this message is reinforced when the new phase of history is once again inaugurated by a single family. In the beginning, God's providence is exercised over a universal, undifferentiated humanity.

As God chose Abraham, and subsequently Isaac and Jacob, he entrusted them with a dual mission: to found the nation of Israel that would inherit, settle and establish a model society in the holy, promised land of Israel, all while serving as a source of light for all mankind.

Ever since, particularly in the aftermath of the destruction of the Second Temple in Jerusalem in 70 C.E. by the Romans, we Jews encountered persecution after exile after persecution. And yet, *the Eternal One of Israel does not lie*,[2] and His eternal covenant with the nation of Israel manifested itself time and again: despite the greatest adversities, our nation has endured.[3] After the darkest hour since the destruction of our holy Temple in Jerusalem, when six million of our brethren were viciously murdered and the embers of their bones were smoldering in the shadows of the Nazi crematoria, God's eternal covenant was once again manifest, as the remnants of Israel gathered their strength and enacted a miraculous reawakening of Jewish consciousness. Communities were reestablished throughout the Diaspora, and many Jews responded to the clarion call to return to Eretz Yisrael, where a sovereign Jewish state arose.

The Jewish people's dual obligations – *to be a light unto the nations*[4] and to secure its own future despite the world's hatred and violence – have been overwhelmingly difficult to fulfill. Despite innumerable obstacles, the Jewish nation has bequeathed many blessings upon mankind, both in the realms of the sciences, culture, philosophy, literature, technology and commerce, and in the realms of faith, spirituality, ethics and morality. These, too, are a manifestation of God's eternal covenant with the Jewish people.

Undoubtedly, the Shoah constitutes the historical nadir of the relations between Jews and our non-Jewish neighbors in Europe. Out of the continent nurtured by Christianity for over a millennium, a bitter and evil shoot sprouted forth, murdering six million of our brethren with industrial precision, including one and a half million children. Many of those who participated in this most heinous crime, exterminating entire families and communities, had been nurtured in Christian families and communities.[5]

At the same time, throughout that millennium, even in very dark times, heroic individuals arose – sons and daughters of the Catholic Church, both laymen and leaders – who fought against the persecution of Jews, helping them in the darkest of times.[6]

With the close of World War II, a new era of peaceful coexistence and acceptance began to emerge in Western European countries, and an era of bridge-building and tolerance took hold in many Christian denominations. Faith communities reevaluated their historical rejections of others, and decades of fruitful interaction and cooperation began. Moreover, though we Jews had achieved political emancipation a century or two before, we were not yet truly accepted as equal, full-fledged members of the nations in which we lived. Following the Shoah, Jewish emancipation in the Diaspora, as well as the right of the Jewish people to live as a sovereign nation in our own land, finally became obvious and natural.

During the ensuing seven decades, Jewish communities and spiritual leaders gradually reassessed Judaism's relationship with the members and leaders of other faith communities.

TURNAROUND – *NOSTRA AETATE*

Fifty years ago, twenty years after the Shoah, with its declaration *Nostra Aetate* (No. 4),[7] the Catholic Church began a process of introspection that increasingly led to any hostility toward Jews being expurgated from Church doctrine, enabling trust and confidence to grow between our respective faith communities.

In this regard, Pope John XXIII was a transformative figure in Jewish-Catholic relations no less than in the history of the Church itself. He played a courageous role in rescuing Jews during the Holocaust, and it was his recognition of the need to revise "the teaching of contempt" that helped overcome resistance to change and ultimately facilitated the adoption of *Nostra Aetate* (No. 4).

In its most focused, concrete, and, for the Church, most dramatic[8] assertion, *Nostra Aetate* recognized that any Jew who was not directly and personally involved in the Crucifixion did not bear any responsibility for it.[9] Pope Benedict XVI's elaborations and explications of this theme are particularly noteworthy.[10]

In addition, basing itself on Christian Scriptures, *Nostra Aetate* asserted that the Divine election of Israel, which it calls "the gift of God," will not be revoked, stating, "God ... does not repent of the gifts He makes or of the calls He issues." It issued the injunction that "the Jews should not be presented as rejected or accursed by God." Later, in 2013, Pope Francis elaborated upon this theme in his apostolic exhortation Evangelii Gaudium: "God continues to work among the people of the Old Covenant and to bring forth treasures of wisdom which flow from their encounter with His word.[11]

Nostra Aetate also paved the way for the Vatican's 1993 establishment of full diplomatic relations with the State of Israel. Through the establishment of this relationship, the Catholic Church showed how it had truly repudiated its portrayal of the Jewish people as a nation condemned to waqnder until the final advent. This historic moment facilitated Pope John Paul II's pilgrimage to Israel in 2000, which served as another powerful demonstration of a new era in Catholic-Jewish relations. Since then, the last two popes have also made similar state visits.

Nostra Aetate strongly "decries hatred, persecutions, displays of anti-Semitism, directed against Jews at any time and by anyone" as a matter of religious duty. Accordingly, Pope John Paul II repeatedly affirmed that anti-Semitism is "a sin against God and humanity." At the Western Wall in Jerusalem, he recited the following prayer: "God of our fathers, You chose Abraham and his descendants to bring Your Name to the Nations. We are deeply saddened by the behavior of those who in the course of history have caused these children of Yours to suffer, and asking Your forgiveness we wish to commit ourselves to genuine brotherhood with the people of the Covenant."

Pope Francis recently recognized a new, pervasive and even fashionable form of anti-Semitism, when he told a World Jewish Congress delegation: "To attack Jews is anti-Semitism, but an outright attack on the State of Israel is also anti-Semitism. There may be political disagreements between governments and on political issues, but the State of Israel has every right to exist in safety and prosperity."[12]

Finally, *Nostra Aetate* called for fostering "mutual understanding and respect," and for conducting "fraternal dialogues." In 1974, Pope Paul VI heeded this call by creating the Pontifical Commission for Religious Relations with the Jews; the Jewish community, in response to this call, has met regularly with Church representatives.

We applaud the work of popes, church leaders, and scholars who passionately contributed to these developments, including the strong-willed proponents of Catholic-Jewish dialogue at the end of World War II, whose collective work was a leading impetus for *Nostra Aetate*. The most important milestones were the Second Vatican Council, the establishment of the Pontifical Commission for Religious Relations with Jews, the recognition of Judaism as a living religion with an eternal covenant, the appreciation of the significance of the Shoah and its antecedents, and the establishment of diplomatic relations with the State of Israel. The theological writings of the heads of the Commission for Religious Relations with the Jews have contributed much to the Church documents which followed *Nostra Aetate*, as have the writings of numerous other theologians.

In its recent reflections on *Nostra Aetate*, "The Gifts and Calling of God are Irrevocable," the Pontifical Commission unambiguously endorsed the notion that Jews are participants in God's salvation, calling this idea "an unfathomable divine mystery."[13] It further proclaimed that "the Catholic Church neither conducts nor supports any specific institutional mission work directed towards Jews."[14] Though the Catholic Church has not disavowed witnessing to Jews, it has nonetheless shown understanding and sensitivity towards deeply held Jewish sensibilities, and distanced itself from active mission to Jews.

The transformation of the attitude of the Church toward the Jewish community is strikingly exemplified by the recent visit of Pope Francis to a synagogue, which renders him the third Pope to make this highly significant gesture. We echo his comment, "From enemies and strangers we have become friends and brothers. It is my hope that closeness, mutual understanding and respect between our two communities continue to grow."

These welcoming attitudes and actions stand in stark contrast with centuries of teachings of contempt and of pervasive hostility, and herald a most encouraging chapter in an epic process of societal transformation.

EVALUATION AND REEVALUATION

Initially, many Jewish leaders[15] were skeptical of the sincerity of the church's overtures to the Jewish community, due to the long history of Christian anti-Judaism. Over time, it has become clear that the transformations in the Church's attitudes and teachings are not only sincere but also increasingly profound, and that we are entering an era of growing tolerance, mutual respect, and solidarity between members of our respective faiths.

Orthodox Judaism – through the American Orthodox Union and the Rabbinical Council of America – had already been a part of the International Jewish Committee for Interreligious Consultations (IJCIC) set up in the late sixties, as the official Jewish representative for relations with the Vatican. A new page in the relations of Orthodox Judaism with the Catholic Church was turned with the establishment of the bilateral committee of the Chief Rabbinate of Israel with the Vatican, commencing in 2002 under the chairmanship of the chief rabbi of Haifa Rabbi She'ar Yashuv Cohen. The published declarations from the thirteen meetings of this bilateral commission (alternating annually between Rome and Jerusalem) carefully avoid matters pertaining to fundamentals of faith, but rather address a broad spectrum of contemporary social and scientific challenges, highlighting shared values while respecting the differences between the two faith traditions.

We acknowledge that this fraternity cannot sweep away our doctrinal differences; it does, rather, reinforce genuine mutual positive dispositions towards fundamental values that we share, including but not limited to reverence for the Hebrew Bible.[16]

The theological differences between Judaism and Christianity are profound. The core beliefs of Christianity that center on the person of "Jesus as the Messiah" and the embodiment of the "second person of a triune God" create an irreconcilable separation from Judaism. The history of Jewish martyrdom in Christian Europe serves as tragic testimony to the devotion and tenacity with which Jews resisted beliefs incompatible with their ancient and eternal faith, which requires absolute fidelity to both the Written and Oral Torah. Despite those profound differences, some of Judaism's highest authorities have asserted that Christians maintain a special status because they worship the Creator of Heaven and Earth Who liberated the people of Israel from Egyptian bondage and Who exercises providence over all creation.[17]

The doctrinal differences are essential and cannot be debated or negotiated; their meaning and importance belong to the internal deliberations of the respective faith communities. Judaism, drawing its particularity from its received Tradition, going back to the days of its glorious prophets and particularly to the Revelation at Sinai, will forever remain loyal to its principles, laws and eternal teachings. Furthermore, our interfaith discussions are informed by the profound insights of such great Jewish thinkers as Rabbi Joseph Ber Soloveitchik,[18] Rabbi Lord Immanuel Jakobovits,[19] and many others, who eloquently argued that the religious experience is a private one which can often only be truly understood within the framework of its own faith community.

However, doctrinal differences do not and may not stand in the way of our peaceful collaboration for the betterment of our shared world and the lives of the children of Noah. To further this end, it is crucial that our faith communities continue to encounter and grow acquainted with one another, and earn each other's trust.

THE ROAD FORWARD

Despite the irreconcilable theological differences, we Jews view Catholics as our partners, close allies, friends and brothers in our mutual quest for a better world blessed with peace, social justice and security.[20]

We understand our mission to be *a light unto the nations*, which obliges us to contribute to humanity's appreciation for holiness, morality and piety. As the Western world grows more and more secular, it abandons many of the moral values shared by Jews and Christians. Religious freedom is thus increasingly threatened by the forces of both secularism and religious extremism. We therefore seek the partnership of the Catholic community in particular, and other faith communities in general, to assure the future of religious freedom, to foster the moral principles of our faiths, particularly the sanctity of life and the significance of the traditional family, and "to cultivate the moral and religious conscience of society."[21] One of the lessons of the Shoah is the obligations, for Jews as well as gentiles, to combat antisemitism in particular, especially in light of once again growing antisemitism. These lessons have to be expressed both in the educational and in the legal spheres of all nations, without compromise.

Furthermore, as a people who suffered from persecution and genocide throughout our history, we are all too aware of the very real danger facing many Christians in the Middle East and elsewhere; as they are persecuted and menaced by violence and death at the hands of those who invoke God's Name in vain through violence and terror.

We condemn hereby any and all violence against any person on account of his beliefs or his religion. We similarly condemn all acts of vandalism, wanton destruction and/or desecration of the hallowed places of all religions.

We call upon the Church to join us in deepening our combat against our generation's new barbarism, namely the radical offshoots of Islam, which endanger our global society and does not spare the very numerous moderate Muslims. It threatens world peace in general and the Christian and Jewish communities in particular. We call on all people of good will to join forces to fight this evil.

Despite profound theological differences, Catholics and Jews share common beliefs in the Divine origin of the Torah and in the idea of an ultimate redemption, and now, also in the affirmation that religions must use moral behavior and religious education – not war, coer5cion, or social pressure – to influence and inspire.

We ordinarily refrain from expressing expectations regarding other faith communities' doctrines. However, certain kinds of doctrines cause real suffering; those Christian doctrines, rituals and teachings that express negative attitudes toward Jews and Judaism do inspire and nurture anti-Semitism. Therefore, to extend the amicable relations and common causes cultivated between Catholics and Jews as a result of *Nostra Aetate*, we call upon all Christian denominations that have not yet done so to follow the example of the Catholic Church and excise anti-Semitism from their liturgy and doctrines, to end the active mission to Jews, and to work towards a better world hand-in-hand with us, the Jewish people.

We seek to deepen our dialogue and partnership with the Church in order to foster our mutual understanding and to advance the goals outlined above. We seek to find additional ways that will enable us, together, to improve the world: to go in God's ways, feed the hungry and dress the naked, give joy to widows and orphans, provide refuge to the persecuted and the oppressed, and thus merit His blessings.

The 13th of Iyar, 5777 (May 9th 2017)

For the CER

| Rabbi Pinchas Goldschmidt, CER President | Rabbi Riccardo Di Segni, CER Vice President | Rabbi Arie Folger, Chairman of the *Nostra Aetate* Response Committee |

For the Chief Rabbinate

| Chief Rabbi David Lau, Chief Rabbi of Israel | Chief Rabbi Yitzchak Yosef, The Rishon le-Tziyon |

For the RCA

| Rabbi Shalom Baum, RCA President | Rabbi Mark Dratch, RCA Executive Vice President | Rabbi Dr. David Berger Senior Advisor on Interfaith Affairs |

About the Signatory Organizations

CER The Conference of European Rabbis (CER) is the primary rabbinical alliance in Europe. It unites more than 700 religious leaders of the mainstream synagogue communities in Europe. The conference is designed to maintain and defend the religious rights of Jews in Europe and has become the voice of Judaism for the European continent.

Chief Rabbinate of Israel The Chief Rabbinate of Israel is recognized by Israeli law as the head of religious law and spiritual authority for the Jewish people in Israel. A Chief Rabbinate Council assists the two chief rabbis, who alternate in its presidency. It has legal and administrative authority to organize religious arrangements for Israel's Jews. It also responds to *halakhic* questions submitted by Jewish public bodies in the Diaspora. By law, the chief rabbinate has jurisdiction over marriage and divorce, burials of Jews, conversion to Judaism, establishing Jewish identity, supervision of the rabbinical courts system, kosher certification and supervision of holy sites.

RCA The Rabbinical Council of America, with national headquarters in new York City, is a professional organization serving more than 1000 Orthodox Rabbis in the United States of America, Canada, Israel, and around the world. Membership is comprised of duly ordained orthodox Rabbis who serve in positions of the congregational rabbinate, Jewish education, chaplaincies, and other allied fields of Jewish communal work.

Endnotes to Appendix II

1. The following individuals represented the three organizations that are signatories to this document in the committees that authored the document:

For the Conference of European Rabbis: Rabbis Pinchas Goldschmidt (CER president), Arie Folger (chairman of the committee), Yaakov Bleich, Riccardo Di Segni, Bruno Fiszon, Jonathan Gutentag, René Gutman, Moché Lewin, Aryeh Ralbag & Yihyeh Teboul.

For the Rabbinical Council of America: Rabbis Shalom Baum (RCA president), Mark Dratch (RCA executive vice president), Yitzchok Adlerstein, David Berger & Barry Kornblau.

For the Chief Rabbinate of Israel: Rabbi David Rosen and Mr. Oded Wiener.

2. I Samuel 15:29

3. Cf. Genesis 17:7 & 17:19, Leviticus 26:42–45, Deuteronomy 20:3-5, etc.

4. Isaiah 49:6

5. Pope John Paul II wrote: "It is appropriate that, as the Second Millennium of Christianity draws to a close, the Church should become more fully conscious of the sinfulness of her children . . ." (Pope John Paul II< Apostolic Letter *Tertio Millennio Adveniente*, 10 November 1994, 33: Acta Apostolicae Sedis 87 (1995), 25.)

The Pontifical Commission for Religious Relations with the Jews wrote: "The fact that the Shoah took place in Europe, that is, in countries of long-standing Christian civilization, raises the question of the relation between the Nazi persecution and the attitudes down the centuries of Christians towards the Jews." (*We Remember: Reflections on the Shoah*, 16 March 1998.)

6. Two examples among the many such heroes of history are the abbot Bernard of Clairvaux during the Crusades and Jules-Géraud Cardinal Saliège of Toulouse during World War II. When, during the Crusades, a fellow Cistercian monk began exhorting Germans to destroy the Jews before waging war on the Muslims, Abbot Bernard of Clairvaux went personally to put a stop to it. As Rabbi Efraim of Bonn wrote:

430

One decent priest by the name of Bernard, a great figure and master of all the priests, who knew and understood their religion, said to them: ... "My disciple who preached that the Jews should be destroyed spoke improperly, for it is written of them in the Book of Psalms, 'Do not kill them lest my people forget.'" All the people regarded this priest as one of their saints, and our investigation did not indicate that he took bribes for speaking well of Israel. When they heard this, many of them stopped their efforts to bring about our deaths. (*Sefer Zekhirah*, ed. by A.M. Haberman, p. 18.)

Jules-Géraud Saliège (February 24, 1870–November 5, 1956) was the Catholic Archbishop of Toulouse from 1928 until his death, and was a significant figure in Catholic resistance to the pro-Nazis regime in France. He was made cardinal in 1946 by Pope Pius XII. Yad Vashem recognized him as a Righteous among the Nations for his efforts to protect Jews during the Shoah.

7. The main subject of this section is *Nostra Aetate*'s fourth section, which deals particularly with the Catholic Church's relationship to the Jews. So as to read less tediously, henceforth reference will be made to just *Nostra Aetate*, however, throughout our document, it is particularly section 4 that we refer to.

8. *Nostra Aetate*'s assertion is rooted in earlier church teachings, such as the Catechism of the Council of Trent, from 1566. Article 4 of that document's section entitled The Creed, relativizes the Jews' imputed guilt by proclaiming that the sinfulness of Christians contributed even more to the crucifixion. Nonetheless, accusations of deicide toward Jews continued for several more centuries. If the accusations became dulled over time, it was more likely on account of the Enlightenment, during which Jew-hatred lost some of its religious character in Europe. *Nostra Aetate*, on the other hand, coming on the heels of a Western desire to disavow the kinds of intense Jew-hatred that contributed to the Shoah, was nothing less than revolutionary in bringing about meaningful change in the Catholic Church in this regard.

9. The degree to which even first-century Jews played a role in the crucifixion of Jesus is itself a matter of scholarly controversy, but in terms of internal Christian doctrine, we recognize that absolving all other Jews from any responsibility for the crucifixion is an extremely significant step for the Church.

10. In his book *Jesus of Nazareth*: Holy Week, 2011

11. Pope Francis, *Evangelii Gaudium*, Vatican 2013, §247, §249

12. Http://www.worldjewishcongress.org/en/news/pope-francis-to-make-first-offi-cial-visit-to-rome and http://edition.cnn.com/2015/10/28/world/pope-jews/.

13. *The Gifts and Calling of God are Irrevocable*, Pontifical Commission for Religious Relations with the Jews, 2015, §36–§39.

14. Ibid. §40

15. See for example Rabbi Moshe Feinstein , *Responsa Iggerot Moshe*, *Yoreh De'ah* Vol. 3, §43, as well as French Chief Rabbi Jacob Kaplan in his remarks cited in *Droit et Libertée*, December 1964, and in Hamodia, 16th of September 1965. Each identified areas where skepticism was warranted.

16. *Commentary to Song of Songs* (attributed to Nahmanides), in *Kitve ha-Ram-ban*, ed. Chavel, vol. II, pgs. 502–503; Ralbag, Milhamot, ed. Leipzig, pg. 356 and Commentary to the Torah, ed. Venice, pg. 2.

17. Tosafot *Sanhedrin* 63b, s.v. *Asur*; Rabbenu Yeruham ben Meshullam, *Toledot Adam ve-Havvah* 17:5; R. Moses Isserles to Shulhan Arukh, *Orah Hayyim* 156:2; R. Moses Rivkes, Be'er ha-Golah to Shulhan Arukh *Hoshen Mishpat* 226:1 & 425:5; R. Samson Raphael Hirsch, *Principles of Education, "Talmudic Judaism and Society,"* pgs. 225–227.

18. Most notably in his essay "Confrontation," *Tradition: A Journal of Orthodox Thought*. 6.2 (1964).

19. See, for example, his *The Timely and the Timeless*, London 1977, pgs 119–121.

20. The press statement issued at the fourth bilateral meeting between the Chief Rabbinate of Israel and Holy See, in *Grottaferrata* (Rome, October 17–19, 2004) is particularly notable in this regard. It stated: "Conscious of the fact that there is not wide enough awareness in our respective communities of the momentous change that has taken place in the relationship between Catholics and Jews; and in light of our own committee's work and our current discussions on a shared vision for a just and ethical society; we declare: We are not enemies, but unequivocal partners in articulating the essential moral values for the survival and welfare of human society."

21. As formulated in Jacobovitz, ibid.